A NEW HISTORY OF PORTUGAL

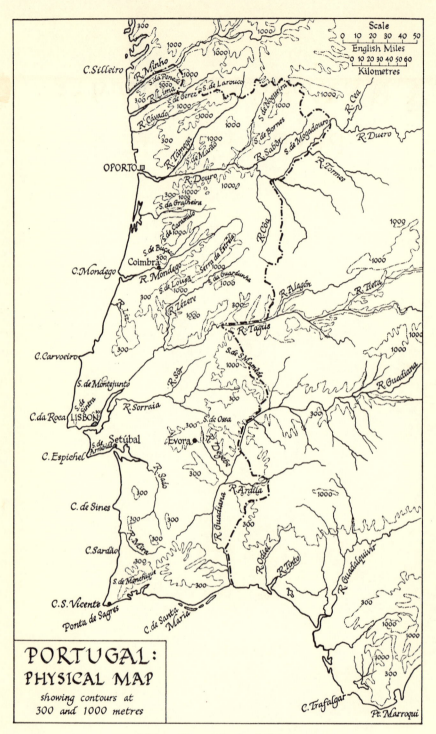

Map 1. Portugal: physical map.

A NEW HISTORY OF PORTUGAL

H. V. LIVERMORE

CAMBRIDGE

AT THE UNIVERSITY PRESS

1966

PUBLISHED BY
THE SYNDICS OF THE CAMBRIDGE UNIVERSITY PRESS
Bentley House, 200 Euston Road, London, N.W. 1
American Branch: 32 East 57th Street, New York, N.Y. 10022
West African Office: P.O. Box 33, Ibadan, Nigeria

©

CAMBRIDGE UNIVERSITY PRESS
1966

LIBRARY OF CONGRESS CATALOGUE
CARD NUMBER: 65–19147

Printed in Great Britain
by Blackie and Son Ltd., Bishopbriggs, Glasgow

CONTENTS

ILLUSTRATIONS

vii

ILLUSTRATIONS

MAPS

PREFACE

In the following pages I have attempted to give an account of the history of Portugal from its emergence as a nation until the present period. It is perhaps necessary to say how this work differs from my earlier book, since it appears from the same press with only a slight change of title.

My interest in Portugal dates from about 1936 and was stimulated two years later by an award from Cambridge which permitted me to spend some time in the country. The first *History of Portugal* was begun at Coimbra and completed after our return to England; it was finally published in 1947, and was awarded the Camões Prize in the following year. At that time, no history of Portugal had appeared in English for about half a century, though much important historical investigation had been carried out by Portuguese and other scholars, and in England especially by Professor Edgar Prestage, who kindly read my text and offered a number of suggestions. The inclusion of material which had not previously been gathered together or which had not been made available in English made the book longer than I had originally meant. Consequently, when it had been out of print for a number of years and the question arose of making it available again, the Cambridge Press ascertained that the cost of reprinting it with some necessary changes would be excessive, and I agreed that it would be preferable to prepare a new book, shorter and shaped on rather different lines. It seemed that the part dealing with the Roman, Germanic and Muslim periods might be greatly abbreviated, partly because I had given a general account of them in a more recent book on Spain, and partly because I intended to write a separate account of the Peninsular societies before and after the Muslim invasion. The first part of the present book is therefore much briefer, though it says a little more about Portuguese prehistory and about the Swabian kingdom. The Reference Index contained in the earlier book has

ix

also been dispensed with, since it is available in most reference libraries. In general, the medieval period has also been compressed: it has seemed preferable, within the limits of proportion, to pay more attention to the events of the nineteenth and twentieth centuries on which relatively little has been published in English.

I have taken it as axiomatic that the history of a nation deals with the life of a society and is concerned chiefly with the distribution of power and the use made of it. If this is a political rather than an economic interpretation, this is because the study of decisions seems to me to embrace the study of possibilities rather than the reverse. It follows that for a society all periods of history are important, though they are not necessarily equally interesting to the historian or the reader. It therefore seemed to me best to adopt a simple division by reigns or regimes throughout. This sort of articulation may perhaps give the misleading suggestion that the Roman, Germanic or Muslim periods are compartments, whereas they are evidently beginnings, but not endings. A similar objection may be made against reigns, when the ruler may represent the use of power without necessarily exercising it, and his appearance or removal does not always imply a real shift of authority. However, it is no less unsatisfactory to disintegrate purely conventional periods into a larger number of inconsequent topics, and the traditional procedure has at least the merit of symbolizing the transmission of authority and the constant renewal of society in the succession of the generations.

I should add finally that although the preparation of this book was contemplated much earlier, it became possible for me to embark on it only in 1961, when the University of British Columbia kindly granted me a leave of absence and the Gulbenkian Foundation made it possible for me to spend a substantial period in Portugal. By chance, my stay there coincided with events not without importance in Portuguese history; in dealing with these I have been unable to go into details of international organization or to explain the inadequacies of western diplomacy, now so evident as to dispense with comment.

I wish to express my thanks to many who have helped me in many ways and in many places; I should refer especially to the two institutions mentioned above, and in particular to the chairman and officers of the Gulbenkian Foundation in Lisbon and London, to those of the British Council in Lisbon and to the Cambridge University Press, and to Professor Virgínia Rau for bibliographical assistance and to Carlos Azevedo for advice and help in obtaining photographs. For permission to reproduce the illustrations my thanks are due to Mário de Novais, the Museu Etnológico, the Archivo Nacional da Torre do Tomba, the Museu Nacional de Arte Antiga, the Palácio Nacional da Ajuda, Secretariado Nacional de Informação and the British Museum.

Lisbon,   H. V. L.
London,
Vancouver.

I

INTRODUCTORY

The metropolitan territory of Portugal consists of the Atlantic sea-board of the Iberian Peninsula from the mouth of the Minho to that of the Guadiana: it lies between 42°91′ and 36°58′ north, and between 6°11′ and 9°30′ west of Greenwich. Its area is 34,216 square miles (88,684 sq. km.). Its greatest length is about 350 miles from north to south, and its width varies between 70 and 140 miles. In addition to this mainland territory, metropolitan Portugal includes the 'adjacent' islands of the Madeiras and the Azores, first settled in the fifteenth century: the eleven inhabited islands have a total area of 1,192 square miles (3,088 sq. km.).

The Portuguese part of the Peninsula is about one-fifth of the whole. In general, the land frontier only occasionally follows defin-able physical features: thus in the north it begins at the mouth of the river Minho, follows the stream for some distance and then moves across country to the massif of Gerez, which forms an effective barrier to communications. To the east of Portugal lie the mesetas of Leon and Castile, a system of high plains tilted gently towards the Atlantic. Three of the five great rivers of the Peninsula, the Douro, Tagus (Tejo) and Guadiana, rise in eastern Spain, cross the Penin-sula and flow through Portuguese territory, each forming the political frontier for a part of its course. Only the rugged gorge of the Douro forms an effective natural barrier.[1] But none of the rivers is navigable in an international sense. The most significant aspect of the frontier area is its relatively low density of population and frequently its barrenness: in places Portugal is separated from Spain by a rock-strewn waste.

The great majority of the population of Portugal lives, and has always lived, close to the ocean, and the most important frontier has therefore been the open boundary of the Atlantic. Castile, the domi-nant region of Spain, is almost entirely continental. Portugal is

---

[1] The electrification of the 'international Douro' which now provides power for both Portugal and Spain is evidently a reversal of natural conditions.

essentially maritime: the proportion of its coastline to its area is thrice the European average. The estuaries of the Douro and Tagus provide excellent ports, and it is here that the great capitals of Oporto and Lisbon have emerged. However, they have enjoyed an absolute pre-eminence only in relatively recent times. From the Minho to Setúbal, the coasts are usually low and sandy, and in the Algarve they are fringed with sand-banks and sea-marshes, and the estuaries, beaches and coves are dotted with fishing-villages and small ports.[1]

The presence of the ocean is not only felt on the coast, but pervades the western half of the country. Over most of Portugal winds from the Atlantic bring sufficient moisture and moderate the extremes of temperature of the meseta. The Iberian Peninsula is divided into two zones, one humid all the year round and the other virtually without rain in summer. The mesetas of Leon and Castile are arid, but most of Portugal belongs to the humid region. The average rainfall may exceed 100 inches; it rarely falls below 35. In Lisbon it is 47, of which nearly two-fifths falls in summer. Nor is the extreme cold of winter on the mesetas felt near the coast: at Lisbon frosts are almost unknown and snow is rarely seen, though it abounds on the high slopes of the serras.

A climate so temperate and moist favours a varied and even luxuriant vegetation, and Portugal has places of notable profusion, such as the northern terraces of the Sintra hills. But these are few, and advantages of climate are often annulled by the poverty of the soil. In the north and centre much high mountainside serves only for rough grazing, and to the south of the Tagus the sandy heaths of the Alentejo defy cultivation. Much of the country is more suited to forestry than to agriculture; about a quarter of it is sylvan, but only the pines occur generally.

Most of the natural features of Portugal, geological, climatic or vegetable, can be paralleled in other parts of the Peninsula. Its distinction lies rather in the variety of its landscape, the mildness of its seasons and the wide range of its botanical species. The scene is pleasantly diversified, but without extremes. Its natural regions are not at first sight sharply defined. There are, however, three generally

---

[1] A number of medieval ports have disappeared owing to the invasion of dunes or the silting of river-mouths.

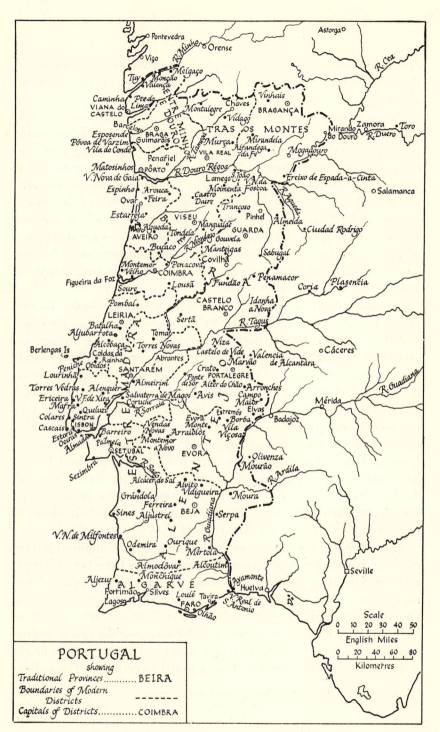

Map 2. Portugal, showing traditional provinces, etc.

distinguishable zones. In the first place, the country to the north of
the Tagus is relatively mountainous, with an average height of about
1,200 feet and numerous serras of 3,500 feet or above. By contrast,
the average for southern Portugal is scarcely more than 700 feet, and
there is very little land above 1,500. Secondly, in the higher north
the conflict between the moderating effect of the ocean and the
extreme continental climate of the mesetas is more strongly felt, and
it is possible to distinguish two zones, a milder and moister western
division which embraces the fertile coastal plains, and a drier, more
rugged and relatively thinly populated eastern half which the sea
winds scarcely reach. These three constitute the main natural zones
of Portugal—the Atlantic north-west, the semi-continental north-
east, and the south, in which gradations of climate are latitudinal
rather than longitudinal.

The traditional regional division is into six provinces: Entre-
Douro-e-Minho, Trás-os-Montes, Beira, Estremadura, the Alentejo
and the Algarve. Of these the first two clearly reflect the differences
of the two natural zones of the north-west and north-east. The second
pair cover central Portugal, and the third the south, Portugal 'beyond
the Tagus' (Alentejo) and the southern coastal strip (Algarve). These
provinces were the administrative divisions of Portugal until the
nineteenth century, when the country was separated into districts
which received their names from their chief towns. Thus Entre-
Douro-e-Minho consists of the districts of Oporto, Braga and Viana
do Castelo; Trás-os-Montes of Bragança and Vila Real; Beira of
Aveiro, Viseu, Guarda, Leiria, Coimbra, Castelo Branco and
Portalegre; Estremadura of Lisbon, Santarém and Setúbal; Alentejo
of Évora and Beja; and the Algarve of Faro.[1]

These districts remain the general administrative divisions of the
country, but in the present century the provinces have been revived
and remoulded as geographical, economic and social regions. The
six traditional provinces have been subdivided or supplemented, so
that the new division is more sensitive to areas of transition than the
old. Thus the valley of the Douro, which cuts across the two northern
zones, forms the two regions of Upper and Lower Douro, while Beira
is divided into three, Litoral, Upper and Lower Beira. The valley

[1] In addition to the eighteen districts, Madeira forms one district (Funchal), and the
Azores two (Horta and Angra do Heroismo).

of the Tagus forms a natural area, the Ribatejo, and the Alentejo is divided into two, Upper and Lower.

The northernmost of these eleven provinces, the Minho, forms (with Baixo Douro) the historical nucleus of Portugal, which takes its name from Portucale, the city now known as Oporto (*o Pôrto*, the port): the first Portuguese dwelt on coastal plains and among undulating hills rich in timber, meadows and springs. In medieval times, it had a handful of market-towns and ports, but most of the population dwelt in villages or in clusters of farms and cottages, and its nobility built fortified manors or *torres* surrounded by vineyards, grainfields and pastures. The countryside is soft, green and misty, and its people pious, sentimental, industrious and prolific. It has been over-populated since the eighteenth century, or earlier, and has now above 170 persons to the square kilometre, as compared with a national average of 100. The land is therefore excessively subdivided, and there has long been emigration to other parts of Portugal and to Brazil.

Lower or Litoral Douro is even more heavily populated. Oporto and its vicinity, now separated to form a small 'region', have a population of a million and a half, with densities exceeding those of Belgium and Holland. Here the countryside has been drawn into the orbit of the city, which it provides with daily supplies: in return, factories and canneries appear among the farmsteads, and the nearer villages are transformed into suburbs, though they remain jealous of their autonomy and identity.

These animated scenes extend to the valley of the Tâmega, beyond which the lofty Serra do Marão and its northern continuations isolate the interior from the busy coast. Trás-os-Montes ('behind the mountains') is two and a half times as large as the Minho, but only two-thirds as populous. It consists of mountain, plateaux (the 'cold land') and river-valley ('warm land'). Resettled in the twelfth and thirteenth centuries, its people are still concentrated in villages of stone houses and practise collective forms of stock-farming and agriculture. The 'cold land' gives rye and chestnuts, and the 'warm' valleys wine and olives. The *transmontanos* are considered to be independent, wilful and dour.

The 'warm land' of the Douro valley forms the region of Alto Douro. The river here runs through a deep declivity, and the steep slopes are everywhere lined with neat terraces to form the vineyards which produce Port-wine.

Below the Douro begins Beira ('the side'), the centre and heart of Portugal. Here the Atlantic coast and the interior are not so sharply divided, despite the fact that the region is crossed by the highest range in Portugal, the long ridge of the Serra da Estrela (6,500 ft.). The three parts of Beira have neither the teeming countryside of the Minho nor the isolation of Trás-os-Montes, though the coastal region is again the more populous and the interior the less. Together they possess a variety of natural features: around the Serra are ranged the high pastures of Beira Baixa, the picturesque forests of Bussaco, the bucolic valleys of the Vouga and the Dão, the waterfields of the Mondego, the longest river that rises in Portuguese territory, and the lagoons and beaches of Beira Litoral. The chief city of Beira, Coimbra, was once the capital and is still the seat of a famous university and in many ways the centre of intellectual life. It rises in academic severity above the charming valley of the Mondego, but is not divorced from its rural context, nor does it claim to dominate the other towns of Beira, the fishing-port of Aveiro with its lagoons and salt-pans, Viseu, the capital of the vineyards of the Vouga and Dão, Guarda, the ancient fortress for the defence of the frontier perched on a high spur 3,000 feet above sea-level, Covilhã, the centre of the woollen industry, and Castelo Branco, the commercial centre of Beira Baixa. If Beira remains the heart of the country, this is in part because the balance between town and countryside has not here been disturbed by the inordinate expansion of Lisbon to the south or Oporto to the north.

The transition from the two zones of northern Portugal to the flatter territory of the south is provided by the valley of the Tagus, which, unlike the Douro, opens out into a broad valley, forming the main feature of the Ribatejo. It is famous for its irrigated fields and its extensive pastures. Here the small-holdings and mixed farming of Beira go side by side with large estates similar to those beyond the Tagus. The cattle, which in the north draw the ox-cart and plough and are sheltered in stables, are here the *gado bravo*, bred on the range in half-wild herds and herded by mounted cattlemen armed with long lances. Santarém, now the capital of a farming district, was formerly the seat of the court: a city of monuments, it commands with dignity the long stretches of the Tagus.

Further down, the great river opens into an inland sea, the salt Mar de Palha, on which stands the city of Lisbon. The country to its north and south, from Leiria to Setúbal, forms the region of Estremadura, whose unity is imposed by the presence of the capital. To the north it is essentially an extension of the domesticated dependencies which have long supplied the city with produce and building-materials. To the south the industrial suburbs have now spread round the shores of the inland sea and include the port of Setúbal in the estuary of the Sado. The building of a bridge across the Tagus at Lisbon, the longest in Europe, completes the unification of the area.

Southern Portugal consists of two strongly contrasted regions, the Alentejo and Algarve. The first of these covers 10,186 square miles (26,400 sq. km.), or more than all the Beiras, but has little more than a third of their population. Here alone in Portugal the maritime area is as sparsely settled as the interior, and the long sweep of coast that runs from Setúbal to Cape St Vincent has only one fishery. Inland, much of the Alentejo is 'charneca', flat, dry heath, intensely hot in summer. In places this desolate landscape is varied by groves of oak and holm-oaks which provide cover and fodder for cattle and swine. Further east, towards Évora and Beja, there are extensive wheat-fields, but the southern part of the Baixo Alentejo is again heath, this time laid over long stretches of small hillocks, never high, but rough and poorly communicated. In most of the Alentejo there is 'no shade but what comes from the sky'. Most of the population is congregated in towns or large villages, and isolated dwellings are infrequent. In places water is distributed in summer by cart or mule. Large estates owned by a few individuals cover a great part of the region. Social discrepancies are resented, but borne: the people of the Alentejo are attached to their own world and rarely emigrate.

Finally, the coastal strip of southern Portugal is the Algarve (*al-garb*, 'the west' of Muslim times). It is a fifth the size of Alentejo, but about half as populous. It is divided from the Alentejo by low ranges of mountains which form a series of amphitheatres facing the sea and the sun. The upper slopes are thinly populated, but the foot-hills and the coastal plain have a dozen towns and scores of villages and hamlets and the countryside is intensively cultivated. The most important crops are almonds, figs and oranges, but there are also olive-groves, wheatfields, vegetable fields and flower-gardens, and the coastal towns have fisheries of tunny, anchovies and sardines. This busy countryside resembles a southern Minho. It is divided into two sub-regions, the western or windward (Barlavento), less sheltered from the storms of the Atlantic which sweep across Cape St Vincent, and the eastern or leeward (Sotavento), which is warmer and more akin to neighbouring Andalusia.

II

THE ORIGINS OF PORTUGAL

The birth of the Portuguese state is conventionally dated from 1139, when Afonso I Henriques for the first time assumed the title of king of Portugal. Forty years later the Portuguese monarchy received from the Papacy formal recognition of a status it had long enjoyed in fact. It thus became one of the Five Kingdoms into which the Christian-dominated part of the Peninsula was divided during the later middle ages.[1]

The country of which Afonso I became king stretched from the Minho to the Mondego, or a little beyond. Below Coimbra, Santarém, Lisbon and the land beyond the Tagus formed part of the Muslim territory of al-Andalus, which had been annexed to the Moroccan empire of the Almoravids, then in decline. In 1147 Afonso was able to take Santarém and Lisbon, carrying his frontiers below the Tagus, and succeeding rulers completed the occupation of the Algarve by about 1250, since when the frontiers of Portugal have undergone only minor alterations.

Successive generations of historians have endeavoured to explain the emergence of the monarchy of Afonso Henriques in different ways. In the sixteenth century it was held that Ulysses had founded Lisbon (Olissipo), or that a legendary Lusus had established the kingdom of the Lusiads, the 'sons of Lusus', or that Tubal, son of Cain, had built Setúbal. In the seventeenth century, with the restoration of the Portuguese monarchy, it was believed that Afonso Henriques had miraculously defeated the Muslims in battle, and that his declaration of independence had divine authority. Later writers

---

[1] It is consequently the older of the two states into which the Peninsula is now divided. Of the other four kingdoms, Leon and Castile were finally united in 1230, and these joined with Aragon in 1479. The fifth kingdom, Navarre, was annexed by conquest in 1512.

In medieval times the Five Kingdoms all regarded themselves as Hispaniae, the successors of the Roman provinces. When Ferdinand and Isabella appropriated the name of Spain for the union of Aragon and Castile, the king of Portugal vainly protested against what he regarded as a solecism. Thereafter the Portuguese identified their country with the Roman Lusitania.

vindicated the legality of the monarchy by showing that autonomy was implicit in the granting of the county of Portugal to the parents of the founder. The greatest of the Portuguese historians, Alexandre Herculano (1810–77), having examined minutely the records of the age of formation, did not hesitate to assert that Portugal owed her national existence to the strong arms and resolution of Afonso I and his barons.

It is indeed evident that the Portugal of Afonso Henriques was not a mere restoration of Roman Lusitania, and that his assumption of sovereignty was an act of political inauguration. But the thesis of a simple decision by one ruler and his liegemen does not by itself suffice to explain the emergence of a nation. Such a declaration is unlikely to succeed unless it is made in the name of a unanimous society, or to prosper unless it takes account of geographical and historical factors. Long before there was a kingdom of Portugal there were Portuguese. The county which was bestowed on the parents of Afonso Henriques can be traced back for at least two centuries, though it was only in the time of his father that it had been made to include the territory of Coimbra, reconquered from the Muslims in 1064. The original nucleus of Portugal was the area between the Minho and the Douro, the Territorium Portucalense, which derived its name from a Roman, and possibly pre-Roman settlement on the north bank of the Douro, the site of the present Oporto. The name Portucale meant the port or ferry of Cale, by which the traveller from Roman Lusitania crossed into the north-western province of Callaecia or Galicia. It refers therefore not to a specific Roman province but to the place, town and border where two provinces met. The territorium is not recorded, and perhaps did not exist before the ninth century, and its evolution, like that of the Portuguese state, is evidently closely related to the Christian reconquest. In earlier times the same society or its ancestors had been known by other names.

The birth of a distinct culture on the Atlantic edge of the Peninsula may be ascribed to the Mesolithic period (8000–3000 before Christ). Portugal was inhabited during the Palaeolithic, both by pre-sapiens

[1] The first discovery of a pre-sapiens man was made in 1847 at Gibraltar, nine years before the appearance of the skull at Neanderthal. In 1929 a child's skull of the same stock was found at Gibraltar, and in 1954 parts of a similar skull appeared in a Mousterian level in Granada. A child's maxillary from Furninhas (Peniche), also from a Mousterian level, represents the first known inhabitant of Portugal.

creatures and by early ancestors of modern man.[1] Implements of the Upper Palaeolithic are fairly numerous and widely distributed. But there is no trace in Portugal of the cave-paintings of the Magdalenians (15,000–12,000 before Christ): their world was essentially a northern one and the animals they depicted at Altamira and Lascaux are associated with the cold phase following the final glaciation. The great Ice Ages scarcely touched Portugal, and it was only after the disappearance of the Palaeolithic hunting cultures that a warmer climate gave rise to a different way of existence. The earliest perspectives of Portuguese life are estuarine or maritime.

The general type of these cultures was established in north-western Spain and denominated 'Asturian'. The Mesolithic peoples dwelt near the mouths of rivers or on the coast, and their characteristic implement is a pick for prising shellfish from rocks and opening them. They have left huge middens of shells and fishbones, mingled with other garbage and also human remains. Sites of this kind have been investigated in Galicia and northern Portugal, but the 'capital' of the Portuguese mesolithic was the lower valley of the Tagus. The middens (*moitas*) of Muge, fifty miles north of Lisbon, were noted in 1863 and first excavated in 1880–85, when they yielded about 120 skeletons. They were generally short in stature, of both broad and long-headed types. Their middens were large (one is 95 metres long, 40 metres wide and 5 deep) and they contain shellfish and crustaceans, as well as bones of the ox, deer, sheep, horse, pig, wild dog, badger and cat. Human remains are found buried in an artificial posture. The implements are scrapers and microliths. They date from 7700–7000.[1]

The primitive peoples of the Iberian Peninsula appear to have remained in isolation until the first achievements of the Neolithic began to reach them, probably not before 3000, at which time the civilizations of Mesopotamia and Egypt were already highly developed. Now agriculture was practised and animals domesticated: pottery was made, and dwellings built, and there had ensued vast advances in social organization. The first Neolithic achievements appear to have reached the south-eastern part of the Peninsula from

---

[1] Abbé J. Roche excavated the Moita de Sebastião in 1954, and obtained this radiocarbon dating. Mendes Corrêa gave the men of Muge the name *Homo afer taganus: afer*, suggested by supposed negroid features, is supererogatory.

across the Mediterranean. The oldest known city of the Peninsula is at Los Millares, near Almería, and it possesses already a necropolis of passage-graves, domed cells entered from a flagged antechamber, walls and gate, and fields protected by hilltop forts. It is unlikely that the Almerían Neolithic and Copper Age reached its full development much before 2000. The appearance of the bell-beaker, probably the earliest item of trade in the west, marks a new phase from about 1600 (?): the earliest bronze axes and knives are probably rather later.

From this site and its neighbours the new cultures spread slowly across the southern part of the Peninsula and up its western coast. From the ancient passage-graves of Almería there developed the megalithic cultures of Andalusia and Portugal in which flagged corridors give access to subterranean chambers lined with stone. The Neolithic and Copper Age cultures of Almería are summarized at Vila Nova de São Pedro, which, like Los Millares, stands on the edge of a small plateau and commands extensive views down the valley of a small river: it may date from 1500.[1]

Portugal is rather rich in megalithic necropolises, of which the best known are at Palmela, Alcalar, Reguengos, Monsaraz and Alapraia. By about 1500 the quest for metals played a dominant part in Peninsular civilization, bringing new settlements over a wide area. Perhaps half a millennium elapsed between the appearance of Bronze Age cultures in Almería, and their prevalence in the west, but by 1000 it is likely that bronze had become generalized, and that gold was mined and worked. During the same time megalithic constructions were raised in many places, and the Portuguese cists and dolmens (*antas*) are associated with a wide range of artifacts, including the microliths and flint edges of a bygone age, axes of polished stone and plain copper of the Neolithic, cylindrical pots, bell-beakers, gold diadems and bracelets.

During the first millennium before Christ, the human stock of the Iberian Peninsula and its customs and culture were modified by a long series of Indo-European infiltrations or invasions. These peoples advanced across or round the Pyrenees in successive waves, and having settled the central mesetas, hitherto sparsely peopled, pressed into

[1] The earliest level appears to precede the introduction of the bell-beaker. V.N. de São Pedro is five miles from Cartaxo to the south of Santarém: it is therefore not far from Muge, but on the opposite bank of the Tagus and further from the river.

northern and central Portugal, and penetrated the south in smaller numbers. Most of these peoples were Celts: they may have included some Germanic groups, but the evidence for this is doubtful. They brought with them the skill of iron-founding and a new arms industry. They preferred a military or pastoral existence. In the north-west it appears that they formed a dominant nobility and made the indigenous peoples their subjects or serfs, implanting their culture and their gods. Elsewhere, they settled with their herds and flocks on the highlands and raided the cultivators of the valleys.

But in the south the peoples of the Peninsula still followed Mediterranean patterns of life. The towns of the valley of the Guadalquivir joined together to form federations or kingdoms, of which the chief was the city and state known as Tarshish or Tartessos, at or near the mouth of the river. On a promontory not far away, at Cádiz, the Phoenicians had established a trading-post, probably as early as 800. They or their native factors traded with the peoples of the interior, taking out silver, copper and tin, and bringing in eastern trade-goods: the oldest datable objects of eastern origin include a scarab of Psammeticus I found at Aliseda (province of Cáceres, near the Portuguese frontier): these venerable beads date from about 600.

With the decline of Tyre, the Phocean Greeks reached Andalusia and traded with the Tartessians (before 546), but by 535 the Carthaginians had taken the place of the Phoenicians at Cádiz and closed the Straits of Gibraltar to the Greeks. There are no Phoenician or Carthaginian records, and the earliest Greek writers know little about the west, now forbidden to them. Herodotus refers to the domination of the Celts outside the Pillars of Hercules, and to the Cinesioi as the westernmost people of Europe: these must be the Cynetes of the Algarve. Later writers from Aristotle to Polybius know only that gold, tin and copper filtered through 'Celtica' to the Tartessian peoples of Andalusia.

Little is known of the influence of the Carthaginians during this long period. Confused legends of the foundation of Setúbal and Lisbon probably relate to their ventures in the Atlantic: they must have known Galicia and may have built the Pharos of Corunna to guide their ships. But it was only after the first defeat of Carthage by Rome that the Barcas attempted to create a Carthaginian empire in the Peninsula, desiring treasure and mercenaries for a war of revenge.

This new phase began with the arrival of Hamilcar at Cádiz in 237 and ended with the defeat of Carthage and the annexation of Africa and Spain by Rome (202). The Carthaginian armies had winter-quarters in the Algarve, and with the capitulation of Cádiz it is probable that southern Portugal passed under Roman rule.

The Romans constituted the former Carthaginian territory into a new province, Hispania Ulterior, corresponding at first to the modern Andalusia. The interior was still little known, though the Carthaginians had marched through the central tableland in their search for allies. In its eastern part there dwelt the federation of the Celtiberians, a powerful alliance of some fifty towns, in which the Celtic and indigenous, or Iberian, elements were already fused. The centre of the Peninsula was less thickly inhabited and less able to resist: in 193–2 the Romans defeated the Carpetani and advanced to the line of the Tagus. They were then confronted with three tribal groups, the Vaccaei, collective farmers who tilled the cornfields of the upper Douro (Palencia); the Vettones, pastoral people in what is now Leon and Spanish Extremadura; and the Lusitanians, who dwelt in central Portugal. These last proved the most formidable of the native peoples. They or their leaders were Celts, and less miscegenated with the indigenous population than the Celtiberians. They appear to have had few towns, and they carried on their long struggle against the Romans not from their own tribal lands but in long ranging campaigns across the centre of the Peninsula and into Baetica, or Roman Andalusia. They were led by the greatest of the native soldiers, Viriatus, 'the Hannibal of the Iberians', the most notable exponent of irregular warfare.[1]

The Lusitanian chieftains had varied their pastoral life by making war for or against the more settled peoples of the valley of the Tagus, and from time to time raiding Baetica for booty. In 193 they resumed these attacks against peoples now under Roman protection. They inflicted heavy losses on Aemilius Paulus in 191, and then came to terms. The Romans were then chiefly concerned with the Celtiberians, who capitulated in 178. In 154 the Lusitanians again marched south, invading the land of the Conii and taking their city

---

[1] Lucilius' phrase, 'the Hannibal of the Iberians', is evidently incongruent. Viriatus is probably from *viria*, a bracelet, as Torquatus, from *torca*, a Celtic torque.

of Conis-torgis.[1] The Romans gathered their forces and in 150 entered the valley of the Tagus. The tribes agreed to capitulate in return for land, but the Roman commander Servius Sulpicius Galba chose to slaughter and enslave them. He was accused by Cato of treachery, but was acquitted after delivering three speeches. Meanwhile, the Lusitanians prepared to fight to the last. When they were almost surrounded and about to surrender against a new promise of land, there appeared Viriatus, who reminded them of the faithlessness of the Romans and undertook to save them from the encircling legions. He took a thousand men, opened a breach by a surprise attack and enabled the main body of the Lusitanians to escape. He then made for the mountains of Ronda, a Celtic stronghold, and killed 4,000 of the 10,000 men sent in pursuit. His victories were halted only when the Roman Senate sent Q. Fabius Maximus; but by 147 Viriatus had established a ring of hostile tribes round Roman Andalusia. When the Celtiberians again rose in revolt, he occupied the valley of the Guadalquivir and forced the Romans to make terms, acknowledging him as king and 'friend of the Roman people'. But the terms were disregarded, and in 139 Q. Servilius Cæpio occupied the territory of the Vettones and established a permanent camp at Castra Servilia, near Cáceres. Viriatus was thus confined to what is now central Portugal. He opened negotiations, and the Romans demanded the delivery of certain rebels. He agreed, and they made new demands. When finally they asked that the Lusitanians should deliver all their weapons, Viriatus refused. But his people were tired of the struggle, and the Romans at last bribed his three negotiators to kill him while he slept. The resistance of the Lusitanians was thus brought to an end.

Like Hannibal, Viriatus appears as the great leader of a losing cause. The Roman view of his career was that he had begun as a shepherd from the Mons Herminius, the Serra da Estrela, 'first a shepherd, he turned to hunting, then from a hunter he turned robber, and soon became the general of a veritable army and occupied the whole of Lusitania'. He was thus from one of those pastoral hill-peoples, who either raided or sold protection to the wealthier inhabitants of the lowlands. He married the daughter of the rich Astolpas, and the bride's family displayed their gold vases, and other

---

[1] Mentioned by Appius and Strabo: it remains unidentified.

possessions at a feast. Viriatus stood by, leaning on his spear, and would take only a little bread and meat, and when the feast was over, he rode back to his fastness. He had a gift for allegory; when the people of Tucci wavered between him and the Romans, he reminded them of the fate of a man who had two wives, one old and one young: the old one pulled out his black hairs and the young one pulled out the white, so that he was left bald. The Lusitanians commemorated his funeral, which was also the end of their independence, by raising a great pyre and sacrificing many animals, whilst the army, horse and foot, marched round the flames singing his praises. After the blaze had died down they sat round the dim ashes in silence, and when they had built his tomb, two hundred pairs of warriors fought a mock combat in his honour.

2. ROMAN PORTUGAL

The Romanization of central Portugal began in 137, when Decius Junius Brutus marched through it without meeting any serious resistance. He occupied Olissipo, the modern Lisbon, and it is likely that this served as the centre of administration and supplies until the foundation of Emerita in 25. As he moved northward, he destroyed the strongholds of the Lusitanians in or near the Serra da Estrela and built a fortified camp at Viseu. He then advanced towards the Douro and crossed it, marching towards the Lima and the Minho. The territory of the Lusitanians had never extended beyond the Douro. But it seems that the Lima was regarded as a tribal frontier: according to legend, long before, a horde of Celts had come from the south and crossed it; they had not returned. Either because of this, or of some other superstition, Brutus' troops became convinced that the Lima was the river of Forgetfulness and refused to enter it until their leader had gone over. He went beyond the Minho into Galicia; and from his time the whole north was called Callaecia; he himself received the cognomen of Callaecus, 'the Galician'.

At the opening of the first century, southern Portugal had already been drawn into the province of Hispania Ulterior; the valley of the Tagus was occupied, and the region to the north of it had been recently subjected and was under military government. When, as a result of the social struggles in Rome, Sertorius attempted to restore the fortunes of the Marian party in Spain (80 B.C.), he revived the native names of Lusitania and Celtiberia, and set up a form of senate at Ebora (Évora). By appealing to local sentiment, he established a personal ascendancy over the natives. If Viriatus had been the last hero of barbarian tradition, Sertorius was the forerunner of the new provincialism, as much Roman as native. But like Viriatus, he was killed by treachery, his regime having lasted less than a decade.

A little later, in 60, Julius Caesar, while pro-praetor in further Spain, was faced with a rebellion in the country of Viriatus, the Mons Herminius, and beyond, and reduced the native town of Brigantium, proceeding to collect great sums in tribute, with which he appeased his creditors in Rome and purchased the consulate in 59. It is hardly surprising that when he fought Pompey ten years later, the Lusitanian auxiliaries sided with his rival. After his victory, Q. Cassius Longinus carried out a severe repression in Lusitania: he perished by shipwreck on returning with his plunder to Rome.

It appears that the port of Olissipo was at this time the centre of Roman rule in Portuguese territory. In Caesar's day it was the only city in the west with Roman rights, and he bestowed on it the title of Felicitas Julia, probably in recognition of its loyalty during his wars. Latin rights were conferred on Ebora and Myrtilis (Mértola), and to the first of these Caesar gave the title of Liberalitas Julia, possibly an allusion to his generosity in providing land to the warlike hill-peoples of the north, now resettled on the plains. He was the founder of Pax Julia (Beja), whose name refers to his pacification. He established colonists of Italian origin in the course of the Tagus at Colonia Scallabis Praesidium Julium (Santarém) and C. Norba Caesarina (Cáceres). He also gathered the native people in *conventus*, or jurisdictions, each having a Roman centre of administration and justice, to which the surrounding tribes were made amenable.

It was left to Augustus to complete the occupation of the Peninsula and to give it a civil administration. Only the Cantabrian mountaineers had remained unsubdued. They were at length conquered, their territory being incorporated in Hispania Citerior, now known also as Tarraconensis, from its military headquarters on the Mediterranean coast. At the same time Hispania Ulterior was divided into two parts, Baetica, or Roman Andalusia, and Lusitania (27 B.C.). The Lusitania of Sertorius was now given a new capital, Emerita Augusta (Mérida,

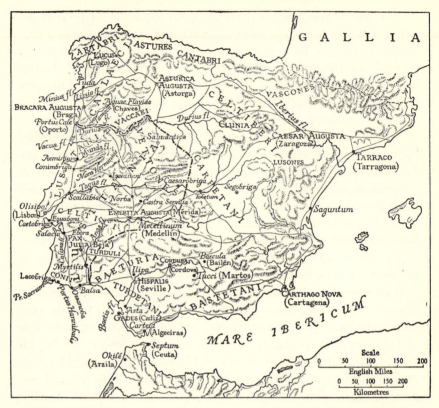

Map 3. The Western Peninsula in Roman times showing roads, towns etc.

in Spain), founded in 25 to reward the veterans, *emeriti*, of the fifth and tenth legions. It stood on the banks of the Guadiana and commanded a great stretch of irrigable farmland at the entrance to the new province of the west. Some years later (7 to 2 B.C.), the Callaeci and Astures were attached to Tarraconensis: this and Lusitania were kept under the authority of the emperor, while Baetica was administered by the Senate. Thus the emperor appointed a 'proconsular legate' to Tarraconensis and a 'propraetorial legate' to Lusitania, each with *procuratores*, or fiscal assistants. This division persisted until the time of Caracalla (A.D. 212), who separated the region of the Gallaeci and Astures to form a new province 'Antoniniana', or Galicia.

The imperialism of Augustus was a military and administrative

18

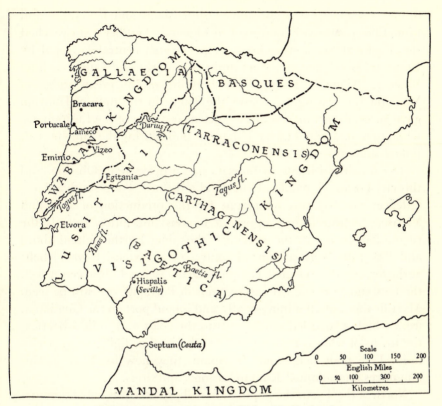

Map 4. The Swabian and Visigothic Peninsula

mantle lightly but firmly drawn over a vast assemblage of towns and tribesteads. The universal city served as a model for provincial municipalities which attained its free institutions: they in turn served as beacons of justice and culture for their rural dependencies. Every free citizen enjoyed a double franchise, that of Rome and that of his birthplace, and he recognized this dual loyalty, universal and local, when he worshipped the gods of Rome and its emperors beside his own deities. Emerita became a great capital comparable with the cities of Corduba and Tarraco, and was endowed with notable monuments. Its great bridge across the Guadiana, still in use, was indispensable in the Roman system of communications. The high-road from the cities of Baetica crossed it and went thence northwards to the garrison-towns of Asturica (Astorga) and Lucus (Lugo) in distant Galicia. It was also linked with Ebora and Pax Julia, and from Ebora the road continued to Olissipo. Another road reached the Tagus at Scallabis, whence it penetrated central Portugal by Conimbriga (Condeixa), Aeminium (Coimbra) and Cale, reaching Braccara Augusta (Braga). The building of the great bridge of Valentia (i.e. Alcántara) across the Tagus in the time of Hadrian gave access from Emerita to the ancient territory of the Lusitanians, while that at Aquae Flaviae (Chaves), built during the same period, linked Braccara with Asturica.

The provincial legate in Emerita had a delegate in Olissipo, and this city possessed temples, baths, and a theatre. To its south Salacia (Alcácer do Sal) was important for the production of salt, and Vipasca (Aljustrel) for copper: a famous inscription records the regulations governing the working of the mines. Further inland Ebora and Pax Julia were provincial centres of an extensive wheat-belt: at the former, the so-called Temple of Diana (second–third centuries), the best known of the Roman remains in Portugal, can still be seen. Myrtilis was a small mining-centre and inland port on the Guadiana, from which a road led southwards to the coast and so into Baetica, the towns of what is now the Algarve being thus linked with Andalusia. Like their neighbours in Spain, they now lost their native languages and adopted Roman customs and dress.

North of the Tagus the population still preserved its tribal organization. Although in the Romanized areas the loyalty of the inhabitants was to their cities and their provinces, the immediate reality in tribal territories was the *conventus*. According to Pliny, Lusitania consisted of three of these—Emerita, Pax Augusta (Beja) and Scallabis (Santarém)—and Callaecia of two—the Callaeci Lucenses with their capital at Lucus, and the C. Braccarenses with their capital at Braccara. The nucleus of Portuguese territory consists of the southernmost of the two *conventus* of Callaecia and the northernmost of the three *conventus* of Lusitania. Although the tribal groupings of this area were the work of the Romans, the territory was relatively lightly Romanized. It was, however, heavily settled by the barbarian invaders in the fifth century, who superimposed on it a new tribalism.

Of Roman Braccara little is known. It may have been settled by bringing down the inhabitants of the primitive hill-top towns, the *citânias*, such as Briteiros and Sameiro, to lower ground. To its east the old tribal divisions survived until very late. Further south Conimbriga (Condeixa) was a Roman town with good houses, supplied with hot baths and mosaics, as recent excavations have shown. But the chief concentration of Roman or Romanized settlement and agriculture was in the valley of the Tagus and in Alentejo, where there are fairly general remains of Roman estates. One of these has yielded mosaics portraying the favourite horses of the farm with their names: it will be recalled that the valley of the Tagus was famous for its mares, which, according to legend, were fertilized by the wind.

By the third century the long age of peace was passing and the empire had begun to undergo great changes. The emperors were now generals and the imperial bureaucracy was militarized. The cities had ceased to generate civilization: the senatorial class became a closed oligarchy, and the municipality served only to control the economy and collect tribute. The ritual of emperor-worship prepared the way for more systematic universal religions, born outside the Roman world, and non-conformist or even anti-imperialist in their implications. The most vital of these was Christianity, which now successfully defied the formal cult of the emperors. It probably entered the Peninsula from Africa by way of Baetica, and was diffused through the Roman capitals and garrisons in the third century. During the persecution of Decius in 250, the bishops of Christian communities in Emerita and Asturica were accused of obtaining false certificates of sacrifice, and were condemned by St Cyprian in Africa. The first council of the church in the Peninsula was held at Iliberri (Elvira, near Granada) in 300–14, and the western provinces were represented by bishops from Emerita, Ebora and Ossonoba (Faro). This was in the years immediately before Constantine ended the persecution with the edict of Milan. In the following years, Arius, a priest of Alexandria, preached a simplified form of Christianity which rejected the consubstantiality of Christ. In 337 he baptized Constantine, who soon after died. His successor, Constantius II (342–54) defended Arianism, whose teachings spread among the Visigoths in Pannonia. They also reached the Iberian Peninsula: the first known bishop of Lisbon, Potamius, accepted Arianism before his death in about 360.

But in northern Portugal Nicene orthodoxy was opposed by a

different doctrine, taught by one Priscillian, a young and wealthy nobleman from Gallaecia, who had studied with the rhetorician Elpidius. He became the leader of a movement which placed great emphasis on asceticism, continence and Bible-readings. He was vehemently accused of gnosticism by Itatius, bishop of Ossonoba, and some of his doctrines were condemned at a council at Saragossa in 380. But Priscillian was elected bishop of Avila and his teaching spread far and wide in Portugal and Galicia, his pupil Paternus being elected bishop of Braga. The Emperor Gratian favoured the Priscillianists, but he was murdered in 383: and his successor, the usurper Maximus, a Spaniard, had Priscillian tried for heresy, and he was condemned and burnt at Trier (385 or 386). But his beliefs were still widely held, and Braga became the stronghold of Priscillianism, while Mérida upheld the orthodox belief.

3. THE KINGDOM OF THE SWABIANS

During the fourth century, the emperors had first repressed Christianity, then tolerated it, then embraced it, surrendering their own sacred status. Finally, Theodosius, born a pagan at Cauca (Coca, near Segovia), but converted to Christianity, sought to make Nicene orthodoxy the sole religion of his subjects, suppressing paganism and destroying the temples of the old gods. On his death in 396 the east and west were again divided, between his sons Arcadius and Honorius, and it was not long before the Roman army resumed its practice of setting up anti-emperors. The pick of the army now consisted of semi-Romanized barbarians, who were treated more favourably than most Roman subjects.

On the last day of 406 several barbarian tribes in Germany crossed the Rhine and forced their way into Gaul. An anti-emperor proclaimed in Britain diverted them into the Iberian Peninsula, which had remained loyal to Honorius. They crossed the Pyrenees in 409 and for two years subsisted on the wheatlands of the northern meseta. It was then arranged that they should be assigned territories and become *federati* or allies. They consisted of four groups, the two branches of the Vandals, the Suevi or Swabians, and the Alans. The Swabians were established in the southern part of Gallaecia, the *conventus* of Braga, corresponding to the province of Entre-Douro-e-

Minho. The Asdingian Vandals were placed to their north, in the *conventus* of Lugo. The Silingian Vandals were given land in Baetica, probably poor tribal territory in the west. The Alans, a non-Germanic people of Iranian stock, who had attached themselves to the Vandals in central Europe, were placed in Lusitania. The numbers of these people are not known, but when the Vandals departed for Africa in 429, taking with them the remnants of the Alans, they were estimated to number 80,000, of whom about a fifth might be warriors. The greater part of these were Asdingians, who by themselves out-numbered the Swabians. It is improbable, therefore, that these last numbered more than 40,000 all told.

The division did not bring peace. The Swabians, under their king Hermeric (*c.* 410–40), claimed the territory of Orense, and were blockaded there by the king of the Asdingians, Gundered. Meanwhile, further south, the Silingians and the Alans proved unwelcome visitors, for Roman billeting laws permitted them to take one-third of their hosts' property. But now the Emperor Honorius found more powerful allies in the Visigoths, formerly settled in Thrace, where they were converted to Arian Christianity. Theodosius had made allies of them, but after his death they had forced their way into Italy. His son persuaded them to settle in Gaul, where they were to give military service and were duly attached to the Roman admin-istration at Toulouse. Their first task was to impose order in the Peninsula. The king of the Silingians was captured by a ruse, and his followers were cut to pieces. The Alans suffered a similar fate, and on the death of their king, they decided not to elect a successor, but to join with the Vandals. These, in turn, were separated from their Swabian neighbours and moved to Baetica. The Visigoths then returned to Gaul. But in the following years the Vandals supported another anti-emperor, and having overrun Baetica, they finally crossed to Africa, supposedly to serve the eastern emperor, but in fact to establish a German kingdom in the ancient territory of Carthage (429).

The Swabians were now the only Germanic people left in the Peninsula. They had come first from the region of the Spree, and had been known to Caesar, who notes that they were good horsemen but fought on foot, and wore few clothes, mainly skins. In Pliny's day they had wooden huts which they dismantled and carried with them in carts: they had no private fields, only folkland. Two centuries later they maintained their military organization and travelled with their women and children riding in carts. They were still pagans. With the departure of the Vandals, they attempted to occupy the Galician garrison-towns, such as Astorga. This led to a series of missions between Gallaecia and Gaul, in which one of the negotiators was the bishop of Aquae Flaviae (Chaves), Hydatius, whose chronicle is the only source for the history of the Swabian kingdom. With the virtual disappearance of Roman administration, the Swabians treated the bishops as the heads of the Roman civil hierarchy and probably regarded those in their territory as removable officials: they also tolerated the Priscillianists, who were still numerous.

In 435 a number of priests reached Gallaecia from Jerusalem: they were mainly Greeks, and it is probable that the Galician see of Iría or Padrón dates from this period. In 447 Pope Leo I sent letters condemning Priscillianism to Bishops Turibius of Astorga and Hydatius of Chaves, and synods were held in Toledo and in Galicia, which resulted in the expulsion of some of the heretics. Meanwhile, Hermeric had reached some sort of settlement about the Galician towns. By 438 he was incapacitated, and had delivered the military command to his son Rechila, who raided the province of Baetica and in 440 captured the Roman legate Censorius at Mértola. On his father's death in 441, Rechila entered Seville, where he replaced the bishop, and also occupied part of Carthaginensis. At this time, eastern Spain was in a turmoil owing to the revolt of the peasants, who left the Roman estates, formed armed bands of *bagaudae* (Celtic, 'rebels'), and raided farms and towns. In 446 a Roman general tried to recover Baetica and Carthaginensis, but failed, being abandoned by his Visigothic auxiliaries.

When Rechila died in 448, his son Rechiarius succeeded. He was converted to Catholicism and became an ally of the Emperor Honorius: coin was minted at Braga in the name of Honorius and Rechiarius. He made an alliance with the Visigoths and married the daughter of their king Theodoric I. However, he also raided the still pagan peoples of the north and sought to extend his authority in Spain. This was opposed by the Romans, who sent missions to persuade him to evacuate Carthaginensis. In 456 Theodoric marched across Spain, defeated Rechiarius near Astorga, and entered Braga.

Rechiarius retreated to Portucale (Oporto), where he was captured and executed at the end of the year.

The Visigothic king left one of his followers, Aiulf, to govern the Swabians, and marched on to Mérida, whence he returned to Toulouse. But the Swabians did not accept the reverse. One party supported a certain Framtane, and another Maldras. It seems that Framtane was killed, and that Aiulf attempted to declare himself king, but was murdered in Oporto (June 457). Then Maldras became sole ruler, occupying the towns of Galicia, and entering Lusitania, where Lisbon was surrendered to him. But in 458 the Visigoths, still ostensibly upholding Roman rule, sent troops to occupy Seville and blocked any further expansion of the Swabians.

At this time the Vandals, from their kingdom in Africa, and supported by the eastern emperor, attempted to form a coalition with the Swabians in opposition to the western Romans. They also hoped to draw in the Visigoths, who had hitherto been loyal to the western emperors, but who now quarrelled with them. The (western) Emperor Majorianus defeated the Visigothic king Theodoric at Arles, and sent a general as ambassador to the Swabians, apparently to persuade them to respect the towns of Lugo and Orense. Early in 460 Maldras was killed. His son and successor Remismund attacked the Galician towns, while another leader Frumarius raided Chaves and arrested Bishop Hydatius. In May Majorianus arrived in Spain and sent a Visigothic general, Sunyeric, against the Swabians. He occupied Santarém in the south and expelled them from Lugo. But when Majorianus went to Cartagena, intending to sail for Africa to attack the Vandals, his fleet was destroyed by them, and his plan having failed, he was soon deposed and died (August 461).

The Swabian kingdom was reunited under the rule of Remismund on the death of Frumarius in 464. The Visigoths were now in effective control in Spain and southern Gaul, and Remismund made an alliance with them, married a Visigothic princess, and was presently converted to the Visigothic religion of Arianism by a Bishop Ajax, an Anatolian who had apostasized from Catholicism. With this support he was able to enter Conimbriga (Condeixa). He also occupied the town of Aunona (Aurona, Orense), whose people, as in the past, sent protests to the authorities in Gaul.

But at this moment the Visigoths at last decided to break with the western emperors and to establish themselves as an independent kingdom. Theodoric II was murdered by his brother Euric, who refused to recognize the western emperor Artemius and sent messengers to Leo, the ruler of Byzantium, and sought an alliance with the Vandals. Artemius appealed to the Swabians for support. They sent a mission to Toulouse; but Euric was already in power and refused to receive it. As it returned, he sent an army hard on its heels to occupy Mérida. The Swabians now made peace with the people of Orense and sent a force to occupy Lisbon. Meanwhile, Euric had garrisoned Astorga and Mérida. Thus in 468 the Swabian kingdom found itself hemmed in by its more powerful rivals. It stretched from the Minho to Condeixa and Lisbon, and may have included Évora and Beja. But Lugo and Astorga in the north and Mérida in the east were firmly held by Visigothic garrisons. In 475 Euric produced a code of laws without reference to a higher authority, and in the following year the last emperor was overthrown in Rome.

During the period of Visigothic hegemony little is heard of Swabian Portugal. Bishop Hydatius died in 468, scarcely surviving the apostasy of the ruling house. Such Arian writings as existed were destroyed after the second conversion of the Swabians to Catholicism. An inscription of 485 from Veirão, near Braga, alludes to a king Veremundus (Vermudo).[1]

The Visigothic ascendancy established by Euric lasted for thirty years. In 507 the power of the Visigoths in Gaul was broken by the Franks, who defeated them in the battle of Vouglé and entered Toulouse. The Visigothic state was saved only by the intervention of the Ostrogoths of Italy and by the removal of their court, first to Barcelona and then to Toledo. Now the eastern empire under Justinian overthrew the Vandal kingdom and regained control of Africa, and Justinian gave instructions for the fortification of Ceuta, commanding the Straits of Gibraltar. The two Gothic peoples alone continued to practise the Arian religion, and they were faced with a powerful array of Catholic enemies, the Franks in Gaul, the Byzantines in Africa, and the subdued Hispano-Roman population in the Peninsula. In 544 the Visigoths seized Ceuta, only to lose it in a short time: a second attempt to take it was unsuccessful. During the short reign of Agila (549-55), the people of Baetica began to rebel

---

[1] Its authenticity was doubted by Hübner.

against Visigothic rule. A Visigothic pretender, Athanagild, accepted the support of the Byzantines, who sent an army against Agila. He was defeated at Seville and retired to Mérida, where he was murdered, leaving the throne of the Visigoths in the hands of the protégé of Justinian (555).

During these years constant attempts had been made to revive the Catholic faith in the west. Paul, a Greek doctor who had settled in Mérida, was made bishop there: Pope Hormixta sent letters to Seville about the condition of Lusitania (517); Pope Vigil addressed Profuturus, bishop of Braga, in 538. Finally the king of the Swabians, Chararic, was converted to Catholicism during the illness of his son (c. 550). His successor Theodomir brought his people back to the orthodox church soon after his accession (558 or 559). Under Arianism, Catholic synods had been prohibited, but in 563 eight bishops gathered at the first council of Braga, presided over by Lucretius, formerly bishop of Iría (Padrón). But the chief architect of the conversion was Martin, a native of Pannonia, who had come to Portugal from the east and founded a monastery at Dume, near Braga. This was possibly the residence of the Swabian rulers. The first council set about defining the errors of Priscillianism, and it does not seem that this heresy long survived. Pagan beliefs were still widespread, and St Martin refers to them in his *De Correctione Rusticorum*.

St Martin founded or rebuilt a basilica, which he dedicated to his namesake, Martin of Tours (d. 400), and during the following years at least fifty churches between the Minho and the Mondego were placed under the patronage of the same saint.[1] The ecclesiastical organization of the Swabian kingdom is shown in a parochiale of about 569, when the metropolitanate of Braga included the sees of Lamego, Viseu, Conimbriga and Idanha. The second council held at Braga, in 572, was presided over by the metropolitan, Martin of Braga, and was attended by bishops of Oporto, Lamego, Viseu, Conimbriga and Idanha, in Portugal, and Tuy, Orense, Iría, Mondoñedo and Astorga, in Galicia.[2]

Of the secular administration of the Swabians almost nothing is known. The concentration of Germanic toponyms in the district

[1] Whence the frequency of the name Martim, Martins.

[2] The see of Oporto was then known as Magnetensis (now Meinedo, near Penafiel) and that of Mondoñedo as Britonensis, from the Celtic tribe of the Britones.

between the Douro and the Minho shows clearly where they dwelt: about 2,000 names of Germanic origin are recorded in Portugal. Coins were minted at Bracara (Braga), Cale or Portucale (Oporto), Aeminio or Imino, the present Coimbra, which now replaced the ancient Conimbriga, Viseu, Lamego, Évora and Beja.[1]

The independent kingdom of the Swabians did not long survive. In 570 Theodemir was succeeded by his son Miro, who attacked and conquered the Rucones, a tribe in Cantabrian territory. But at this time the Visigothic monarchy passed to the most energetic of its rulers, Leovigild (569?–586), who recovered central Baetica from the Byzantines, and also subdued the peoples of Cantabria and the north. In 573 he annexed the Asturians, and Miro sought an alliance with the Franks, but without effect. Leovigild then invaded the territory of Galicia and occupied Orense, long claimed by the Swabians. Miro asked for terms and apparently obtained a truce of short duration (576).

But Leovigild's great design was to restore the ascendancy of the Visigoths throughout the Peninsula and to wean the Spanish Catholics from their alliance with the Byzantines. He allowed his son Hermenegild to marry a Catholic and sent him to govern Baetica. But St Leander, the metropolitan of Seville, converted Hermenegild to Catholicism, and the young man presently sought the help of the Byzantines in rebelling against his father. He also appealed to Miro, the king of the Catholic Swabians, who marched to Seville. But Leovigild advanced on Baetica, and defeated and captured his son, who was executed. Miro had led his army to Seville, but was driven back, and apparently fell ill during the expedition. Leovigild pursued him to Mérida and forced him to make an oath of submission. Shortly after, Miro died, and was succeeded by his young son Eboric (583). It appears that one faction of the Swabians was anxious to end their subjection to the Visigoths and gave its support to Andeca, who had married Miro's daughter:

---

[1] These are the centres of ecclesiastical administration. Coins are also known from Beriso, Lancia (Guarda), Maurelos (Mourelos) and Senabra (Puebla de Sanabria). In Galicia, coins were minted at a number of small towns or villages, but apparently only in Visigothic times.

Few Swabian words have survived in Portuguese. They include: *britar*, to break (stones); *laverca*, lark; *lóbio*, vineyard. It is supposed that the Swabians introduced the heavy northern plough into Portugal, and it is probable that other agricultural practices and local customs can be traced to them.

he now deposed his brother-in-law and had him tonsured and confined in a monastery. In 585 Leovigild again intervened, deposed Andeca, put him in a monastery and suppressed the Swabian monarchy.

Nothing is heard of the Swabian kingdom for more than a century. Leovigild died in 586, and his son Reccared was converted to Catholicism, summoning a council at Toledo at which he urged the Arian bishops to follow him. Not all were willing to do so: there was a brief rebellion in the west and one Witeric attempted to murder the Catholic bishop of Mérida. In 589 St Leander celebrated another council at Toledo, at which the Portuguese sees were represented: Braga, Dume, Portucale, Laniobrensis (Feira, south of Oporto), Viseu, Lamego, Eminio, Idanha, Évora, Beja and Ossonoba.[1]

The religious distinction between the Swabians and the Visigoths was thus obliterated. However, the consociation of the Gothic monarchy and the Catholic church was a lengthy process, which reached its apogee only in the time of St Isidore, metropolitan of Seville and restorer of classical learning (d. 636). In the first years of the seventh century the Visigothic traditionalists overthrew Reccared's successor and brought to the throne Witeric, during whose reign no council of the church was held. It was left to Sisebut (612–21) to make peace with the church, suppress rebellions in Galicia, Asturias and Cantabria, and negotiate the evacuation by the Byzantines of their remaining strongholds in the Peninsula. Thus St Isidore, in extolling the greatness of the Goths, asserted that Sisebut's general and successor Swinthila (621–31), was the first ruler 'to receive the monarchy of all the Spains', and in 624 dedicated to him an enthusiastic eulogy as 'prince of peoples and father of the poor'. In praising the Visigoths, he noted that they had hemmed in the Swabians among the 'inaccessible corners of the Spains' and finally deprived them of the kingdom 'which they held in slothful idleness' and gave up 'without any attempt at defence'.

But St Isidore's enthusiasm for the Visigoths as defenders of the faith would certainly have been tempered if he could have foreseen the events of the rest of the century. The much-praised Swinthila fell from grace when he tried to associate his son as his successor.

[1] Eminio is the see of Conimbriga, whose name it will later adopt. Lisbon is conspicuous by its absence, and reappears in the episcopal lists only in 633.

One of his nobles Sisenand made a *pronunciamento* in Septimania and entered Toledo in triumph, Swinthila being abandoned by his men. Sisenand apparently ruled mildly and favoured the church, but 'the people of the Goths are impatient when they do not have a strong yoke over them'.[1] In 642 power was seized by Khindaswinth, an elderly noble, who arrested and tonsured his young predecessor and executed 200 nobles and 500 others who were opposed to him. He also deprived the metropolitanate of Seville of the primacy of the Spanish church and bestowed it on the metropolitan of Toledo, a see of overwhelmingly Visigothic tradition. From this time the church became increasingly Gothicized, and far from representing the interests of the Hispano-Roman population, it became involved in the struggles of the Gothic nobility. Khindaswinth died in 653, at the age of ninety, and his son Recceswinth, who had been 'associated' with him since 649, repressed the rebellion of Froya in the north and celebrated a council of Toledo (VIII, 653), at which it was agreed that when a king died, his successor should be elected in the palace or wherever the court was by the nobles and bishops. In effect, the kings were appointed by a small oligarchy of officials and prelates.[2] In 654 (?) Recceswinth promulgated a new code of laws, the Liber judiciorum, which survived into the middle ages as the Fuero Juzgo, the code of medieval Galicia and Leon. A year later, a new Council of Toledo (IX) further identified the church with the state by enacting that the king alone should have power to punish the metropolitans, and these to punish the bishops.

During all this time little is heard of the Swabian kingdom. Fructuosus, who occupied the see of Braga until his death (665–7), was the son of a Visigothic noble from Bierzo in Leon and had studied in Baetica. A letter from his friend, St Braulio, (Visigothic) bishop of Saragossa, shows that he had complained of the backwardness of his flock, 'an extremity of the west, an ignorant country where naught is heard but the sound of tempests'. Braulio reminded him that the

---

[1] Fredegarius, IV, 82, 162–3, on the deposition of Sisenand's young son Tulga.

[2] The chief secular figures of the court were not more than fifteen or twenty, described as *dux*, governor, general, *comes*, governor, companion, or *procer*, noble. Specific offices were the *comes cuobiculariorum*, or governor of the palace; *c. patrimoniorum*, treasurer; *c. notariorum*, chancellor; *c. scanciarum*, cup-bearers; *c. spathariorum*, head of the bodyguard; *c. stabularum*, master of the horse. There also appears a *comes* or governor of the city of Toledo.

west had been evangelized by learned Greeks, and had produced such men as Paulus Orosius, Toribius, and Hydatius of Chaves. Fructuosus' contribution was two rules, the *Regula communis* and *Regula monachorum*, which governed monastic life in the west for some four centuries. Of particular interest is the 'pact of St Fructuosus' by which the abbot and monks exchanged oaths of loyalty in terms which clearly reflect Germanic customary law.

In 672 Recceswinth died, and the electors passed over the younger sons of Khindaswinth and chose as king one Wamba, who was apparently favourable to the church. He is traditionally credited with having established the ecclesiastical divisions of the Peninsula.[1] Before his election he presented the testament of St Martin at the Council of Toledo,[2] and may therefore have governed the Swabian kingdom. He was faced with a rebellion led by Ranosind, *dux* of Tarragona, and part of Recceswinth's court, and carried his campaign against them into Septimania, capturing the ringleader Paul, who was executed in Toledo. In 680 Wamba fell ill and was persuaded to take the tonsure, as though he were about to die: he recovered, but was disqualified from ruling, and remained in a monastery near Burgos. According to the chronicler, his deposition was a plot by Ardabast, a Greek who had married a relative of Khindaswinth, and his son Erwig, who thus seized power (680–687). In 681 a Council of Toledo (XII) accepted the deposition of Wamba and the succession of Erwig, and pardoned those who had been excommunicated for siding with Wamba. It also gave the metropolitan of Toledo the power to appoint successors to all the bishoprics.

Erwig completed his reconciliation with the partisans of Wamba by marrying his daughter to Wamba's nephew Egica. When in 687 Erwig fell ill, he in turn was tonsured and clad as a penitent, and on dying left the throne to Egica (687–702). There were, however, descendants of Khindaswinth. One of these, Theudefred, had apparently been blinded, and dwelt in Córdoba with his son Roderic: another, Favila, had a palace at Tuy in the confines of the Swabian kingdom. Erwig now associated his son Witiza with his rule, and sent him 'to reside in the city of Tuy in the province of

---

[1] The 'divisio Wambae' in its known form is a later sophistication.

[2] The celebration in 675 of the XI Council of Toledo and III Council of Braga implies the duality of the Visigothic kingdom.

Gallaecia, so that the father should have the kingdom of the Goths and the son the kingdom of the Swabians'.[1] It seems that the son of Khindaswinth named Favila who had his palace at Tuy was the father of Pelayo, the leader of the Christian resistance after the Muslim conquest.

The last decade of the Visigothic monarchy is extremely obscure. Like his predecessors, Egica despoiled his rivals and enriched himself by confiscating their estates. He also sought to frustrate the elective tradition by bestowing the throne on his son. He died in 702, having already made Witiza regent. The new king relaxed his father's oppression; he also sent assistance to Ceuta, now threatened by the Muslims. But when Witiza died, early in 710, the Visigothic nobles rejected the succession of his sons, who were minors. They drove his widow and children out of Toledo, and elected as their ruler Roderic, the son of the blinded Theudefred, who had been living in Córdoba, and was perhaps duke of Baetica. He defeated his rivals, and in the spring of 711 marched northward to put down a revolt of the Vascones at Pamplona. As he did so, his enemies, the faction of Witiza, sought the help of the Muslims, whose expansion across North Africa had recently brought them to the Straits of Gibraltar.

4. THE MUSLIM INVASION AND THE CHRISTIAN RECONQUEST

While St Isidore was celebrating the merits of the lately converted Visigoths, the prophet Muḥammad was preaching a doctrine of pure theocracy in distant Arabia. After his death the desert peoples had overrun Syria and Egypt, and after a long struggle had driven the Byzantines out of Libya and Tunis. They were bitterly resisted by the Berbers of Tunisia, and it was only towards the end of the first Muslim century that they reached the Atlantic plains of Morocco, entering Tangier. Ceuta had remained in Christian hands: its count, one Julian, was a subject of Witiza, but the merchants and ships that frequented the port were probably Byzantine or Syrian. It seems that Julian invited the Muslims to intervene in Spain against Roderic and on behalf of the family of Witiza. They landed near Algeciras

---

[1] Chronicle of Alfonso III (c. 890) and Epitome Ovetensis (c. 883).

and occupied the surrounding district in the spring of 711. Roderic hastened southwards and gave battle in July. He was abandoned by some of his followers in the field; the rest were overrun, and he himself perished in the fray. The Muslims advanced to Córdoba, and then marched on Toledo. They occupied it without a further struggle, and seized there the treasure of the Visigoths.

The heirs of Witiza had hoped that the Muslims would overthrow Roderic and then depart, having restored them to power. They did indeed recover vast estates, but the newcomers, far from relinquishing their conquest, garrisoned Toledo and descended on the provincial capitals, obtaining the capitulation of the authorities as they went. The last real resistance of the Visigoths was made at Mérida, which was besieged for months and fell in June 713. The first conquerors were mainly freedmen and Berbers, but the Arab governor of Ifrīqiya, Musa ibn Nuṣair, now arrived, and having entered Mérida, wintered in Toledo. In the spring of 714 he advanced to Saragossa, and then marched across the north: he or his generals now entered Leon and Astorga. He was recalled to Damascus, and his son, who had probably already entered southern Portugal, seems to have occupied Évora, Santarém and Coimbra in 714–16; but there are no details of these events.

In the north and west, the Muslims, who were few in number, were content to receive the capitulation of the Visigothic governors, leaving only small garrisons in the centres of administration. These would be largely of Berbers only newly converted to Islam. Some were followed by their families and kinspeople, who established themselves on the central tableland and in Galicia. They were nomadic pastoral peoples, not yet Arabic-speaking: it is improbable that they contributed anything towards the implantation of an eastern culture.

The seeds of the Christian reconquest were sown in about 718, when one Pelayo, apparently a son of Favila, the son of Khindaswinth who had had his palace at Tuy, placed himself at the head of the tribes of the Asturias. About four years later, he defeated a force of Berbers near Covadonga. Nothing is known of the appearance of the Muslims in northern Portugal or neighbouring Galicia, but if the family of Witiza retained or recovered their states there, it is probable that there was little settlement by the newcomers. These last were intent on invading France, and their extraordinary expansion was checked only by their defeat near Poitiers in 732. Seven years later they were faced by a formidable rebellion of the Berbers in Africa. It spread to the Berbers of the Peninsula, and in 741 those of Galicia marched on the Arab-occupied cities of Toledo and Córdoba. The caliph sent Arab reinforcements, and the Berbers were defeated, but there followed a great famine, in the course of which many returned to Africa. Meanwhile, the contingents newly-arrived from Syria were given land in the Peninsula. They were spread from the Portuguese Algarve to Murcia, and the old Roman territory of Baetica thus became the heart of the Muslim Peninsula, al-Andalus. In the distribution (753), the Egyptians were settled in the Algarve between Beja and Ossonoba, and the Syrians from Emesa between this and Seville.

These events drew off most of the small Muslim population of the north and west. Pelayo had died in 737, and his son Favila was killed in 739. His daughter had married Alfonso, the son of an independent leader in Cantabria. He joined the two provinces and profited by the discord of the Muslims to recover Astorga and Galicia. By 753 he had entered Lugo, Tuy, Braga, Oporto and Viseu, and had raided as far south as Mérida. In 755 the Muslims sent an expedition into Galicia, but it appears to have failed. However Alfonso had not the resources to occupy and defend all these places, and instead he carried off the inhabitants to be resettled in the north, How complete this depopulation was remains doubtful: the Christian chronicles say that he *eremavit*, or created a no-man's land, between his territory and that of the Muslims. He may well have destroyed the towns and broken up the civil and ecclesiastical administration by removing the nobles and prelates. But it is unlikely that the whole countryside was abandoned, and in places at least the parochial divisions survived. Documents of 747(?) and 760(?) show how one Odoarius, bishop of Lugo, had been obliged to leave the town, of which he was a native, and to 'dwell in waste places': he now returned, found Lugo uninhabited, and settled 'many of our families, both noble and common' on land in its vicinity, providing them with oxen and beasts of burden. He refers expressly to Provecendi (Provezende, Vila Nova de Cerveira), Desterit (Desteriz, Orense), Avezaria (Abação, Guimarãis), Guntini (Gontim, Fafe) and Veremundi (Vermoim, Famalicão): it seems that he intended to restore the see of Braga, but died before he could do so. Rural resettlement continued to take place under the patronage of the kings of Asturias, nobles or prelates, and unoccupied land (*pressúrias*) was peopled with clients, free settlers or fugitives or captives from the south.

In 756 an Arab prince, 'Abdu'r-Raḥman, the sole surviving member of the caliphal family of the Umaiyads, arrived in the Peninsula, entered Córdoba, and set up a separate Muslim dominion in the west, thus restoring the fortunes of his house. For many years he was forced to struggle with enemies, often stirred up by the ʿAbbāsid caliphs of Bagdad. He was therefore rarely able to intervene in the affairs of his Christian neighbours. In 768 a Berber reformer rebelled in central Spain and held the line of the Tagus, occupying Mérida and other towns: he was not reduced for nine years. The princes of Córdoba held effectively only the south and east. The cities of Saragossa, Toledo and Mérida became the frontier between the two civilizations, and these were still populated overwhelmingly either by Christians or by new Muslims whose attachment to Islam was often dubious. In 778 Charlemagne embarked on his famous expedition against Saragossa, the consequence of an intrigue by the caliph of Bagdad. It failed, but it was followed by a series of campaigns by both sides. In 791 a Muslim was able to force his way into Galicia, and in 795 another commander from Córdoba occupied Astorga. But three years later Alfonso II advanced through Portugal and entered Lisbon. He still could not occupy it. A few years later a rebel named Tumlus seized power there: he was finally defeated and executed by an Umaiyad prince (809). During the same period there were constant revolts in Mérida and Toledo, where the Muslims maintained their authority by dint of bloody repressions.

During these years there occurred an event of far-reaching importance in the evolution of the west, the discovery of what was believed to be the tomb of the Apostle St James the Greater at the Galician fishing-port of Padrón. The tomb was transferred to Compostela, where a church and shrine were built. Successive rulers of the Asturian kingdom conferred privileges and prestige on the sanctuary of the Apostle, which thus came to take the place of the five ancient metropolitanates. Of these, four were in cities now occupied by the Muslims, and the fifth, Braga, had been abandoned. It is probable that the effect of the Muslim invasion and of the policy of resettlement pursued by the Asturian monarchy was to concentrate the Christian population in the northern part of Galicia. Of northern Portugal little is heard: it appears that Alfonso II convened a council of counts and bishops at Guimarãis in 840 with a view to the restoration of Braga, but this had not been achieved when he died two years later. At this time the Muslims held Coimbra and Viseu, from which they attempted to invade Christian territory in 825 and 838. They were driven back, but it is uncertain where the Christian defences began. During the following decade, the Christians were beset from another direction when the Norsemen, who had raided the estuaries of western France, appeared in the *rias* of Galicia and raided villages in the interior. The bishops and counts raised local forces and drove them back to their ships. They sailed on, putting in at Lisbon to plunder, and finally reached the Guadalquivir, sacking Seville (840).

After the middle of the century, the Christians began to occupy the abandoned frontier. Ordoño I (850–866) advanced out of the Asturian mountains to resettle the Roman city of Leon. To the east a new frontier had been peopled, and it was known as 'the castles' or Castile. To the west, Ordõno restored Astorga and Tuy, then the western defences of his kingdom. In 868 one Vimara Peres undertook the rebuilding of Portucale, thus occupying the line of the Douro. The town itself must have been small, but the surrounding district was settled and brought under cultivation, to be known as the 'territorium Portugalense'. This term was soon applied to the whole region from Minho to the Douro, and was extended southwards to the Vouga to include the territory known as Feira. Nothing is yet heard of the restoration of Braga.

We have no continuous account of the restoration of the old Swabian territory. The administrative divisions of the revived Gothic monarchy were governed by bishops or counts, who might be appointed from court or be members of powerful local families. In Castile, there were at first several counts, whose territories were united in the hands of a single family, which finally claimed hereditary office and made a dynastic alliance with the ruling dynasty. In Portugal, the territorial unity of the area seems to have been preserved, and there the counts were for long drawn from a single house. We hear of a Count Mendo, or Hermenegildo Gonçalves, and his wife Mumadona in 931. On Mendo's death Mumadona held the county for her two sons, Gonçalo and Diogo. During the last third of the century, her heir Gonçalo Mendes acquired great influence in the affairs of Leon, seeking either an alliance with its kings or virtual autonomy. The counts of Portugal supported Ordoño III (951–7) and must have participated in his attack on Lisbon. But on his death, his brother, Sancho I the Fat, thrust aside his young heir, and the barons of the west, in conjunction with the bishop of Santiago, defended the principle of primogeniture and drove out the usurper. However, Sancho went to Córdoba and obtained the help of the Muslims to recover his throne. When he died, the barons accepted the succession of his son Ramiro III, a boy of five.

At this time, the Vikings appeared in the *rías* of Galicia (968). They killed the bishop of Santiago in battle, but his successor St Rudesind rallied the forces of the region and finally killed the Viking king, Gundered.

But now the Umaiyads of Córdoba had assumed the title of caliphs, and sought to establish their ascendancy over the Berber kingdoms of northern Africa and over the Christians of the Peninsula. As 'Abdu'r-Rahman III invaded Leon, the barons of the west declared for Vermudo II, the heir of Ordoño III, who was proclaimed king in Santiago. For a time he ruled in the west and Ramiro III in Leon: a first battle between them was indecisive, but in 984 Vermudo succeeded in entering Leon: he had probably obtained help from the Muslims.

Prominent among his supporters was Gonçalo Mendes, count of Portugal, whose son Mendo Gonçalo became tutor to Vermudo's heir, Alfonso V (b. 994). But when Vermudo attempted to disentangle himself from his engagements towards the Muslims, he was attacked by the new master of Córdoba, the all-powerful dictator known as al-Manṣūr, who unleashed a series of devastating campaigns against the Christian west. In 987–8 he sacked Coimbra, which had passed under Christian rule: it lay abandoned for several years and was then reoccupied by the Muslims. In 997 he attacked both Leon and Santiago, and carried off to Córdoba the gates and bells of the basilica of Saint James. The Christian kingdoms were still in subjection when Vermudo died in 999: his heir Alfonso V was a child of five.

At this time Mendo Gonçalo enjoyed great influence in the kingdom or empire of Leon, and hoped to perpetuate it by betrothing the little king to his daughter. During his absence, his county was governed by a delegate, Magister Everardus (1004). But in 1008 the Vikings again raided the north-west and Mendo was killed in a campaign against them. His widow Tuta Mendo then governed the county, and married her daughter and heiress Ilduara to one Nuno Alvito, whose father had been governor of Vermoim. He himself is described as *dux magnus* and he lived until 1028. After this, Ilduara shared the government of Portugal with their son Mendo Nunes. This Mendo died in battle between 1050 and 1053, leaving a young son named Nuno Mendes. Dona Ilduara still survived, and it appears that she governed Portugal and the borderland of Feira. Alfonso V had laid siege to Viseu in 1028, and was killed by a bolt from the walls. There were no further royal campaigns in the west for a quarter of a century, but in 1034 a Portuguese frontiersman named Gonçalo Trastemires recovered the castle of Montemór, between Coimbra and the sea, thus carrying the frontier down to the level of the Mondego.

The rise and decline of the first dynasty of counts of Portugal is clearly associated with the organization of the military frontier against Islam and with the struggle of the large and populous west to maintain its influence in the councils of Leon. But these designs were frustrated by the weakening of the old kingdom of Leon, and the association of Castile and Navarre, which now combined to overthrow the neo-Gothic dynasty, the leaders of the reconquest for three hundred years. Navarre, the territory of the Romanized Basques of Pamplona, became an independent monarchy in the early tenth century, with the support of Leon. Later, it had made alliances with the caliphs of Córdoba and with the counts of Castile, who since 950 constituted an hereditary dynasty. Its most ambitious ruler, Sancho III the Great (1000–39), the son of a Castilian mother, succeeded to the county of Castile and bestowed it on his second son Ferdinand in 1034. After his death, Ferdinand assumed for the first time the title of King of Castile and defeated and killed the last of the rulers of the neo-Gothic dynasty, uniting the territories of Leon and Castile, and taking for himself the title of emperor.

The consequence of the hegemony of Castile was to diminish the influence of the western barons, and to replace the old houses by nobles of the second rank, or *infanções*, or by royal officials. Thus in 1050 an *infanção* named Gomes Eitaz appears as governor in Guimarãis, and others are recorded as 'holding the land of Portugal' in 1062. In the following year the 'land of Portugal' was governed by maiorini (*meirinhos do rei*) or *vicarii*, 'noble and of great dignity', possibly a triumvirate of administrators. This was the earliest Portuguese experience of Castilian centralization. There are now no references to 'counts of Portugal'.

Ferdinand I—unlike his father, who had never drawn sword against the Muslims, but devoted his reign to the aggrandizement of his house at the expense of his Christian neighbours—was a crusader. Since the death of al-Manṣūr, the rulers of Córdoba had lost control of their Berber generals, who raised up caliphs and pulled them down, and finally sacked Córdoba and created their own anti-caliphate. At length in 1031 the citizens of Córdoba, weary of civil strife, proclaimed the end of the Umaiyad caliphate and set up a municipal republic. The rest of al-Andalus fell into its component divisions or *taifas*. Ferdinand I seized the opportunity to lay tribute on these Muslim principalities, and to extend his frontiers at their expense when they refused to pay.

In Portugal, Montemór had been taken in 1034, the year in which the Navarrese dynasty invaded Leon. There followed a long lull. Now Ferdinand was able to occupy the outpost of Sena (Seia) and to enter the towns of Lamego (1057) and Viseu (1058). Smaller places—Tarouca, Travanca, Penela—fell into Christian hands or offered tribute. In 1064 Ferdinand raised forces for the conquest of Coimbra: it fell on 9 July after a siege lasting six months.

The territory of Coimbra was not attached to Portugal, but erected into a new county and entrusted to Sisnand ibn David or Davidiz, a native of Tentúgal, between Coimbra and Montemór, and a Mozarab, or Christian who had lived under Muslim domination. He long governed Coimbra, serving Ferdinand and his sons as ambassador in their negotiations for tribute with the princes of al-Andalus. His city was the first Muslim fortress of any consequence to fall under Christian rule, anticipating the conquest of Toledo by a generation. In contrast to Portugal north of the Vouga, which had hardly known Muslim occupation, and was in essence a reconstruction of the old Swabian kingdom, the region of Coimbra had long been a Muslim frontier. While further north there are no traces of Muslim architecture, Coimbra still possesses the gate of its madina, the Arco de Almedina, parts of its Muslim walls, a small gate now incorporated in the Museo Machado de Castro and the characteristic *couraças*, or steep roads of access built under the shadow of the walls.

After its conquest, the Mozarabic population replaced the Muslims as the predominant class. There was probably no general exodus of citizens. The institutions of the Muslims remained. The governor was called an *alcaide*, not a *tenens*. His assistants were two *alvazirs*, not *consules*. At least part of the Muslim system of inspectors, police and market officials survived. Many of the inhabitants continued to be known by their Arabic names, even though they were Christians, and including Mozarabic priests. Thus members of the same family bore either Muslim or Christian names: Marwan Menendiz, Pelagius Abu Nazar presbyter, Martinus ibn Tomad, Zoleiman Leovigildis presbyter, Exeixa Alvara and her children, Abdirahman, Justa and Maria. The will of Bona Menendez shows that she had come from Zorita in the Muslim kingdom of Toledo to settle in Christian territory, bringing her servants and household goods. These last are referred to by their Arabic names, and the document is confirmed by a priest named Petrus Zoleima and witnessed by Calaf, Levita and Merwan. Later documents provide a varied Mozarabic vocabulary for garments, musical instruments, household goods, domestic beasts, food-plants and herbs.

5. FROM COUNTY TO KINGDOM

In the year following the conquest of Coimbra Ferdinand I died, and his realms were divided among his three sons and two daughters. His eldest son, Sancho II, inherited Castile; his second son Alfonso VI received Leon, and his youngest son García was made king of Galicia. The elder daughter Urraca received the town of Zamora, and the younger Elvira that of Toro, both using the title of queen The separation of Leon and Castile was followed by a series of struggles between the elder brothers, culminating in the death of Sancho and the triumph of Alfonso, who in 1072 again united the kingdoms and took the title of emperor. The division of the west led to further, but obscurer, strife. The border county of Coimbra was still governed by Sisnand, the loyal servant of Ferdinand and Alfonso. The Portuguese barons were thus excluded from direct participation in the perils and profits of the frontier war. Worse still, they were now subordinated to the new ruler of Galicia. It appears that Nuno Mendes, the descendant of Mumadona, resisted the new order: he was defeated and killed in a battle with Galicians between Braga and the river Cávado in January 1071. But two years later, when Alfonso had eliminated Sancho, he decided also to regain possession of Galicia, and invited García to an interview, arrested him and held him prisoner in a castle in Leon, where he died in 1090. Galicia thus ceased to be a kingdom.

But while Alfonso VI looked towards the eventual restoration of the old Visigothic 'empire', the church began to press for a different and more meticulous reconstruction. The rulers of the Asturo-Leonese monarchy, following the late Visigothic tradition, had regarded themselves as patrons of the church, appointing prelates and even abbots. But the reformers of Cluny now sought to make the monasteries independent of the civil power, to replace the old Visigothic rite by the universal Roman liturgy and to establish the supremacy of the papacy above kings. Hildebrand, the great proponent of papal supremacy, was elected pope as Gregory VII in 1073. In Leon, the Cluniac reformers were favoured by Alfonso VI, who had married a Burgundian wife and soon requested the pope for assistance in establishing the Roman liturgy in his realms (1078); two years later a council was held at Burgos at which the change was formally adopted.

The revival of the church implied the re-creation of the ecclesiastical organization of the Peninsula as it was deemed to have existed before the Muslim conquest. Of the five metropolitanates only Braga was in Christian hands, and it had been restored as a bishopric in 1070, an event possibly not unconnected with the clash between Nuno Mendes and the Galician barons. The main resistance to the restoration of the pre-Muslim order proceeded from the church of Santiago, which had come into existence only with the invention of the Apostle's tomb and could claim no pre-Muslim ancestry except by identifying itself with the minor see of Iría or Padrón. It had received many privileges and now governed places that had once belonged to Braga. The obstacles to the restoration of the metro-politanate of Braga were thus considerable, and they were not diminished when in 1081 the Mozarabic bishop of Coimbra, Paternus, gained control of the churches of Lamego and Viseu.

In 1085 the processes of restoration, secular and ecclesiastical, were carried rapidly forward with the reconquest of Toledo. Alfonso gained great prestige, and entrusted the restored see to a Cluniac named Bernard. Three years later, in 1088, he ordered the arrest of Diogo Pais, bishop of Santiago, on a charge of high treason, alleging that he had proposed to betray Galicia to the Norman king of England; whether there were grounds for the accusation is doubtful, but it is significant that at this time the papacy was claiming tribute from various princes, including Alfonso and William the Conqueror. Diogo Pais confessed his unworthiness and resigned his see. Soon afterwards it was awarded to a Cluniac, Dalmatius. When King García died, still in prison, two years later, it seemed that Galician autonomy had been stifled.

But now Alfonso VI and his empire suffered an astonishing reverse of fortune. His conquest of Toledo not only horrified the Spanish Muslims but undermined the authority of the princes of al-Andalus, who had purchased security by paying tribute to him. They were now compelled by their subjects to seek help from the Muslims of Africa. The new rulers of the Magrib were the Almoravids, a Berber people who had gone out into the desert, converted the Senegalese and returned to seize power in their own country, founding the new capital of Marrakush and implanting a fanatical and puritanical reform. Their leader Yusuf ibn Tashfin now responded to the appeal from al-Andalus, crossed the Straits and defeated Alfonso in a battle fought at Sagralias or Zallaka, near Badajoz, in 1086. The tributary system Alfonso had built up collapsed, and the danger of an invasion of Leon itself caused him to appeal to France for help. In May 1087 a large number of French knights entered the Peninsula. They included Eudes, duke of Burgundy, a nephew of Queen Constance. His cousin Raimund, had probably preceded him; both visited the court in Leon. The danger of further Almoravid attacks disappeared when Yusuf returned to the Magrib, and most of the French went back to their own country, but Raimund was to settle in Spain and indeed to become the stem of the royal house of Leon and Castile: in

1090 he married Alfonso's legitimate daughter Urraca. In the same year Yusuf returned to the Peninsula and attacked Aledo, a Christian outpost in the territory of Murcia. This time, he took advantage of the support of the Muslim populace to depose the princes of al-Andalus and to annex their territories to his African empire. As he did so, the ruler of Badajoz appealed to Alfonso for protection, offering to cede Santarém, Lisbon and Sintra as the price of Christian support.

It was therefore necessary to strengthen the west. This consisted still of three territories, Galicia, whose deposed king now died in prison, Portugal, long out of favour, and Coimbra, where Sisnand governed until his death in 1092, when he was succeeded by his son-in-law Martim Moniz. Neither the resources of Coimbra, nor the prestige of the new governor sufficed to meet the threat of the Almoravids. Alfonso's first plan was simply to reinforce Coimbra. A document of 22 April 1093 shows that Raimund, described as the son-in-law of the king, was placed in charge of the county of Coimbra, Moniz being relegated to the minor governorship of Arouca. Raimund then appointed one Sueiro Mendes to govern the three places ceded by the emir of Badajoz: between 30 April and 8 May Santarém, Lisbon and Sintra were garrisoned by Christian troops. By the end of the year Raimund's jurisdiction had been extended to include Galicia, and a document of 2 February 1094 refers to him for the first time as Count of Galicia: a little later he was 'lord of Coimbra and all Galicia'.

His rapid rise was followed by an equally rapid eclipse. Early in 1094 an Almoravid army descended on Badajoz and took it. Its prince and his sons were murdered before Raimund could intervene. By November he had assembled a force of Galician barons and knights, including the bishops of Lugo and Santiago, at Coimbra. But he failed to hold the new frontier. Lisbon was soon lost, and the last evidence of Christian control in Santarém is a document of 9 August 1095, in which Raimund still uses the style 'lord of Galicia and Santarém'. By the end of the year Santarém had fallen, and the defence of Coimbra had passed into other hands.

Raimund's cousin, Henry of Burgundy, the founder of the royal house of Portugal, had possibly arrived in the Peninsula by the beginning of 1095, but the earliest surviving document in which his name appears is dated 18 December 1095.[1] Here he is called Count of Coimbra, but by the following year his authority extended to Portugal, and in 1097 he was styled Count of Portugal, and ruled over all the territory from the Minho to the Muslim border. Later documents describe the domain as 'Portugal and Coimbra', but as the Portuguese took over the defence of the frontier their name was applied to the whole.

Henry's aunt, Queen Constance, had died in 1093, but he soon entered the royal family by marrying Alfonso's other daughter, Teresa (Tarasia, Tareja), a bastard by Ximena Nunes. It is not certain when or where this marriage took place, but it appears that the county of Portugal was conferred on him as Teresa's dowry. But Henry also made an agreement with Raimund, in which he promised to support the latter's claim to the succession in return for certain advantages. This 'pact of succession' is undated, but was negotiated by one Dalmatius Gevet, representing Abbot Hugo of Cluny, almost certainly the Cluniac Dalmatius who was elected bishop of Santiago in 1095. By this agreement Henry promised to help his cousin against anyone who might dispute his claim, in return for which Raimund would grant Henry Toledo, but would retain two-thirds of its treasure, or, if he could not give Toledo, then Galicia. The context of this pact is probably the fourth marriage of the Emperor Alfonso VI to a daughter of the deposed ruler of Seville: by this Muslim wife Alfonso had his only son, Sancho, born probably in 1097, and heir to the Leonese throne until his death in battle at Uclés in 1108, a year before the death of his father. It seems, therefore, that when he arrived in the Peninsula, or soon after, Henry hoped either to assume command of the frontier regions, or to attach Galicia to Portugal.

Little is known of Count Henry's government in Portugal. He set up his court at Guimarãis (Vimaranes), near Braga: he gave it a charter and put aside a street or ward for foreigners, probably retainers or merchants who came to serve or supply him. He favoured French Cluniacs in the church, but surrounded himself with Portuguese barons and appointed them to the chief offices and rewarded

---

[1] Herculano supposed that he arrived about a year earlier, but on no tangible evidence. The loss of Santarém appears the most plausible motive for the appointment of a more effective commander.

them with estates. A document of 1096 shows that his jurisdiction extended into Trás-os-Montes.

Braga had been restored as a see in 1070, but had not recovered its metropolitan rank, owing to the opposition of Lugo and Santiago. After its conquest, the primacy of Toledo had been recognized by the pope, but Braga was still unreinstated; when its bishop obtained recognition from an anti-pope, he was deposed for his pains. But in 1096, with the restoration of the county of Portugal, a new bishop was appointed, a Cluniac from St Pierre de Moissac named Gerald. His fellow-Cluniac, Dalmatius of Santiago, had taken the precaution of obtaining a bull of exemption for his diocese, but with the disappearance of Dalmatius, Gerald at last obtained papal recognition of the metropolitanate of Braga (1099–1100). He was strongly opposed by the administrator, and subsequent bishop and archbishop of Santiago, Diego Gelmírez, the most militant churchman of his day, who descended on Braga and carried off the relics of St Victor and St Fructuosus by force in 1102. Gerald had recourse to Rome, and obtained a reproof for his rival and confirmation of his supremacy over all the sees of the west as far as Coimbra, with the sole exception of Santiago. Thus Portugal enjoyed ecclesiastical autonomy until the death of St Gerald in December 1108.

But the secular and ecclesiastical independence of the territory were both compromised by the death of Alfonso VI (1 July 1109). The old emperor who had subdued half Spain and lost it again and had brought in the Cluniac reform and the Burgundian counts, had at last married a Muslim and recognized as his heir her son Sancho. The birth of this heir (1097) may explain the journey of Henry and Teresa to visit Raimund and Urraca at Santiago in 1098. But ten years later, the prince died in battle against the Almoravids, and it seems that the emperor blamed Count Henry, who was in command, for negligence. Count Raimund had died in the previous year, leaving an infant son known as Alfonso Raimúndez, who was thus the indisputable heir to the throne, and was so declared by Alfonso, who bade the Galicians serve and defend him and his mother against all comers.

Thus Henry saw the pact he had made with his cousin rendered valueless. He visited Leon a little before the death of the old emperor, and although it is not known what passed, the chronicle of Sahagún alludes to 'discord and wrath' and says that Henry 'departed in anger against the king'. He had evidently failed to obtain concessions. Urraca became heiress, and arrangements were begun for her marriage to the king of Aragon, Alfonso the Battler, then regarded as the leading warrior in the Peninsula. They were concluded by October, and the Battler assumed the title of Emperor.

This caused great dissatisfaction in the west, where the child Alfonso VII Raimúndez was proclaimed king of Galicia by his guardian, Pedro Froilaz, count of Trava. Count Henry went to France in search of support, but was arrested and returned empty-handed. Soon after Urraca quarrelled with her new husband, and the archbishop of Toledo pronounced the marriage incestuous. The Battler refused to be disqualified and attempted to carry Urraca off to Aragon, but she escaped and rejoined her supporters. The Aragonese sought the aid of Count Henry, and defeated the Castilian barons at Candespina (October 1110). But Urraca persuaded Henry to change sides, offering him the command of her army and other inducements. Henry laid siege to the Battler at Peñafiel, without success, yet in the following year he and Teresa demanded an immediate partition of territory as the price of their continued support of Urraca. She replied by seeking a reconciliation with the Battler. Henry now made common cause with Pedro Froilaz, who again proclaimed Alfonso Raimúndez in Galicia. Urraca then left the Battler and joined the party of her son in Galicia (November 1111). The Battler next won over Henry by granting him the towns of Astorga and Zamora in Leon. He succeeded in capturing Pedro Froilaz. Urraca resumed negotiations with Henry and Teresa, who visited her in Galicia early in 1112. On their return Henry went to Astorga, where he died on 30 April. His unedifying pursuit of personal advantage had brought no positive gains.

He left a young son, Afonso, known as Henriques, who was not more than five years old. Dona Teresa therefore governed Portugal, calling herself variously queen, as the daughter of an emperor, or infanta, or countess. She was unable to prevent the return of Astorga and Zamora to her half-sister Urraca, with whom she had a series of violent quarrels. Moreover, the new metropolitan of Braga, Maurice Bourdin, formerly bishop of Coimbra, had gone to Rome in 1109 to secure confirmation of his rights, and during his absence the archbishop of Toledo had appointed a successor to Coimbra. So, after the death of the count, Maurice came to terms with Diego Gelmírez, whose archdeacon Hugo he appointed bishop of Oporto; Teresa was persuaded to grant the new prelate full jurisdiction over the town. Thus the unity of the Portuguese sees was broken.

The quarrels of the emperor's family continued for a further decade. In 1114 Pedro Froilaz proclaimed Alfonso Raimúndez in Leon and made alliance with the countess of Portugal. The Aragonese Battler retired to his own realms, and presently reconquered Saragossa. But in 1116 the Almoravids attacked in the west and occupied Miranda and Santa Eulália, two of the approaches to Coimbra; a third, Soure, was abandoned, and in 1117 the Almoravid caliph laid siege to Coimbra, surrounding it for twenty days, and sacking the suburbs and neighbouring villages, while Teresa took refuge in the keep.

It seems that Pedro Froilaz, her ally, sent his son Fernando Peres to Portugal, probably to organize the defences. He abandoned his legal wife and joined Teresa, by whom he had a daughter. In 1121 he is described as lord of Oporto and Coimbra, and his or Teresa's forces briefly occupied the southern frontier of Galicia, Tuy and Orense. But Diego Gelmírez had now gained an ascendancy over the Portuguese church, and Maurice of Braga had carried his case to Italy, where he crowned the Emperor Henry V in March 1117: he was excommunicated, became anti-pope and was finally unfrocked. Thus in 1118 Diego Gelmírez was presented with a perfect opportunity to crown his struggle for supremacy. He sent a mission to Rome with a present of 120 ounces of gold, surely sufficient to doom the claims of Braga. But as the mission crossed Aragon, it fell into the hands of the Battler, who detained it and relieved it of its treasure. It finally reached Rome empty-handed: a new pope refused to decide, and the independence of Braga was saved.

The ancient metropolitan rights of Braga were confirmed to a new bishop, Pelagius, in 1118; but Gelmírez was granted a bull of exemption for Santiago, and awarded the titular metropolitanate of Mérida until such time as it should be reconquered from the Muslims. Countess Teresa, engaged in her own intrigues, arrested Pelagius, but was obliged by the pope to release him (1122). Even so, Diego Gelmírez obtained the titles of archbishop and metropolitan in perpetuity (1124), thus reaching the height of his power.

While Fernando Peres flourished, the authority of Countess Teresa waned, and the Portuguese barons began to look towards the succession of her son Afonso Henriques. In 1124 his cousin Alfonso VII of Leon armed himself knight in the cathedral of Santiago, and a year later Afonso Henriques performed a similar ceremony at Zamora. When Urraca died (1126), Alfonso VII made peace with Teresa and Fernando Peres, and confirmed his aunt in the possession of her territories. She refused to do homage, and Alfonso VII invaded Portugal in September 1127. He was supported by Gelmírez and the barons of Galicia. The invasion lasted six weeks: Teresa was forced to give homage and to surrender the territory she had acquired in southern Galicia. Little is known of the campaign, but various sieges took place, including that of Guimarãis, held by adherents of Afonso Henriques. The defenders found resistance impossible, and undertook to do homage in the name of their prince. One of the barons, Egas Moniz, became surety for the oath, and when later the prince disregarded the promise of vassalage, presented himself haltered and barefooted to redeem his honour with his life: according to legend, Alfonso's anger was appeased and Egas was pardoned.

The Portuguese barons blamed the intrigues of Teresa and her Galician favourite for the decline of their fortunes. They therefore ranged themselves behind her son. The first reference to the exercise of power by Afonso Henriques is in a Galician document of 7 September 1127, which alludes to Alfonso VII as king, and adds 'imperante Portucalis Adefonsus filius Henrici comes'. By the end of the year various castles on the Lima and Neiva were being governed in his name, and as late as 31 March 1128 Teresa and her son appear together to confirm the same document. But in April the two factions were separating. On 27 April Afonso Henriques confirmed the charter his father had granted to Guimarãis, without reference to his mother. On 26 May he appointed the Archbishop of Braga, Pai Mendes, to be his chaplain, and promised to deliver the city of Braga to him when he should come into possession of the government. In July his authority extended to Bragança. On 24 July the army of Teresa and Fernando Peres approached Braga and faced Afonso's barons on the field of São Mamede, near Guimarãis. The young count was victorious, and captured his mother and her favourite. They were expelled to Galicia, and Afonso Henriques remained in possession of the county of Portugal.

III

THE AGRARIAN MONARCHY

Afonso Henriques was now a youth of twenty to twenty-four; he had been educated among the barons of the Douro and consolidated his authority in his father's castle at Guimarãis. His usual capital was to be Coimbra, from which he launched his campaigns against the Muslims, but he first occupied the territory to the north of the Minho annexed by his mother (1130). Diego Gelmírez was lying ill in Santiago, and the Galician barons did not react with any energy. But at this time Teresa died, and Fernando Peres joined Afonso: his brother Vermudo Peres was married to Afonso Henriques' sister and held the town of Viseu. Not long after Fernando's return, Vermudo was involved in a plot and expelled from Portugal. Fernando then attached himself to Alfonso VII in Leon and was placed in command of the Galician frontier. Afonso Henriques retorted by entering Galicia and building the fortress of Celmes in his cousin's territory. Alfonso VII then appeared in Galicia, captured Celmes and garrisoned it.

Alfonso VII was now secure in the possession of Leon and Castile and bent on acquiring fame as a warrior. His chief competitor was his stepfather the Battler of Aragon who, since losing his matrimonial campaigns in the west, had conquered Saragossa (1118) and marched through the Muslim south (1125-6). But he was now defeated by the rising star of Leon and retired to Aragon to die. Thus in 1135 Alfonso VII, now entitled Emperor, convoked a great assembly in Leon, and the other rulers of the Peninsula appeared to do him homage. They included the new king of Aragon, the dispossessed Muslim ruler of Saragossa, the king of Navarre and the counts of Barcelona, Toulouse and Montpellier. Afonso Henriques was conspicuous by his absence.

The count of Portugal had still not accepted the loss of the territory beyond the Minho, and he again advanced and defeated Fernando Peres. This brought to the scene the emperor, who recovered Tuy and ordered the Galician barons to make war on Portugal. But negotiations were opened, and the *Historia Compostelana* includes a treaty by which Afonso Henriques undertook to aid his cousin and to restore on demand the fiefs received from him: the pact of homage was to be ratified by 150 vassals of Afonso Henriques.[1] Having apparently obtained his cousin's submission, the emperor took his departure.

But now the ecclesiastical dispute took a more favourable turn. When the see of Coimbra again fell vacant, Bishop Paio of Braga promptly consecrated his archdeacon, Bernard, and stood his ground when Gelmírez carried his complaints to Rome. The new bishop of Coimbra gained the goodwill of the pope by admitting the Cluniac reformers, who established the first monastery 'of the protection of St Peter', subordinated directly to Rome, at Santa Cruz: this foundation undertook to pay tribute to the Holy See. These negotiations were successfully concluded by John Peculiar, who was to become Afonso Henriques' principal ally. When the 'Galician' bishop of Oporto died in 1136, Afonso Henriques obtained the installation of John, who two years later succeeded to Braga: he remained archbishop for thirty-seven years, continuing to intervene in the affairs of Coimbra, despite the protests of Toledo and Santiago, and playing an important part in the conquest of Lisbon and the restoration of its see. Although the tangle of claims of the ecclesiastical authorities was not adjusted to the national frontiers until the later Middle Ages, the spiritual ties of the Portuguese were reconciled to the political largely through John Peculiar's long collaboration with Afonso Henriques.

The independence of Portugal, like the imperial title of Leon, had to be vindicated on the field of battle. Count Henry had been entrusted with the defence of the western frontier when the power of the Almoravids was at its summit: after his death the Muslims had destroyed the outposts of Coimbra, and the defences had been stiffened in 1128, when Soure was placed in the hands of the Templars. But the Almoravid empire was now threatened by a new Muslim reform, that of the Almohads, or 'uniters'. Its founder, the mystic

---

[1] The pact, known only from the chronicle, lacks the signatures. Gonzaga de Azevedo (*História*, IV) argued that the treaty was only a negotiators' draft. But the fact that the emperor departed immediately after the negotiations indicates that he regarded them as completed, and had achieved the object of his campaign.

ibn Tumart, propounded a Berberized form of Islam. When he died in 1130, it was still confined to his immediate disciples, but during the following years it gradually gathered momentum under its champion, 'Abdu'l-Mu'min. The Almoravid caliph still appeared formidable, and his son Tashfin governed al-Andalus from Granada. In the west there was a lull until 1134 when the Leonese attacked Badajoz: they were defeated, but when Tashfin took the offensive, he in turn suffered a heavy defeat at Qaṣras (Cáceres?), and his father recalled him to Africa (January 1138).

In the following year Afonso Henriques gained his most famous victory. According to tradition, it was fought on the day of Santiago, 25 July, at a place called Oric or Ouric. The early writers do not suggest that the battle was on anything but a modest scale, though later authors were to develop it to majestic proportions and to introduce the favourite theme of visible divine intervention. Even its place remains doubtful: the present town of Ourique was far too deep in Muslim territory, and of the alternative sites, the most plausible is the Chão de Ourique, near Santarém. The chronicles refer to the flight of a prince called 'Ismar' or 'Ismal Auzein', probably Abu Zakariya, the governor of Santarém. It is probable that in consequence of the battle the Muslims of Santarém resumed the payment of tribute and obtained a truce.

Until July 1139 Afonso Henriques appears in documents as *infans* or *Portugalensium princeps*. After this date he is king. A document of 1 October 1139 (wrongly dated 1149) bears the proud title 'Alphonsus gloriosissimus princeps et Dei gratia Portugalensium rex'. The resounding adjective may reflect the glow of victory: the usual title thereafter is 'rex Alphonsus'. Its sense is difficult to ascertain. The emperors of Leon regarded themselves as 'kings of kings' and conferred the title of king or queen on their children. Thus Alfonso VI's heiress Urraca was called queen, and her bastard sister, Teresa of Portugal, sometimes used the title.[1] Urraca's son Alfonso VII was proclaimed king as a boy, and assumed the title of emperor only when he had defeated the Battler of Aragon and received the homage of his neighbours. Although Afonso Henriques had refused to attend the coronation of his cousin, he had later been forced to do homage. However, the assumption of the title of king was not necessarily a

[1] Afonso's heir, Sancho, is called *infans*, but he died in battle before coming of age.

repudiation of homage, for the king of Navarre was a vassal of the emperor. It seems, therefore, that in assuming the royal title, Afonso Henriques established his claim on his descent as grandson of an emperor, and on his recent success in battle: the element of rivalry with his cousin must have been present, and also the consideration that his father County Henry had had the advantage of Count Raimund as a warrior.[1]

At the end of 1139 or beginning of 1140 Afonso Henriques renewed his claim to his mother's territory in southern Galicia, and his cousin replied by raising his followers in Galicia and crossing the Minho into Portugal. The two forces met near the border and engaged in a tourney, one of those ritual contests which had often decided the fate of the crowns of Leon and Castile. The chronicle of Alfonso VII says that 'without awaiting the emperor's order many leaders and men joined battle with the followers of the king, who came down from their camp: many were unhorsed, brought to earth and captured on either side'. According to this source, the Portuguese sued for peace, while the Portuguese chronicle says that the Portuguese knights had the advantage, and included among their captives Bernardo Peres. But the settlement made at Val-de-Vez was evidently inconclusive.

In 1143 there arrived in the Peninsula Cardinal Guido, who had negotiated with John Peculiar in 1135. He now conferred with Afonso Henriques and with the emperor in a council at Zamora. As a result the king of Portugal declared himself a liegeman of St Peter and the pope, and promised to pay four ounces of gold a year in return for protection. On 13 December 1143 Afonso Henriques sent a letter of oblation to the Holy See, and in the following year the new pope Lucius II accepted his service and repeated the promise of protection. He refers to Afonso as *dux Portugalensium*, not as *rex*: it was only in 1179 that the Holy See began to use the royal title. However, Afonso Henriques had won recognition of independence, and the church of Leon and Castile accepted the fact at a council in Valladolid; neither

---

[1] Afonso Henriques' heir, Sancho I, speaks of his sons as kings and his two daughters as queens in his will. One of the daughters was the repudiated wife of the king of Leon, but the other had never been anything but a princess.

The looser use of the title is perhaps not unrelated to Muslim usage. The title caliph has the same connotation of uniqueness as that of emperor, though since the tenth century the title had been duplicated. The Almoravid caliphs appointed their sons governors of territories or emirs, and this title was conventionally translated by *rex*.

this nor any subsequent council in Castile was attended by John Peculiar, who continued to negotiate directly with Rome.

Shortly afterwards, in 1146, Afonso Henriques renewed the connexion with Burgundy by marrying Mafalda, daughter of Amadeus III, count of Maurienne and Savoy. His first son, named Henry, was born on 5 March 1147, five days before Afonso set out to conquer Santarém, but died in infancy. The eventual successor, Sancho, was born in 1154.

2. THE CONQUEST OF LISBON

The domains of Afonso Henriques are briefly described by the Muslim geographer Idrisī, who completed his work in Sicily in 1154. Coimbra, he says, is 'a small city, flourishing and well populated, rich in vineyards and orchards of apples, cherries and plums. Its fields are very fertile. From the west almost to the city there are many tilled fields, and the inhabitants, who are the bravest of the Christians, possess many cattle great and small: the Mondego moves many mills and bathes many vineyards and gardens'. Twenty miles north of the castle of Montemór on the Mondego was the mouth of the Vouga, beyond which lay the land called Portugal, 'a populous land with towns, castles and many tilled fields. It has many warriors, horse and foot, who raid the country of their neighbours not of the same party. The Vouga is a big river, entered by trading-vessels and galleys, for the tide goes up it many miles. From it to the mouth of the Douro is fifteen miles. The Douro is also a big river with a rapid, rushing current, full and deep. From this to the mouth of the Minho is sixty miles: this is also a large, wide and deep river: the tide goes far up it, and vessels that go up it stop often because of the great number of villages and castles on its banks'. This description clearly shows that in the eyes of the Muslim geographer the most important thoroughfares of Portugal were its rivers and coast, already much frequented by shipping.

To the south of Coimbra Soure was firmly held, but Leiria had been raided and sacked by the Muslims in 1137 and 1140 and was rebuilt for the third time in 1144. Further east, the Christian outpost was at Germanelo, near Penela, built in 1142. South of this was Muslim territory. In 1140 (or 1142) the first opportunity had offered for Afonso Henriques to strike at Lisbon. A fleet of some seventy ships carrying English and Norman crusaders, men of Southampton and Hastings, bound for Palestine, sailed into the Douro and agreed to join Afonso Henriques in a combined attack. The suburbs of Lisbon were sacked, but the city itself resisted and probably offered to pay tribute to the Portuguese, who accordingly departed.[1]

Muslim Portugal was governed from Seville, the great port on the Guadalquivir held by an Almoravid general and garrison. The capital of the western frontier was Badajoz, which had replaced Roman Mérida, though there were towns and castles further north facing Coimbra and Salamanca. The west was divided into several zones. The southern coast, al-Qunu (the Conii?) or al-Garb, 'the west' (the Algarve), had its capital at Shalb (Silves), which Idrisī describes as 'fine in appearance, with attractive buildings and well-furnished bazaars'. It possessed a port and a ship-yard, and was defended by stout walls. It had been occupied by the jund from the Yemen, and its people continued 'to speak pure Arabic and compose poetry, and are eloquent in speech and elegant in manners, both the upper and the lower classes'. It traded in fruit and fish with the African and Mediterranean ports. Further north, Beja and Évora were the centre of a farming district. Beja had Almoravid troops and settlers, and relations between them and the older families were strained. To the west was the fortress and port of Qaṣr Abi Dānis (Alcácer do Sal). The chief town of the Tagus valley was Shantariya (Santarém). Both ar-Rāzī (tenth century) and Idrisī (twelfth century) refer to the great fertility of the region, which produced crops forty days after sowing and yielded a hundredfold. Of Lisbon, Idrisī says little, digressing on the legend of the Wanderers who left it to explore the Atlantic: it was a compact and well-defended town on the site of the present castle of St George, with dependent fishing-villages across the Tagus. Sintra was a small fortified town with tilled fields stretching towards the sea. There were Muslim villages

---

[1] The chronicle of the Goths gives the date as 1140. The English account of the conquest of Lisbon places it five years before the successful attack of 1147. The chronicle of the Goths notes that Afonso received tribute from Lisbon and Santarém in 1142, while the English account notes that there was opposition to the agreement with Afonso in 1147 from some crusaders, William and Ralph Veal (Vitulus) and others, who had participated in the previous attempt and blamed the Portuguese for the circumstances in which it was abandoned. The recent acquisition of tribute must have served to impress Cardinal Guido in 1143.

further north, but the region towards Leiria was precariously held and often raided. In the intervals between royal campaigns, which were not lightly undertaken, relations between Christians and Muslims were usually governed by a truce, in which case the weaker party would pay tribute, or were dominated by raids for booty or for the destruction of the opponent's crops. Some Christian frontier-towns organized regular expeditions, but these were rarely intended to bring territorial gains: the towns on both sides were proof against anything but formal siege or surprise.

But now the defences of the Muslims were weakened by internal strife. The Almoravid caliph died early in 1143, being succeeded by Tashfin, who recalled his son from the Peninsula to fight the enemies of their house. The people of southern Portugal were disillusioned with their defenders, and in 1143-4 a native of Silves named ibn Qasi, who, after a prodigal youth, had performed the pilgrimage and returned to install himself as a hermit at Arrifana, near Aljezur, gathered a following and sent seventy men to capture Mértola. He claimed to be the Mahdi and distributed money which he said came from God: he was acclaimed in Silves, Beja and Evora. But the 'Mahdi' was only the tool of the native Muslims in throwing off the rule of the Almoravids. He was soon deposed by ibn Wazir of Évora: other families seized towns in Andalusia and appealed to Alfonso VII for protection. Ibn Qasi departed for Africa, and offered himself to 'Abdu'l-Mu'min, the leader of the Almohads, now master of Fez. He greeted the seer from Silves with the words: So you claimed to be the Mahdi?, and ibn Qasi replied: You know that there are two dawns, the true and the false: I was the false.

In consequence of this incident, the Almohad ruler agreed to intervene, and in the summer of 1146 he sent troops which proclaimed ibn Qasi governor of the Algarve. They entered Mértola and Silves, and as they moved northward, ibn Wazir submitted with Beja and Badajoz. They wintered at Mértola, but then received news that Alfonso VII was attacking Almería and therefore marched on Seville.

Thus in the spring of 1147 the opportunity offered for Afonso Henriques to seize Santarém.[1] On 10 March Afonso Henriques left Coimbra, being joined by the Templars from Soure. He camped at

---

[1] The ancient Scallabis, renamed after St Iria, or Eiria, supposedly burned there after her martyrdom in 653.

Pernes, and sent a messenger to announce the end of the truce, for which three days' notice was required. On the eve of the expiry ladders were hidden in fields near the walls. The assault was made before dawn, and the scalers found the sentries drowsing, forced a way to the gate, and admitted the main force. After a struggle in the streets, the defenders capitulated.[1]

Two months later, a large company of crusaders arrived in the Douro on its way to the Holy Land. The fleet had assembled at Dartmouth, and consisted of 164 vessels, carrying about 13,000 men. They were in three groups: English under four constables, Germans under Arnold, count of Aerschot, and Flemings and Boulogners, under Christian of Ghistelles. A very full account of the expedition has been preserved in the letter of an English crusader, probably a priest, addressed to a correspondent at Bawdsey in Suffolk.[2]

The crusaders were organized in national groups, and had two judges to every thousand men, who were to apply strict laws of an eye for an eye, to keep the peace. Each ship was treated as a parish with its priest. After being separated by a great storm, during which at intervals the Sirens were heard ('a horrible sound, first of wailing and then of laughter and jeering, like the clamour of insolent men in a camp'), at last Galicia was sighted, 'a mountainous province, very famous for the hunting of beasts and for the manifold fruits of its soil, and quite delightful were it not defiled by its inhabitants'— an allusion to the approach to Muslim territory. The lighthouse tower at Corunna was seen, 'a wonderful work formerly built by Julius Caesar in order that it might serve as a centre through which the revenues and interminable lawsuits of Britain, Ireland and Spain might pass'. Rivers and towns of Galicia and northern Portugal are named. The ships put in at Portugala on the mouth of the Doyra.[3] It was some days before they were collected. The bishop of Oporto,

---

[1] In the same month the Almohads captured Marrakush after a siege of nine months, and thus completed the overthrow of the Almoravid empire.

[2] The manuscript at Corpus Christi College, Cambridge, has been edited by Stubbs, and by C. W. David, *De expugnatione Lyxbonensi*, New York, 1936. The incipit *Osb.*, Osbern, Osbert?, may refer to the sender or the recipient. The constables were Hervey de Glanvill (Norfolk and Suffolk), Simon of Dover (Kent), Andrew (London), and Saher of Archelle (the rest).

[3] In the bar of the Douro were sands in which the sick were enveloped until the rising tide washed them off and healed them: this form of bathing was supposed to have cured the last bishop of a black and blue spot 'like leprosy'.

Pedro Pitões, conveyed a proposal of alliance from Afonso Henriques (who had left on campaign) in a sermon in the cathedral cemetery, since the crusaders were too many for the church to hold. The bishop's message was translated into the various tongues of the audience. He mentioned that, some years before, the Muslims had raided Oporto and carried off vestments and vessels and killed and captured clergy all the way up to Santiago (a century and a half ago . . .). If the crusaders would help, Afonso would give such money as he could afford, and they might take hostages. It was agreed to send for Archbishop Peculiar, who sailed with the fleet to Lisbon. At the entry of the Lisbon river, after a heavy squall, a wondrous portent was beheld in the shape of great white clouds bespattered with blackness coming from the mainland: it was felt that this symbolized the Muslim foe, and it was duly vanquished by a cloud from the sea. On 28 June some crusaders landed and skirmished with the Muslims, but only two tents with thirty-nine men spent the night ashore: the writer was among them, 'not without fear'. Next day, Afonso Henriques and his army arrived, and a great meeting was held to discuss the collective contract. 'As the king approached, we almost all went out to meet him, rich and poor mixed up together'. The king asked who the chief men were, and on being told, congratulated them on the appearance of their army. He could not offer gifts, 'for having been constantly harassed by the Muslims so that sometimes not even our life has been safe, it has surely not been our fortune to amass wealth'. He appealed to their piety. At this point there must have been some expressions of disapproval, for he continued: 'But lest our discourse be disturbed by the shouting of your people, choose from among you those whom you wish in order that we may withdraw together and quietly and in good temper mutually define the conditions of our promise.' There followed much 'beating of the air': William Veal and the old hands thought that Afonso was not to be relied on, and that they should sail on and raid Muslim shipping between al-Andalus and Africa. Eight or ten shiploads took this view, but they were persuaded to remain. The contract was then drawn up, by which all the spoils of the city were to go exclusively to the crusaders, and the inner city if they conquered it, and the ransom of the captives. Afonso offered land to any crusaders who might desire to stay in Portugal, with the right to enjoy the liberties and customs of their own countries. He gave his pledge not to desist from the undertaking, unless from mortal illness or invasion of his kingdom from another quarter. Twenty hostages were exchanged.

Afonso then sent Archbishop Peculiar and Bishop Pitões to demand the surrender of Lisbon. They approached the wall and held speech with the governor, *qaḍi* and bishop, saying, 'Surely, if a natural sense of justice had made any progress among you, you would go back unbidden to the land of the Moors whence you came, with your baggage, money and goods, and your women and children, leaving to us our own'. The Muslim spokesman was said to have replied: 'I cannot wonder enough concerning you, for while a single forest or district suffices for many elephants and lions, neither the land nor the sea is enough for you. Verily, it is not the want of possessions, but ambition of the mind that drives you on.'

The military operations began on the following day. Afonso Henriques occupied the height of the Graça, behind the city: to the west were the English, and to the east the Flemings and Germans. Muslim forces came out of the suburb to attack the English slingers, but were driven back behind the walls. Towards evening the outer defences were carried, but it was too late for a general attack, and Afonso ordered a withdrawal till next day. But by now many of the English were fighting in the suburb, and Saher of Archelle called up others, so that when night fell there were 3,000 men in the outer defences, and the Muslims had retired to the madina. The attackers camped in the cemetery, while abandoned houses blazed around them.

Next day the defenders made a sortie to try to recover the western suburb, but were driven off by the Portuguese and English. The eastern suburb was occupied by the Flemings and Germans. The besiegers thus gained access to the storage-caves tunnelled in the side of the hill; they contained 100,000 loads of wheat, barley, millet and pulse. But the madina made a long resistance. Mangonels were built but burnt down. A tower built by the English got stuck in the sand and was fired. The men of Cologne began five mines, but were driven off. Six weeks passed, and the besiegers began to waver. The defenders derided them from the parapets, 'taunted us with the numerous children about to be born at home in our absence' and

59

made remarks and gestures offensive to their religion. But one night a skiff was seen slipping across the water towards Palmela. Its occupants were attacked and fled: in the abandoned boat letters were found begging ibn Wazir of Évora to send help. Some days later, it was rumoured that a messenger from Évora had been captured: he carried a letter saying that no help could be sent.

The plight of the besieged was becoming desperate. Food was placed outside the walls, and poor Muslims who tried to slip out to take it were netted like birds. The neighbouring villages had been destroyed: eighty heads from Almada were impaled before the walls. But the various machines and mines were still not successful. Catapults pelted the city with stones: an engineer from Pisa directed the construction of a movable wooden tower on the western side, while the Germans and Flemings tried to lay a long mine under the walls: it was fired on 16 October, but the breach was occupied by the defenders, and the English and Germans quarrelled about access to it. Three days later the English tower was finished and brought up against the wall on the river-side. It was the scene of heavy fighting, But the Muslims failed to burn it, and at last it was brought near enough for a drawbridge to be dropped on the parapet. The besieged then asked for a truce.

Those deputed to negotiate were Afonso Henriques' general Fernando Cativo and Hervey de Glanvill. They agreed to suspend the attack and give the besiegers the night in which to decide whether to surrender; meanwhile, hostages were delivered to Afonso. This aroused the suspicions of the crusaders, who flocked towards the royal enclosure, evidently fearing that the king would accept tribute and depart. A rascally priest of Bristol, of the worst morals, for he was later arrested among thieves, stirred up an uproar against the leaders and an attempt was made to lynch Hervey. The Germans and Flemings came out of their quarters to try to seize the hostages. Afonso Henriques prepared to resist by force, and threatened to abandon the siege if there was any further commotion. Calm was restored, and next day the leaders of the allies renewed their oaths to the king and made plans for the entry. A force of 140 English were to lead, followed by 160 Germans and Flemings. They would advance to the gate of the keep, where the Muslims would hand over all their possessions: if anything was withheld, the penalty was death. After the sack, the Muslims should depart freely. Despite these plans, the Germans and Flemings entered first, and others pushed their way through the abandoned breach. There was much violence before the inhabitants streamed away from three of the gates, from Sunday 25 October to the following Wednesday. The siege had lasted seventeen weeks. Both shores of the Tagus were abandoned by the Muslims: Sintra, now isolated, capitulated, while the rock-fortress of Palmela was abandoned, and the Muslims were thrust back on Alcácer and Évora.

3. AFONSO I AND THE ALMOHADS

Afonso Henriques now proceeded to organize his new conquest, appointing as governor Pedro Viegas and as bishop Gilbert, a priest from Hastings, who was consecrated in the mosque of the *qaṣba* as soon as this had been converted to Christian use: Archbishop Peculiar took care to extract an oath of obedience to Braga despite the fact that Lisbon had in ancient times formed part of the metropolitanate of Mérida. Alfonso VII supported the protest of Toledo, complaining that his rights and dignity had been impaired by the mutual concessions of the papacy and the Portuguese. The pope, a refugee in France, ordered that the primacy of Toledo should be respected and that Archbishop Peculiar should comply within three months. But Peculiar ignored the decree, and in 1148 went to Lombardy and was absolved. It seems that Gilbert of Lisbon sent a representative to Toledo, but the matter rested there until the death of Alfonso VII.

Meanwhile, Afonso Henriques was faced with the problem of re-settling what he had won. A number of crusaders had accepted offers of land in or near Lisbon, one William Lacorni and his men at Atouguia, Jourdan at Lourinhã and Allard at Vila Verde. Bishop Gilbert set up a confraternity for the English settlers in the church of Nossa Senhora dos Mártires, at one of the two cemeteries of those who died in the siege.[1] The other was on the site of São Vicente de Fora, where a monastery was founded in November 1147. But the occupation of the valley of the Tagus and the thinly peopled

---

[1] It was removed to the church of Santo Domingo in 1241. Bishop Gilbert introduced at Lisbon the Use of Sarum, promulgated by Bishop Osmund of Salisbury in 1085; it survived until 1536, when the Roman rite was brought in.

territories of the Alentejo was beyond the resources of private magnates or foreign colonists, and called for the collective energies of an
institution. The Templars had been entrusted with the defence of
Soure in 1128, and had occupied Pombal and other places: Afonso
Henriques had bestowed on its Master Hugo the churches of
Santarém, but with the restoration of the see of Lisbon, they were
claimed by Bishop Gilbert, and the contention ended with the
Templars being granted Cera, a castle on the river Tomar, where in
1162 the Master Gualdim Pais founded the town of Tomar. The
Templars thus took over the defence of the Tagus valley, holding
the castles of Almourol, Zêzere and Idanha.

The sudden advance from Leiria to Lisbon left a hollow frontier,
and the repopulation of the intervening lands was undertaken by the
Cistercians, who in 1153 took over the territory of Alcobaça. They
were of Burgundian origin, like Afonso's father and wife, and they
devoted themselves to agriculture, working the land among their
peasants. Their domains, stretching from Leiria to Óbidos, came to
include the townships of Alcobaça and Aljubarrota, with finally
thirteen smaller places and the ports of Pederneira (later replaced
by Nazaré) and Selir (São Martinho).

Meanwhile, Afonso Henriques took advantage of the prostration
of the Muslims to make a further advance. Soon after the conquest
of Lisbon, his men attacked Qaṣr Abi Dānis, but without effect. In
1150 (?) Bishop Gilbert went to England to preach the Crusade,
'urging many to go to Spain to besiege and conquer Seville'.[1] He
returned with some ships in 1151, and in 1157 a further attempt was
made on Alcácer with the aid of a new band of crusaders, perhaps
those of Thierry of Alsace, Count of Flanders, whose son later
married Teresa, a daughter of Afonso. It failed, but in the following
year Alcácer fell to the Portuguese.

The Almohads had now established their rule in Africa and
occupied Seville; but there were still Almoravids in Granada, while
Alfonso VII had seized the port of Almería, and a Spanish Muslim
ruled over eastern Spain. But now the Almoravids of Granada submitted to the Almohads, who took the opportunity to reconquer
Almería (1157). In the west, ibn Wazir placed Beja and Évora under

---

[1] John of Hexham, Twysden, *Hist. Ang. Script.*, Anno 1157, 278.

Almohad protection, but ibn Qasi of Silves appealed to Afonso Henriques, offering to pay tribute. The people of Silves then rebelled, entered the castle and emerged with ibn Qasi's head on the point of a lance, crying: 'Behold, the Mahdi of the Christians!' It was probably during these troubles that Afonso Henriques was able to enter Alcácer. And soon ibn Wazir began to fear the consequences of the Almohad expansion: in 1159 Afonso Henriques succeeded in obtaining the submission of Évora and Beja.

On the death of the Emperor Alfonso VII, his domains were divided; his elder son, Sancho III, received Castile and the younger, Ferdinand II, Leon and Galicia. In May 1158 these two made a pact for the conquest of Portugal, whereafter Ferdinand would divide it in half and Sancho would take his choice. The threat was perhaps intended to force Afonso Henriques to come to terms, but within three months Sancho had died, and the throne of Castile passed to his infant son, Alfonso VIII. The proposed partition of Portugal was forgotten, and Ferdinand of Leon tried to seize Castile during the minority of his nephew. In December 1160 Afonso Henriques was able to make peace with Ferdinand, who in 1165 married his daughter Urraca.

This alliance was of short duration. The claims of Portugal and Leon against the Muslim kingdom of Badajoz were unresolved. The Portuguese had held Beja for only two months, and Évora for two years, when it was recovered by the Almohads. But in September or October 1166 an adventurer named Geraldo Sem Pavor, apparently banished from the Portuguese court, took Évora by a surprise attack, formed a troop of free-booters, and occupied Cáceres, Montanches, Serpa and Juromenha. Across the frontier in Leon, Ferdinand II had founded Ciudad Rodrigo in 1160, and its inhabitants lived also largely by raiding the Muslims. A crisis was provoked in 1169, when Geraldo laid siege to Badajoz, still Muslim, but under Leonese protection.

Afonso Henriques had quarrelled with his son-in-law, Ferdinand II, two years earlier, and had invaded Galicia, seizing Tuy and building a castle at Cedofeita. Ferdinand had attacked it, and its main tower being struck by lightning, the garrison gave in at this display of divine dissatisfaction. When Geraldo attacked Badajoz, the inhabitants appealed to Ferdinand and Geraldo to Afonso Henriques, who presently appeared on the scene. It was soon reported that Ferdinand was approaching, and in the confusion Afonso was caught in the gate of Badajoz and his right leg broken. His followers got him as far as the Caia, where he was captured. He remained two months in the hands of his son-in-law, and was then ransomed, undertaking to abandon all claim to Galicia. The Muslims of Badajoz continued to pay tribute to Leon, while Geraldo returned to his frontier fortress at Juromenha.

But Afonso Henriques was not able to ride again. His military career came to an end, and in August 1170 he knighted his son Sancho, now sixteen, at a ceremony at Coimbra, and began to associate him with the government of Portugal. In the following year the Almohad caliph, Abu Ya'qub Yusuf, arrived in the Peninsula, where he was to spend five years (June 1171–March 1176). His African commanders dismissed ibn Wazir from the government of Beja, and appointed two intriguers as vizir and qaḍi: most of the noble families of the place followed ibn Wazir to Seville (February 1172). Six months later, a band of Portuguese scaled the walls and seized the castle by surprise, the new defenders fled pell-mell, but the Portuguese could not occupy it and merely destroyed its defences, carrying off such of its population as had not already fled. Meanwhile, the caliph had prepared an army which occupied Alcántara and other places near the frontier. Both Portugal and Leon came to terms with him, Afonso Henriques making a truce for five years (1172–7). The Muslim chronicle tells how Geraldo Sem Pavor denaturalized himself and went to live in Seville, possibly as a hostage. But when he began to receive letters from Afonso, the caliph became suspicious and arrested him, sending him to Sijilmassa: he was killed while trying to escape.[1]

The Almohad reform brought with it the persecution of the Mozarabic Christians still dwelling in al-Andalus, and it was probably because of this that the monks of Cape St Vincent brought the relics of their patron to Lisbon in 1173. He had been martyred in Valencia in 304, and his relics were brought to the Cape in the

---

[1] *Bayān al-mugrib*, which calls Geraldo the head of Afonso's army. His denaturalization has recalled that of the Cid, a century earlier, cf. D. Lopes, 'O Cid português, Geraldo Sem Pavor', *Revista Port. de História*, I, 93. See also E. Lévi-Provençal, *Documents inédits d'histoire almohade*, 216.

eighth century. Idrisī refers to the shrine built there, and to the traditional hospitality of the Mozarabic monks and to the considerable revenues they derived from land in the Algarve. It is said that when Afonso Henriques sent to obtain the relics, these were conveyed to Lisbon by sea and attended by two of the ravens which never left the church. The ship, with two birds, fore and aft, came to form the crest of Lisbon.

During the truce, the Almohads restored Beja. In December 1174 a contingent of 500 men arrived from Silves with rations for a month, being then relieved by others. By March they had completed the wall of the *qaṣba* and the outer walls were in progress. When the truce ended, Beja was strongly held. The Portuguese began a series of vigorous campaigns directed chiefly towards Almohad Seville, the richest prize in al-Andalus, though seventy years were to pass before its conquest. The Portuguese armies laid waste the fields of Beja, but its new fortifications were too strong for them. They then swept into the outskirts of Seville and burned galleys in the river. When the Almohads of Beja and Serpa struck at Alcácer, they were defeated and the two governors paraded in chains through the streets of Coimbra. By contrast, the king of Leon remained at peace and even sought the help of the Almohads against his rivals.

This was the context of Alexander III's recognition of Afonso Henriques' claim to the title of king. Toledo had continued to maintain its pretentions to primacy, and in 1163 Archbishop Peculiar had paid his seventh visit to Rome, bearing a letter from Afonso Henriques in which the king reiterated his obedience and described the extent of his conquests: the existing arrangements were then confirmed. In 1172 Alexander III sent his legate Jacinth to the Peninsula: he conferred with Afonso Henriques at Braga (January–February), and the pope thereafter ruled that as long as Braga held (illegally) the Portuguese dioceses claimed by Santiago, the sees of Leon claimed by Braga might obey Santiago. This compromise maintained ecclesiastical theory while adapting ecclesiastical practice to political realities. Afonso Henriques then forbade his bishops to obey Santiago, and Ferdinand forbade his to obey Braga. John Peculiar died on 3 December 1175: his successor Godinho visited Rome in 1177. On 23 May 1179, by the bull *Manifestis probatum*, Alexander confirmed Afonso in possession of all his conquests and recognized the rights of his successors. The 'intrepid extirpator of the enemies of the name of Christ' was assured of papal protection, and of the kingdom of Portugal in the full royal honour and dignity pertaining to kingship: including all conquests over which neighbouring Christian princes could not prove rights. In return, the tribute to be paid to the curia was quadrupled, from four ounces of gold to two marks, and a single payment of a thousand ounces was sent as a gift. Thus the secular independence of the Portuguese monarchy was established. The rival historical claims of the archdioceses became the subject of an interminable and insoluble lawsuit in which only ink was shed.

During the last years of Afonso Henriques, the struggle with the Almohads was sustained by land and sea. An Almohad fleet from Ceuta raided Lisbon, but was defeated by the Portuguese sea-commander Fuas Roupinho off Cape Espichel (15 July 1180). Fuas was himself defeated in the following year, and finally perished in a raid against Ceuta. On land, the Portuguese army advanced from Santarém and raided the suburbs of Seville and western Andalusia. In 1183 the king of Leon undertook not to renew his truce and alliance with the Almohads, due to expire at the end of the year: he was finally reconciled with his Castilian neighbour. But as he laid siege to Cáceres, the caliph again crossed to Spain and advanced to Badajoz, and the Leonese withdrew. The main object of the Almohad campaign was to punish the Portuguese for their attacks on Seville, and at the end of June 1184 the caliph laid siege to Santarém. Its suburbs were destroyed and the rich farmlands of the Tagus laid waste, but the keep of Santarém held out, and in one of the attacks the caliph was wounded. His armies began to withdraw, and he died on the road. His court returned to Africa: five years passed before his successor was able to resume the Holy War.

Afonso Henriques died on 6 December 1185: he was probably nearly eighty years of age and had reigned for fifty-seven. He was buried with his wife Mafalda at Santa Cruz in Coimbra. No contemporary depiction of him has survived, but the tradition that he was endowed with gigantic stature, a flowing beard and Herculean strength goes back at least as far as the time of King Manuel, who placed the recumbent statue over his tomb.

Of his children, Teresa had been married to Count Philip of

Flanders, a match arranged by Henry II of England; Urraca had been queen of Leon, but on being repudiated retired to a convent; Mafalda died young. Of the king's three bastards, Fernando Afonso was *alferes* (general, champion) of the army, a position later held by his brother Pedro Afonso: the third Afonso was elected Grand-Master of the Hospitallers in Palestine, but forced to resign because of his excessive worldliness.

4. SANCHO I, 1185–1211; AFONSO II, 1211–23; SANCHO II, 1223–46

Afonso's heir, Sancho I, was now thirty-one, and had been associated with the government for fifteen years. The English chroniclers Robert du Mont and Roger Hoveden evidently regarded him as king during his father's lifetime, speaking of 'the king of Portugal, whose father still lived, though of a great age'. The administration of the old king, derived from Leon, but with Burgundian modifications, was thus continued in the new reign. The chief officers were the *maiordomus*, the head of the administration, the *signifer* or *alferes*, who led the army in the king's absence or bore the royal standard in his presence, the chancellor or notary, and the *dapifer*, the master of the royal household. These officers, together with whatever members of the royal family, barons, governors or prelates might be present, formed the council, and confirmed documents issued by the crown. The office of chancellor had been held by Mestre Alberto from 1142 to 1169: his successor, Mestre Julião, was now one of the most influential figures at court. A document of the first month of Sancho's reign is attested by: the present and former *alferes*, the *dapifer*, *comes* Velasco, the governors of Viseu, Lafões, Lisbon and Santarém, four other nobles, Archbishop Godinho, the bishops of Oporto, Lamego, Viseu and Coimbra and bishops-elect of Lisbon and Évora. The groups represented by these, together with the masters of the military orders and certain abbots, formed the first rank of society; the great nobility, or *ricos homens*, possessing many followers, great estates and wide jurisdiction over them: they were barons of *pendão e caldeira*, banner and cook-pot, enrolling men under their pennant and feeding them. Below these, the lesser nobility, *infanções*, held smaller estates or were entrusted with the defence of castles and towns, but did not possess private civil or military jurisdiction. Below them, the highest class of free commoners was that of the villein-knights, *cavaleiros-vilãos*, who were able to maintain a horse and arms of their own. They were often attracted to settle in or near the towns of the frontier, where they were granted the privileges enjoyed elsewhere by *infanções*. They organized raids against the Muslims for their own profit, and gave a military character to towns in eastern and southern Portugal. Most free men were *malados*, or clients, who received protection from an overlord and paid taxes or performed services in return. The *juniores* were free men without full liberty of movement. Serfs existed on the estates of the crown, nobility and clergy, and free men often lapsed into serfdom through capture, indebtedness, crime or personal preference. Slaves, not attached, but saleable, were usually Muslim captives.

This population was very unevenly distributed. Northern Portugal, comprising the coast, the plain, the river-valleys and basins between the Minho and the Douro, was thickly settled and dotted with villages and small fortified baronial houses or 'towers'. The northern frontier was defended by castles on the Minho and the Lima, and the chief towns were Guimarãis, Count Henry's capital, Braga, the ecclesiastical centre, and Oporto, 'the port' by antonomasia. All these places were quite small. The majority of the population was rural, and occupied in agriculture, stock-raising or village crafts: the valley of the Douro was already planted with vineyards.

Further south, the county of Coimbra still retained its Mozarabic traditions though it was increasingly dominated by the court and by barons from the north. The town was larger than those of the north and had a greater concentration of artisans; between it and the sea the lower valley of the Mondego was irrigated and intensively cultivated. Leading families of the city owned estates here, or in the fertile basins of the interior. Small craft came up the river to trade.

The interior province of Trás-os-Montes and inland part of Beira were sparsely populated, and it is here that the process of resettlement is most visible. In Trás-os-Montes new village societies were established which administered the land, herds and flocks, implements and facilities collectively: such communities still survive. In Beira the resettlement took the form of the restoration of ancient towns:

Covilhã, Guarda and Idanha were all re-created in the reign of Sancho I with the evident intention of strengthening the eastern frontier.[1]

In order to attract settlers to these underpopulated places, it was the practice to establish *concelhos*, or units of self-government, offering privileges to those who dwelt in them. The privileges and usages of such places were recorded in charters (*forais*). These traditions (*foros*) derived from local conventions and from Germanic customary law, influenced by Roman usage and, increasingly, by current practice transmitted from one *concelho* to another. In old Christian territory the *concelho* might be a township or a rural community: in reconquered areas it could be a new foundation or the former Muslim administrative capital together with its dependent territory or *alfoz*. The territory was divided into six parts, each with a *sesmeiro:* these officials regulated the disposal of unoccupied land. The *concelhos* were required to provide military service. The *cavaleiros-vilãos*, gave a period of service each year and thus gained relief from tribute. The *peões*, who could not provide a horse, served under varying conditions, in some cases being obliged to defend only their own *concelho*, and in others being required to participate in an annual expedition, the *fossado*. Settlers were attracted by the offer of freedom to serfs or slaves either on arrival or after a year's residence.

Although most charters were issued by the crown, the task of resettlement was shared with the nobles, prelates, military orders and abbeys. The hollow frontier caused by the sudden advance from Coimbra to Lisbon was filled by the great abbey of Alcobaça, where the monks taught, tilled and traded on behalf of their settlers. Beyond the Tagus the rural population probably changed little with the reconquest. The defence of the Alentejo was largely undertaken by the military orders, which occupied citadels and castles and drew revenues from broad estates tilled or grazed by Muslim serfs. To towns such as Lisbon, Santarém and Évora there was a stream of

[1] Against Leon rather than against the Muslims. In Muslim times the concept of the frontier was latitudinal, the defences of the west ('the lower frontier') being coordinated at Badajoz. With the Christian reconquest, and especially with the dissolution of the old 'empire' of Leon, new frontiers were created running north and south. The Leonese foundation of Ciudad Rodrigo in 1160 was followed by the unsuccessful Portuguese attempt to seize Badajoz in 1170, and the repopulation of eastern Beira from 1185.

Christian settlers. The free Muslims retained their own quarter, their *qaḍis* and mosques, and had their *foral* (Lisbon, 1170). In other districts *forais* contain clauses guaranteeing the security of Muslim merchants and travellers.

The opportunity to carry the reconquest into the Algarve was provided by the Third Crusade, following the fall of Jerusalem in 1187. In July 1189 a fleet put into Lisbon, bringing the Landgrave of Thuringia and two Flemish counts with their men, together with a party of Londoners. They made a bargain with Sancho for the conquest of Silves, left Lisbon with a Portuguese fleet and reached the Algarve in four days. Entering the river Arade, then navigable, they anchored off Silves, a city of twenty or thirty thousand inhabitants with a strong keep and stout walls within which gleaming minarets rose above the flat roofs. The suburb was entered, and the inhabitants retired within the fortress, where they were besieged. On 1 September some offered to surrender if they were allowed to keep their possessions: Sancho was anxious to accept, but the crusaders refused to forgo their booty for an indemnity. However, on 3 September the defenders capitulated and evacuated Silves, most of them departing for Seville. The crusaders looted the houses and shops amidst scenes of great disorder. Finally, Sancho drove them back to their ships where they divided the spoils after their own fashion.

The Muslims of al-Andalus at once appealed to the Almohad caliph, who crossed to Tarifa on 1 May 1190. He negotiated truces with Castile and Leon, sent his fleet to invest Silves, and detached an army to raid Portugal. Sancho held Santarém and the Templars their headquarters at Tomar. At this time, Richard Lionheart's fleet appeared at Lisbon on its way to the Holy Land. The first ship with a hundred men-at-arms from London sailed on to Silves and contributed to its defence. A force of 500 men went to the relief of Santarém, and the Almohads retired from both places.

But in April 1191 the caliph left Seville with his main force and advanced on Alcácer do Sal, where he was joined by his fleet. A general assault on 10 June brought the fall of the place: Palmela was razed and Almada left in ruins. On 27 June the Almohads arrived before Silves; it surrendered in the following month and the caliph retired in triumph to the Magrib, having recovered all the Portuguese gains south of the Tagus with the exception of Évora. In 1194 the truce between the Almohads and Castile expired, and the caliph prepared a new invasion. His victory at Alarcos in July 1195 was the greatest triumph of the Almohads in the Peninsula, and it was followed by a series of raids to the east and west of Toledo: great havoc was caused but no major town was taken.

The Christian states were now in disarray. The concept of a single Leonese 'empire' had long been replaced by that of Five Kingdoms. This arrangement told against Leon, and favoured Castile, now firmly in control of the ancient imperial capital of Toledo, and Portugal. Ferdinand II of Leon had vainly attempted to intervene in the affairs of Castile, and his son Alfonso IX had sought to unite the other Peninsular states, Portugal, Aragon and Navarre, against his more powerful neighbour. This alliance was completed in February 1191, when Alfonso married the daughter of the king of Portugal at Guimarãis. The Castilians protested, and a papal legate forced the king of Leon to separate from his queen and reconciled Portugal with Castile. Thus Portuguese troops appeared with the Castilians at Alarcos, while the Leonese sought help from the Almohads. Pope Celestine III accordingly excommunicated the king of Leon (October 1196) and authorized the other Christian princes to crusade against him. Castile and Aragon invaded Leon (1197), and the Portuguese occupied Tuy. But by the end of the year the Leonese had come to terms with Castile by means of another un-canonical marriage. They also lost their Muslim ally, the victorious caliph, who returned to the Magrib, where he died (1199).

During the following years, the kingdom of Leon, now deprived of its imperial pretensions by papal policy, strove desperately for survival. It first attacked Portugal, besieging Bragança while Sancho I marched on Ciudad Rodrigo. Neither side gained ground, but these campaigns provide the context of the *forais* now granted to Belmonte and Guarda for the defence of the Portuguese frontier. In the following years Leon resumed the war with Castile (1200, 1203, 1207, 1209). At the end of 1208 Sancho had married his heir Afonso (II) to a daughter of the king of Castile, and fought another brief campaign on the Leonese frontier; the only permanent result was the repopulation of the borderlands of Beira.

In March 1211 Sancho I died in his capital at Coimbra, aged fifty-seven, and was succeeded by Afonso II, now twenty-five. Sancho had been a successful soldier,[1] a founder of towns and a patron of court poetry: the earliest datable *cantar de amigo* in the Galaico-Portuguese lyrical tradition is ascribed to him. He also accumulated great wealth. His will distributed a million *morabitinos* or gold *dinars*, as well as jewels, plate, cloths, furniture, hangings, arms and horses, held in the castles of Coimbra, Guimarãis and Évora or deposited with the Templars at Tomar. To his heir he gave 200,000 *morabitinos* stored at Coimbra, 6,000 at Évora, the royal cloths at Guimarãis, all his arms and his five best horses. To the other seven children of Queen Dulce he left 40,000 *morabitinos* each, together with quantities of silver. Two illegitimate families, numbering eight persons, received seven or eight thousand apiece, and various castles and towns. The religious bequests included 100 gold marks for the pope, 10,000 *maravedies* each for three Cistercian foundations (Alcobaça to found a leper-house, Santa Cruz at Coimbra, with other bequests), 2,000 to the cathedral of Braga, 1,000 each to the other Portuguese sees, 3,000 to Tuy, and various gifts to monasteries and churches. As if aware that his heir might contest this munificent distribution of the royal patrimony, Sancho extracted from him an oath of obedience and appointed guarantors, while the beneficiaries hastened to obtain the pope's confirmation.

Afonso II had apparently survived with difficulty an illness in adolescence and was incapable of military exertions, being known as 'the fat'. His affairs were managed by the chancellor Mestre Julião who had served his father and grandfather. In the first year of the new reign a council was celebrated at Coimbra in which the nobility and prelates were called upon to approve the dispositions of Sancho I. This assembly was a consultative meeting of the privileged classes: it also ratified many concessions to the church. Ecclesiastical law was to be considered inviolable, and all governors, judges and royal officials were required to protect monasteries and churches against the encroachments of nobles or institutions. The mode of presentation to benefices under royal patronage was established, and the clergy exempted from *colheita*, the entertainment of the king; *anuduba*, the maintenance of fortifications; and the royal 'service', or annual grant. The only concession obtained by the crown was a prohibition

---

[1] The 'ibn ar-Rink', i.e. Henriques, referred to with such bitterness in the *Bayān al-mugrib* is Sancho I rather than his father.

on the purchase of land by the church (but presumably the church acquired most of its new wealth by gift). In the secular sphere, the crown undertook to limit oppressive taxation and to protect payers of tribute against the impositions of nobles or clergy. Every free man might choose his own master unless he resided on another's land. He might sell his property freely, though his relatives should have preference as purchasers. The payment of a third on sales of foodstuffs to king or overlord was abolished. The crown undertook not to constrain any subjects to marry against their will, to appoint royal judges to decide suits, and to grant twenty days' stay before executing death-sentences.

Afonso now received papal confirmation of his kingship from Pope Innocent III, together with a reminder of his obligation to pay tribute (April 1212). In December 1213 he sent fifty-six gold marks, representing arrears of tribute for twenty-eight years, the period of his father's reign. Having satisfied the church and made concessions to his subjects, Afonso was unable to maintain the members of his family in the state to which they were accustomed. His two brothers took their departure; Fernando to Paris, where he joined his aunt, the widowed countess of Alsace, and married the heiress to the county of Flanders; Pedro to Aragon and later to Marrakush, where he commanded the Christian contingent in the service of the Almohad caliphs. Their three sisters, awarded towns and convents in Portugal, carried on a lengthy correspondence with Afonso, and one of them, the repudiated queen of Leon, appealed to her former husband, the king of Leon, who seized several frontier castles, only to be attacked in turn by the Castilians and so forced to retire. In these disputes, Afonso maintained that his father had had no right to alienate the royal patrimony, and therefore challenged the validity of the will. In 1216 the papacy upheld the integrity of the royal patrimony, but recognized the right of the princesses to the usufruct of the disputed places, which were to be occupied by the Templars. Thereafter, from 1216 until 1221, the crown asserted its general right to maintain the royal patrimony by requiring those who had received donations from previous kings to apply for letters of confirmation: it thus reserved the power to revise grants to nobles, ecclesiastics or corporate bodies.

This process was soon carried a stage further. In the territory north of the Douro, the tenure of land antedated the independence of Portugal, and documentary evidence of possession was not seldom lacking. In 1220 royal commissions were instituted to investigate the nature of land ownership. These *inquirições* consisted of depositions taken from the oldest or most experienced men in each parish: lords were not usually consulted, and it appears that the lands of the archbishopric of Braga were singled out for special attention. The inquiry revealed numerous abuses, the improper extension of boundaries and conspiracies to defraud the crown of revenue. While these probings offended both privileged classes, the reaction of the church was the sharper. In 1219 the archbishop of Braga had excommunicated the court and laid an interdict on the whole kingdom. Royal officers seized his properties and he fled the country. At the end of 1220 the pope deprived Afonso of his patronage of the churches of Portugal, confirmed the excommunication of the king, ordered the bishop of Coimbra to leave the court and relieved the Portuguese of their oath of fealty. Six bulls were issued in three weeks, the last bidding Afonso to dismiss his advisers 'or deceivers', 'frogs lurking in the royal penetralia'. The court ignored these commands: Afonso's will, drawn up at Santarém in 1221, contains no bequests for any of the bishoprics, except the newly founded see of Guarda, and Tuy and Santiago in Galicia: the chief beneficiaries by this exclusion were the military orders. In 1222 the king of Leon contributed forces for an invasion of Portugal, occupying Chaves and assisting Afonso's half-brother, Martim Sanches, who raided Guimarãis and Braga. In June the pope made a further attempt to reduce Afonso to obedience, in which case the archbishop of Braga was empowered to absolve him. It appears that Afonso was now ill, and slowly dying of leprosy. His chancellor came to terms a little before he expired in March 1223. He was still excommunicate, and the archbishop refused to give him an ecclesiastical burial until an agreement had been reached between the court and the church. In June 1223 the chancellor agreed to set aside moneys to indemnify the losses of the church, to revise the *inquirições* and to respect ecclesiastical law and refrain from violence and abuse. Thus the church secured a complete victory at the expense of the new ruler.

Afonso II had left four children, the eldest of whom, Sancho II, could not have been more than twelve years old. It does not appear that any members of the royal family formed a regency, and the government remained in the hands of officials of the court. The reign of Sancho II is the obscurest in the history of Portugal; the chronicle is meagre, and many documents were probably destroyed after his deposition. During the early years of the reign there was a civil war, in which one party seems to have sought to remove Sancho in favour of his younger brother Afonso, who now or later left Portugal. In 1228 a papal legate, Jean d'Abbeville, held a council in Coimbra, seeking to pacify the kingdom and to divert the barons from internal strife to the war against the Muslims.

The Almohad empire was now in full decline. In 1212 the caliph had attempted a major campaign in the central meseta, and had been heavily defeated at Las Navas de Tolosa. This victory had opened the gateway of Andalusia to the Castilians, and by the middle of the century all that survived from the old caliphate of Córdoba would be the Naṣrid kingdom of Granada, now tributary to Castile. Portuguese troops had participated at Las Navas, and in 1217 they inflicted a heavy defeat on the Muslims at Alcácer do Sal, which was now restored to Portuguese control. In the following years pretenders struggled for power in Marrakush, and a Spanish Muslim from Murcia, ibn Ḥud, drove the Almohads out of al-Andalus. In 1230 the Leonese entered Mérida; and a band of Portuguese knights found Elvas abandoned by the Muslims. In the same year the death of the king of Leon finally reunited the crowns of Leon and Castile in the person of Ferdinand III, whose followers presently forced their way into the ancient Muslim capital of Córdoba (1236).

The crusade was now preached in Portugal, and Christian forces entered Mértola (1238), and Tavira and Cacela (1239). Soon only Silves and its immediate region remained under Muslim rule. This advance was made chiefly, if not solely, by the knights of the military orders. Those of Santiago, who had been granted Alcácer do Sal, opened the way through Aljustrel to Mértola: their Portuguese master, Pero Pais Correa, later distinguished himself in the Andalusian campaigns.

Sancho II appears to have been incapable of exercising authority. It is probable that as a boy he fell into the hands of a powerful family, the Mendes de Sousa. By 1229 these had given way to a government formed by the chancellor Mestre Vicente and alferes Martim Anes,

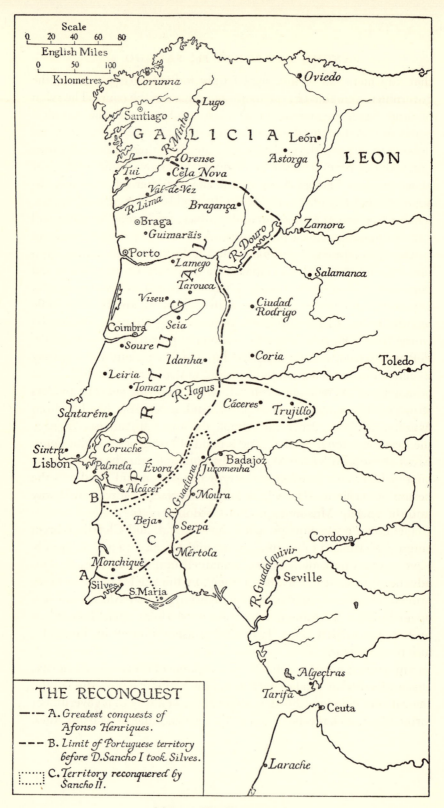

Map. 5. The Reconquest.

both of whom had served under Afonso II. But baronial disorders multiplied, and the king's family participated in them. His uncle, Rodrigo Sanches, governing the Minho, was accused of various excesses in the diocese of Oporto, while his brother Ferdinand, the 'infante of Serpa' (reconquered in 1232), perpetrated several murders and was finally condemned to a spectacular penance. Complaints of abuses of power now fall fast and furious, of abuses by the nobility against royal officers, by the bishops against the populace, by the nobility and clergy against the monasteries, and finally by the crown and the royal favourites against the church. One constant source of irritation was the episcopal control of the city of Oporto, dating from the days of Dona Teresa. This had led to riots in 1209, when the populace sided with royal officials against the bishop, who placed the city under an interdict and remained pent up in his palace for five months: he had then fled to Rome and raised a storm against Sancho I. In the time of his grandson, the bishop of Oporto again complained to Rome of royal interference with the bishop's vassals, and obtained an injunction from the pope. By 1231 the bishop of Lisbon, who had been accused of extortion in his see, departed for Rome with a string of complaints against the crown. The archbishop of Braga had been drawn over to the court party, and it was only after his death that his successor, Archbishop Godinho, began to lead a league of bishops. Archbishop Godinho had been consecrated in Rome, and in 1235 the pope appointed a candidate to the see of Coimbra. In 1237 the new bishop of Oporto, Pedro Salvadores, brought bitter complaints against the encroachments of the crown and the misdeeds of the king's uncle in his diocese, while the king's brother, the infante of Serpa, was accused of seeking to intimidate the chapter of Lisbon to elect a royal nominee. Nevertheless, the papacy was apparently reluctant to take a stand against Sancho while the Portuguese forces were actively crusading against the infidel, and the church itself was by no means free from dissensions: the appearance of the Franciscans in Portugal in 1216, under the protection of the sisters of Afonso II, had been followed by difficulties with the crown; the Dominicans, on the contrary, were admitted in 1237 to the diocese of Oporto, where the bishop hoped that they would fortify his authority— instead they sided with the recalcitrant burghers against him.

Sancho II now passed under the influence of a favourite, Martim

Gil, a son of Gil Vasques de Soverosa and Maria Aires, mistress of Sancho I (possibly the 'witch' kept in the palace and denounced by the Bishop of Coimbra in 1209). Martim Gil evidently personified the resistance of the barons against papal intervention, as represented by the bishop of Coimbra. In 1241 Sancho was married to Mécia López de Haro, widow of a famous Andalusian frontiersman, Alvaro Pérez de Castro, who had died in the previous year.[1] There were no children of this match.

The prelates of Braga, Lisbon and Oporto were in Rome in 1241 and witnessed the election of Innocent IV, whose chief concern was to impose obedience on Frederick II. Pope Innocent took refuge in France and called a further council at Lyons in 1245. It was on this occasion that the conspiracy to depose Sancho was first elaborated. Sancho's younger brother, Afonso (III), had left Portugal and acquired by marriage the title of Count of Boulogne. He now denounced Sancho's marriage to Mécia López as uncanonical: it alone stood between him and the throne. In January 1245 Innocent IV asked Afonso to take succour to the Holy Land, and under this pretext he was able to enlist men and acquire arms. In February the pope ordered Sancho II to abandon Dona Mécia, and in March he delivered a long philippic in which Sancho was accused of committing or permitting every form of crime. The bishops of Coimbra and Oporto carried the message to Portugal, returning to Lyons in May, when they presented a lamentable picture of anarchy. The pope then drew up a bull in which the nobles, knights, *concelhos* and communities were bidden to deliver the kingdom to a more worthy ruler. The catalogue of crimes was repeated, and the favoured successor was named, the legitimate heir and virtuous, religious and prudent count of Boulogne, who was to be received everywhere and to receive all tributes and revenues. In case of hesitation the archbishop of Braga and bishop of Coimbra were empowered to apply the penalties of the church (24 July 1245).

The Portuguese then repaired to Paris. Afonso engaged to restore the good old customs of Portugal and to set aside the bad innovations

[1] In order to marry her, Alvaro had repudiated Aurembiax, Countess of Urgel, who then married Sancho's brother Pedro, former commander of the Christian contingent in Africa. He was offered the islands of Majorca and Minorca by James I of Aragon, and became king of the Balearic Islands.

of his brother and father, to appoint honest judges and to punish crimes, especially against churchmen. In spite of the innumerable accusations made against Sancho, no mention was made of the reform of the government except in general terms. Most of Afonso's promises related to obedience to the papacy and protection of the church. The intent of the papacy was clearly to provide an object-lesson for the contumacious Frederick II, who in a letter to Ferdinand III of Castile observes how the pope 'wielded his sickle in the corn-fields of other men' and how he had arrogated to himself supremacy over the kingdom of Portugal. The point was not lost on Ferdinand, and when Sancho II belatedly appealed to his heir, Alfonso el Sabio, the Castilian prince protested to the pope against the usurpation of the count of Boulogne; and Innocent replied that it was not his intention to depose Sancho or any legitimate son of his, provided he would mend his ways.

Meanwhile, Afonso arrived in Lisbon early in 1246. His reception had been carefully prepared, and he had the support of the Order of Santiago and the *concelho*, whose privileges and *foros* he at once confirmed. He claimed to be 'Procurator of the Kingdom' or 'Defender and Visitor of the Kingdom for the Supreme Pontiff'. Probably most of the south adhered to him. Sancho and Martim Gil held Coimbra. In the previous year they had defeated the king's uncle at Gaia in a fight called the 'lide do Porto' and had killed a number of the northern barons. In Coimbra Martim Gil persecuted the clergy as supporters of the usurper, and one of his henchmen jestingly called himself Bishop of Coimbra. A few miles away, at Montemór, Teresa, the former queen of Leon, welcomed the insurgents, while a brother of the archbishop carried off Dona Mécia, or assisted her to flee from her husband—Sancho pursued her to Ourém, but he could not take it. Afonso's succession was now safe, since no legitimate child could be born to Sancho.

Early in 1247 the Castilian prince and Dona Mécia's brother, Diego López de Haro, entered Portugal and marched on Coimbra. They were duly excommunicated by the Portuguese clergy, and on their protesting to the pope, he raised the ban and sent a negotiator. But he clearly had no intention of preventing the usurpation. Sancho and his party retired to Castile. As they passed Trancoso a knight emerged and challenged Martim Gil, offering to renew his allegiance to Sancho if he would dismiss the favourite: Sancho forbade the combat and went on his way to Toledo: he died there early in 1248. His will shows that he was accompanied into exile by his chancellor and a few adherents. Castilian troops held Coimbra for him, and according to legend its governor refused to deliver the city until he had been to Toledo and seen the body of his master with his own eyes. By July Afonso III had entered the capital.

5. AFONSO III, 1246–79; DINIS, 1279–1325

In the war of the two brothers, Sancho had stood for legitimism, the usual bond of the baronial party, but for a legitimism now much weakened by the individual pretensions and jealousies of the *ricos-homens*. By his subservience to Martim Gil, he had forfeited the support of the *infanções*, the knights of Santiago and the Templars. His brother was the candidate of the papacy, the Portuguese church, the *infanções* and the municipalities, which provided a great part of his troops. The Peninsular kings could best win the unanimous acclaim of their subjects by appearing as crusaders. Afonso III now gathered troops for a final campaign in the Algarve. In November 1248 Ferdinand III of Castile and Leon had completed the conquest of central Andalusia by entering Seville after a long siege: many of the smaller places to its west and south made what terms they could. In 1249 Afonso took Faro: the neighbouring towns probably capitulated when he visited the Algarve in the following year.

The Portuguese reconquest was thus complete except that the jurisdiction of the Algarve was disputed by Castile. The knights of Santiago had obtained bulls from Innocent IV confirming their occupation of Sesimbra, Palmela, Alcácer, Mértola, Tavira and Cacela. The order was still international, but its Portuguese Master Paio Peres Correia had also sought confirmations from Ferdinand III, and a Muslim commander, ibn Maḥfuḍ, who had seized Niebla, with Faro and Silves, had made submission to Castile. The Portuguese protested, but in 1250, after a short struggle, a truce was concluded for forty years.

But in May 1252 Ferdinand III died and was succeeded by Alfonso X, the former enemy of Afonso III. He now annexed the territories of ibn Maḥfuḍ, who departed for Africa. His claim to

Silves provoked new hostilities, and in January 1253 the pope intervened to prevent war. It was then arranged that Afonso III should marry the bastard daughter of Alfonso X, still an infant. The Portuguese would retain the sovereignty of the Algarve and the territory to the east of the Guadiana, but the Castilians would retain the usufruct until an heir of the match reached the age of seven. Afonso was, of course, already married to the Countess of Boulogne, who protested from France against her husband's bigamy and alleged the usual canonical impediment. In spite of this the child Beatriz Guillén was delivered to the Portuguese and treated as queen. The pope eventually ordered their separation in 1258, when the marriage was still unconsummated. But Afonso's wife now died, and in 1260 his prelates made a plea on his behalf. An interdict laid on him was raised in 1263, and the children then born were recognized as legitimate.

Afonso's relations with the church had been regulated before his arrival. In January 1257 he convoked an assembly of barons for the purpose of enforcing order, and established fines for homicide and robbery, and measures for the suppression of banditry and the protection of travellers. Three years later (February–April 1254), he summoned a wider representation to the *cortes* of Leiria, the first assembly in Portugal at which the commons were represented. The towns had first been summoned to attend *cortes* in Leon in 1188, and the need for this form of consultation appears to have arisen from fiscal and monetary questions. Until the time of Alfonso VI of Leon, no coin had been minted, the usual medium of exchange being the measure of wheat (*moio*) or Muslim or even Roman and Byzantine coins. Thereafter the flow of coin had depended on conquest or tribute from the Muslims: in Portugal, Muslim gold became treasure, and the coin circulation came from Leon or France. The growth of trade now stimulated the demand for coin, which ceased to be sufficient to cover needs. It then became the practice to call in silver, debase it and reissue it with the same face value. This process was introduced into Castile as early as 1202, when money was 'broken' septennially. But the process was unpopular, and the towns were willing to pay a large compensation to avoid it. At the end of 1253 it was reported that Afonso III would break the Portuguese coin, and prices began to rise. In this context *cortes* were held at Leiria, and

Afonso accepted *monetágio*, compensation in lieu of debasement. Other measures that were adopted included the introduction of a price-tax in the region of the Minho and Douro, territories which had been Christian before the use of coin became general and customarily paid taxes in kind. There existed a general preference for non-variable contributions established by ancient *foros* and based ultimately on the concept of fixed prices, but this prejudice was now gradually overcome.

One of the questions discussed at Leiria was the status of Oporto, which had remained in the hands of its bishop since the grant of Dona Teresa. The crown had established a royal borough, Gáia, on the opposite bank, and the two places disputed the right to collect toll and disembark merchandise. When the bishop opposed the entry of the royal officers, Afonso had the whole city occupied. At Leiria it was agreed that one-third of the ships descending the Douro and half those from abroad should unload at Gáia. The bishop rejected this and appealed to the pope, but he could not prevent Afonso from formally establishing the *concelho* of Vila Nova de Gáia in 1255.

As the septennium during which the value of the coin was fixed expired, Afonso proposed to raise the face-value of existing coin and to make a new and weaker issue, to the alarm of his subjects. *Cortes* were convened at Coimbra in 1261, and the relationship between the old coin and the new was agreed, but minting was to be suspended for four years and the number of furnaces limited to twenty. Afonso undertook not to break the coin for the rest of his reign, and the septennial debasement was converted into a practice of one devaluation in each reign. In return, it was agreed that the non-privileged classes should pay a tax on their capital. Those excepted were ecclesiastics, sword-bearing knights and their children and noble ladies, unless they were married to commoners. For the rest, those who possessed 10 to 20 *libras* were to pay half; 20 to 100, one; 100 to 1,000, two: over 1,000, three *libras*.[1]

The collection of taxes in coin rather than in kind was now much extended, often in return for some privilege, such as the right of presentation of a governor or the obligation of the lord to pay for

---

[1] The French system of money of account was now adopted: *libras*, *soldos* and *dinheiros* replaced *morabitinos*, *dinars* and *dirhams*. Only *dinheiros* actually were minted. The *morabitino* of Afonso Henriques was set at thirty *soldos*, and that of Afonso III at twenty-two.

goods in money. These changes are possibly also associated with the revival of the *inquirições* in 1258. Commissioners were again sent to take the evidence of the magistrate, priest and good men of each parish, in order to restore land improperly taken from the royal patrimony. Once more, the prelates were aggrieved, and reminded the king of his promises to defend the church. Soon seven of the nine sees were in revolt: the bishop of Silves, the eighth, lived in Castile: only the bishop of Lisbon, the ninth, adhered to the king. In 1267 the archbishop and four of the bishops placed their dioceses under an interdict and went to Rome, where they accused Afonso of laying hands on church property and of misgovernment. In reply, he announced his intention to crusade, and the interdict was raised: the *concelhos* obediently produced a testimonial to the excellence of his government. He then appointed an administrator to the arch-diocese of Braga and took over the revenues of the other abandoned sees. He procrastinated successfully for several years and still resisted when a bull was issued demanding new oaths of obedience and ex-patiating at length on the 'hereditary depravity' of the Portuguese sovereigns (September 1275). Gregory IX was succeeded by Innocent V, Adrian V and John XXI. This last, Petrus Hispanus, was a native of Lisbon, and Afonso was urged to take the chance to negotiate. But he did not give way; in March 1277 the penalties against the king were proclaimed in Lisbon, and in May John XXI died. In October, the final penalty of deposition was pronounced; although a few disaffected persons attempted to start a civil war, nothing had been achieved when Afonso fell ill, promised obedience, received absolution and died.

Afonso had hardly proved the docile instrument of papal policy that his patrons had desired. The thirteenth-century conflict of authority was not confined to Portugal, though it was unusually acute there owing to the special relationship with the Holy See. Until the Roman reform the Peninsular rulers had nominated bishops, and it had been common practice for secular patrons to appoint parish priests on a pittance, retaining most of the revenues of the benefice for themselves. The remedy for these abuses had been to strengthen the authority of the papacy and of the bishops, and to extend the powers of the ecclesiastical courts to embrace all cases which involved clerics. But the crown still regarded itself as the patron of sees, and while the principle that bishops were elected by the chapter was accepted, in practice the crown regularly attempted to secure the election of its own candidate and expected to reward faithful clerks in this way. The conflict of interests was complicated in many ways. The crown inevitably resisted the attempts of the church to secure absolute autonomy for the ecclesiastical courts: Afonso II had reserved serious crimes to the royal judges, and attempted to define cases in which clerics should be judged by ecclesiastical law. But economic questions almost defied elucidation: if formerly the church had too little property, or too little control over its property, to support the clergy, it now threatened to acquire so much land in mortmain that the royal patrimony was seriously diminished, and the crown had to take steps to prevent the purchase of land by the church and to annul legacies and donations. The papacy had condemned the practice of inducing testators to bequeath a fixed proportion of their property to the diocese, but it still continued. Finally, the tithes were a fruitful cause of disputes, for they were sometimes gathered by a church, sometimes by a diocese, and sometimes shared between the chapter and the crown. The crown had in fact no choice but to determine the rights of the church, and to revise its policy in the light of the general interest.

Afonso's heir Dinis was eighteen years of age and was excommunicate when he began to reign. His advisers were in no hurry to come to terms with the Holy See and ten years had passed before a concordat was reached in 1289. By then the weapons of the church had lost a good deal of their effect: Dinis had succeeded, been crowned and married Isabel of Aragon (1282) without inconvenience. In 1285 he celebrated *cortes* in Lisbon and obtained support for laws which forbade the religious corporations to purchase land and ordered the sale of land purchased since the beginning of his reign. In 1284 he launched a new series of *inquirições*, and they received the approval of *cortes* despite the opposition of the nobles and the clergy.

The responsibility of the crown to determine questions of jurisdiction was asserted in 1282, when Dinis reserved the right to judge appeals: this had been asserted by Afonso II, but often usurped by the magnates. Dinis' grandfather, the learned Alfonso X, had attempted to draw up a systematic work of reference, intended to serve as a basis for a uniform system of royal law. It was bitterly resisted by the Castilian nobles and towns, and in his last days Alfonso's authority was generally repudiated. Dinis, although he had his learned predecessor's works translated into Portuguese, did not seek to emulate him. When in 1288 various ecclesiatics urged on him the need for a Portuguese centre of learning, such as the 'General Studies' that had now come into being in Leon and Aragon, he complied. The Studies were founded at Lisbon and received papal approval in August 1290. Twenty years later they were transplanted to Coimbra, where provision was made for the study of grammar, logic, canon and civil law, and medicine.

Dinis' father had lived in France, and his own education had been entrusted to a Frenchman, Aymeric d'Ebrard, and a Portuguese, Domingos Anes Jardo. His grandfather, Alfonso X, had grown up in Galicia and had written his poems in Galician and his prose in Castilian. King Dinis followed him in writing many poems in the courtly tradition of Provence as well as in the characteristic lyric style of Galaico-Portuguese. Despite the translations ordered by Dinis from the legal works of his grandfather, it can hardly be said that Portuguese prose reaches the maturity of the verse: it begins with the incomparable chronicles of Fernão Lopes at the beginning of the following century.

While still a boy, Dinis had visited the court of Castile and received from his grandfather the territories of the Algarve which had formerly been in dispute. The final annexation of the Algarve added a new dimension to the Portuguese coast: while the whole territory was now completely nationalized, the external relations of the Portuguese kingdom were rendered international in a way that had never been possible before. The military orders, brought to their full development during the period of the great Almohad invasions, and still owing allegiance to the Holy See, now became purely national orders of chivalry. The Order of Calatrava, though founded in Castile, had in fact developed into a Portuguese institution when Afonso II bestowed on it the town of Avis, from which it took its Portuguese name. In 1288 the Portuguese Order of Santiago obtained an independent organization and elected its own Master: its seat was at Palmela. When the Templars were suppressed by the popes of Avignon, Dinis seized the opportunity to replace them with a purely national order. In 1308 Clement V instructed the bishop of Lisbon to hold an inquiry into the activities of the Portuguese Templars, sending a list of their probable offences. Dinis then placed his own officials in their castles and towns, setting up a special court to justify his intervention. The Peninsular prelates held a council at Salamanca and asserted the innocence of the Templars, but the kings of Portugal, Castile and Aragon agreed to adopt a common policy in the event of their dissolution. In 1312 Clement V ordered the suppression of the order and the transfer of its possessions to the Hospitallers, but made an exception in the case of the Peninsular states. Seven years later John XXII authorized the foundation of the new Order of Christ, with headquarters at Castro-Marim, near the mouth of the Guadiana, evidently intended for the defence of the Algarve: the new Order received Tomar, Castelo Branco and other properties of the Templars. Dinis occupied Pombal, Soure and other estates in the region of Coimbra.

In Castile, where the reconquest was still not concluded, the military orders remained on a war footing and in the fifteenth century became private armies in the hands of Masters who sought political pre-eminence. In Portugal, the reconquest was already past, and the Orders tended to become simply corporations of more or less celibate landowners. But the Order of Avis contributed conspicuously to the defence of Portuguese independence in the fourteenth century, and in the fifteenth the resources of the Order of Christ were diverted by its master into the great enterprise of the discoveries.

The existence of a Portuguese navy goes back to the time of Afonso Henriques, whose ships attacked Seville and Ceuta. It is probable that Muslim Lisbon had traded actively with Ceuta, where there was a Genoese merchant colony in the eleventh century. The Genoese had played a part in the decline of the Almohad empire and in the Castilian reconquest of Seville, and they thereafter (1248) reached out into the Atlantic to the western ports of Morocco, the Algarve and Lisbon. The first Genoese to open the sea-way from the Mediterranean to the ports of Flanders and England was Benedetto Zaccaria, later engaged by Alfonso X as admiral of Castile to provide ships for the occupation of the Straits and the defence of Seville.

It is clear that Portuguese merchants were trading in the English ports in the twelfth century and that these contacts increased in the thirteenth. The chief object of the planting of the great pine-forest of Leiria by order of King Dinis, the 'Pinhal d'el-Rei', was to produce timber for ship-building. The creation of a specifically naval tradition is usually dated from the appointment of a Genoese, Manuel Pessagna or Peçanha, to be hereditary admiral of Portugal in February 1322: as usual, the warships were used for trade in time of peace.

The appearance of Italian seamen and merchants is followed by the concession of letters of security and trading-privileges, of which the most important is that of having a particular judge, often the governor of the custom-house, to ensure prompt settlement of cases involving visiting merchants. At the same time, encouragement is given to the construction of larger ships, and a system of mutual insurance against the risk of loss is introduced.

The development of overseas trade is paralleled by the spread of domestic trade and the holding of fairs and markets. In earlier times, the universal place of exchange had been the weekly market, in which transactions had been chiefly in kind. Afonso III had encouraged the payment of tribute in coin and had also stimulated the holding of fairs held under royal charter. The charter gave guarantees of security, together with exemptions from tolls and customs-dues. Afonso granted charters for some sixteen fairs, mostly perhaps with the object of attracting settlers and goods to the still sparsely settled eastern frontier. Dinis gave authority for at least forty fairs, and gradually almost every *concelho* came to have one. By the end of the fourteenth century almost all fairs were 'free'.

The expansion of commerce was accompanied by a growth of the strength and influence of larger *concelhos*, particularly Lisbon and Oporto. Here the royal officials, the governor (*alcaide*) and the consuls or vizirs (*alvazis*) were now closely associated with representatives of the parishes and guilds, *homens bons*. In Christian territory representation in the towns was traditionally based on the parish council, but in Muslim times no representative institution had linked the numerous appointed officials (governor, police, inspectors) with the autonomous guilds traditionally organized in streets or quarters. In fourteenth-century Lisbon the two systems were fused. In 1298, when Dinis desired to raise troops in Lisbon he instructed the authorities and 'good men' to consult the 'good men' of the guilds: the influence of the latter continued to grow during the following century.

Dinis had been born before the papal legitimization of his father's marriage, and his younger brother Afonso, born after the dispensation, claimed on this account to be the rightful heir and rebelled in his town of Arronches on the frontier in 1288; he was attacked from Portugal and Castile, and his mother and the two queens, St Isabel and María de Molina, intervened to negotiate a peaceful settlement. Ten years later, when the crown of Castile was in dispute and the neighbouring kingdom was rent with strife, Dinis was again faced with a rebellion by his brother, who declared for the Castilian pretender. Once more the struggle was ended by the intervention of the queens.[1] By the Treaty of Alcañices (September 1297) Dinis obtained a favourable settlement of frontier questions with Castile and undertook to marry his son and daughter to the young king of Castile, Ferdinand IV, and his sister.

The last years of the reign of Dinis were clouded by new domestic troubles. His heir by Isabel of Aragon had been born in 1291, but he had also several illegitimate children, including Pedro Afonso, whom he made Count of Barcelos in 1314, and Afonso Sanches, who became *mordomo-mór*. Because of Dinis' attachment to the latter, the heir believed, or affected to believe, that Dinis intended to disinherit him. He persuaded his grandmother, Queen Beatriz, now in Castile, to write to his father to ask that the government should be handed over to him (1320). When Dinis refused, the prince raised a rebellion in the north and marched on Coimbra. He finally entered Coimbra and Oporto, and when Dinis sent troops against him, Queen Isabel intervened and made peace. Dinis gave his son the two cities and received in return an oath of obedience (May 1320). By the settlement, the bastard Afonso Sanches left Portugal. When he returned, a year later, the prince again rebelled, and once more Queen Isabel made peace. Shortly after, in the first days of 1325, Dinis died, and the crown passed to Afonso IV.

---

[1] In both countries there was doubt about the legitimate succession. In Castile Alfonso X had pronounced in favour of strict primogeniture, but his heir had died at a time of crisis in 1275 and his second son, Sancho IV, had been given precedence over the infant sons of the heir. In Portugal, the younger brother's claim rested on doubts about the legitimization of Dinis.

6. AFONSO IV, 1325–57; PEDRO I, 1357–67

Afonso IV confiscated the possessions of his half-brother Afonso Sanches, who had gone to live in Castile and had married the daughter of Juan Alfonso de Meneses, lord of the frontier-town of Albuquerque. The pretender gathered a band of supporters and attempted to invade Portugal, but once more peace was restored by the intervention of Queen Isabel. She indeed maintained the balance of peace until she died in her convent of Santa Clara at Coimbra in 1336.

Meanwhile, the long minority of Alfonso XI of Castile had led to a bitter struggle between factions of the Castilian royal family, who sought support from the courts of Portugal and Aragon. The most ambitious of these magnates was Don Juan Manuel, a grandson of Alfonso X, and adelantado of Murcia. The royal tutors had sought to appease him by promising that the king should marry his daughter, but when Alfonso XI came of age, he rejected the match and married instead the daughter of Afonso IV of Portugal. At the same time Afonso's heir Pedro was betrothed to a Castilian princess. But Alfonso XI soon abandoned his Portuguese queen for Leonor de Guzmán (whose children were later to seize the throne of Castile), and Don Juan Manuel contrived to form an alliance with Portugal and Aragon: it was now arranged that his daughter Constanza should marry the Portuguese heir (1336). Thus in 1337 the allies made war on Castile, and Afonso IV besieged Badajoz while Pedro of Barcelos entered Galicia.

The struggles of the Christian princes enabled the rulers of the Magrib, the banu Marin, to attack Tarifa and prepare what was to be the last Muslim attempt to invade the Peninsula on a massive scale. Having recently extended their power in Africa, the banu Marin gathered a vast army and succeeded in destroying the Castilian fleet which now habitually guarded the Straits. The pope granted indulgences for a crusade; peace was made between the Christian princes; a Portuguese fleet was sent forward to defend the mouth of the Guadalquivir, and Afonso IV, with a thousand lances, joined the Castilian host assembled at Seville. In October 1340 Castilians and Portuguese met the armies of the Magrib and Granada on the river Salado, and won a resounding victory. The

Marinid ruler fled to Africa, abandoning his treasure, and in the following years Afonso XI was able to reduce Algeciras after a long siege (1342-4).

The peace of 1340 enabled Constanza Manuel to leave Aragon and cross Castile for her marriage to the Portuguese heir, which took place in Lisbon in August 1340: she gave birth to a prince, Fernando, and died in 1345. But among her court was a Galician lady named Inês Pires de Castro, to whom Pedro became attached. King Afonso, fearing the consequences of this entanglement, banished Inês de Castro, who withdrew to Alburquerque, where earlier his half-brother and rival had established himself. When Constanza Manuel died, Inês was able to return to Portugal and to rejoin the prince, who installed her in a country house near Coimbra, where she bore him several children. During the following years Afonso was unable to persuade his son to make another marriage, and became increasingly alarmed that Inês's brothers would succeed in directing the affairs of Portugal. His advisers finally suggested a brutal method of preventing this. On 7 January 1355, while Pedro was absent, the king rode from Montemór to Inês' estate, accompanied by his chief justice, Álvaro Gonçalves and two others, Pedro Coelho and Diogo Lopes Pacheco: Afonso IV had an interview with Inês, and after he had left, his counsellors returned and murdered her.

Pedro now took up arms against his father and laid siege to Oporto, while the brothers of Inês invaded Portugal from Galicia. The fighting continued during the summer, but peace was restored on 15 August, when Afonso pardoned his son and awarded him the administration of justice in return for an undertaking that the three murderers would be spared. However, when Afonso died, in May 1357, the three culprits immediately fled to Castile. Pedro sought their extradition and in 1360 finally laid hands on Álvaro Gonçalves and Pedro Coelho, who were executed at Santarém, their hearts being drawn, one through the chest, and the other through the back. Pedro proclaimed that he had been married to Inês, and gave her a pompous funeral. The apotheosis of Inês who 'reigned after her death' passed through the chronicle of Rui de Pina to form the subject of the first tragedy in Portuguese, the *Castro* of António Ferreira, and to provide a famous episode in the *Lusiads*. In the abbey of Alcobaça two splendid tombs record the story of Pedro and Inês, concluding with a scene of the Day of Judgement in which the lovers are seen in the company of the blessed and look out from a casement on the agony of Álvaro Gonçalves and Pedro Coelho engulfed in the jaws of hell.

In fact, Fernão Lopes, whose first chronicle is that of Pedro I, says little of Inês de Castro, but a great deal of the king's obsession with the punishment of crime, which emerges as the chief theme of his reign. Nor is the tradition of Pedro as an inconsolable royal lover an authentic one, for soon after his accession Pedro's favourite was one Teresa Lourenço whose son John, the future founder of the dynasty of Avis, was born in June 1358. In the same year, a mission from Castile proposed that Pedro's heir Fernando and the two sons of Inês, João and Diniz, should all marry Castilian princesses.

If in the middle of the thirteenth century, the papacy had demonstrated its authority by deposing the king of Portugal, by the middle of the fourteenth, its secular power was in eclipse; and the monarchy had successfully curbed the jurisdiction of the nobility and the church, and established itself as the final court of appeal. It increasingly had recourse to the code of Justinian, and regularly overrode the ancient particularisms preserved by the nobles and the towns, enacting new legislation for the whole country, for which it sought the consent of the people's representatives assembled in *cortes*. In the settlement of 1355 Pedro took over the administration of justice in somewhat exceptional circumstances. His own reign was that of a supreme judge itinerating on a never-ending circuit; Fernão Lopes depicts a ruler deeply preoccupied with the application of penalties, of which he quotes a number of alarming examples. Pedro expedited the administration of justice by disgracing corrupt magistrates, dismissing advocates and removing other impediments. The *cortes* of Évora of 1381 complained that he had appointed judges who should have been elective. The dramatic incidents related by Fernão Lopes illustrate an energetic campaign to enforce the royal authority at the expense of private or local jurisdictions. Appeals and petitions were delivered to the confidential notary (*escrivão da poridade*), who delivered them to the judges of appeal (*desembargadores*) for submission to the king: decisions were announced the same day or the next. Petitions involving the exchequer were submitted to one of the treasurers (*veedores*) for comment before going to the *desembargador*.

It is with evident approval that Fernão Lopes notes that 'folk said that such years there never were in Portugal as these when Dom Pedro was king'. In the great crisis that was shortly to involve both Portugal and Castile, the unity of Portugal under a single royal jurisdiction would emerge from the ordeal reinforced, not impaired, while in Castile the regalist aspirations of Alfonso the Learned would remain unachieved, and victory would go to the baronial party.

These years saw a rapid expansion of the commerce of Lisbon, Oporto and other places. In the previous century Portuguese merchants were already trading actively in the northern ports, particularly in England: letters of Dinis to Edward I and II show the crown intervening to obtain safe-conducts and protection for Portuguese merchants in England and offering reciprocal rights. In 1353 the merchants and seamen of Lisbon and Oporto made their own treaty on trade with Edward III, negotiating as a corporation with responsibility for its members. The most important single factor in this expansion was the opening of the Straits of Gibraltar following the Christian conquest of Seville and the inception of frequent shipping services between the Italian ports and those of northern Europe; these regular sailings date from the early years of Afonso IV. The appointment of Manuel Peçanha as admiral must have served to stimulate commerce, since it was usual to allow the admiral to use his ships for trade in time of peace. By the middle of the century Genoese and other Italians enjoyed guarantees of security and other privileges in Lisbon.

The expansion of trade was accompanied by that of geographical exploration. The Atlantic coast of the Magrib was not unknown, for the Genoese had long traded through Ceuta with the Moroccan ports and both Castilian and Portuguese soldiers had served the Almohads in Africa: Alfonso X had unsuccessfully attempted to conquer Sallee. In 1291 the brothers Vivaldi left Genoa, apparently in the hope of circumnavigating Africa: they were not heard of again. The Canaries do not appear on a planisphere of 1325, but are shown on a Majorcan map of Dulcert in 1339. A Genoese named Lanzarotto Malocello visited the island still called Lanzarote in these years, and in 1341 it was reported in Florence that the king of Portugal had supplied two ships in which Italian merchants had sailed from Lisbon to 'those islands', bringing back sheepskins, tallow, sealskins and dyewood: a Genoese captain gave a fairly full description of the Canaries which was recorded by Boccaccio. In February 1343 Afonso IV sent the pope an account of his attempts on the Canaries, noting that strife with Castile had prevented their continuance, but this seems to have been without effect, and in November 1344 Pope Clement VI granted the title of Prince of Fortune (i.e. of the Fortunate Islands) to a Spanish nobleman, Don Luis de la Cerda. He took no steps to justify the award, and it appears that Malocello continued to frequent the islands under Portuguese auspices: a map of 1367 records almost the whole archipelago and shows ships with Genoese flags visiting it.

These tentative explorations were to bear fruit later. But the decade of Pedro 'the Justicer' saw the beginnings of a far-reaching political crisis which was soon to spread havoc through the Peninsula. The Black Death had reached the Peninsula in 1348. Among its victims was Alfonso XI of Castile, who died while besieging Gibraltar. He was succeeded by his heir, Pedro, the son of his Portuguese queen. But Pedro had murdered, or countenanced the murder of Leonor de Guzmán, his father's favourite, and he was soon faced with the rebellion of his bastard half-brother, Henry of Trastámara, who was to devote the following decade to a single-minded and finally successful campaign to usurp the throne. This struggle was to involve both Peninsular states in the long conflict between England and France.

As long since as 1336, the French had made an alliance with Castile, but neither it, nor the English attempt to counter it, had borne fruit. On his accession, Pedro of Castile had fallen under the influence of a favourite, Juan Alfonso de Albuquerque, who had married him to a French princess. But he had at once abandoned his queen and come under the sway of a rival faction. When his half-brother Henry of Trastámara made alliance with Aragon, Pedro replied by negotiating a treaty with his namesake of Portugal and opening discussions with England (1358). Thus Portuguese galleys assisted Castile until 1360, when peace was made. It was now clear that Henry would not come to the throne with the help of Aragon alone, and he therefore became a client of France. In 1366 the opportunity offered for him to obtain troops from the king of France, with which he entered Castile and proclaimed himself king. Pedro of

Castile, betrayed by his supporters in Andalusia, now fled to Portugal and appealed for help. The Portuguese Pedro summoned his council at Santarém and discussed what course he should pursue. They decided in favour of prudence and terminated the proposed dynastic alliance with the Castilian Pedro: however, the deposed king passed on to Galicia, which remained constant to him, and so went to Bordeaux, where he successfully invoked his alliance with England. In 1367 he returned to Castile with the aid of the Black Prince. defeated Henry of Trastámara, and forced him to retire to France. As he did so, Pedro the Justicer died in Portugal.

7. FERNANDO I AND THE NATIONAL CRISIS, 1367–83

The decade of Pedro I, with its summary justice and its rollicking festivities, came to an end. The new king Fernando was a youth of twenty-two, handsome, liberal and impetuous. He inherited considerable wealth; Fernão Lopes says that he was the richest king yet to rule in Portugal, and that the tower of Lisbon alone held 800,000 pieces of gold and 400,000 marks of silver. The royal revenues were 200,000 *dobras*, not including the customs of Lisbon and Oporto, and the customs of Lisbon were estimated to bring in 35,000 to 40,000 *dobras* a year. 'The kings in those days had such a way with the people for their service and profit that all perforce were rich and the kings had great revenues', notes Fernão Lopes, 'for they lent money at interest and since everyone paid a tenth of what he earned against his debt, this was gradually discharged and they were still rich, while the king came by his own'. Fernão Lopes was writing from the great inflation of the following reign, and added: 'All this disappeared when the wars began, and a new world was born very contrary to the old, and the easy years of his father's time were gone; and afterwards there came redoubled woes, so that many wept their ill-starred misery. If he had been content to live in peace, well-furnished with his revenues . . . no one in the world would have lived more merry, nor spent his days in such ease: but perhaps it was not so ordered from above.'[1]

[1] The chronicler refers to the great activity of the port of Lisbon, and the numbers of foreign residents, Genoese, Lombards, Catalans, Majorcans, Milanese, Cahorsins, Biscayans and others. Often 450 trading-ships would lie in the Tagus, and 12,000 tuns of wine would go out in a year.

Fernando began his reign by ratifying the existing peace with Castile and Aragon. But Pedro of Castile, though restored to his throne, was unable to pay the Black Prince the rewards he had offered, and the Prince began to intrigue with Aragon for a partition of Castile and finally withdrew his troops. The French immediately renewed their support of Henry of Trastámara, who again entered Castile at the head of a French army. This time, when Pedro advanced from Andalusia to the relief of Toledo, he was taken by surprise, captured and put to death by his half-brother's own hand. Thus the bastard of Trastámara became Henry II of Castile.

The Castilian legitimists now turned to the king of Portugal to defend their cause. Pedro had left only daughters, and the nearest legitimate male claimant to the Castilian throne was the son of his sister, Fernando of Portugal, who was now received in the legitimist province of Galicia with much enthusiasm. Henry at once marched to Galicia and invaded northern Portugal, where he succeeded in occupying Braga. But he could not take Guimarãis, and while he was besieging it, he received news that the king of Granada, the faithful ally of the legitimists, had destroyed Algeciras and was threatening Christian Andalusia. Henry therefore left Portugal, pausing only to occupy Bragança.

Fernando had been unprepared for this energetic campaign, and had left Galicia for Oporto and Coimbra, where he was raising troops. He also made a treaty with the king of Aragon, who agreed to recognize his rights to Castile in return for the cession of Murcia to Aragon: the pact was to be sealed by the marriage of Fernando to an Aragonese princess and by the dispatch of 1,500 Aragonese lances to Portugal, for which Fernando sent 4,000 marks of gold to Barcelona. The treaty was concluded on 29 June 1370, but it was soon undermined. The king of France, who was unable to send more troops to help Henry, enlisted the influence of the pope to calm his adversaries. In March 1371 Fernando suddenly changed his policy and accepted the Treaty of Alcoutim, by which he renounced his claim to Castile and undertook to marry Henry's daughter Leonor.

The change was due partly to the influence of the papacy and partly to the fact that Henry had succeeded in taking Zamora, a legitimist town, on 26 February. Its consequence was that the Aragonese seized Fernando's gold in Barcelona, while in May the legitimist stronghold in Andalusia fell to Henry. With Fernando's relinquishment of his rights, the heiress of the legitimist claim became Pedro's elder daughter Constanza. She had remained in Bordeaux, and in September 1371 John of Gaunt, duke of Lancaster, espoused her and her cause, replacing Fernando as pretender to the throne of Castile. But he could not expect to succeed without an ally in the Peninsula, and a Galician knight, Juan Fernández Andeiro, undertook to negotiate with the king of Portugal on his behalf.

Fernando was now under the influence of the old count of Ourém and Barcelos, D. João Afonso Telo. Although the king had undertaken to marry a daughter of Henry II of Castile according to the terms of the Treaty of Alcoutim, the favourite was reluctant to risk his influence to a Castilian princess. His niece Leonor Teles de Meneses was very willing to become a queen: and when her husband, who was unwilling to arrange a divorce, had fled for his life to Castile, Fernando declared his intention to marry her. The people of Lisbon, led by a tailor, Fernão Vasques, protested; and the king, fearing an uprising, departed for the north. He was then united to Leonor Teles, and the impertinent tailor was executed. The new queen's brother was at once given command of the castle of Lisbon, and her family settled down to enjoy their pre-eminence: Dinis, one of the sons of Inês de Castro, refused to do homage to Leonor and left the court.

When Andeiro arrived in Portugal, he had little difficulty in taking advantage of Fernando's breach with Castile, or in making friends with the new queen. Thus on 10 July 1372, at Braga, he concluded an alliance between Fernando and Lancaster. But Lancaster did not intend to attempt an immediate invasion, and the prospect that he might do so faded when the French obtained the use of Castilian ships and defeated the English fleet near La Rochelle and later blockaded Lisbon. In September the Castilian king invaded Portugal, entered Viseu and marched on Coimbra. Fernando attempted to defend Lisbon and appealed to England for help. Although Lancaster promised troops in January 1373, none had arrived when on 19 March Fernando was obliged to sign a humiliating peace at Santarém. He now became the ally of Henry and France, and the enemy of Edward III and Lancaster, promising to send galleys to join the Castilian fleet in their operations from French ports, to repel the English if they tried to land, to expel the Castilian legitimists who had taken refuge in Portugal, and to marry his half-sister to Henry's brother and give hostages (April 1373).

However, Fernando regarded this imposed peace as no more than an unfortunate accident. Negotiations with England continued, and on 16 June the first Anglo-Portuguese Alliance was sworn in St Paul's. English merchants now frequented Lisbon on an unprecedented scale, for since Lancaster had published his claim to the throne of Castile, trade with the neighbouring country was difficult. On Fernando's side, although the Treaty of Santarém remained in force until 1379, little attention was paid to it, and the period of peace was used to strengthen the defences of Lisbon with a new wall and to pass new laws governing military service. At the same time the building of ships was encouraged: all who built vessels of over 100 tons were allowed to cut timber from the royal forests without payment: no duty was to be charged on the cargoes of the first voyage, and a system of marine insurance was instituted by means of a tax to recompense owners of ships lost by wreck.

Meanwhile, an attempt was made to increase the supply of foodstuffs. The 'leis das sesmerias' of 1375 required that in every village the good men should see that all land was fully utilized, keep inventories of untilled land, and so remedy the 'great lack of wheat and barley and other products with which above other lands this was formerly the best replenished'. The laws attempted to make the ownership of land conditional on tillage, and to constrain all those who had formerly worked on it to return to it. This statute of labourers attributes the lack of cereals to the abandonment of the soil. The decline of serfdom and the increase of trade had evidently drawn many away from agriculture: at the *cortes* of 1377 it was reported that many former labourers and stock-raisers had sold up and become hucksters and merchants and had ceased 'to work and to make things'. These difficulties were accentuated by the Castilian invasions which devastated the frontier areas. The inadequate resistance of fortified towns in the previous campaigns must have been due at least in part to inadequate supplies.

But in 1379 Henry II of Castile died, and his throne passed to his son Juan I, a ruler altogether less formidable than the ruthless bastard of Trastámara. However, Fernando did not at once denounce the onerous Treaty of Santarém. His half-brothers, Dinis and John, the sons of Inês de Castro, both resided in Castile: John had married a sister of Queen Leonor Teles, and had murdered her, and then sought refuge abroad. But Lancaster now reopened negotiations with both Portugal and Aragon, sending Andeiro to propose to Fernando a grand alliance against the new Castilian king.

Two factions existed at Fernando's court. One persuaded the king to renew the understanding with Castile, promising that his heiress Beatriz should marry the newly born son of Juan I (July 1380) and offering assurances to the French. The other opened secret negotiations for a new alliance with England. Andeiro, arriving from England, went in disguise to Estremós, where he arranged that the Alliance of 1373 should be revived: Fernando would declare war on Castile when English aid arrived and would marry his heiress to Edward of Cambridge. After the agreement had been completed (15 July 1380), Andeiro revealed himself and was duly arrested, a manœuvre evidently intended to mislead Castilian spies. The Portuguese council were then informed of what was afoot and expressed their disapproval. But Fernando was ruled by Leonor Teles, who in turn was in the hands of Andeiro: the Portuguese chancellor was sent to England to ratify the pact. There Parliament voted a grant for 'defence', and in June 1381 the earl of Cambridge arrived in Portugal with 3,000 men. A little before they arrived the Queen's brother, João Afonso Telo, had set out to attack the Castilian fleet, but suffered a crushing defeat.

Fernando received Cambridge and obligingly transferred his adherence from Pope Clement VII to Urban VI: his daughter Beatriz, aged ten, was then betrothed to Edward, aged six. But the English troops were of poor quality and had no mounts: it was not until December that they reached the Castilian frontier, unpaid and unruly. In England, Parliament now refused funds for Lancaster, and the London merchants would no longer extend credit. When in July the English and Portuguese troops at last faced the Castilians between Elvas and Badajoz, the campaign had virtually collapsed. On 10 August the Portuguese constable and marshal visited the Castilian camp and negotiated a secret peace: Fernando's heiress would marry the younger son of Juan I and the Castilians would supply ships for the evacuation of the English. Cambridge and his men made demonstrations of anger, but the campaign was clearly incapable of success.

Fernando himself was prematurely decrepit and was governed by Leonor Teles and Andeiro, now count of Ourém. Leonor gave birth to a son in July 1382, but he died within a few days, and the girl Beatriz remained heiress to the throne. In order to secure her succession, and the continuance of his own power, Ourém now proposed that Beatriz should be married not to a prince but to the king of Castile, who had recently become a widower. This arrangement was concluded in March 1383 and ratified on 2 April. It provided that Beatriz should succeed to the throne, and that the king of Castile should be her consort, using the title of King of Portugal. The country would be governed by a council of regency until any children of the match were old enough to succeed. If there were no children, Juan would become king of Portugal and would guarantee that the Portuguese *cortes* should remain separate and that none but Portuguese should be appointed to office in their country. On 14 May Juan received Beatriz as his wife and carried her off to Castile: Fernão Lopes notes that some Castilians observed that 'they would rather castrate their king so that he should remain childless and rule Castile and Portugal together than that he should have a son who would make Portugal independent'. Nevertheless, the guarantees of autonomy were sufficiently convincing to gain the consent of the Portuguese *cortes*. A few weeks later, on 22 October, Fernando died at Lisbon at the age of thirty-eight.

IV

THE HOUSE OF AVIS

1. JOHN OF AVIS, DEFENDER AND KING, 1384–1433

On the death of her husband Leonor Teles assumed the title of 'regedor e governador'. A delegation of the citizens of Lisbon sought an interview with her to protest against the number of foreigners who were associated with her, Ourém and the bishop of Lisbon among them. In fact, Portugal had become a haven for Galician legitimists who had at first supported the Lancastrian claim, but were now disillusioned and prepared to regain favour with the Trastámaras at the cost of Portuguese independence. That they should have come so near success is less surprising when it is recalled that Afonso IV and Pedro I had married Castilian princesses, that Inês de Castro was Galician and her sons now dwelt in Castile, and that influential frontier families such as the Meneses had sought influence in the courts of both countries. This interested internationalism was by no means shared by the Portuguese people, who now looked upon the crown as the symbol of their jurisdictional integrity, that is of their nationhood.

Juan had already sent agents to persuade the Portuguese nobility to accept the union of the two countries, and had ordered the arrest of the two sons of Inês de Castro, lest they should yield to the temptation to present themselves as his rivals. He now added the arms of Portugal to his standard, and sent orders to the Portuguese townships that they were to proclaim Beatriz as queen. His assumption of the royal symbols was taken against the advice of his council. When his heralds appeared in Lisbon, they were mobbed. In December Juan entered Portugal and occupied the city of Guarda near the frontier.

There was consternation in Lisbon, and in particular a wave of hatred against the Galician regime. On 6 December John, Master of Avis, a bastard of Pedro I, broke into the palace and murdered Ourém. There followed tumults in the city, in the course of which the Spanish bishop was flung from the tower of the cathedral.

Leonor fled to the town of Alenquer, by tradition the property of queens of Portugal.

At this time John of Avis had little thought of leading an alternative regime, but the citizens of Lisbon pressed him to accept the office of 'defender of the realm'. He consulted a hermit, Fr João de Barroca, and then undertook the responsibility, appointing a merchant to be *corregedor* of the city and admitting the guilds into the city council. He confiscated the goods of followers of Leonor and Juan, and seems to have thought of offering the throne to his elder half-brother, also John, the son of Inês de Castro, and the husband and murderer of the sister of Leonor Teles.

News of this revolution soon spread to Oporto, Évora and other towns, which expelled the supporters of Castile. Leonor departed from Alenquer to Santarém for fear of being cut off. She urged Juan to advance: he found the gates of Coimbra and Tomar locked against him, but on 12 January 1384 he joined Leonor in Santarém and received the reins of government from her. His intention was to raise an army and crush the centre of resistance in Lisbon. In Castile, the victory of the Trastámaras had favoured the old landed nobility, and many Portuguese members of the same class had already flung in their lot with the invader. Nearly sixty places had declared for Castile, but they were chiefly small towns or castles dominated by rural magnates or governors.

John of Avis and his advisers had already sent a mission to England to seek help. It consisted of a squire and a merchant from Bristol, and it at first achieved little. But now the chancellor Fogaça, who had accompanied Leonor to Santarém, refused to become an official of the king of Castile and joined the resistance. In March he and the Master of Santiago went to England to raise troops. There was little time to lose. Juan had now arrested Leonor Teles and packed her off to Castile. Basque ships and Castilian troops began to arrive in Portugal for the siege of Lisbon. In the Alentejo Nun'Álvares Pereira, one of the innumerable progeny of the Prior of the Hospitallers, had been placed in command of the defenders, despite his youth, and on 6 April he gained a victory at Atoleiros by skilful generalship. But he could not prevent Castilian men-at-arms and archers from reaching Lisbon, which was closely besieged. But fortunately for the Portuguese, the Castilian camp was soon afflicted by pestilence, which claimed two hundred victims a day: they included the famous admiral Sancho de Tovar. Juan decided to withdraw to Seville, preparing a general onslaught for the following year.

The defender and his government were now gaining ground. Permission had been granted for the raising of troops in England, and by February some 800 men had been gathered at Plymouth. Since December Nun'Álvares had taken the offensive and cleared much of the Alentejo, while the castles near Lisbon were all in Portuguese hands. In March 1385 it was decided to summon *cortes* at Coimbra for the end of the same month with a view to the election of John of Avis as king. His chief advocate was Dr João das Regras, who three years before had returned to Portugal after completing his studies at Bologna. There was much hesitation. It was possible to argue that Beatriz had been disinherited by her marriage to a foreigner, the enemy of her country. But there was no other legitimate claimant, and if the crown was to go to a bastard, the sons of Inês de Castro were senior to John of Avis. Furthermore, it was commonly believed that Pedro had secretly married Inês. It fell to João das Regras to prove his client's case. He did so by producing documents which were said to contain the refusal of Innocent IV to recognize the marriage or legitimize the two bastards. This was enough to clinch the case: if the sons of Inês de Castro had no legal claim, the practical advantage lay with John of Avis. They had served Castile and were absent: he was already defender of the realm. On 6 April the opposition ended, and the defender was proclaimed king as John I: he was twenty-six.

Fortified with his title, he sent to inform Richard II and to ask for an alliance, sending six galleys to England as English troops began to reach Portugal. He and Nun'Álvares, whose military abilities qualified him as commander of the Portuguese, marched north and obtained the submission of Braga, Guimarãis and other places. Meanwhile, the king of Castile had appealed to Aragon and France and gathered his army at Ciudad Real, sending a force forward against Viseu. It was brought to battle at Trancoso, where the Portuguese dismounted and adopted a defensive formation: the Castilian troops exhausted themselves in attack and were then routed. But Juan was still intent on marching against Lisbon. He therefore led his army, which contained contingents from the leading families

of Castile and Leon, round Coimbra and continued to march southwards. At Soure he received Nun'Álvares' challenge to pitched
battle. John of Avis was at Abrantes on the Tagus, and his council
was opposed to giving battle against heavy odds. But Nun'Alvares
insisted on engaging the invaders before they could reach Santarém.
On 11 August it was known that Juan was marching direct to Lisbon.
Two days later he was south of Leiria, and the Portuguese were
at Porto de Mós, from which Nun'Álvares occupied a steep ridge
barring the Lisbon road. This position was too strong to be attacked,
and the Castilians marched round it so as to take advantage of a
gentler slope by approaching it from the south. Nun'Alvares advanced a little and threw up rough earthworks at São Jorge. It was
nearly six in the evening when the Castilians came within range
after spending most of the day on the road. Their younger leaders
insisted on attacking, overriding the advice of the more experienced.
They sent their horse against the Portuguese defenders, and the first
impetus was successful. But the Portuguese wings were brought into
play, and the centre stopped the advance with sword and axe. The
attack faltered, then suddenly the Castilian royal standard fell and
the battle was lost. The Portuguese took the offensive, and Juan fled,
followed by all his men. The battle of Aljubarrota, fought on 14
August 1385, secured the independence of Portugal for almost two
centuries, made the Master of Avis a most desirable ally and opened
the way for John of Gaunt to renew his claim to the throne of Castile.
It also saw the fall of the old landed magnates of Portugal (many of
whom had gone over to the Castilians) and assured the rise of the
merchant classes of Lisbon and Oporto, who had thrown in their lot
with John of Avis.

The king lost no time in proposing that Lancaster should join him
in invading Castile. If the Lancastrian claim was ever to be asserted,
no more favourable opportunity could arise. On 17 May 1386 a new
Anglo-Portuguese treaty was concluded in the Star Chamber at
Westminster: it contained political, military and economic clauses,
and above all, it laid down that 'there shall be between the two
above-mentioned kings now reigning, their heirs and successors and
between the subjects of both kingdoms, an inviolable, eternal, solid,
perpetual and true league of friendship, alliance and union, not only
between each other, their heirs and successors, but also between and

in favour of their kingdoms, lands, dominions and subjects, vassals, allies and friends, wherever they may be, so that each of them shall have the obligation to assist and give aid to the other against all people now born or who shall come to be born and who shall seek to violate the peace of others or in any way make bold to offend their states ...'

Lancaster now obtained a grant from Parliament and prepared to invade Castile from Portugal, while John of Avis sent a squadron of galleys for the defence of England. In the autumn Lancaster, with some 5,000 men, landed near Corunna. Juan of Castile had doubted whether the attack would be delivered in Galicia or in Andalusia, the two legitimist regions, and had sent reinforcements in both directions, but had concentrated on the defence of Castile. Meanwhile, John of Avis marched north and met Lancaster on a hill near Ponte do Mouro. In discussions in his tent, he agreed to put 5,000 men into the field at his own expense. Lancaster would cede a strip of territory, roughly corresponding to Extremadura, if he became king of Castile. The question of a dynastic alliance had already been raised: it was now arranged that the Portuguese king should marry Lancaster's daughter by his first wife—he wisely rejected a marriage with Catharine, Lancaster's daughter by Constanza, the legitimist heiress to Castile. Philippa of Lancaster, now aged twenty-six, arrived in Oporto in December, and the marriage was celebrated there at the beginning of February 1387.

In the same month the campaign began. English and Portuguese forces met near Bragança, some 11,000 men, with many noncombatants, but no artillery or siege equipment. If they had hoped for a surge of legitimist sentiment in Leon, they were disappointed. The major castles were adequately held, and little was gained from an excursion behind the main line of defence. Lancaster had insisted on receiving the supreme command, although his forces were in the minority. He did not prove an effective general, and Nun'Álvares was little impressed by Lancaster or by the quality of the English troops. It fell to the hero of Aljubarrota to lead the army back by way of Salamanca and Almeida. Lancaster seems to have done little to prevent the collapse of claims he had doggedly sustained for fifteen years and opened negotiations with his rival. They were concluded at Trancoso, where the pretender agreed to marry his daughter Catharine to Juan's heir, the future Henry III of Castile, receiving a large indemnity in money in return for the surrender of his claims. He seems to have taken no steps to safeguard the interests of John of Avis, despite the terms of the Alliance. He had now no funds, and his Portuguese son-in-law had to supply fourteen galleys in which he sailed from Oporto to Bayonne (September 1387).

This left John of Avis still at war with Castile, and excluded from the negotiations which were resumed at Bayonne. His half-brothers, the sons of Inês de Castro, João and Dinis, had remained in Castile, and João had been responsible for the defence of Salamanca. But Dinis now returned to Portugal, was pardoned and in 1388 was sent to England to obtain ratification of the Alliance and seek the neutralization of the frontier. On arriving at Dartmouth, he was arrested, and when released, captured by Flemish pirates, returning eventually to Castile. Nevertheless, the Alliance was ratified, and Portuguese ships continued to serve in the Channel for the defence of England until the Anglo-French truce of Leulingham in June 1389.

John I had now concluded a short truce with Castile (February 1389). On its expiry, he captured Tuy, and thus forced the king of Castile to accept an exchange of conquests. He then subscribed to the Anglo-French truce (1389–92), having sent an account of his motives to Richard II. In Castile, Juan had performed public penances after his defeat at Aljubarrota, but recovered his mettle since the Lancastrian fiasco. In February 1390 he informed his *cortes* that he had given Lancaster no guarantees about John of Avis and intended still to call himself king of Portugal. But on 9 October he died in an accident, and his son Henry III, a minor, was unable to resume the struggle. In 1393 the truce was renewed for fifteen years, during which the Castilians undertook not to support either Beatriz or the sons of Inês de Castro; judges were appointed to settle frontier-incidents, and trade was resumed.

It was, however, an armed peace. Arbitrators had assessed damages to be paid by Castile at 48,000 *dobras* of gold, but no payment was made. The Portuguese threatened reprisals, and in May 1396 seized Badajoz. Henry III again promised to pay, but his frontiersmen wanted war, and in particular the commanders of his navy, who had not participated in the defeat of Aljubarrota. There followed frontier raids in the Alentejo and naval raids which developed into a regular war of privateers. In 1397 the Castilians urged France to declare war on Portugal and John of Avis applied to England for archers. But France and England were now both seeking to solve the schism of the western church and had no interest in resuming the Peninsular war. In 1398 the legitimists were again active in Castile, and John I besieged Tuy while Henry III recognized Dinis as king of Portugal. But in 1402 negotiations were reopened and resulted in a long truce extending from 1403 to 1413; the Portuguese returned Badajoz and Tuy and the Castilians Bragança and Miranda, while a new commission of arbitration was set up and trade was again restored.

Under cover of the truce negotiations were begun for a permanent peace. Henry III, an invalid, died in 1406, leaving an infant heir, Juan II. The regency was held by his widow Catharine of Lancaster, assisted by his brother Fernando. She at last renounced the demands made by Castile for an indemnity in return for waiving the Trastámaran claims to Portugal, and as Fernando was chiefly anxious to be elected to the vacant throne of Aragon, it was finally possible to reach a settlement in 1411, though even now the royal repudiation of the Trastámaran claim had to await the majority of Juan II in 1419. It was deferred because of troubles in Castile, and although further negotiations took place in 1421–3, the final recognition of the house of Avis was delayed until October 1431. It was ratified by John I in the following year: he himself died on 14 August 1433, the forty-eighty anniversary of the victory of Aljubarrota, having outlived the other heroes of the crisis, João das Regras, who died in 1404 and Nun'Álvares, who founded the Carmelite monastery in Lisbon, abandoned the office of Constable to enter the order and died as Brother Nuno in 1431.

2. CEUTA, 1415

By his marriage to Philippa of Lancaster, John of Avis became the father of a generation of princes who were to be no less famous than the makers of the new dispensation. Philippa brought to the court the Anglo-Norman tradition of an aristocratic education: she herself may have studied the use of the astrolabe with Chaucer. She learned Portuguese, and it is likely that Robert Payn, canon of Lisbon, who translated Gower's *Confessio Amantis* into Portuguese, was associated with her chapel or with the education of her children. Her personal qualities were of the highest order, and her influence was not diminished when her brother usurped the English throne as Henry IV. Her eldest son, Duarte, born in 1391, was the author of a moral work, the *Loyal Counsellor*, and the patron of legal compilations. Her second son, Pedro, travelled 'the seven parts of the earth', and combined an interest in history and geography with the practice of government, as regent after Duarte's death. His fame was eclipsed by that of her third son Henry, born at Oporto in 1394, Master of the Order of Christ, and patron of the voyages of discovery. The fourth son, John, born in 1400, played a less conspicuous part in affairs, and the fifth, Fernando, born in 1402, participated in the ill-fated attack on Tangier in 1437 and died a captive in Morocco. Their sister, Isabel, born in 1397, married Philip the Good, duke of Burgundy, at Bruges in 1429, and played a prominent part in the growth of relations between Portugal and the Low Countries. John I's bastard daughter Beatriz was married to Thomas FitzAlan, earl of Arundel, in 1405. A second bastard, Afonso, married the daughter of Nun'Álvares Pereira and was created count of Barcelos: he and his house came to exercise enormous power at the middle of the century.

It is usually supposed that the victory of Aljubarrota brought the fall of the old landed nobility and gave power to the mercantile middle class whose interest in commerce served as the propelling force of the great movement of exploration and expansion. But the opposition between the crown and the old nobility resided essentially in the question of jurisdictions, and this had been settled in favour of the crown a generation before Aljubarrota, by Pedro I. Nor is it clear that the movement of expansion was the work of a mercantile middle-class. The crown had patronized shipbuilding in the time of Dinis, and owned merchant vessels in the first half of the fourteenth century: its Genoese admiral engaged in trade, and there is no reason why other nobles should not have done so as well. In the time of Fernando, the crown was engaged in money-lending, possibly through the activities of its Jewish tax-farmers: its interest in the custom-house of Lisbon ensured that it would take a favourable interest in the development of trade. It certainly had the strong support of the merchants and the guilds in the struggle for independence, but there is no evidence that those who now held power were overwhelmingly merchants or members of the middle class. The crown had found resources for the Genoese who visited the Canaries in 1345, and it was still the crown that initiated the great movement of expansion.

The long crisis had seen a drastic reduction of the resources of the royal treasury. The wealth accumulated by Pedro I had been spent by Fernando, who had been forced to debase the coin drastically. John of Avis had also paid his debts by constantly depreciating the value of coin: a mark of silver which formerly made 18 *libras*, made 195 in Fernando's time, and 29,000 in John's. Pensions and similar payments lost their value, and during the long struggle with Castile the knights of the frontier maintained themselves by frontier-raids. As in the Castilian war against Granada, there was a vested interest in maintaining the struggle: the problem faced by the crown was not how to pay for its wars, but how to support its dependants in time of peace. During the negotiations with Castile John had proposed a joint crusade against Granada, but this was refused. One impediment was the fact that the two countries obeyed rival popes: another that the regent of Castile, Fernando, though his fame rested on the conquest of Antequera from Granada in 1410, was now only interested in becoming King of Aragon, and therefore made peace with Granada and Morocco.

But in 1411-12 a civil war swept the Magrib, and Fez suffered three sieges in a year. The sultan unsuccessfully sought naval aid from Aragon. He did gradually recover control of his territories, and the rebel leader who had held Ceuta withdrew to Granada, taking with him the fleet of the ancient port, which was thus exposed to attack. Neither Castile nor Aragon could intervene because of their truce with the sultan. The Portuguese however had good reason for doing so, for the Council of Constance, summoned for November 1414, was expected to bring about the end of the schism. By launching a crusade the Portuguese could expect to stand well with the new pope and so clinch the peace with Castile. The suggestion for the campaign of Ceuta came from João Afonso de Azambuja, archbishop of Lisbon and cardinal, John's representative in the negotiations with Castile and at Constance.

The Portuguese campaign was prepared in 1414. Ships were built and freighted abroad. A letter of Henry V of England of 26 September authorizes João Vaz de Almada to raise 400 lances, and another of 26 January 1415 licenses 350 lances and some men-at-arms. The contingents of northern Portugal and Beira were gathered at Oporto by Prince Henry, and those of the south at Lisbon by Pedro. As the expedition was about to leave, Queen Philippa sickened of plague: she gave swords and good counsel to her sons and died on 19 July 1415. Six days later the fleet left the Tagus. It rounded Cape St Vincent and put in at Tarifa. Muslim sources describe a first attack: the mountain *qabilas* came down to defend Ceuta and the attackers withdrew, but when the tribal contingents dispersed, the onslaught was renewed. The Christian chroniclers describe only a single attack, and the fall of Ceuta before a general assault in a single day. John bestowed on Pedro and Henry the titles of Duke of Coimbra and Viseu, the first duchies to be created in Portugal.

The sudden conquest of Ceuta spread alarm throughout the Muslim west. In Granada, the military party brought to power a new ruler, Muḥammad IX, the Left-Handed King, who strove to unify the forces of Morocco and to obtain help from Tunis, but his siege of Ceuta was a failure. However, the neighbouring tribes continued to attack Ceuta, and it was impossible to subdue them or to open trade. The place had to be supplied by sea. Consequently the Portuguese governor built ships, and these began to lay in wait for Muslim shipping frequenting the ports of Gibraltar and Málaga.

Meanwhile, the settlement of the Atlantic islands had been begun. The Canaries and Madeira were known, and in the later fourteenth century the Azores appear on maps. In 1402 a party of Normans attempted the conquest of Lanzarote in the Canaries. Their sailings were soon interrupted by the renewal of war between France and England, and their rights were ceded or returned to the crown of Castile. In 1418 they were transferred to the house of Niebla, the leading family of western Andalusia. In the same year there occurred the first recorded voyage of exploration on behalf of Prince Henry, when João Gonçalves Zarco and Tristão Vaz Teixeira visited Porto Santo and in the following year Madeira. According to Azurara, Henry's chronicler, the colonization of these islands was begun in 1420 by Bartolomeu Perestrelo and others.[1]

In the following years, the prince began to give thought to the

[1] Prince Henry's will gives the date as 1425, which appears too late. Diogo Gomes dates the discoveries from 1415, but there is no other evidence for this. Perestrelo's father was a member of the Pallastrelli family of Piacenza and had settled in Portugal in 1385. Bartolomeu became captain of Porto Santo and his daughter married Christopher Columbus.

exploration of the west African coast. The traditional limit of navigation was Cape Non, where strong adverse currents added to the hazards of the Atlantic coast of Morocco, heavy mists, sudden storms, sand-banks and long reefs. It was now that the prince engaged the services of a Majorcan cartographer, Jaffuda Cresques, the son of Abraham, the author of the atlas of *c.* 1375. However, no appreciable success was achieved in mapping the African coast for ten years.

Meanwhile, in 1424 the prince had sent a force of 2,500 men and 120 horse to occupy the Canaries, but the intention of annexing the whole archipelago appears to have been dropped as a result of protests from Castile. In 1427 or 1431 Portuguese ships were visiting the Azores, which, like the Madeiras, were uninhabited and unclaimed: they were colonized from 1445. Thus while the first voyages under the patronage of Prince Henry, were undoubtedly sanctioned by John I, the grant of the Madeira archipelago and the consequent exploration of the west coast of Africa date only from the reign of King Duarte.

3. DUARTE, 1433–8

The eldest son of John I and Philippa of Lancaster acceded at the age of forty-two. The death of his father so distressed him that his brother Pedro had difficulty in persuading him to assume his duties. He was indeed sensitive to the point of morbidity, and his own premature death was hastened by self-reproach for the fate of his youngest brother in captivity in Morocco. He was well read in the fathers of the church and in the classics, and his *Loyal Counsellor* reveals both his introspectiveness and his strong moral sense. At the *cortes* of Santarém, he obtained popular consent to the compilation of Portuguese royal law, but the work was completed only in the following reign and is therefore named the Ordenações Afonsinas after his son. His father had generously rewarded adherents of the house of Avis with grants of land, and it was now necessary to declare that these awards were not absolute, but subject to confirmation at the start of each reign. This ruling was known as the 'Lei Mental,' on the ground that it had been in the mind of John I, though he had failed to promulgate it. Entailed estates, the *morgados*, continued to be governed by Duarte's principles until 1832.

Duarte had married Leonor, a daughter of Fernando I of Aragon, in 1428. In Castile, the son of Catharine of Lancaster, Juan II, displayed little energy or ability and surrendered power to his resolute constable, Don Alvaro de Luna, without whom he was incapable of governing. But when Fernando had been elected to the throne of Aragon, he had bestowed various properties in Castile on his sons, who for many years kept up a running struggle with Don Alvaro ostensibly to retain their estates, but in fact for political power over their cousin, the otiose Juan II. The marriage of their sister to Duarte had been an attempt to draw Portugal into the Aragonese camp, but Don Alvaro had countered it by offering peace in 1431, thus concluding the ancient quarrel between the two countries. However, the Portuguese princes felt some sympathy for the Aragonese infantes, threatened with dispossession in Castile, and obtained a temporary reconciliation with Don Alvaro in 1432. This lull enabled the Constable to embark on a campaign against Granada on an impressive scale: for a moment Juan II was able to pose as a successful crusader.

At this time the Portuguese were engaged in three enterprises, all interrelated but not necessarily integrated in a wider scheme—the conquest of Morocco, begun with the campaign of Ceuta, the occupation of the Atlantic islands, and the exploration of the west African coast. Of these the first was the most esteemed, but not in itself the most rewarding: the material consequences of the conquest of Ceuta had proved disappointing. The occupation of the Canaries, however, offered other possibilities. The existence of Berbers who were not Muslims and were therefore capable of conversion to Christianity emphasized the fact that Islam had limits to the south and suggested that it might be taken from the rear. Such a prospect had long been cherished. In the twelfth century the imagination of the western world had been disturbed by the idea of Prester John, the Christian monarch of an enormous but shadowy realm in Asia: he was later confused with the Christian ruler of Abyssinia, and his legend was magnified. By the second half of the fourteenth century it was no longer necessary to credit these fantasies. Among Muslim travellers ibn Baṭṭuṭa of Tangier had visited Persia and east Africa and related his adventures in a series of lectures at Granada (1355), and the statesmen and historians ibn al-Khaṭib and ibn Khaldūn knew of the southern and eastern limits of the Muslim world. In the Peninsula the Spanish Franciscan who composed a *Knowledge of the World* in c. 1350 was familiar with the names of the African kingdoms beyond the Sahara. When this mosaic of cosmogony was brought into focus in the west remains obscure. But in 1434 Portuguese seamen under Gil Eanes succeeded in passing Cape Bojador, revealing another stretch of barren and inhospitable shore: in 1435 he reached Angra dos Ruivos, and in 1436 his companion Afonso Gonçalves Baldaia found what he thought was the mouth of the River of Gold, the Senegal, and named it Rio de Ouro, though he was in fact only half way there.

At the same time Prince Henry asked the Castilians to recognize his right to occupy such of the Canaries as were still unsubdued. They refused, and the prince resorted to the pope, who gave his consent. But the Castilians then sent a strong mission to present their case at Bologna, and on 31 July 1436 the pope delivered the bull *Dudum siquidem* in which he exhorted Duarte to respect the rights of the Castilians, though without expressly defining these. The Castilians had acquired merit by their campaign against Granada in 1432, but they now made peace with the Muslims. The Portuguese therefore grasped the opportunity to resume the struggle in the Magrib. According to the chronicler, the idea of an expedition against Tangier arose from the desire of Fernando, the youngest brother of the king, to achieve glory: it is clear, however, that Prince Henry convinced the queen and finally obtained the consent of the king. At a council at Leiria, Pedro and John opposed the plan, and Duarte wrote to Rome for advice. He finally abided by his decision, and preparations were completed by August 1437. But Tangier was defended by Salah ibn Salah, who had formerly governed Ceuta, and he had the support of Granada, now at peace with Castile, and of the *qabilas*. When the Portuguese landed, they were cut off from their ships, and a large part of the army was captured, including Fernando.

The price demanded by the Muslims for the release of their captives was the return of Ceuta. Prince Henry at first accepted, and Duarte was disposed to agree. But Pedro, John and others were opposed to the cession, and the archbishop of Braga held that Ceuta could not be surrendered without the pope's consent. The majority of the council was against cession. Prince Henry, returning to Portugal, proposed a new expedition in the hope of rescuing his brother, but the prospect of this was small, for Fernando had been removed to Fez. Meanwhile, an outbreak of plague caused the court to leave

Évora. Duarte and his family moved to Tomar, where on 9 September 1438 the king died of the infection and of grief that he had found no remedy for the disaster of Tangier. Fernando died, still unransomed, in Fez in June 1443: his chaplain wrote a pathetic account of his suffering and he was popularly canonized as the 'Infante Santo'.

4. AFONSO V, 1438–81; THE REGENCY OF DOM PEDRO

Duarte was buried at Alcobaça in October, and *cortes* assembled at Torres Novas to confirm his testament. His heir was six years old, and Duarte had appointed Queen Leonor regent and tutor of her children, and charged her to ransom Fernando. There was some opposition to the assumption of all authority by a woman and a foreigner, and Leonor agreed that Pedro should be associated with the government. He was opposed by his half-brother, Afonso, count of Barcelos, the eldest bastard of John I. Both aspired to gain influence over the young king, Pedro by marrying him to his daughter Isabel, and Barcelos by a similar union: Barcelos' son had married the daughter of Nun'Álvares Pereira and claimed to have acquired the office of Constable by this match; his daughter had married Prince John, and he hoped to unite their daughter to the young king. He and his friends now insisted on the execution of Duarte's will, and it fell to Prince Henry to put forward a compromise by which Queen Leonor would be tutor of her children and control the treasury, while Pedro would take the title of Defender of the Realm and administer justice. The Barcelos party resisted this division, and Prince Henry put forward a new analysis of the royal responsibilities: (i) the tutelage of the royal family, (ii) the treasury, (iii) the royal council, (iv) justice, (v) defence, and (vi) the question of Fernando and Ceuta. Henry proposed that the queen should remain tutor and have the appointment of officials, that Pedro should take charge of defence, and that the son of Barcelos, the count of Arraiolos, should execute justice. A council of nine, six appointed and one from each estate of *cortes*, would transact all business, and its decisions would be ratified by the queen and Pedro. Although the queen was disposed to accept it, Barcelos rejected the agreement and persuaded her to withdraw. The struggle between him and Pedro was thus joined. The populace of Lisbon was strongly in favour of Dom Pedro, and acknowledged him as regent, with his brothers Henry and John as his successors. The queen had the support of the archbishop, a relative of Barcelos, and of part of the nobility. She now retired to Alenquer and, with the Barcelos party, declined to attend *cortes*, which accordingly appointed Pedro sole regent.

During these events, the Trastámaras of Aragon resumed their struggle for power in Castile, and succeeded briefly in forcing the king to dismiss Don Alvaro de Luna. Having achieved this, they attempted to restore the regency to their sister in Portugal, aligning themselves with Barcelos against Dom Pedro. In 1440 a Castilian mission arrived in Portugal ostensibly to seek satisfaction for alleged attacks by the Portuguese on Castilian shipping, but in fact to demand the restoration of Queen Leonor. The mission produced a violent letter in which Juan II demanded also that she should visit Castile and that Castilian representatives should visit the cities and towns of Portugal to explain her rights in public. All this recalled the use the first of the Trastámaras had made of Leonor Teles, and Pedro asked the mission to leave the country and that Leonor should return to the court. Instead she departed clandestinely for Crato, where she met adherents from Castile. Pedro then ordered the frontiers to be manned and cut off supplies from Crato, and Leonor crossed into Castile (29 December 1440). Barcelos now submitted, embraced Dom Pedro and was pardoned.

But in Castile the struggle between Don Alvaro and the Infantes of Aragon continued, and in January 1442 the Aragonese party was able to convoke *cortes* and obtain a subsidy for a war against Portugal on the pretext of recovering the regency for Dona Leonor. Dom Pedro retorted by summoning the Portuguese *cortes* at Evora and obtaining confirmation of his own regency. But in the following year the Aragonese princes were less formidable: the Constable of Castile regained ground and finally defeated his rivals in the battle of Olmedo (19 May 1444). The Portuguese regent gave his support, sending his son, also Pedro, whom he had made Constable of Portugal, with a band of troops. One of the Aragonese princes, Henry, had died at Olmedo, and it seemed that their faction was in dissolution. Queen Leonor applied to return to Portugal, but died at Toledo in the following year.

Dom Pedro appeared to have triumphed; he paved the way for the continuance of his power by arranging the marriage of Afonso to his daughter Isabel; when the young king reached his majority in January 1446, he consented to the match and requested his uncle to retain power for the time being. The Barcelos faction had not put aside its ambitions. The old count had been granted the title of Duke of Bragança, and his son the county of Ourém as well as that of Arraiolos. In 1442 Prince John, the fourth son of John I and Philippa, had died, and the Mastership of Santiago passed to Ourém, his wife's brother. But the office of Constable, which Barcelos claimed to be hereditary, had gone to the regent's son. The bastard branch was still not satisfied, and it was shortly to achieve its ambitions. In Castile Juan II, now a widower, married in 1447 the daughter of Prince John: she was to become the mother of Isabella the Catholic. In Portugal Afonso V married the regent's daughter, but having done so, was persuaded by the Barcelos faction to declare the termination of the regency. The old duke of Bragança pressed home his advantage, and secured the dismissal of Dom Pedro, who soon retired to Coimbra: his friends were removed from office, and accusations were put about that he had poisoned Duarte, Leonor and John, and had plotted to remove Afonso and his brother and to seize the throne. The young king was induced to forbid all his nobles to visit his uncle, who was confined to his estates. His son Pedro was deprived of the office of Constable, and his intimate friend Álvaro Vaz de Almada was dismissed from the governorship of the castle of Lisbon. In October 1448 Afonso V arrived in Lisbon and summoned the duke of Bragança to his side. Rumours soon reached Pedro of a plot against him. It was demanded that he should hand over his arms; on the advice of Álvaro Vaz, he decided to resist. He also appealed to Prince Henry to intervene, but the prince's negotiations produced no result. The court, from which the remaining friends of Pedro had been expelled, remained at Santarém, while the duke of Bragança marched down from his estates in the north. Pedro arrested a royal messenger in the hope of discovering his enemy's intentions: he was then warned that he was deprived of his estates. On Good Friday 1449 his forces and the duke's were close together, and a battle seemed inevitable. But the duke suddenly crossed the mountains to Covilhã and so reached the court. The object of this manœuvre was to ensure the consent of Afonso V for the final struggle. Dom Pedro also moved south, and decided to go to Lisbon, where he could count on the support of the populace. He found his way barred at Alfar-robeira by troops of the king and duke. The fight was brief: Dom Pedro was shot through the heart with an arrow, and Álvaro Vaz fell by his side (24 May 1449).

The bastard line now enjoyed unlimited power, increasing its possessions enormously and making the fortunes of its followers. It continued to overshadow the royal house for thirty-five years. Its victory gave new courage to the enemies of Don Alvaro de Luna in Castile. The understanding maintained by Dom Pedro with the Castilian Constable was terminated, and in April 1453 Juan II was persuaded to arrest his favourite: he was executed two months later. Dom Pedro's son, now deprived of the office of Constable of Portugal, remained in exile in Castile until 1461, continuing the literary traditions of his family. In 1464, when the people of Catalonia rebelled against the surviving infante of Aragon, they offered to make him king: he accepted and campaigned for a year there, but was defeated and died in 1466.

5. PRINCE HENRY AND HIS EXPLORATIONS

After the disaster of Tangier, there was a halt in the process of exploration for some four years. When the voyages were resumed in 1440, the Portuguese seamen were using a new type of ship. The old *varinel* had combined sails and oars, and was therefore low and heavily manned: it was, in fact, suitable only for coasting. The *barca* was a heavy cargo-ship, slow and difficult to handle. There now appeared the *caravela*, which was light, long and high. Relying entirely on sails, it could be worked by a small crew and was not weighted down by supplies: its speed enabled it to cover great distances, and it was sufficiently manœuvrable to stand little danger from the shoal-bound and foggy Atlantic shores, and stout enough for ocean sailing.[1]

In 1441 Nuno Tristão and Antão Gonçalves were sent by Prince Henry to explore beyond the Pedra da Galé, the limit of the previous voyages. The first of these was a 'young knight, stouthearted and enterprising, brought up since a lad in the Prince's chamber': he

---

[1] The word is apparently a diminutive of the *carabo*, a transport ship used in the Mediterranean.

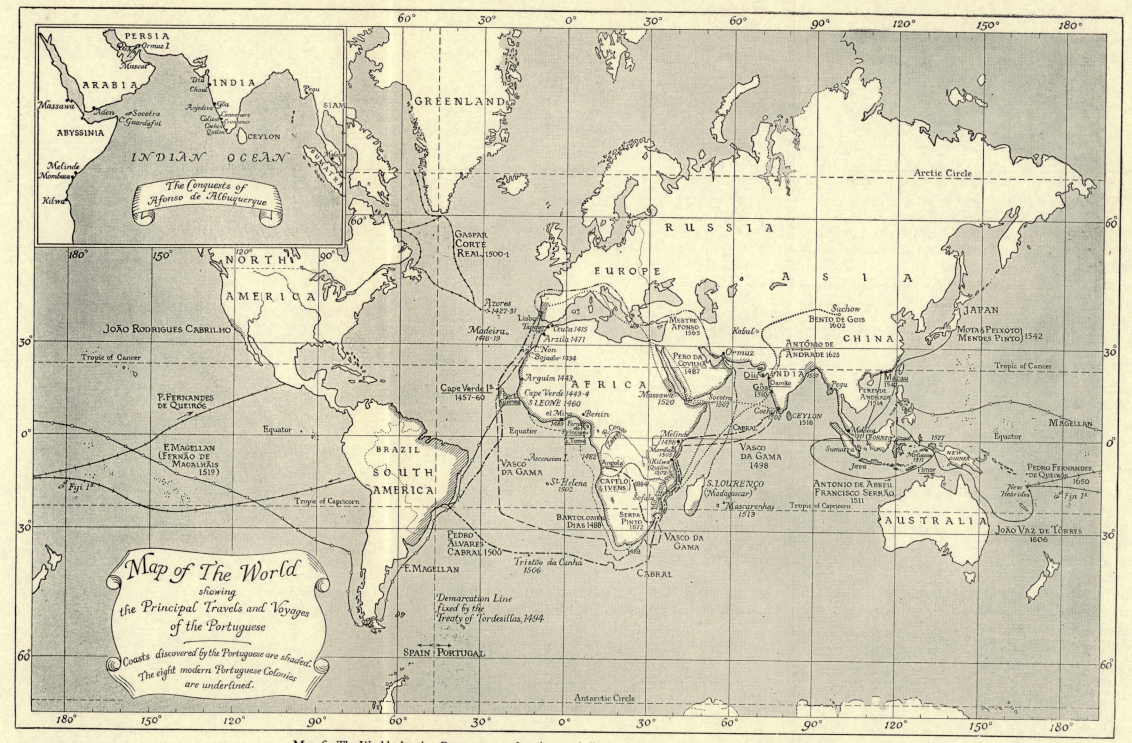

Map 6. The World, showing Portuguese explorations and discoveries, and the Portuguese territories at 1960.

reached Cape Branco. The second, Henry's 'master of the wardrobe (*guardaroupa*), a rather young man', was to load sealskins and oil at the 'River of Gold': he brought back the first captives, Azenegues, who were familiar with the caravan-routes of the west coast. In 1442 Gonçalves returned and exchanged some Muslim captives for negroes and gold dust. The importance of these undertakings was clearly realized by 1443, when Prince Henry, then residing at the village of Rapouseira, between Lagos and Sagres, received from his brother Pedro the regent a monopoly of trade with lands he might discover, together with the right to build a town 'on the other cape that is before the cape of Sagres to those going from west to east'. This was Cape St Vincent, which in ancient times had been the site of a monastery and a beacon for navigation: it does not seem, however, that this authorization was used. The chief port for the adventurers was Lagos, and the organization of the expeditions was under the control of the prince's treasurer, Lançarote. In 1443 Nuno Tristão sailed as far as the isle of Arguim, and in 1444 to Senegambia, while Dinis Dias passed Cape Verde. During the following two years, Álvaro Fernandes, a nephew of Gonçalves Zarco, sailed 100 leagues beyond Cape Verde, receiving rewards from both Pedro and Henry.

These explorations enhanced the value of the Canaries, and in 1448 Prince Henry unsuccessfully attempted to buy the rights of Bethancourt over Lanzarote. In July 1449 the duke of Medina Sidonia obtained from the Castilian crown a concession to explore or trade on the African mainland as far as Cape Bojador. Meanwhile in 1448 or 1449 the Portuguese had established trading-posts on the coast, and Henry gave orders for a fort to be established on the island of Arguim. According to Cadamosto, who saw it a few years later, it had been let out to a private contractor on a lease for ten years, and many caravels visited it every year, taking away gold, some 700 or 800 slaves, silk and cotton, which were exchanged for corn, cloth and horses. In 1448 Azurara's account of the discovery of Guinea comes to an end, and there is only piecemeal evidence of the last twelve years of Prince Henry's work.

The colonization of Porto Santo and Madeira had begun in about 1425: 'I began to people my island of Madeira now some thirty-five years ago', according to Prince Henry's will. João Gonçalves Zarco, 'a *cavaleiro*, familiar and servant of the Prince' asked to be appointed captain of Madeira, 'saying that he would go with his wife and family to settle it'. Thirty years later Cadamosto found four settlements with about 800 persons, who exported wood, wax, honey and sugar. Of these products the most valuable was sugar, which had been grown in southern Portugal at least as early as the beginning of the century and was introduced into Madeira by 1433. In Cadamosto's day the production was already 400 *cântaros* (or about 2,000 tons), and by the end of the century it was 100,000 *arrobas*.

The discovery and occupation of the Azores is more obscure. Martin Behaim, who married a daughter of the donatory of two of the islands, mentions a voyage of discovery in 1431 and the landing of domestic animals in 1432. A royal letter of 1439 authorizes Prince Henry to settle 'the seven islands of the Azores' where he 'had had sheep put down'. Azurara says nothing of the discovery, but notes that Frei Gonçalo Velho settled two islands for the Prince in 1445. An island tradition places the discovery of Santa Maria in 1432, and the settlement of São Miguel in 1444. The map of Gabriel de Valsequa (1439) depicts the islands, and bears the legend that they were discovered for the king of Portugal in 1427 by Diogo de Silves (? or Sines?). All these references apply only to the seven easternmost islands: the two westernmost islands appear to be first recorded between 1448 and 1453.

These events, which fall within the period covered by Azurara, receive scant or no notice from him, and we must conclude that they were considered unimportant in relation to the theme of the 'conquest of Guinea'. Prince Henry hoped to reach 'the Indies', and his immediate objects were to obtain a foothold in the Canaries and to achieve papal confirmation of his monopoly of commerce on the African coast. As regards the Canaries, the Castilians had refused to give way, and the papacy offered no encouragement. But in January 1454 Pope Nicholas V granted the Portuguese the monopoly of navigation to Guinea, and a reference of 1458 states that Prince Henry had sent his caravels to 'all the land of Barbary, Nubia and so into the land of Guinea full 300 leagues'. By this time several of the Cape Verde Islands were known: like the Madeiras and Azores, but unlike the Canaries, they were uninhabited. But this did not prevent their serving as a feasible alternative to the Canaries, and in September 1460, just before his death, Prince Henry granted the spiritual dominion of the islands to the Order of Christ and the temporal to the crown.

The last of the voyages described by Azurara was commanded by a Scandinavian nobleman, Valarte or Abelhart, who had come to Portugal to participate in the discoveries. In 1453 one Cid de Sousa sailed to Guinea, but the results of the expedition are unknown. Two years later, the Italians Alvise de Cadamosto and Antoniotto Usodimare sailed, and in 1456 they reached the Bijagós islands and the rivers of Portuguese Guinea, which are described in Cadamosto's account. These rivers are also mentioned by Diogo Gomes, who must have sailed in the same year. At about the time of Prince Henry's death, one of his followers, Pedro de Sintra, reached Sierra Leone, which constitutes the limit of his explorations.

6. AFONSO V 'THE AFRICAN' AND THE CASTILIAN SUCCESSION

The king was now a man of twenty-eight. His queen, Isabel, had been able to do little to protect her father's followers: it fell to the heir, the future John II, born in 1455, to curb the power of the Braganças. This now reached its height: the title of marquis was introduced into Portugal for the eldest son of the duke, while his ally Dom Jorge da Costa succeeded in accumulating the three archbishoprics of Braga, Lisbon and Evora, the bishopric of Coimbra and finally in removing the abbot of Alcobaça. The *cortes* of Lisbon of 1461 urged Afonso to show 'a firmer hand in the affairs of the crown, with which he should sustain his estate as his predecessors had done, and not give them away with such freedom and so unnecessarily'. He swore to mend his extravagance, but did not do so.

In his relations with his neighbours, Afonso was now drawn into alliance with Castile, where Juan II had been succeeded by his son Henry IV, who had inherited his father's *aboulia*. The surviving prince of Aragon John (II) now succeeded to the throne of Aragon, and devoted his long life to schemes to gain control of Castile, which were to bear fruit with the marriage of his heir Ferdinand to Isabella, the half-sister of Henry IV. But in 1455 Henry's advisers arranged for his marriage to Joana, a sister of Afonso V, and in the following year Afonso and Henry met on the frontier and swore a faithful alliance. The western world had been alarmed by the fall of Constantinople to the Turks in 1454, and both rulers now resumed the crusade against Islam, Henry opening a series of campaigns against Granada, while Afonso undertook a new expedition in Morocco. In 1458 he crossed the Straits with 25,000 men and captured Alcácer-Seguir (al-Qaṣr aṣ-ṣaghir): it was placed under the command of Dom Duarte de Meneses, who successfully withstood two sieges.

In the Magrib the last of the Marinids had long ruled under the tutelage of the powerful Waṭṭāsid clan: he was now murdered, and the Waṭṭāsids were able to make themselves sultans, but only after a bitter struggle. In November 1463 Afonso again crossed to Africa in the hope of winning Tangier, but his attempts were unsuccessful and he returned to Portugal at Easter 1464.

Meanwhile, in Castile Henry IV remained unfitted to rule, yet unable to find an Alvaro de Luna. His favourites João Pacheco and Pedro Girão, brothers, were of Portuguese families established in Castile in 1398. But their ascendancy was now challenged by Beltrán de la Cueva, whom Henry created duke of Albuquerque. When Queen Joana gave birth to an heiress, also Joana, in 1462, it was popularly rumoured that Beltrán was the real father. A faction of the barons upheld this report, and attempted to get Henry's half-brother, Alfonso, declared heir to the throne of Castile. But Henry's advisers sought to preserve the succession by arranging a closer alliance with Portugal, and when the two kings met at Gibraltar (1464), it was arranged that Afonso V, now a widower, should marry Henry's half-sister Isabella and that Afonso's heir John (II of Portugal) should marry Joana 'la Beltraneja'. This did not satisfy the Castilian barons, who demanded that Henry should dismiss Beltrán and declare Alfonso his heir: when he refused they declared Henry deposed, and proclaimed Alfonso 'XII' at Avila. The Portuguese queen of Castile, Joana, appealed to her brother Afonso V for help. He was disposed to comply, but the Portuguese *cortes*, now meeting at Guarda, was against intervention.[1]

---

[1] At this time John II of Aragon, under the influence of his second wife, Juana Enríquez, persecuted, arrested and probably poisoned his son by his first wife, Carlos, prince of Viana, who had been declared primogènit, or heir, in Catalonia. On his death, the Catalans invited Pedro, the former Constable of Portugal, to rule them. He struggled against the Aragonese Trastámaras until his death in 1466. John II was then able to overpower the Catalans and return to his schemes in Castile.

When two years later the boy Alfonso 'XII' died, the Castilian succession lay between Henry's infant daughter, Joana, whom he had earlier repudiated, and his half-sister Isabella. For a moment, Henry thought of declaring Isabella his heiress, but he then again favoured his daughter and reverted to the double marriage with Portugal. This gave John II of Aragon the opportunity to arrange for Isabella to marry his heir Ferdinand, who in 1469 travelled clandestinely to Castile to make the match. By this move John made himself arbiter of the destinies of Castile. Under the influence of the opposing faction, Henry IV at once proposed to recognize Joana as his heiress, and to marry her to Afonso V, but although the two kings met on the frontier, the Portuguese was restrained from committing himself by the opposition of his people.

The crisis came at the end of 1474 when Henry IV died. Isabella and Ferdinand took possession of Castile, but the anti-Aragonese party urged Afonso V to marry Joana and claim the throne. Several towns in Leon were willing to recognize Afonso, who at last obtained the consent of *cortes* to throw his cap into the ring. It was not the first, nor the last time that a ruler of Portugal was tempted to seek the throne of Castile, exalting his house at the expense of the autonomy of his subjects. Castile itself was distraught with feuds, and it seemed at first that the legitimist areas might carry the day. Having sent his claim to his rivals, who rejected it, he crossed the frontier, married Joana and assumed the title of King of Leon and Castile. Zamora opened its gates to him, and Ferdinand and Isabella came to Toro. Ferdinand challenged Afonso to single combat, apparently as a cover for negotiations in which Ferdinand would have compounded for the recognition of Joana as queen of Galicia, but Isabella's advisers refused to cede a stone of Castilian territory.

By 1476 Afonso's claim was in decline, and his rivals were in effective control of Castile. He was defeated at Castro Queimado, near Toro, and now held only Toro itself and a group of castles. But he did receive what he understood to be an offer of support from the king of France, and in August he sent messengers to announce his impending arrival; leaving Lisbon with twenty ships, he sailed to Collioure whence he travelled by land to Tours. But although Louis XI had offered to approach the pope to legitimize Afonso's marriage to Joana and to secure the cession of certain

Spanish towns by corruption, in fact he passed Afonso on to Charles the Bold of Burgundy, in the hope that he might furnish artillery. Charles received Afonso at Nancy, but was killed shortly after. Afonso then returned to France, where in May 1477 he received news that the pope would legitimize the marriage only if Louis XI made war on Castile. Another interview with Louis removed any lingering illusions Afonso may have had. The king errant decided to sail from Honfleur, but as he waited for ships, he was overcome by the vanity of human wishes and disappeared, sending letters to his son and to the king of France to announce his intention to become a monk. He was soon traced to the village of Robinet-le-Bel and persuaded to return to Portugal.

He had entrusted his kingdom to his heir, John II, born in 1455 and married to Leonor, a daughter of Afonso's younger brother. To this resolute prince fell the task of raising troops for the unpopular war in Castile. On receiving his father's renunciation, he had declared himself king: although he now returned the title to Afonso, he continued to bear the brunt of authority. His father was discredited, Toro had been lost, and in February 1479 the bishop of Évora was defeated and captured. In March negotiations were opened between Beatriz, duchess of Viseu, and Queen Isabella. By the Treaty of the Alcáçovas peace was restored, and Afonso forwent his claim to Castile: Joana was deprived even of the title of princess. The heir of the Portuguese prince (Afonso, born in 1475) would marry the eldest daughter of the Catholic Monarchs; their eldest son might marry Joana, but if he did not she would receive a dowry or might retire to a convent. In fact, she refused to accept her exclusion and lived in a convent in Portugal until 1530, referred to as the 'Excellent Lady', though she called herself queen. The royal children, whose destinies were thus disposed of, were educated together in a little court at Moura near the frontier, where the Portuguese heir was in fact under the supervision of a mediator on Portuguese soil. It remained for John to extricate himself from this situation of dependence.

Afonso V was 'never again merry, and always went withdrawn, musing and pensive, like a man that abhorred the things of the world rather than a king who prized them'. He had resolved to abdicate in 1481, but died before *cortes* could assemble to give their consent.

royal apartment was closed, and when it opened again the duke was dead, stabbed 'without many words' by the king's own hand. Several other conspirators were punished and some fled: these last included the Jewish treasurer, Isaac Abarbanel, who escaped to Venice.[1] Viseu's remaining brother, Manuel, gave his allegiance to the crown, and in due course succeeded John II.

This drastic assertion of royal supremacy was accomplished without much interference from the friends of the Braganças. In Spain Ferdinand and Isabella had embarked on the war of Granada in 1481, and were engrossed in it for a decade. In Rome the pluralist Archbishop Costa, formerly of the Bragança faction, was now a cardinal; and the regalism of the Portuguese king had reached the point where the *cortes* of Évora of 1481 had enjoined that papal letters should not be published without royal consent. The papacy denounced the 'new laws daily passed in Portugal contrary to papal authority and established custom', and in May 1483 Sixtus IV condemned John's 'new and unheard of constitutions' which usurped the liberty of ecclesiastics and attempted to 'extinguish the church'. But in 1485 John sent an embassy to Rome to protest his loyalty: he withdrew from his previous stand, but he was now master in his own house.

In 1490 the marriage between the heir to the throne Afonso and the eldest daughter of the Catholic Monarchs, Maria, was celebrated with lavish rejoicings at Évora. But in June 1491 while John was swimming in the Tagus at Santarém, Afonso challenged a companion to race to where his father was, fell from his horse and was killed. John's nearest legitimate male relative was now Manuel, duke of Beja and Master of the Order of Christ, his cousin and brother to Queen Leonor.

One far-reaching consequence of the Castilian marriage was John's submission to the religious policy adopted by the Catholic Monarchs. Throughout the Peninsula the Sephardic Jews had retained their separate communities and autonomy as provided under Muslim law until the fourteenth century. Little is known of the early history of the Jews in Portugal, but it does not appear that there were more than small groups of merchants in the ports and other towns until the thirteenth century: in Lisbon and southern Portugal, which had

---

[1] His son, Leon Hebreo, was the author of the neo-Platonic *Dialoghi d'amore*.

been under Muslim rule, these *aljamas* were probably rather larger. During the thirteenth century the Jews attained considerable economic and political influence as tax-collectors, court doctors, astrologers and intermediaries between Christians and Muslims, and their influence in these capacities extended to Portugal in the early part of the fourteenth century: Dinis made the chief rabbi, Dom Judas, administrator of his treasury. The suppression of the Templars, formerly bankers and moneylenders to the crown, enabled the Jews to extend their activities. Moises Navarro and his son Judas served Pedro I and Fernando as chief collectors.

But in Spain the tricommunal society of al-Andalus began to decline, particularly after the pogrom of Seville of 1391, which spread through Andalusia. After this date many Spanish Jews accepted conversion, whether sincerely, out of fear or for interested motives. The converts attained high positions in the state, and being now cut off from their former co-religionists, they often put pressure on them. But after the Turkish conquest of Constantinople, the Spanish rulers began to fear a general revival of Islam, and were reminded of the part commonly attributed to the Jews in the events of 711. Thus in 1478 the Catholic Monarchs obtained from the pope the right to establish an Inquisition similar to those used by Rome in the Middle Ages to destroy heresy, but designed especially to compel Spanish Jews who had accepted Christianity to observe its obligations. In 1480 the *cortes* of Toledo pressed that the Jews should again be compelled to reside in Jewries, but as soon as the Granadine war was over, the rulers decided on the expulsion of all Jews (31 March 1492): they were accorded four months in which to sell up and leave the country.

In Portugal the Jewries had survived with little change, enjoying the protection of the crown and nobility, to whom they paid tribute. The Portuguese Jews were physicians, astrologers, tax-gatherers and especially artisans. A small Jewish aristocracy had great influence at court—Duarte had deferred his coronation on the advice of his Jewish physician and astrologer. It is likely that their numbers increased as conditions in Castile became less favourable. There is no doubt of their contribution to the growth of science and culture in Portugal. Prince Henry had summoned the cartographer Cresques from Majorca; a generation later three of the earliest Portuguese printers were Jews: Rabbi Eliezer of Lisbon, 1489–92, Abraão Samuel d'Ortas at Leiria, 1492–4, and Samuel Gascon at Faro, 1487–94. All of the first eleven Portuguese incunables are in Hebrew. Few of the Portuguese Jews were wealthy, but in some crafts their predominance was considerable: thus the Lisbon goldsmiths and lapidaries were headed by officials elected by a committee of six 'New Christians' and six Old Christians.

It was therefore not unnatural that the Spanish Jews should seek refuge in Portugal. Although there had been popular complaints against Jewish tax-gatherers at the *cortes* of 1490, John had rejected them, and he had no hesitation in negotiating for the entry of more Jews: 600 wealthy families purchased the right to settle in Portugal for a payment of 60,000 *cruzados*. The rest were to be admitted for a stay of eight months on payment of eight *cruzados* a head: five stations were opened at the frontier, and the customs officers issued receipts which served as passports. In theory the Portuguese crown was to provide transport at the end of the permitted period, but in fact the crown was not anxious to keep this part of the bargain, and the only facilities provided were for the fortresses of Tangier and Arzila in North Africa. About 60,000 individuals were admitted, perhaps a third of the total number expelled from Spain.

2. THE VOYAGES OF DISCOVERY, 1460–95

Since the death of Prince Henry, the exploration of Africa had been continued, though without the singleness of purpose of the initiator: the prince had devoted the revenues of the Order of Christ to the enterprise and received large subsidies from the state, but he died indebted to the crown, the count of Arraiolos, the abbey of Alcobaça and the Jews. His mantle now passed to his nephew Fernando, the younger brother of Afonso V.

During his later years the prince had hoped to reach the 'Indies': Marco Polo had described three Indies, and it is likely that the planisphere obtained by Dom Pedro in Venice in 1428 showed the land of Prester John and India as contiguous. Azurara, referring to the expedition of Antão Gonçalves (1442), notes that the Prince sought information 'not only about that land' (Rio do Ouro), 'but also about the Indies and the land of Prester John'. Similarly, an inscription on the tomb of his chancellor and treasurer, Fr Gonçalo de Sousa (1469?), refers to 'the whole coast of Guinea as far as the *Índios*'. Ethiopians had visited Europe in the previous century, and a Portuguese document of 1452 alludes to the entertainment of 'George, ambassador of Prester John'. If this was an Ethiopian, the distinction between the land of Prester John and India must have been clear, though the word Indies seems still to have been loosely applied to Africa.[1] Prince Henry's testament refers only to the exploration of 'three hundred leagues of the coast of Guinea'.

In November 1469 the crown leased to a citizen of Lisbon named Fernão Gomes the monopoly of trade with Guinea for a period of five years: he was to pay the crown 200,000 *reais*, and not to trade on the main before the Cape Verde Islands, which belonged to Dom Fernando, or to the castle of Arguim, which Afonso V had granted to his son, Prince John. According to João de Barros, Gomes undertook to explore 100 leagues of coast a year. During this period João de Santarém and Pero Escobar reached the Costa da Malagueta, or Pepper Coast, and Mina do Ouro, the Mine of Gold, later to become the chief centre for the gold-trade. The islands of São Tomé and Principe were discovered in 1471 and 1472. Fernão do Pó found the island which bears his name, and Rui de Sequeira reached Cape St Catharine (now Cape Catharine) in November 1474 or 1475.

Nothing appears to have been added to these achievements during the period of the war with Castile, but with John II the crown once more took an active part in explorations and commerce. In December 1481 Diogo de Azambuja was sent to Mina do Ouro with men and materials to build a fortified factory, and in the following year Diogo Cão reached the mouth of the Zaire, or Congo. He visited the coast of northern Angola, and hearing news of a chief in the interior, sent a party to find him. It was delayed, and he therefore took several natives back to Lisbon, promising to return with them in the following year: their visit to Europe, their treatment and what they saw soon caused their chief, the 'Manicongo', to seek conversion and close relations with the Portuguese. When, in 1485, John II sent a mission to Rome to explain his achievements, his ambassador claimed that the Portuguese had almost attained the Arabian gulf:

[1] The Papal bull of 1456 refers to 'that southern shore as far as the Indians'.

shortly before, Cão had sailed forth again, this time reaching Serra Parda (22° 10′ S.), where he is supposed to have died.

During these voyages, the ships carried *padrões*, stone pillars surmounted by a cross and the arms of Portugal, to be erected as markers, evidence of priority and beacons. That of St George at the mouth of the Congo served as a fetish until 1859 when some British seamen, attempting to remove it, dropped it overboard. The *padrão* of St Augustine (Cape Santa Maria, 13° 26′ S.) and another from Cape Negro (15° 42′ S.) were brought to Lisbon in 1892, while a fourth from Cape Cross (12° 15′) was carried to Germany.

But in 1487 a Portuguese factor at Benin brought news of the existence of a priest-king called Ogané twenty moons march inland; he was thought to be a Christian and therefore identified with Prester John. In consequence, John II sent two expeditions, one designed to continue the explorations of Cão and the other to attempt to locate Ethiopia and India by land. The first of these consisted of two caravels and a supply-ship commanded by Bartolomeu Dias. It left Lisbon in August 1487, reached the gulf of Santa Maria (Walvis Bay) in December, and Serra dos Reis on 6 January. It then sailed out to sea and lost sight of land for almost a month. When it turned north and again touched land on 3 February, the coast was running northeast. Native herdsmen and cows were seen on shore, and the place was named Terra dos Vaqueiros, now Mossel Bay. Dias had doubled the Cape without seeing it: he continued as far as the Great Fish River and then turned back, reaching Lisbon in December 1488 after an absence of seventeen months and seventeen days. He had at last demonstrated that the African continent could be rounded and the Orient reached by sea.

The travellers by land were Pero da Covilhã and Afonso de Paiva, men versed in warfare, diplomacy and Arabic, They went to Rhodes, whence they passed to Alexandria in the guise of honey-merchants. Passing through Cairo, Sinai and Suakim, they reached Aden, where they parted company, Pero da Covilhã for India and Afonso de Paiva for Ethiopia. The former reached India in a year, landing at Cannanor and seeing Calicut and Gôa, the former an emporium of the oriental spice-trade, and returned to Ormuz. He travelled thence with the monsoon at the end of 1489 to Sofala in Africa and so by Aden to Cairo. Here he found two Jews, the Rabbi of Beja and José de Lamego, a cobbler, who had been sent by John II to search for the wanderers. They were able to tell him that Afonso de Paiva had died in Africa. José de Lamego then returned to Portugal with the news, while the Rabbi went on to Ormuz. Pero da Covilhã reached Ethiopia and was honourably received by the emperor, but not allowed to depart: he settled there, married and raised a family, being seen by the Portuguese mission of Dom Rodrigo de Lima in 1526.

The information collected by the expeditions of 1488 threw new light on the cosmography of the east and vindicated Prince Henry's design to seek the Indies and Prester John by rounding Africa. But the possibility that Asia might be reached by crossing the Atlantic had not been overlooked. The settlement of the Madeiras and the Azores had prompted voyages of exploration into the middle Atlantic in quest of semi-legendary islands, the Seven Cities, St Brendan, Antillia and Brazil: all these were probably chartmakers' reduplications of the known Atlantic Islands. There is evidence of voyages westward from the Azores in 1486. Further north, English and other merchants traded with Iceland. The Viking settlements in America of c. 985 had disappeared, but the memory of them lingered in the early fifteenth century in Iceland. The Norwegian monarchy had treated its settlements in Greenland as a royal monopoly: that in western Greenland died out in the fourteenth century; that in eastern Greenland survived into the fifteenth, though in decline.

The possibility of a westward voyage to Asia across the Atlantic depended on calculations of the probable distance between the westward and eastward limits of the known world. A Florentine physician, Paolo Toscanelli, discussed this with a canon of Lisbon, Fernão Martins, who on returning to Portugal reported the conversation at court. He was asked for further information, and in June 1474 Toscanelli replied with a calculation that Marco Polo's Quinsay would be 5,000 miles west of Lisbon: Cipango or Japan would be only 3,500 miles and the legendary 'Antillia' 1,500. The reckoning seems not to have impressed the Portuguese, but it came to the notice of Christopher Columbus who at this time had settled in Portugal and married the daughter of Bartolomeu Perestrelo, captain of Porto Santo. In 1481 or 1482 Columbus put forward a plan for the discovery of the Indies from the west, but it was rejected, and he therefore approached the courts of England and Spain. On 28 March 1484 John II wrote, in reply to a lost letter from Columbus, inviting him to return to Portugal, but he did not do so: this may be the context of the grant to a group of Azoreans of an island to be found at the end of forty days' sail (Antillia?, Cipango?). After the failure of this project, John II returned to his African schemes, while Columbus remained at the Spanish court, where, after the fall of Granada, he finally obtained Isabella's assistance. He sailed in the autumn of 1492, and returned at the beginning of the following year, believing that he had discovered India. On his arrival in Lisbon, he saw John II, who at once prepared a fleet under Dom Francisco de Almeida to make a Portuguese claim. When Columbus reached Spain, the Catholic Monarchs took measures to prevent this, obtaining papal backing for their own claims from the Aragonese pope Alexander VI in the bulls of 3 and 4 May, which awarded them all lands discovered or to be discovered lying more than 100 leagues west or south of the Cape Verdes or Azores. This dispensation would have confined the Portuguese to African waters, leaving the whole of the supposed Indies to Castile. A later bull of 26 September virtually rescinded the rights recognized as Portuguese since 1454. However, this was mainly designed to strengthen the bargaining power of the Castilians; negotiations had already been proposed, and John II obtained by dint of argument and bribery a very different settlement in the Treaty of Tordesillas of 7 June 1494. Instead of the containment of the Portuguese zone put forward in 1493 a dividing-line was to be drawn 370 leagues west of the Cape Verdes and running north and south. All to the west of this would go to Castile and all to the east would fall to Portugal. The effect of this was to reserve Brazil for Portugal, a fortunate stroke of policy which affords supposititious evidence for the theory, so far quite unproven, that the Portuguese court had foreknowledge of the existence of Brazil, to be discovered six years later.

3. MANUEL I, 1495–1521

John II, the 'Perfect Prince', fell ill of dropsy in 1494 and died in October 1495. His only legitimate son, Afonso, had predeceased him, and John himself is said to have remarked that he would not have made a king: the chronicler Rèsende notes that Afonso resembled his grandfather more than his father. John had a bastard, Dom Jorge, born in 1481, whom he took into his own household and hoped to make his successor. Queen Leonor was bitterly opposed to this, and John and she were reconciled only on his deathbed, when he recognized the succession of his cousin and his wife's brother, Manuel, duke of Beja and Master of the Order of Christ. Manuel was the youngest of a family of nine: four of his brothers had died young, and the fifth, the duke of Viseu, had been murdered by John II. He was now twenty-six, fair, rather thin, diligent, sparing in his food and drink, musical, vain, and fond of display. He rewarded his servants and minstrels lavishly, and at once pardoned the nobles who had been exiled ten years before, returning fifty properties to the new duke of Bragança. He made the nobility into a court circle, recognizing seventy-two families, whose coats of arms were placed in the Sala dos Brasões of the palace at Sintra. Many of these families were now established in Lisbon or its neighbourhood, receiving grants or pensions from the royal household or the military Orders. The masterships of the Orders were now assimilated by the crown: Manuel was already Master of the Order of Christ and recommended in his will that Avis and Santiago, which had passed from Prince Afonso to Dom Jorge, should be incorporated in the crown.[1] In 1496 the papacy granted members of the Orders of Christ and Avis the right to contract marriage without forfeiting their ecclesiastical privileges, thus the crown was free to avail itself of the orders of knighthood to reward its servants.

The monarch was no longer a defender or justicer, but the embodiment of the state, and his specialized functions were increasingly discharged by functionaries at court or royal officials distributed through the country. The royal supremacy was provided with a constitution by a new compilation of the laws and a reform of the ancient charters of the *concelhos*. The Ordenações Afonsinas begun by Duarte and Dom Pedro were now replaced by the Ordenações Manuelinas, which received a third and last revision in 1521. The five sections of the original work (a simplification of the seven *partidas* of Alfonso X) were preserved: Book I, the judicature, magistracy, treasury; Book II, privileges of the crown and of the two

---

[1] The process was completed by John III in 1551.

privileged classes; Book III, procedure; Book IV, law of inheritance and contract; Book V, crime and penal law. As the codification of law was extended and Roman precedent invoked, the administration passed into the hands of a professional class, and the *cortes* relinquished rather easily the right of requesting new legislation. The *cortes* were now in eclipse: the founder of the house of Avis had celebrated 25 *cortes* in his reign of 48 years; Duarte 4 in 6 years; Afonso V 22 in 44 years; John II 4 in 13 years: Manuel held 4 *cortes* in 26 years and John III 3 in 31 years. This was partly because new forms of revenue had reduced the importance of the *subsídio* voted by *cortes*, and the method of collection had been sufficiently standardized. Moreover, the economic interests of the country were more diversified, and urban life had become more complex, so that questions of war, peace and commerce came to rest in the hands of professional advisers. New institutions and offices were described in *regimentos* which established their functions, duties and privileges, often in meticulous detail. By contrast, the revision of the *forais*, attempted by Afonso V and John II, and achieved only in 1498, purged the charters of local privileges, and expressed all payments in terms of contemporary currency, simplifying difficulties that impeded collection: the reformed charter of Lisbon came to consist almost entirely of tributary regulations.

The assumption by the crown of responsibility in questions of policy also affected the organization of the municipalities. In Lisbon, the municipal council had long been dominated by the guilds: the 'good men' of the guilds had played a prominent part in bringing the house of Avis to the throne, and had retained their representative body, the House of Twenty-four. This was suppressed in 1506, as a punishment for popular participation in a massacre of the Jews. An outbreak of plague led to processions to implore divine mercy; a discussion about a supposed miracle ended in the murder of a New Christian, after which two Dominicans ran through the streets and incited the mob to violence. The riots lasted three days, and several hundred persons were said to have been killed. Manuel gave orders for the execution of some fifty culprits, the closure of the Dominican monastery, the suppression of the House of Twenty-four and the extension of the period of grace for the Jews.

On Manuel's accession it was at once proposed that he should

133

marry Isabel, the eldest daughter of the rulers of Spain, the widow of Prince Afonso. Once more Ferdinand and Isabella made the condition that Portugal should expel the Jews. Thus in December 1496 Manuel ordered that all Jews and Muslims who refused baptism should be expelled, undertaking to provide ships at the end of ten months. The marriage was duly celebrated in October 1497. But Manuel had no intention of parting with a large and valuable community, and attempted to force the removal of Jewish and Muslim children and their education as Christians at the expense of the crown. Some Jews were thus forcibly converted: the threat against the Muslims was dropped for fear of reprisals against Christians in Muslim territory. It was then announced that unbaptized Jews must embark in Lisbon: about 20,000 congregated in the city and attempts were made to induce them to be converted by threats, promises and force. On accepting a technical 'conversion', they were granted twenty years' grace, during which no inquiry was to be made into their beliefs. A handful resisted this treatment and departed: they included the king's mathematician and astrologer, Abraão Zacuto, and a doctor Abraão Saba. Pressure for rigorous measures came from the monastic orders, especially the Dominicans, the patrons of the Inquisition, and from Spain. After the troubles of 1506, Manuel renewed his guarantee to the New Christians in 1507 and later prolonged it for sixteen years.

Manuel's deference towards the Catholic Monarchs was inspired by the hope that he or his heirs might rule over the whole Peninsula.[1] On the death of the Spanish heir, his queen became the heiress. Having obtained the consent of the Portuguese *cortes*, Manuel and Isabel travelled to Toledo, where they were duly recognized. But when they reached Saragossa (July 1498), the Aragonese refused recognition. The queen gave birth to a son, Miguel da Paz, but died in doing so. The Aragonese now recognized the infant prince, but he remained with his grandparents in Castile while Manuel returned to Portugal. When in March 1499 the Portuguese *cortes* met in Lisbon to discuss the succession, they now expressed misgivings about the Spanish inheritance, feeling evidently that a prince educated in

---

[1] The word Spain or the Spains had hitherto been applied to the whole Peninsula. When Ferdinand began to call himself King of Spain and was granted the title by Alexander VI, Manuel vainly protested against the misuse of the word.

Castile would be a different matter from one brought up in Portugal: they demanded guarantees that if the two crowns were united, only Portuguese should control the treasury, justice, the towns and castles of Portugal and the possessions overseas. But in July 1500 the infant prince died and the prospect of union faded. The Castilian succession now passed to the second daughter of the Catholic Monarchs, Juana, who had married the heir to the Emperor Maximilian; her son Charles would inherit the crown of Spain, the archduchy of Burgundy, the imperial title and the remaining possessions of both parents. Meanwhile, Manuel married the fourth daughter of Ferdinand and Isabella, Maria, by whom he had ten children, his heir, the future John II, being born in 1502.

At the opening of the reign of Dom Manuel, the Portuguese were consolidating their three enterprises, the conquest of the Magrib, the occupation of the Atlantic Islands and the exploration of the west African coast. In Morocco, John II had received the fortresses of Ceuta (1415), Alcácer-Seguir (1458), Arzila and Tangier (1471), and had made only one attempt to extend these, by building the fortress of Graciosa at the mouth of the Lukkus: this would have dominated the town of Alcácer-Quivir (al-Qaṣr al-kabir), but it proved impracticable and, on the withdrawal of the Portuguese, the sultan built Larache (al-Araish) to defend the estuary. Under Manuel, the Portuguese supplemented these four conquests in northern Morocco with a chain of fortresses down the Atlantic coast. However, these last were originally factories now taken over and fortified for the purpose of asserting Portuguese trading-rights against the Genoese and Catalans. Because of Castilian activity at Agadir, a Portuguese merchant named João Lopes de Sequeira built the fortified factory of Santa Cruz on Cape Guer in 1505. In the next year Diogo de Azambuja established the Royal Castle at Mogador, while Safi (which had recognized Portuguese sovereignty in 1488), was occupied in 1508. To these were added Azammur (1513) and Mazagão (1514): these remarkable fortified harbours are still largely intact.

Although the beginnings of this enterprise were mercantile, the fortresses were able to dominate Atlantic Morocco. The climax of the Portuguese expansion was reached in 1515, when the governor of Safi, Nuno de Ataide, fought his way almost to Marrakush, only to be driven off. He then built a fort at Ma'mura and prepared an assault on Fez: this was defeated and he was killed in the following year in the course of a raid near Marrakush. The conquest of the Magrib, which had seemed within reach, became impossible, and the unprofitable exercise of the Holy War was eclipsed by more useful ventures.

The colonization and settlement of the Atlantic Islands had now been under way for three-quarters of a century, and brought important new sources of wealth. In particular Lisbon became the great market for sugar, which now became a staple of western diet. By 1498 there were 220 estates in Madeira, and the production was limited to 120,000 *arrobas* a year to halt the fall in price of what had lately been a luxury.[1] Cultivation was almost entirely on small estates by Portuguese emigrants from the Minho and the Algarve.[2] Of the 120,000 *arrobas*, only 7,000 were consumed in Portugal, the chief market being Flanders (40,000), Italy (Venice, Genoa, Leghorn, 31,000), France (16,000), Chios and Constantinople (15,000) and England (7,000). There existed a flourishing Portuguese factory at Bruges, while branches of the German banking houses were established in Lisbon by 1504, together with merchants from Flanders, Italy, France and England.

In west Africa the main trading posts were Arguim and Mina, both of which were chiefly important for the purchase of gold. In each case the factors either visited the neighbouring villages or employed native agents: these last often settled at the factories, detribalizing themselves and adopting the Portuguese language, religion and customs, and therefore considering themselves as Portuguese. Further south, the most fruitful contact was with the Manicongo or 'king of the Congo', whom Cão had visited at his village, Mbanza. The Manicongo had asked for teachers, builders and farmers, and in 1490 there arrived three ships with priests, artisans and soldiers. The rulers were converted; and the next king, Afonso I (1505 or 1506–1540), showed every desire to adopt Portuguese ways. Manuel now sent priests, a lawyer to describe the functioning of the Portuguese government and

[1] In *c.* 1445 Sicilian sugar cost 1080 *reis* the *arroba* of 32 lbs: by 1493 the *arroba* of Madeiran sugar cost 300 *reis*.

[2] Of the 220 estates, only three produced as much as 1000 *arrobas*: the average being 345. Only a few were owned by foreigners, but the export trade was very largely held by foreigners and Jews, or by clients of the duke of Bragança.

a resident, Simão da Silva, who was to govern the Portuguese in the Congo and conduct trade. Unluckily Silva soon died, as did many of his compatriots, and the small band of survivors were left without authority. The subjects of Afonso were raided by the coastal peoples, who sold slaves to Fernão de Melo, now engaged in occupying the island of São Tomé, which had been found uninhabited. In 1521 Afonso I's son, Henrique, returned to the Congo after spending thirteen years in Europe: he had been appointed Bishop of Utica, but he achieved little among his own people, and in 1526 Afonso asked for fifty more missionaries. By now a new Portuguese resident had arrived and imposed order on his compatriots, while Afonso set up a commission to ensure that no free natives were sent to São Tomé. From the first the Portuguese treated the Manicongo as a free and independent sovereign, though they seem to have exaggerated his power, probably for reasons of prestige: he was in fact only the nominal head of a tribal confederation of six provinces which were not always disposed to obey him. It was therefore inevitable that the Portuguese should be drawn into the domestic differences of the BaCongo, and the problem was complicated by the appearance of a *mestiço* race, not amenable to either authority. Afonso's death was followed by a civil war. In 1548 the Jesuits built three new churches, but did not succeed in establishing themselves.

Meanwhile, the Portuguese navigators had achieved the final stage of the opening up of the sea-way to the east. John II had appointed an admiral for an expedition to complete the work of Dias, but it was only in the next reign that a start was made. The new admiral was Vasco da Gama, governor of the small fishing-port of Sines, and he sailed from Lisbon on 7 July 1497 with three ships and a supply-boat, his own *São Gabriel*, his brother Paulo's *São Rafael*, and Nicolau Coelho's *Berrio*, carried about 148 men with supplies for three years, stone markers and letters addressed to Prester John and the King of Calicut. From the Cape Verde Islands, they sailed out into the ocean, battling for three months with gales and downpours, after which they put in at Angra de Santa Helena, just short of the Cape. For four days they were unable to pass the Cape because of the strength of the wind, but on November 25 they found Dias' Bay of Cowherds. They then passed Dias' furthest point, reaching a new coast on Christmas Day which they called Natal. Somewhere near the mouth of the Zambesi they saw two men who differed from the natives, and must be from or have visited Arab settlements. On 2 March they put into Moçambique and found some Arab merchantmen at anchor. They obtained pilots for Mombasa, but when they had been recognized as Christians an attempt was made to ambush them there and they sailed on to Melinde. Here the sultan proved friendly and found them a pilot for India. A month later they sighted Calicut (18 May 1498).

Vasco da Gama opened relations with the ruler of Calicut, the Samorin, and his factors were able to buy a quantity of spices. There followed some disagreeable incidents, which the Portuguese attributed to the intrigues of Muslim merchants, who were well aware that the establishment of these rivals would be to their disadvantage. On 29 August Gama left Calicut, coasted to Angediva (Gôa), where he took on water, and on 5 October sailed for Melinde. The crossing was very difficult, and thirty men were lost from disease. The survivors reached Melinde on 7 January 1499, and the Cape Verdes by the end of April: Nicolau Coelho sighted Lisbon on 10 July, two years and two days after the departure. Gama lingered at the Azores, where his brother died, arriving at Lisbon some weeks later.

His exploit had crowned three-quarters of a century of endeavour: it turned the course of European history. The hold of the *São Gabriel* was stuffed with specimens of pepper, cloves, nutmeg, cinnamon and precious stones. Europe, poor, enterprising and resolute, was no longer separated by the hostile confraternity of Islam from the splendid despotisms of the east.

Already in August, Manuel had written to Rome to obtain a papal confirmation of his claims, and within six months he had assembled the largest and finest fleet yet provided for a voyage of discovery. It consisted of thirteen ships, placed under the command of a young nobleman, Pedro Álvares Cabral, who was to establish relations with the rulers of India. It was now realized that Columbus's 'Indies' were in fact a new world, though the visionary Genoese persisted until his death in believing that he had been to Asia. Spain's hopes of trade and treasure were dashed: Gama, not Columbus, had glimpsed the fantastic world of Marco Polo.

The new expedition included Nicolau Coelho, Bartolomeu Dias and his brother Diogo, Duarte Pacheco Pereira (author of the

Esmeraldo), various nobles, nine chaplains and a total of some 1,200 men: it carried provisions for eighteen months. From the Cape Verdes, it sailed south-west for a month, and on 22 April sighted a new land, the coast of Brazil. On the previous day floating weeds had been seen, and now in the evening a long line of mountains was descried with woods at their foot and in front a flat stretch of beach.[1] Next day, Coelho put out in a boat and found a band of natives, naked, but armed with bows and arrows. They exchanged a feathered headdress for three Portuguese caps. After sailing a little to the north, Cabral sent a ship to report his discovery of a large island, which he called the land of Vera Cruz. Brazil had been reserved for Portugal by the Treaty of Tordesillas, and it is probable that in sailing so far to the south-west Cabral was deliberately crossing the zone of discovery defined in the treaty. But for the moment Brazil remained no more than a savage shore marked with a single wooden cross.

Cabral's voyage round the Cape was an unfortunate one. Half his ships were lost, including that of Bartolomeu Dias, who perished in the seas he had been the first to sail. The six surviving vessels reached Sofala in July and Calicut on 13 September 1500. The Samorin allowed some of the Portuguese to land and trade for pepper, but there was a disturbance in which the factor Aires Correia was killed. Cabral replied by bombarding the city, and transferred his attention to Cochin and Cannanor, whose sultans were hostile to the Samorin. Having left a group of Portuguese to maintain a factory at Cochin, Cabral departed from India in January 1501, bringing three ambassadors from the Indian states.

Although Gama had at first supposed that the Samorin was a Nestorian Christian, he was soon disabused. He also discovered that most of the foreign trade of Calicut was in Muslim hands. In opening his factory, Cabral informed the Samorin that his people were enemies of the Muslims, though they would give no offence in Calicut. But the Muslims were unwilling to surrender their monopoly, and it was therefore almost inevitable that the Portuguese should be drawn towards the princes opposed to the Samorin. When Gama made his second voyage to India in 1502, with a fleet of fifteen ships, followed by five more under his cousin, he first made an alliance with

---

[1] The discovery of Brazil is conventionally celebrated on 3 May, the day of the Invention of the True Cross.

the ruler of Kilwa in East Africa, who paid tribute to the Portuguese, and on reaching India again bombarded Calicut and strengthened relations with Cochin and Cannanor. As soon as he left, the Samorin attacked Cochin, and forced its ruler and the Portuguese to retire to the island of Valpi, where they were found by Francisco de Almeida's fleet in 1503. From this point the ruler of Cochin became a client of Portugal, and Duarte Pacheco was detached with 160 men and three ships to ward off the next attack from Calicut. He succeeded in this, and when the next Portuguese fleet arrived, Calicut was again bombarded and a Muslim fleet was destroyed at Cannanor. Now the Portuguese factories were guarded by 300 men and five ships.

The Portuguese attributed the hostility of the Samorin to Muslim intrigues: if they had at first thought of obtaining concessions for factories like those of foreign powers in Lisbon or of the Italians in the Muslim ports of the Mediterranean, they were now obliged to adopt a plan more resembling the fortified ports in Morocco. In 1505 Dom Francisco de Almeida was accorded the title of Viceroy and instructed to conclude alliances with the Indian rulers, setting up factories and forts on the east and west coasts of Africa. He was also to build a fort near the mouth of the Red Sea to intercept the Muslim spice-trade, which had hitherto been transacted through the ports of the Red Sea, by caravans to Alexandria and so connected to the European centres of consumption by Venetian and other merchants.

In order to achieve this commercial revolution, Almeida was given a fleet of twenty-two ships with about 2,500 men, of whom 1,500 were soldiers contracted for three years' service. Almeida duly built a fort at Kilwa and burnt hostile Mombasa in Africa. At Cochin he gave the ruler a golden crown and built a stone fort instead of the wooden one. He then imposed a system of licences on trading-ships, thus threatening to ruin the Muslims. The Samorin gathered a fleet, but it was beaten off by the artillery of eleven Portuguese ships. In consequence, the Muslims began to seek spices in Malacca and the Sunda Islands and to sail by Ceylon or the Maldives to the Persian Gulf and the Red Sea, avoiding western India. Meanwhile, the Egyptians, with aid from Venice, built a fleet to defend the Red Sea.

Almeida's instructions were to suppress the trade of the Muslims and to secure the preponderance of Portuguese commerce. He sought to achieve this by control of the sea, believing that too many fortresses would disperse the Portuguese forces. Now two more fleets were sent, under Tristão da Cunha and Afonso de Albuquerque: the latter held powers to succeed Almeida at the end of his viceroyalty. Cunha explored the coast of Madagascar and part of East Africa, occupied the island of Socotra and built a fort to control the mouth of the Red Sea, before sailing on to India. But Albuquerque ravaged the cities of the Oman coast, some of which surrendered, while others were captured and sacked. In September 1507 he appeared off Ormuz at the mouth of the Persian Gulf and demanded tribute. After attacking ships in the harbour, he was given some gold and began to build a fort. But his men were unwilling to toil as stone-masons, and when three of his ships slipped anchor, he was obliged to retire to Socotra. In 1508 he returned to Ormuz to find that Almeida had sent a letter of protection to its regent. He therefore went to India to claim the governorship, but Almeida refused to acknowledge him as successor, since he himself had received no letters of recall. At this time the new Egyptian fleet made its appearance. The fort of Socotra proved too distant to pen it in the Red Sea, and early in 1508 it intercepted Almeida's son, who was mortally wounded at Chaul. The viceroy then gathered nineteen ships and 1600 men, while the Muslim armada crossed the ocean to Diu, where it was reinforced by the Samorin. On 2 February 1509 a great battle was fought off Diu in which Almeida destroyed the enemy fleet and succeeded in retaining command of the sea.

On his return, his authority was again challenged by Albuquerque, whom he arrested. But in October a new fleet under Dom Fernando Coutinho brought confirmation of Albuquerque's succession and orders to attack Calicut. Almeida then surrendered his command, and set out for Portugal, being killed by natives in a skirmish near the Cape. Albuquerque set out to conquer Calicut in January 1510, but he suffered heavy losses and was himself wounded. He then decided to establish a capital at Gôa, an island site which could be defended from attack by land or sea. Its ruler, the Hidalcão, at first drove Albuquerque back to his ships, but a second expedition at the end of the year resulted in the conquest of the city, which was garrisoned and fortified.

It was now necessary to trace the spice-trade back to its source, for the Muslims had already congregated at Malacca, the emporium for the spices of the Moluccas and the trade with China. It had been reached by Diogo Lopes de Sequeira in 1509: Albuquerque conquered the city in August 1511, built a fort and sent messengers to Siam, to Pegu (Burma), to the Moluccas and to China.

On his return Albuquerque lost his flagship and treasure off Sumatra and escaped on a raft. When he reached Cochin, he heard that Gôa was besieged. But new forces had arrived from Portugal, and he was able to relieve it. He then made peace with the Samorin and built a fort at Calicut. In 1512 he laid plans for the occupation of strategic positions in the Persian Gulf and the Red Sea, sailing in February 1513. He failed to take Aden, but spent three months in exploration before returning. He began his last expedition in 1515, attempting to reduce Ormuz and Aden, and intending to proceed from this to the conquest of Mecca. Ormuz agreed to pay tribute and to restore the Portuguese fort, but, after garrisoning the place, Albuquerque fell ill and returned to Gôa, where he died shortly after his arrival, having learned that his rival Lopo Soares had been appointed to succeed him.

Apart from his conquests, his governorship had seen the foundation of a capital at Gôa, of an administration and of a Luso-Indian population: shipbuilding and other industries had been founded and forts had been built at Gôa, Calicut, Malacca and Ormuz: those of Cochin and Cannanor had been reconstructed. Relations had been begun with western India, Ceylon, Bengal, Burma, Siam and the Spice Islands. Albuquerque had assured the supremacy of Portuguese sea-power in the Indian Ocean for a century and came near to creating a monopoly of the spice-trade at its source. His unrealized aspirations included the conquest of Mecca and the exchange of the tomb of Muḥammad for Jerusalem.

Manuel was now for a time the wealthiest ruler in Europe, 'Lord of the Navigation, Conquest and Commerce of Ethiopia, Arabia, Persia and India', according to his own resounding titles, or King of the Spices, according to the envious ruler of France. The first pepper was bought in Cochin for 2 *cruzados* the *quintal* and sold in Lisbon for 80. In consequence Gama's first expedition was paid for sixty times over by a relatively small cargo. As the volume of trade grew, the price fell to 40 and later to less than 20: a royal order forbade its sale at less than 20, and the price was later stabilized at 30. The crown also monopolized the import of cloves and cinnamon and collected a tribute of 30 per cent on other spices, of which 5 per cent was set aside for the building of the Jerónimos monastery at Belém. In 1502 Gama induced the ruler of Kilwa to pay a tribute of 200 gold *mithkals* a year, and the first-fruits of this was converted into the great gold monstrance of Belém, the work of Gil Vicente, the court dramatist and master of the mint. A few years later Albuquerque assessed the annual revenue of the crown at a million *cruzados*, discounting the loss of ships and other charges: he asserted that India had made Manuel the richest of rulers. In fact, the advantage to the crown declined steeply, and the cost of expeditions soon exceeded returns, and the toll in men and resources became increasingly onerous.

In comparison with these spectacular fortunes, the growth of Portuguese interests in the New World was slow. The eastern coast of South America had been explored in 1501–2 by Amerigo Vespucci, who demonstrated that it was not an island, but a continent: it was in future to go by his name. But no high civilizations and no great treasure had been discovered. In 1502 Fernão de Noronha, a New Christian, was granted the monopoly of dyewood in return for pursuing the exploration of the coast. The cultivation of sugar was introduced in about 1516, but it was the intensification of interloping by French privateers that finally led to the distribution of the terri-tory among captains, or *donatários*, in 1534.

The Portuguese were precluded from sailing in the area of the Caribbean by the Spanish grant, but they were interested in explor-ations further north. By the beginning of 1500, it was realized that a continental territory existed to the west and south of the Caribbean, but it was not known how far this extended to the south or north. It seems that a ship from Faial in the Azores had set out to look for a territory in the north-west (Greenland?) as early as 1452. Even earlier Bristol merchants were sailing to Iceland for cod, and by 1480 the Portuguese were frequenting Bristol: they may have gone to Iceland and may have learned about Greenland and have picked up the memory of Icelandic voyages to the lands beyond. The sailors of Bristol, for their part, searched for the 'Isle of Brasile' as early as 1481, and had found a Brazil 'believed to be the mainland' before 1497. Sebastian Cabot may have attempted to persuade the Portu-guese to attempt this discovery when he was in Lisbon, presumably before his arrival in England in 1495. In 1497 Cabot sailed from Bristol in search of a north-west passage and touched either Labrador, Newfoundland or the mainland of Canada. In May 1502 Manuel issued a licence to Gaspar Corte-Real, a nobleman with lands on Terceira in the Azores, to search for islands or mainland: he visited both coasts of Greenland and returned to Lisbon. Another inhabitant of Terceira, João Fernandes, known as 'o lavrador' (the farmer), possibly the 'Johannes Ffernandus' who exported goods from Bristol to Lisbon in 1493, may have visited these parts earlier: he certainly sailed from Bristol in the service of Henry VII in 1500. His name was applied to Greenland in maps of 1503 onwards: it was transferred to the present Labrador only in about 1570. Meanwhile, Gaspar Corte-Real and his brother Miguel made other voyages to western Greenland, the present Labrador, Newfoundland and Nova Scotia. Both were lost at sea, and after 1503 Manuel gave up the idea of a north-west passage. However, the Cantino map of October (?) 1502 shows Portuguese flags on Greenland, Newfoundland and Labrador, and is inscribed 'Terra del Rey de Portuguell'. Portuguese ships began to harvest the Newfoundland fisheries, and dried codfish became a staple diet in Portugal and on Portuguese ships. The departure of the Portuguese codfishing fleet for the banks of Newfoundland is still celebrated every spring in Lisbon.

During the following decade the energies of the Portuguese were concentrated in their struggle to obtain control of the sea-ways of the East, while the Spaniards explored and settled the lands of the Caribbean area. The logical conclusion of the cycle of voyages of exploration was achieved by a Portuguese sailing under the Spanish flag. This was Fernando de Magalhãis, or Magellan, who had served under Albuquerque at Malacca, but in 1517 left the Portuguese court, taking with him Rui Faleiro, an astronomer and cartographer: they had offered their services to the Spanish crown, proposing to discover new spice-lands. In 1519 Magellan sailed from Spain, passing through the Straits which bear his name and crossing the Pacific. He himself perished in a skirmish in the Philippines, but his Basque companion Elcano completed the first circumnavigation of the world. It was just a century since Prince Henry's caravels had begun to venture to the Madeiras.

4. JOHN III, 1521–57

When Manuel died in December 1521, his successor, John, was aged
nineteen, a shy and retiring youth, on whom his father had hesitated
to confer a separate household. Some four years earlier Manuel had
become a widower for the second time. The young Charles V had
recently become king of Spain and was about to be elected emperor,
and Manuel asked for the hand of his sister Leonor for John: when
Leonor arrived in Portugal, he changed his mind and married her
himself (1518). When John came to the throne, negotiations were
opened for another double marriage with Spain: Charles was now
emperor and desperately in need of money, and he demanded a
dowry of 900,000 gold *dobras* for his marriage to John's sister Isabel.
The municipality of Lisbon urged John to marry his father's widow,
Leonor, whose dowry would then remain in Portugal, but John rejected this plan and Leonor returned to Castile. He then married
Charles' sister Catarina, and Charles married his sister Isabel. Fifty
years later, these marriages were to enable Philip II of Spain to lay
claim to the Portuguese throne on the extinction of the male line of
Avis. But now the Portuguese succession appeared to be safe, and the
need for a firm friendship with Spain was apparent: by the papal
dispositions and by the Treaty of Tordesillas, the New World had
been partitioned among them, and their monopoly was increasingly
contested by other powers.

These claims were not formally questioned, but French and later
English ships began to interlope in the African and American trade.
In Manuel's day the French pirate Mondragon had stood off the
Azores to intercept ships from the Americas. Complaints to the
French court brought no redress, but he had finally been captured,
only to be set free. The corsairs continued their work, sailing to
Brazil. When they were attacked by the Portuguese, they obtained
letters of marque from the French council: by 1531 they were said
to have seized three hundred ships. Thus harassed, it was natural
that the court of John III should seek an understanding with Castile.
The chief bone of contention between the Peninsular states was the
possession of the Spice Islands, which the Portuguese had reached
from the east and the Spaniards from the west. It was now necessary

to draw a line of Tordesillas in the orient. This was finally achieved by the Treaty of Saragossa of April 1529, by which Portugal retained the Moluccas, but paid Charles V 350,000 *cruzados* for the cancellation of the Spanish claim.

In the following year, John III took the decision to occupy Brazil, and divided the coast into strips, each of which was granted to a donatory, who undertook to found settlements and to open up trade. The first of these donatories, Martim Afonso de Sousa, founded the colony of São Vicente near the present port of Santos, and a village in the interior called Piratininga, now São Paulo. He also drove off the corsairs. But during the following years John III continued to make representations to the court of France, urging it to investigate the seizures and withdraw the letters of marque it had issued. In January 1535 John reminded Charles V of these complaints, pointing out that 'the cause was also his'. Only in 1539 did the French king forbid his subjects to go to Brazil or the Malagueta coast, thus affording a temporary relief.

The Portuguese crown no longer drew great revenues from its oriental enterprise. The cost of spices in the east had not greatly altered, but European prices had sharply fallen. The expense of expeditions continued to rise, and if Manuel had given many pensions to nobles, courtiers and functionaries, John III paid Spain an enormous dowry when his sister became empress (900,000 *dobras*) and a heavy indemnity for the Moluccas (350,000 *cruzados*). Manuel had already sold *juros* (bonds): John III did the same, and contracted large loans from his bankers. The profits of the spice-trade, at first divided between the crown (the Casa da India) and the private importer, passed to the mesh of interests surrounding the Portuguese factory at Antwerp, the Feitoria de Flandres, with ramifications in Germany, Spain and Italy. The pepper-trade had to support heavy purchases of silver, copper, cereals and arms. Over the twenty years from 1523 to 1543 there were deficits of over 3m. *cruzados* and interest on loans was 2,200,000: the total of 5,300,000 is equivalent to £2,377,550 in gold.

The sums voted by *cortes* now formed only a minor part of the income of the crown. In 1534 the annual budget stood at 620,000 *cruzados*, but ten years later the *cortes* of Almeirim were informed that total expenses since John's accession had been 4m. *cruzados*, out of which only 1,180,000 had been met: sums of 250,000 (twice) and 100,000 had been voted by *cortes*, but over 2,200,000 remained to be found. Of this debt almost 2m. was owed in Flanders and Spain, and the factor in Flanders reported in 1544 that the rate of interest was 25 per cent.

Meanwhile, in June 1532 the 'converted' Jews or New Christians were forbidden to leave Portugal, and captains of ships were ordered not to carry out gold or valuables belonging to them. The period of grace during which they were free from molestation had now expired, and the Portuguese court applied to Rome for permission to establish an inquisition. The requisite bull was issued at the end of 1531, but the New Christians made representations to the pope, who suspended the bull and issued a general pardon to all New Christians: this was renewed in October 1535. But in May 1536 a new bull finally instituted the Inquisition to investigate offences of heresy, apostasy, and the performance of Judaic, Muhammedan, Lutheran or magical rites. Confession and denunciation were required in cases of keeping the Sabbath on Saturday or Friday, fasting for Ramadan, praying shoeless, bathing the whole body, refusal to consume bacon or wine, the denial of hell, paradise, mass, absolution, the virgin birth or the articles of faith, and bigamy, witchcraft or the unauthorized possession of the Bible in Portuguese. The first inquisitor, the bishop of Ceuta, had little intention of using his powers, and the Inquisition remained inactive until 1539, when he was succeeded by John's brother, Henry, then archbishop of Évora, a zealot. In September 1544 the pope ordered the suspension of all sentences of the Inquisition: John III expelled the nuncio, who in turn excommunicated the inquisitors. In 1548 the papacy laid down conditions for the resumption of the Inquisition: full pardon for all those so far condemned, secrecy of abjurations, delayed execution of sentences. Henry, now raised to the cardinalate, stood out for public confession and immediate execution, but finally agreed to the pope's conditions and assumed office.

Inquisitions functioned in six Portuguese cities, Lisbon, Coimbra, Évora, Oporto, Lamego and Tomar: in the last three the tribunals were suppressed in or before 1547. In Lisbon the first *auto-da-fé* occurred in 1540: there were few in the reign of John III. In Coimbra the tribunal functioned only from 1567. Évora had its first *auto* in

1542 and six more in the next fifteen years: this unusual activity was due to the association of Cardinal Henry with the diocese. In general, neither the clergy nor the people at first displayed enthusiasm for the institution.

Since the time of Dom Manuel Portuguese scholars had gone to Italy or France, no longer simply to study theology, law or medicine, but for the humanities, philosophy and art. The circulation of printed books had greatly stimulated the desire for humanistic studies, while the new-found wealth of the spiceries enabled Manuel to build new monuments or restore and improve old ones in the style associated with his name. Among his reforms was that of the Augustinian monastic school of Santa Cruz in Coimbra (c. 1513 onwards). But the favourite resort for Portuguese scholars was now Paris, where the College of Ste-Barbe was leased and placed under a Portuguese master Diogo de Gouveia: in 1526 John III provided fifty scholarships for Portuguese to study in Paris. However, in the following decade, as Paris was rent by religious differences, the Portuguese court began to think rather of reviving learning at home. The Portuguese university founded by Dinis at Lisbon in 1290 had twice migrated to Coimbra in the fourteenth century, but had been in Lisbon since 1377: in 1537 it was finally re-established in Coimbra, where it undertook the teaching of law, rhetoric and mathematics, in addition to theology, medicine, grammar and Greek, taught since the reform at Santa Cruz. Ten years later a College of Arts was created at Coimbra to teach Latin and philosophy: it was headed by André de Gouveia, who brought teachers from Paris and Bordeaux, and had an enrolment of 1,200 in 1548 and of 1,500 by 1550. But on the death of Gouveia, it was divided by factional quarrels, intensified by accusations of heresy, in which the Inquisition intervened. In 1558 John III ordered the College of Arts to be handed over to the Jesuits.

The Society of Jesus had been introduced into Portugal through the favour of the court. In Spain the king regarded it as an enthusiasm whose energies might best be diverted to the mission field. In Portugal the royal council discussed whether the first Jesuits should go straight to the Indies. This was what Cardinal Henry then desired, but John III decided that they might establish a college at Coimbra, and in 1543 he selected Simão Rodrigues, St Ignatius' first Portuguese follower, as tutor to his son, Prince John. Cardinal Henry insisted on holding an inquiry into the orthodoxy of the Jesuits, but the society was vindicated, and he soon after took a Jesuit as his confessor. At this time Henry was piqued by the failure to set up what he regarded as a true Inquisition, and St Ignatius interceded in Rome on behalf of the Portuguese Inquisition. Henry gradually became a fervent supporter of the Jesuits and in 1558 founded a Jesuit university in his own diocese of Évora. For the next two centuries the Jesuits remained the strongest single influence in Portuguese education.

Their most famous achievements were in the missions. The Franciscans had reached Gôa in 1532, and the first Jesuits arrived in May 1542. St Francis Xavier, the Apostle of the Indies, preached in India and the Spice Islands, and in 1549 reached Japan, where he spent two years. He had intended to continue his work in China, but died in 1552, being buried in Gôa. In Brazil the first six Jesuits, led by Fr Manuel de Nóbrega, reached Bahia in 1549, accompanying the first governor-general, Tomé de Sousa. He and his followers evangelized northern and central Brazil, while further south, Fr José de Anchieta opened a school for the Indians at São Paulo: from this the famous missions of Paraguay were inaugurated in 1586.

The overseas policy of the Portuguese had now been modified. The eight fortresses in North Africa required to be heavily garrisoned and were of no economic value, with the exception of Ceuta and Tangier. In view of the financial difficulties and of the need for men, it was decided to abandon Safi and Azammur in 1542. When in 1549 the Saadian sharif of Marrakush conquered Fez and unified the Magrib, the possibility of a Christian conquest of the Magrib vanished. The garrisons were withdrawn from Alcácer-Seguir (1549) and Arzila (1550), leaving only four fortresses, Ceuta and Tangier, Santa Cruz de Guer and Mazagão. During the same period it became necessary to establish a central administration in Brazil, and in 1549 Tomé de Sousa was appointed governor of the whole area and entrusted with the task of establishing a capital at Bahia de Todos os Santos. The rich plains of the neighbouring *recôncavo* were planted with sugar, and negro slaves were introduced from West Africa. By about 1560 Brazil had overtaken Madeira as the chief source of sugar-production; the number of *engenhos* or mills was

60 in 1570 and 122 in 1585. Meanwhile, in the east, the Portuguese had reached China in about 1514 or 1516, and in 1557 their merchants were granted the territory of Macau as a factory for trade with Canton. In the previous year a Dominican, Frei Gaspar da Cruz, had attempted to preach in China, but had been forced to leave, but in 1565 the Jesuits established themselves at Macau, and the celebrated Matthew Ricci was able to reach the court of Pekin (1583).

But many of those who went to occupy the Portuguese city of Gôa or to man the factories beyond returned, like Camões, in abject poverty. Many more were lost by disease or shipwreck: Diogo do Couto set out for India with 4,000 men, and says that only half reached Gôa. The same writer notes that in 1538 when John III hoped to send forty ships to the east, he could raise only twelve, because the nobles maintained that India was not for fighting the infidel, but only for trade: the crown threatened to deprive them of their *comendas* in the military orders, but they appealed and were upheld. But many of these nobles were now uprooted from their estates, and lived, not by fighting the infidel, but off the court in Lisbon.

The wealth of the capital attracted many peasants from the land, who preferred to become servants rather than till the soil. In 1535 the Belgian humanist Cleynarts noted that agriculture was despised, and the Portuguese chose to live in indolence.[1] The *cortes* of 1525 and 1535 presented complaints of the number of court parasites, their extravagance, the redundancy of offices, the maintenance of unnecessary servants, the prevalence of gambling and so on. In 1538 a series of laws attempted to deal with these questions, forbidding the wearing of gold, silver or silks, requiring masters to pay their servants and forbidding mendicancy to those who were able to work.

By 1557 the population of Lisbon had risen to 100,000. Many of these had been drawn to the city by reports of its great wealth. Others were slaves, estimated to number a tenth of the population: they were porters, messengers, water-carriers, washerwomen. Cleynarts remarks, with exaggeration, that they and the captive Muslims

---

[1] He notes that his remarks apply to 'those who live beyond the Tagus and breathe most nearly the air of Africa'. 'If agriculture was ever despised, it is certainly in the parts where I reside': he taught at the Jesuit university at Évora.

did all the work. But more serious than the growth of the capital was the depopulation of the countryside. Many Portuguese had left the land for Seville, where it was said, again with much exaggeration, that a quarter of the population had been born in Portugal. In consequence of the drain there was a shortage of meat, corn, cheese and butter, all of which were imported. So too were stockfish, cloth, metalwork and furniture. In 1549 the factory at Antwerp was abolished, being insolvent, and in 1560 it was necessary to cease payments from the Casa da Índia: hitherto it had been the practice to pay interest on loans by notes against the Casa or the custom-houses. Now all loans were reduced to 5 per cent. In fact, this measure, like the parallel step of Philip II in Spain, was designed to check the ruinous interest-rates charged by the bankers. However, as the treasurer, the count of Castanheira, noted, 'so many motives for despair appear before me when I consider the things Your Highness must sustain and the state of your treasury that it often seems that they come more from my melancholic humour than from anything else'.

The favourites of John III were the counts of Castanheira (Dom Antonio de Ataide) and of Vimioso (Dom Francisco de Portugal). The latter had quarrelled with John's secretary, the bishop of Viseu, and raised up in his place Pedro de Alcáçova Carneiro, whose father had been a royal secretary. He established a long ascendancy at court, continuing into the following reign.

John's heir, also John, had been married in December 1552 to his cousin, Juana, the daughter of Charles V. He died in the first days of 1554, and shortly after, on 19 January, his widow gave birth to a son, Sebastian. When John III died of a stroke on 11 June 1557, after reigning for thirty-six years, Sebastian succeeded at the age of three.

5. SEBASTIAN, 1557–78

Sebastian's mother had already returned to Spain, and it was declared, on the evidence of some notes recorded by the royal secretary, that John's will had been that his widow Catarina should act as regent for her grandson. Her brother, the Emperor Charles V, who was now in retirement at Yuste, at once sent the Commissary-General of the Jesuits, St Francis Borja, to inquire about the

Portuguese succession. He was told that both Catarina and her advisers considered that Sebastian's heir was Don Carlos of Spain, the pathetic result of the marriage of Philip II to John III's sister, Maria, but that it was impossible to publish a pragmatic to this effect, since the Portuguese would go to all lengths to defend their independence.

The only surviving legitimate male members of the house of Avis were King Sebastian and his great-uncle, the Cardinal Henry, now heir-presumptive. John's other brother, Luis, had left a bastard, António, known as the Prior of Crato. Cardinal Henry soon became the centre of opposition to the regency of Queen Catarina, who was thought to be too attached to Spain: she had chosen a Spanish Dominican to be tutor to the young king. Henry gave his support to a Portuguese Jesuit and eventually won the day. Soon after, Catarina announced her intention of relinquishing the regency, though at the same time she took steps to sound opinion and found it favourable. She retained the regency until December 1562, when *cortes* met in Lisbon: she then agreed that the cardinal should govern while she remained in charge of Sebastian's education. The immediate background of this change was the great siege of Mazagão. The sharif had sent a large army against the fortress, and the governor had held it for more than two months with a garrison of 2,600 men—the last famous feat of arms of the Portuguese in the Magrib. The only reinforcements had come from the Algarve; appeals to Lisbon had failed to stir the regent in time. The same *cortes* displayed anxiety that Sebastian should be educated as a good Portuguese, and adjured the regent and tutor to bring him up 'in the customs of old Portugal ... Give him back the guard of cavalry and remove this [of halberdiers] that more befits the king of the Congo ... Let him dress Portuguese with his *camareiro-mór*, eat Portuguese, ride Portuguese, speak Portuguese, all his acts be Portuguese, and thus you will accustom him to have great love for the kingdom and its affairs.' The *cortes* also thought that great economies could be made during the minority, and urged that the university of Coimbra 'be done away with as noxious to the kingdom, and the revenues be applied to the war, and whoever wishes to learn, let him go to Salamanca or to Paris, and there will not be so many graduates in excess, or so many suits'.

The cardinal's administration lasted just over five years. *Cortes* had recommended that he should be guided by a council of twelve, and presented names: he instituted the council, but did not accept any of the nominees. He recalled Pedro de Alcáçova Carneiro, John III's secretary, who had been dismissed by Catarina, and entrusted the education of his grandnephew to a Portuguese Jesuit, the ascetic Fr Luis Gonçalves da Câmara, whose brother Frei Martim, also a Jesuit, acted as administrator of the royal household. They isolated him from possible favourites and endeavoured to train him for his duties. But he proved inexperienced about real situations, obstinate rather than resolute, and arrogant in his solitude. He practised a sort of military asceticism which included swimming and riding, the use of arms and spiritual exercises. Out of this was to emerge an obsession with the idea of becoming Christ's captain against the infidels. In 1565 he suffered from a disease which was thought to portend impotence. He improved under treatment, but in January 1567 he resumed the violent exercise to which he was addicted and again grew worse. In 1569 the doctors thought that he was better, but unfit to marry before he was eighteen.

This difficult and self-opinionated youth reached his majority at fourteen in 1568. His great-uncle the cardinal ceased to have any influence over him, and he showed little desire to consult his grandmother. In 1569 he suddenly changed his ministers, and ordered the restoration of the old palace of the Alcáçovas, where he began to reside. However, an outbreak of plague drove him from Lisbon, and he went to Sintra and Alcobaça, where he ordered the tombs of the kings of the House of Avis to be opened so that he might contemplate their bones. By the spring the plague had abated, and Sebastian returned to the capital to review the new militia, organized for the defence of Lisbon against a possible Protestant invasion (October 1570). At this time the Turks had invaded Cyprus, and the pope had appealed to the Peninsular rulers for succour. Philip II's half-brother, Don John of Austria, won the naval victory of Lepanto in 1571. The Portuguese responded by raising a fleet, but it was destroyed by storm in September 1572.

Sebastian, inspired by the example of Don John, began to dream of victories in Africa. The influence of the Câmaras was now supreme at court. His grandmother had announced her intention to return to Spain, but had been persuaded to stay, though Sebastian's visits to her were irregular and not always peaceful. The Senate or municipality of Lisbon urged that he should give up hunting, marry and set up a larger royal council, but to little purpose. In 1574 his grandmother sounded Philip II with a view to marrying Sebastian to his daughter, but Philip was cautious: in 1576 his ambassadors reported that Sebastian was being attended by many doctors. At the same time, Sebastian sent to ask Philip for an interview.

Three years earlier, after witnessing an *auto-da-fé* at Évora in which seventeen persons were burned, Sebastian had made his first visit to the Algarve. The approach to Africa excited his desire for glory; he appointed Rodrigo de Sousa, the hero of Mazagão, to govern Tangier, but was disappointed with his efforts and taunted him, as a result of which Sousa threw himself into battle and perished. Sebastian then appointed his relative the bastard prior of Crato to command Tangier. But then Sebastian returned to the Algarve, and himself crossed to Ceuta and Tangier, where he dismissed the prior. He had, in fact, slipped away from Lisbon, and wrote letters from the Algarve announcing his intention of crossing to Africa and asking his great-uncle to act as regent. He made an improvised attempt to summon the nobility of the Algarve for a campaign, but nothing had been prepared, and it took the combined efforts of his grandmother and Philip II to get him back.

In the first years of Sebastian's reign the Portuguese had been granted the territory of Macau for their trade with China, and their expansion in the east reached its fullest extent. They were already trading with Japan, and had visited the islands of Oceania, but the great sources of oriental wares were now known and as supply balanced demand, the flow of commerce became regularized: the rarity value of eastern products diminished, and the Portuguese adventurers drew most of their profit from the normal transport of goods between the ports of the east and their shipment to the west. In this network of trade-routes, east Africa came to play an important part. When the Portuguese arrived, these places, Moçambique, Kilwa, Malindi, Mombasa, Mogadishu, Patta, Pemba and Zanzibar, were ruled by Arabs and frequented by Arab, Persian and later Indian merchants, while Swahilis carried on trade with the peoples of the interior. The most prosperous was Kilwa, which then obtained gold from Sofala. As early as 1505 Almeida had built a fortress at

Sofala to seek the 'gold of Ophir', but receipts were small, and the gold collected was not enough to finance the purchase of spices in India. In the following years Sofala was eclipsed by Moçambique, which was the regular station for ships sailing to and from India. Here in 1558 was built the fortress of St Sebastian, with quarters for 1,000 men, a chapel, hospital and storehouses. Its captain, though subject to the viceroy of India, was placed in charge of the trade of the Zambesi. But although captains were placed at Sena, Quelimane and elsewhere, little advance was made into the interior, which was known to be ruled over by a potentate, the Monomotapa. In 1569 the Portuguese court sent a large expedition to trace the source of gold, but its leader and many of the men died. From 1570 Zambezia was overrun by the invasions of the Zimba, and although the Portuguese reached Manica in 1574, they found little gold.

Meanwhile, further north, the old kingdom of the Congo, which had been the first to obtain the friendship of the Portuguese, was now declining into anarchy. In 1556 the ruler of the Congo was defeated by his former vassal, the Ngola, the chief of the Kimbundu, whose title was applied to the territory of Angola. The Jesuits then persuaded the Portuguese government to send a mission to the rising power, and in 1560 Paulo Dias de Novais was sent to establish relations. He did not at this time set up a permanent factory or mission, but on his second expedition in 1574, he founded the town of São Paulo de Luanda, which thus became the first European city in West Africa south of the equator.

Still further north, Portuguese trade was centred on the fortified factories of Mina and Arguim and on the islands off the west coast, Madeira, the Cape Verdes and São Tomé and Príncipe. The first of these had been settled by Portuguese, chiefly small-holders, in the early days of the expansion. The Cape Verdes were colonized by a mixed population, partly Portuguese, partly African, while the tropical islands were settled chiefly with slaves and consisted of large estates for the production of sugar. On the mainland, the Portuguese maintained friendly relations with the peoples near their factories; their practice was not to attempt conquest but to obtain the goodwill of the native rulers, and so to send merchants and missionaries into the interior.

But the monopoly of trade to which they aspired was challenged by other nations. When the French crown forbade its ships to visit the Malagueta coast and finally suspended all letters of marque (1552), their place was taken by the English. John III had protested to Queen Mary, who replied using arguments hitherto employed by the French, that her ships traded only in places not frequented by the Portuguese. In 1555 John had taken advantage of the marriage of the English queen to the Spanish Prince Philip, and Mary had forbidden illicit voyages to Guinea, Benin and Mina. But after 1559 the French again permitted privateering, and the English, as usual, followed their example. In 1560 Elizabeth expressly denied the Portuguese monopoly, and English sailors opened trade with Guinea and attempted to set up their own factories: the protagonist of these intrusions was Sir John Hawkins, who sought control of the supply of slaves to Spanish America. He soon found that the most profitable trade was on the unfrequented coasts of Senegal and Sierra Leone, where slaves could easily be captured: thus almost all the English ships which visited the West African coast in 1569–71 were slavers.

In 1567 George Fenner had attempted to seize the port of Santiago in the Cape Verde Islands, but was beaten off. In May 1568 the Portuguese threatened war, and in 1569 confiscated the property of the English in Portugal. For two years legitimate trade between England and Portugal was suspended, and the Portuguese ordered all their ships to sail in convoy and all ships of thirty tons or more to be armed, offering inducements for the building of larger ships. But the English merchants engaged in legitimate trade with Portugal were opposed to the breach, and in February 1572 an Anglo-Portuguese treaty was negotiated: it was not concluded until 1576, when the English were granted the right to trade in the Madeiras and Azores, but no reference was made to Barbary or Guinea: in fact, the interloping voyages now dwindled away.

These difficulties were thus smoothed away when Sebastian found an opportunity to intervene in the affairs of the Magrib. The Saadian ruler had been driven out of Fez and fled to Mazagão, which he had besieged when he was still heir to the throne in 1562. He appealed for help, and Sebastian heeded. In December 1576 the king of Portugal met Philip II at Guadalupe: he appeared without advisers, though Philip was accompanied by the duke of Alba and Cristóvão de Moura. Sebastian asked to marry Philip's daughter and to receive help in an expedition against Larache. Philip finally agreed to find galleys, men and supplies for an expedition. Thus encouraged, Sebastian returned to devote himself to raising an army, borrowing money from the merchants of Lisbon, Christians and Jews, and seeking troops in Rome and Spain. The cardinal resigned his inquisitorship on hearing that Sebastian had sold favours to the New Christians and vainly urged the Lisbon municipality to intervene. The royal council consisted of young noblemen who sought to flatter the king: Queen Catarina died in February 1578, having been unable to influence him. In May a band of 2,800 Germans and Netherlanders arrived in Lisbon: they had been engaged by Conrad Roth, a German merchant who had lent Sebastian 400,000 *cruzados* at 8 per cent on the security of the royal imports of pepper. There followed an English desperado, Sir Thomas Stukeley, who had obtained ships and men from the pope on the pretext of raising Ireland against the protestant queen. Philip II had prohibited the participation of the Spaniards, though he sent a military adviser, Francisco de Aldana, and about 1,000 Andalusians ignored his ban. The Portuguese troops included 2,000 adventurers, and four regiments raised in Lisbon, Estremadura, the Alentejo and the Algarve. In June Sebastian sailed to Tangier and Arzila, leaving a council of regents, from whom he took care to exclude his great-uncle, the cardinal. His fleet of 500 ships landed the army at Arzila, where it bivouacked in 2,000 tents, unprotected by ramparts or ditches. Sebastian called a council and decided to march overland to Larache. It was only at the end of July that ox-carts were ready to carry biscuit, water and powder. He set off with about 15,000 foot and 1,500 horse, with nearly 1,000 carts and several thousand camp-followers, servants, priests and women. News was received that the sharif had left Sallee with 17,000 horse, 7,000 arquebusiers and many thousands of foot, as well as cannon. Sebastian refused to believe these reports. His army left Arzila on 29 July and reached Alcácer-Quivir on 3 August: it had consumed its rations, was overcome by heat, and was out of touch with the fleet. On 4 August Sebastian's force was faced by a vastly greater Moroccan army, but it had no choice but to fight. The battle was joined in the morning as the Moroccan cannon fired and their arquebusiers harassed the infantry. Sebastian ordered his cavalry to attack, and the adventurers almost reached the sharif, who died of a heart-attack in his litter. But his household concealed his death, and the captain of Sebastian's adventurers was shot. The whole Christian army, left with no plan of campaign, was slowly engulfed. In the 'Battle of the Three Kings', Sebastian, the sharif, the former sharif (Sebastian's protégé) all perished, as did Aldana, Stukeley, the commander of the Germans, and some 8,000 of Sebastian's army. Nearly 15,000 fell into the hands of the Moroccans: barely a hundred succeeded in escaping to Arzila or Tangier.

6. HENRY, CARDINAL-KING, 1578–80

The first reports of the disaster of Alcácer-Quivir reached Lisbon on 10–11 August, and although the governors withheld the news, rumours quickly circulated. The cardinal was summoned from Alcobaça, and on his arrival the fact of the defeat was made public, though the fate of the king was still unknown: it was only on 24 August that it was learned that Sebastian's body had been buried in the house of the governor of Alcácer The legends of his survival probably took root during the period of doubt. On the night of the defeat some refugees reached Arzila and clamoured to be admitted: the guards were at first afraid to open the gate, but one of the party shouted that the king was there, and another wrapped himself in a mantle, and so passed in. This incident may be the origin of the lore of Sebastianism, the consecration of the national love of rumour.

The cardinal was now proclaimed king. He had been born in January 1512 and was the last surviving son of Manuel. Two of his brothers had issue; one had left a legitimate daughter Catarina, married to the duke of Bragança: the other, Luis, was the father of the bastard António, prior of Crato, who had long attempted to divest himself of his ecclesiastical status, but now succeeded in escaping from Morocco in the guise of a parish priest. A daughter of Manuel, Leonor, had married the Emperor Charles V, and was the mother of Philip II of Spain, who had strengthened his ties with Portugal by marrying a daughter of John III; but both she and her son Don Carlos were dead, and Philip was now married to Elizabeth of Valois, so that Philip's claim lay through his mother, not through his wife.

Although the cardinal was of advancing years and in declining health, he announced in January 1579 that he was disposed to seek a papal dispensation to leave the church and marry. The only way of reconciling independence with legitimacy appeared to be the union of the cardinal with the daughter of the duchess of Bragança, a girl of thirteen: that this disparate match should have been seriously considered is an indication of the power of the monarchical principle and of its identification with legalism. But the cardinal's attempts to obtain a dispensation were easily thwarted by the king of Spain, who now sent the duke of Osuna to Portugal to assert his rights, 'clear and evident in the light of general law and of that peculiar to the kingdom of Portugal'. Philip's representative, Cristóvão de Moura, set about bribing influential Portuguese, a task much facilitated by the concentration of authority in a few hands. He won over Pedro de Alcáçova Carneiro, part of the nobility and the municipality of Lisbon, which two hundred years before had identified itself with the resistance to the Spanish succession. On 1 March *cortes* assembled in Lisbon, the nobles in the church of the Carmo, the clergy in the cathedral, and the commoners in the convent of São Francisco. The ostensible purpose was to support the dispensation for Henry's marriage, but the Cardinal-King asked each arm to elect a small permanent committee of *definidores*, intending that they should in-vestigate the rival claims to the throne. The commoners were at first reluctant to reduce themselves to a committee and elected forty. But by 1 June, when *cortes* were again convoked, they readily undertook to obey Henry, to accept the governors he should nominate, and to maintain order: they were then dismissed. On 12 June Henry ap-pointed five governors to act as regents on his death.

Shortly before, on 30 May, Philip II had declared before the *cortes* of Castile that his claim was supported by the most expert Spanish, Italian and Portuguese jurisconsults: the evidence was presented in Lisbon in the following month. The only active opposi-tion came from the prior of Crato, who was cordially disliked by Henry, not approved of by the nobility or clergy, but favoured by the populace, if only for lack of any other national candidate. His friends put it about that his parents had been married, and this had caused Henry to banish him from court and publish a declaration of his bastardy, later withdrawn. He went to Coimbra, where he was warmly received by the students. When Edward Walton arrived in Lisbon on 14 July with gifts from Queen Elizabeth for Dom António and the duchess of Bragança, he soon formed the opinion that there was no likelihood of opposing Philip, who would, if necessary, use force. Henry himself had suggested that Philip should avoid the union of the two crowns by presenting one of his children as candidate, but this had been in vain: Osuna and Moura continued an intensive campaign of bribery in order to gain control of *cortes*, even proposing that commoners should be ineligible to elect the successor.

Meanwhile, the kingdom was drained of money for the ransom of the victims of al-Qaṣr. The sharif demanded the cession of the Portuguese fortresses in return for Sebastian's body: this was refused, and he accepted 60,000 *cruzados*. Eighty live nobles held at Fez were valued collectively at 400,000: the crown contributed a quarter, and the families sent jewels, cloth and letters of credit. When the ambassador, Dom Francisco da Costa, had sold these, he was still 120,000 *cruzados* short, but sixty-nine survivors were released in November 1579: Costa remained as a pledge for what was owing, but died unredeemed. Of the captives at Marrakush, forty nobles were released at from 2,000 to 10,000 a head. Thousands of less fortunate prisoners were scattered over the country, and redeemed themselves piecemeal out of a common chest: one of the pledges offered by Philip II was that he would complete the redemption of the prisoners.

On 11 January 1580 the Portuguese *cortes* assembled at Almeirim and Santarém. They were to elect judges who would decide the succession. The first two were supporters of the duchess of Bragança, and Osuna and Moura protested and obtained their removal. The commoners had now been largely purged of adherents of Dom António. When the patriot Febo Moniz demanded a wider consultation, the Cardinal-King proclaimed penalties for all who gave shelter to the prior of Crato. On 15 January the bishop of Leiria appeared at Santarém, and urged that the commoners should come to terms with Philip: he held that Henry was entitled to designate his successor. This provoked great protests, and Febo Moniz went to Lisbon to remonstrate with the king. But Henry was now moribund. He could only advise the commoners that he thought that Philip's claim was the best. The same night consent was sought for negotiations with Spain: the clergy were in favour; the nobility were now divided, but finally agreed by a majority of one; the commoners declared that they would die rather than obey Philip II. The representatives of the chief towns were called to Henry's bedside and urged to come to heel. The Spanish representatives redoubled their pressure. On 28 January Henry fell into a coma. The same night António, who had been deprived of his titles and rank in November, appeared in Almeirim. He was followed next day by the duchess of Bragança. On 31 January the Cardinal-King expired.

It now fell to the five governors to preserve order until the judges should determine the succession. Three of the governors had been suborned by Moura; one was undeclared, and one was against the Spanish succession. They had at their disposal 2,000 soldiers, but they feared that the appearance of António would lead to popular disturbances and urged the commoners to work with them. In reply, Febo Moniz demanded an inquiry into the cases of bribery, and urged that embassies be sent to Spain to assure Philip that justice would be done, and to Rome to ask that Philip should be restrained from violence. No precedent existed of the death of a monarch during the sessions of *cortes*: the closure was a prerogative of the crown, but the governors decided that they were entitled to exercise it. The commoners then appointed a standing committee.

Philip II sent soothing offers to the governors, the *cortes*, the cities, the Braganças and the prior. He promised to dismiss no one appointed to office by Henry, to receive Portuguese in his household, to defend Portugal, India and Africa, to have his son educated in Portugal, to ransom the prisoners in Morocco, to supply corn. At the same time, he prepared troops under the duke of Alba for the occupation. He himself waited at Guadalupe, where two Portuguese emissaries asked for an undertaking that he would not use force. He kept them waiting for more than two weeks, and then informed them that he refused to allow anyone to pronounce on the rights of his case. In May he gave the governors a month in which to obey. Their chief fear was of losing control of the people. They therefore decided to summon *cortes* once more, hoping to ensure the election of procurators favourable to Philip. The first choice of Lisbon showed that this was not possible. On 18 June the frontier town of Elvas declared for Philip: this was a concealed invasion, and it provoked a general commotion.

Next day António was proclaimed king at Santarém amidst scenes of popular enthusiasm. He entered Lisbon, the governors having retired to Setúbal. On 27 June Spanish troops occupied Évora, Arraiolos and Montemór and reached Setúbal, whence they were carried by ship to the mouth of the Tagus. Antonio's forces were mainly improvised, and he had few officers and little money. Alba reduced the fortress of Cascais with cannon-fire, and hanged its governor and three others. His troops met António's irregulars on the western outskirts of the capital and had little difficulty in putting them to flight in the battle of Alcântara. After his defeat, António fled northwards to Santarém and Coimbra, where the students enlisted with him. He then retreated to Oporto, but could not hold it. For several months he remained in Portugal in hiding, and in May 1581 he left for France. Philip had entered Portugal in December 1580 and received the homage of the duchess of Bragança by proxy, together with that of the other nobles and ecclesiastics. Only the Azores remained loyal to Dom António.

VI

THE THREE PHILIPS

The crown of Portugal was thus annexed by force. If there was no national uprising like that which had brought the house of Avis to power in 1383, this was partly because the Spain of 1580 was far stronger than the Castile of 1383, while the defeat at Alcácer-Quivir had weakened and discouraged the Portuguese. Moreover Philip II played his hand with far greater skill than Juan I: he himself was half Portuguese and he made full use of his Portuguese intimates, and of the Hispanophile members of the Portuguese nobility and church. Furthermore, the growth of autocracy, of the machinery of government and of new devices of war conspired to limit the possibilities of improvised resistance. The Cardinal-King himself had effectively neutralized his unruly nephew, the prior of Crato, the only possible actor for the part of John of Avis.

The champions of Portuguese independence had for a moment looked to the English treaty and sought help from Elizabeth, but the prudent queen had little confidence in her power to face Philip on land, and she could not bridge the gulf now opened between her national religion and the counter-reformed faith of the Portuguese, a gulf far more profound than the schismatic aberrations of the fourteenth century. For half a century the interests of Portugal had seemed to lie with the Spanish Habsburgs rather than with their rivals. Portugal and Spain had shared the first-fruits of the expansion of Europe and must together defend the settlement made by the papacy in their favour.

Philip issued letters convening *cortes* for the end of January 1581, and instructed the towns that no one who had been a follower of Dom António, or favoured by him, was either to elect or be elected. This made it necessary to delay the opening until 25 March. The *cortes*, meeting at Tomar, then declared Philip II to be Philip I of Portugal, and he issued a pardon to those who had sided with António, with rather numerous exceptions. His guarantees of Portuguese autonomy were published only late in 1582. In theory the

163

union of the two crowns was a purely personal affair. In Philip's absence he would be represented in Portugal by a governor, who would be either a member of his family no further removed than cousin, or in default of this, a Portuguese. He himself would be accompanied by a Council of Portugal of six members, through whom he would transact all Portuguese affairs. *Cortes* should meet only in Portugal, and all existing officials, civil, military or ecclesiastical, and all existing rights and privileges were confirmed. The language, administration of justice, coinage and military organization would remain entirely autonomous. However, Philip rejected requests to withdraw the Spanish garrisons and reduce taxation, and gave no reply to others: that he should marry a Portuguese, that his heir should be brought up in Portugal, that the New Christians should be excluded from office.

Philip now began to look for a governor. The widowed Empress was called and spent a few months in Lisbon, but Philip finally appointed his nephew, the Cardinal-Archduke Albert of Austria. Three Portuguese were appointed as his advisers, the archbishop of Lisbon; the inveterate placeman Pedro de Alcáçova Carneiro; and Miguel de Moura. In February 1583 Philip ended his long stay in Portugal, taking his Council of Portugal with him.

He had already prepared a fleet to reduce the Azores. Seven of the islands, under a magistrate, Dr Ciprião de Figueiredo, with headquarters at Angra on Terceira, had declared for António: two, São Miguel and Santa Maria, had recognized Philip. A first expedition against Terceira had a rude reception when the half-wild bulls of the island were driven into the troops as they sought to land. Meanwhile, António had reached England, and failing to persuade Elizabeth to make war on Philip, passed on to France, where Catharine of Medici, in return for the promise of the cession of Brazil, sent 800 men to reinforce Terceira and gathered a fleet of fifty ships and 5,000 men under Philippe Strozzi. In June 1582 this expedition departed, hoping to reduce the two islands which adhered to Philip and to capture the Spanish treasure-fleet. The Spanish admiral, Alvaro de Bazán, marquis of Santa Cruz, sailed to São Miguel and reinforced its capital, and on 26 July routed the French fleet and killed Strozzi. António left Terceira for France in November: he succeeded in sending small reinforcements, but Santa Cruz had little difficulty in reducing Terceira. After this the pretender led a shifting life in France and England, threatened from time to time with assassination. In 1584 his prospects seemed to brighten, for Elizabeth found herself unable to avoid a breach with Spain, and Philip began in 1586 to prepare his Invincible Armada for the conquest of England. It was built largely in Lisbon under the supervision of Santa Cruz, who died before the departure. The expedition sailed and failed in 1588. In the following year Elizabeth sent Drake with thirty ships and 15,000 men to attempt to establish António at Lisbon. The invaders sacked Corunna, and coasted southwards to Peniche, which they raided. But the forts of the Tagus were too strong for them to enter the river, and Lisbon was well defended. António's supporters were cowed by a few acts of terrorism, and gave no response as he approached. The expedition therefore retired. António's attempts to raise further expeditions in France came to nothing: he died in Paris in 1595.

Meanwhile, Philip favoured in Portugal the institutions which might tend to link the two countries together, the Society of Jesus and the Inquisition in particular. In 1580 he had sent Filippo Terzi to complete the Jesuit church of São Roque: on this church was bestowed the collection, of unprecedented size, of relics assembled by the third son of St Francis Borgia. Duly authenticated, they were carried through the streets in a veritable march of the saints to confound the heretics as the Armada was made ready.

The annexation spread alarm among the New Christians, who certainly expected that under Spanish rule the Inquisition would become more rigorous. In the popular belief that Sebastian was not dead, but that he would return to rule again, there is a strong element of New Christian Messianism, expressed in prophetic and political poems and songs. In 1591 the Archduke Albert appointed a visitor of the Inquisition to Brazil, where the New Christians, some wealthy merchants who financed the sugar- and slave-trade or farmed taxes, and some poor craftsmen, were subjected to a severer control and obliged to conform. In Lisbon one of the main functions of the Inquisition was now the repression of protestantism: its familiars closely watched, and at times persecuted the foreign merchants, and regularly searched ships for illicit religious or political propaganda.

The national rumour of Sebastianism had now taken firm root.

The pitiful reality of the foolhardy prince who had led his people to disaster was forgotten. Sebastian was thought to have been a hero, who would one day reappear, the one possible deliverer from the Spanish yoke. As early as 1503 the Jew Isaac Abarbanel had foretold the coming of the Messiah, and in 1526 a claimant had been revealed. In 1541 a cobbler from Trancoso, Gonçalo Anes, had been brought before the Inquisition because of the strange prophecies and portents revealed in his *Trovas*. This mystical hope was now transmuted into Sebastianism: it was not long before a series of impostors transmuted themselves into Sebastians.

The first, a mysterious and handsome youth, appeared at Penamacor, where he put it about that he had been in Africa and was doing a penance for seven years: he described the battle of Al-Qaṣr and spoke a gibberish he said was Arabic. He soon formed a little court, calling one of his followers Cristóvão de Távora, Sebastian's favourite, and another the bishop of Guarda. Probably, he intended only to draw on local charity, but news of his doings reached Lisbon and an inquiry was ordered. Philip was highly sensitive to displays of national feeling, and Spanish troops were detached to arrest the band. The 'king of Penamacor' was shown to have been born at Alcobaça and to have gone with a maker of rosaries to Lisbon, where he had been adopted by a rich widow of one of the victims of the disaster: the parish priest had dismissed him, and he had gone to remote Penamacor. He was exhibited in Lisbon for the space of a morning and then sent to the galleys.

The second false Sebastian was the son of a stone-mason in the Azores. After being a novice in two monasteries, he set up as a hermit at Ericeira. He did penance with groans and cries, claiming to be Sebastian. He conferred the titles of marquis, count and governor of Lisbon on a wealthy farmer, who became commander of his 'army', said to number 800, but equipped only with agricultural implements. His 'royal letters' led to an inquiry, but two magistrates were killed by his followers, who fought a sharp engagement with the troops: he was hanged and quartered, and about 200 of his allies were executed for their part in the rebellion.

Two other 'Sebastians' never came to Portugal. One of the dead king's confessors, who had supported António, Fr Miguel dos Santos, was confessor to the nuns in a convent at Madrigal, the birthplace of

Isabella the Catholic, where there lived an illegitimate daughter of Don John of Austria. He presented to her one Gabriel de Espinosa, a pastry-cook, who pretended to be King Sebastian, and obtained some jewels from her, which he foolishly allowed to be seen: the element of political intrigue was supplied by the confessor, who corresponded with sympathizers in Portugal. The last Sebastian appeared in 1598 in Venice, where there was a colony of adherents of Dom António and Portuguese Jews. He did not speak Portuguese—owing to a vow he had taken, he said. At the behest of the Spanish ambassador, he was arrested. Dom João de Castro, an opponent of Philip II, took up his case, and it was arranged to get him to Paris, but he was captured in Tuscany and carried off to Naples, where he was identified as a Calabrian, Marco Tullio Caltizzone, and condemned to the galleys for his imposture. Funds were collected to rescue him, and he was executed in 1603.[1]

During the reign of Philip II (I), the conditions of autonomy agreed at Tomar were in general adhered to. The Portuguese may have noted with concern that in 1590 Philip insisted on the appointment of a Castilian as viceroy of Aragon and swept away much of the autonomy of Aragon. But in Portugal he continued to appoint Portuguese, as he had promised. What could not be preserved was an independent foreign policy: the enemies of Spain became the enemies of Portugal, and the consequences for Lisbon, with its heavy dependence on foreign trade, were much graver than for land-locked Castile. In the years after the Armada, Philip prohibited the use of Portuguese ports by English ships, thus suspending the legitimate trade and reviving the activities of the English corsairs. Five years later, the same policy was applied to the Dutch; fifty Dutch ships in the Tagus were seized, and all further trade was forbidden. The consequence was that a Dutch resident in Lisbon named Cornelis Houtman, who had visited the east in Portuguese ships, now offered to show his compatriots the route to the east. He sailed for Java in 1595; five years later forty ships were freighted, and the spice-trade was gradually wrested from the Portuguese. In 1602 the Dutch East India Company was launched: it soon rewarded its shareholders with ample dividends.

---

[1] Sebastianists continued to appear from time to time. In 1666 the Inquisition punished the daughter of a guitar-player in Lisbon, who claimed to have visited the Hidden Isle and spoken to Sebastian and seen King Arthur, Enoch, Elijah and St John.

However, the trade of the east no longer dominated the Portuguese economy as it had for a time in the days of Dom Manuel. In the second half of the sixteenth century the settlement of Brazil proceeded apace, and its sugar-mills increased from five to 125. A succession of caravels and hulks delivered chests of sugar at Lisbon, whence it was distributed far and wide. If Portugal as a whole seemed impoverished and inert, the causes do not lie solely in the Spanish occupation. Since the time of Manuel, the practice of entailing estates had greatly increased, and many elder sons, having spent or distributed their fortunes, possessed quantities of land which they could neither alienate, nor afford to improve. The religious revival which followed the Counter-Reformation drew many younger sons and daughters into the church and led to the founding of many new monasteries and convents—some 350 in a century—with a further reduction in the active population and of revenues to the crown. Attempts were now made to limit the litigation arising out of entailments and to enable families to make provision for younger sons, but without conspicuous success.

Writers of the period refer frequently to the depopulation of the countryside and to the high proportion of uncultivated land. For a century the city, the sea, the army and the church had drawn men from the soil, and for much of that period the country had been obliged to import cereals and other staple foods. The new compilation of the laws of Portugal, ordered by Philip II and completed in 1602, the Ordenações Filipinas, reveal a general concern to protect agriculture and to lessen the burdens borne by the farmer. Attempts were made to control hunting, still the favourite occupation of the nobility, to limit seigneurial rights, to prevent the pledging or seizure of farm equipment, to enable village assemblies to settle disputes which might otherwise go to court, and to induce the *corregedores* to put idle land to use.

The death of Philip II (I) in 1598 and the accession of his son Philip III (II) brought with it a less respectful attitude towards the autonomy of Portugal. The young king had none of his father's industry and devotion to duty, and left the affairs of government to a Valencian nobleman, the duke of Lerma, who scandalously enriched his family and friends and resorted to endless devices to raise money, but did nothing to stimulate prosperity. His most positive achievements were the negotiation of peace with England in 1605 and the conclusion of a twelve-year truce with the Dutch in 1609—not applicable to the Portuguese east.

The second Philip did not hold *cortes* in Portugal on his accession and did not visit the country at all until 1619, towards the end of his reign. He soon appointed Spaniards to the Council of Portugal in Madrid, as auditors of the Portuguese treasury and as permanent inspectors of the treasury and Casa da Índia in Lisbon (1602). In 1615 he attempted to nominate the count of Salinas, a Spaniard, to govern Portugal, but in the face of general protests, he gave way and appointed the archbishop of Lisbon. However, in 1617 he nominated the same count, bestowing on him the Portuguese title of Marquis of Alenquer. Two years later, he paid his only visit to Portugal, swore to uphold the privileges and attempted to allay popular discontent by distributing largesse.

The receipts of the Spanish crown from American silver were now dwindling sharply, and although the revenues to be drawn from Portugal were in theory limited, Lerma was soon tempted by the prospect of special transactions, such as the sale of privileges to the New Christians. They first offered 170,000 *cruzados* for permission to leave Portugal, and this was favourably received. They were then offered the right to remain, together with a general pardon and admission to all offices in Portugal: the fee demanded was ten times that for departure. By this device the Spanish crown would raise a vast sum in Portugal and also get a Portuguese administration of its own choosing. The Portuguese were bitterly opposed to the scheme, and the protest of the governors being ignored, the three archbishops went to Spain to lodge their objections. They offered to find 800,000 *cruzados* in compensation; but the Portuguese towns refused to pay, and the Spaniards reopened negotiations with the New Christians. The right to office was dropped, and the New Christians were offered only absolution and toleration for the full sum of 1,700,000 *cruzados*, which was in fact converted into an exaction. In 1610 all privileges granted to the New Christians were withdrawn and the Inquisition was resumed.

Philip III (II) died in 1621, and the crown passed to his son Philip IV (III), who, though much better able to rule than his spiritless father, entrusted power to the count-duke of Olivares, and devoted himself to the pursuit of pleasure. Unlike Lerma, Olivares strove to maintain the power of the Spanish monarchy and recommended his master to pursue a policy of rigorous centralization, assimilating all his kingdoms to Castile, by persuasion or corruption, or if necessary by force.

The truce with the Dutch now expired; and Olivares aligned himself with those who were in favour of renewing the war. The Dutch, who had had designs of seizing part of Brazil, now formed a West India Company, which began to prey on Portuguese and Spanish shipping. In 1624 it seized Bahia, the capital of Brazil, and occupied the neighbouring sugar-plantations. In reply, Olivares organized the 'expedition of the vassals' of Spaniards and Portuguese. In March 1625 it drove out the invaders, who again returned to privateering. On this occasion, the Portuguese nobility and towns contributed their share, and the success of the operation encouraged Olivares to press forward his design for unification in the Peninsula. He proposed to denationalize the Portuguese nobility by calling it to serve in Madrid and by intermarriage with the houses of Castile, to impose new taxation in Portugal without reference to *cortes*, and to enforce a general military service. Thus in July 1628 he demanded a forced loan for defence, which was to be extended to the clergy, and also reopened negotiations with the New Christians. His underlying intentions had been revealed in his dealings with the Catalans, and they spread consternation in both the autonomous areas. Thus when, in 1630, the Dutch West India Company seized Pernambuco, the second city of northern Brazil, the Portuguese no longer displayed any eagerness to collaborate with Olivares for its recovery. It remained in Dutch hands, and in 1636 the States-General appointed Johan Maurits of Nassau as its governor. He sent forces to Africa which captured Mina and part of Angola; and during the following years the Dutch exploited 120 of the 166 sugar-mills in the province, introducing some 2,300 slaves.[1] They were unable to take Bahia, but the governor of Bahia was also unable to dislodge them.

In Portugal the realization of Olivares' aims was brought nearer by the appointment as governor of the widowed duchess of Mantua,

---

[1] The Portuguese Brazilians continued to own 60 per cent of the *engenhos;* the Dutch owned 32 per cent, and the Jews 6 per cent. The farming of taxes was largely in Jewish hands.

a cousin of the king of Spain. Her secretary, Miguel de Vasconcelos, was regarded as a tool of Olivares in his policy of unification. In previous years Lisbon had resisted the imposition of new taxes, and in 1637 attempts to collect them by force had led to a revolt in Évora. In 1638 Olivares summoned a number of prominent Portuguese to Madrid in the hope of furthering his aims, and of raising troops in Portugal for service against the enemies of Spain. These now included France; and Richelieu, aware of Olivares' difficulties, sent to Lisbon a former consul, Saint-Pé, with instructions to make soundings about a revolt and to offer support to a Portuguese pretender, such as the duke of Bragança, with men and ships.

The duke was the nearest collateral of the house of Avis, being the son of John III's daughter Catarina: he was also the leading aristocrat and greatest landowner in Portugal, and overlord of some 80,000 people. His palace was at Vila Viçosa in the Alentejo, the region of great estates, and his willingness or refusal to act would undoubtedly influence the attitude of his countrymen. The reigning duke was a prudent fellow and refused to be involved in Richelieu's intrigues. But a group of Portuguese nobles began to conspire together, and approached his brother Dom Duarte, who had served in the forces of the Empire: he also refused, and returned to Germany. In 1639 Olivares attempted to force the duke's hand by declaring him 'Governor of the Arms of Portugal' and asking him to raise 1,000 men. The cautious duke made objections, but these were overruled, and he began to equip his private army.

But in the middle of 1640 the Catalans rebelled against Philip IV and murdered his viceroy in a popular tumult. Agents of Richelieu had been busy in the Principality, which duly offered its allegiance to Louis XIV. It was now urgent for Olivares to obtain reinforcements to put down the Catalan rebellion. It was also the time for the Portuguese to make their decision. The group of conspirators, nobles and officials, negotiated with Dr João Pinto Ribeiro, the agent of Bragança in Lisbon, and persuaded the duke to take the throne. In November there were clandestine meetings, and it was decided to strike on 1 December, at nine in the morning. In view of the duke's caution, he was not told of the advanced stage of the plot. The word was spread among numbers of patriotic citizens at the last moment, but many of these were not optimistic of success. However, on the morning of 1 December the conspirators assembled in the Terreiro do Paço, and as nine sounded from the cathedral clock, they swarmed up the palace staircase, dispersed the guard and sought out Vasconcelos, who was shot and defenestrated. The duchess screamed for help from the palace windows, but without effect: she was arrested. There was no further resistance, and three governors were appointed until the duke should arrive.

VII

THE RESTORATION

1. JOHN IV, 1640–56

John IV arrived in Lisbon on 6 December and was crowned on a platform erected in the Terreiro do Paço on the 15th. At Vila Viçosa his favourite occupations had been the chase and musical composition, 'adjusting the consonance of the solfa'. He might not have risked his vast possessions in a long and arduous struggle for the throne had it not been for the resolution of his Spanish wife, Luisa de Guzmán, a sister of the duke of Medina Sidonia, the leading nobleman of Andalusia, and no friend to his distant relative, Olivares. The heir-apparent, Teodósio (born in 1634), was to predecease his father, but Luisa's other sons, Afonso (b. 1643) and Pedro (b. 1648), were both kings of Portugal: and her daughter Catharine (b. 1638) was to be queen of England.

The new king confirmed all existing officials in their posts: the few Spanish garrisons, in the forts defending the Tagus and at Setúbal and Viana, had quickly surrendered. For the moment an invasion was improbable since the Spaniards were deeply engaged in Catalonia, where the rebellious Catalans were about to proclaim Louis XIII of France Count of Barcelona. Two Portuguese envoys, both Jesuits, arrived there the following day, and reported great enthusiasm for the Portuguese revolution, adding that if they had arrived a few days earlier the Catalans would have aknowledged John IV.

But John had no army, no other allies, and only limited resources. The national studs had been discontinued after 1580, and there was a lack of horses; the navy was in disarray; the frontier fortifications had long been neglected. A Council of War, created on 11 December, appointed a governor and staff to each province, with powers to conscript all able-bodied men between the ages of fifteen and seventy, exempting farmers and the only sons of widows. The defence of each province was entrusted to its own recruits. *Cortes* assembled at Lisbon on 28 January 1641, to provide funds for troops and warships. The cost of raising 4,000 horse and 20,000 infantry was set at 1,800,000 *cruzados* (later increased), and this was to be met by a property-tax of 10 per cent applicable to all classes except the clergy, which would contribute a lump sum according to the resources of each diocese: there were also duties on trade and taxes on holders of public office.

The new government needed allies. The enthusiasm of the Catalans was shared by the French and the Dutch, who at first supposed that the separation of Portugal would bring Spain to her knees. When in February 1641 John sent missions to these countries, great things were expected of Richelieu, in view of the offers extended by Saint-Pé in 1638, and the ambassadors were instructed to ask for men and ships and also for a 'league' which would bind France to Portugal and might include Holland and other allies. A favourable result seemed assured since Richelieu had sent Saint-Pé to Lisbon with a promise that France would include Portugal in any treaty with Spain.

But even more urgent than an agreement with France was the question of a settlement with the Dutch. During the Spanish occupation, the Dutch East India Company had made inroads against the Portuguese settlements in the East, while the West India Company still held Pernambuco, where Johan Maurits had established a splendid, but precarious military administration. To an independent Portugal with a hostile Spain to her east, the security of the seas was imperative, and John IV therefore sought to conciliate the Dutch by assuring them of the commercial privileges they had formerly enjoyed at Lisbon, while attempting to divert their rapacity from Brazil toward the Spanish treasure-fleet and the port of Cádiz. In order to avoid recognizing the Dutch seizure of northern Brazil, the Portuguese ambassador to Holland was to ask not for a formal commercial treaty but for a truce for ten years. But the Dutch, though they had greeted the Portuguese revolution as a blow to Spain, were not disposed to pay anything for a triumph which they regarded as a free gift. When John restored the privileges of the Dutch merchants, the States-General prohibited the seizure of Portuguese ships, but affected to consider the Portuguese colonies as still under Spanish control and the supposedly autonomous West India Company instructed Johan Maurits to try to occupy Bahia.

By May 1641 Richelieu, unwilling to compromise his influence over the Dutch by giving guarantees to John IV, retracted his

promise and informed the Portuguese that he could not enter a formal league without the concurrence of Holland and Sweden. The
Portuguese protested, but finally accepted the treaty of 1 July, in
which a secret article limited the aid of the French to what their
allies would agree to. This at least enabled the Portuguese negotiators
to return to Lisbon accompanied by a French fleet under the command of Richelieu's nephew, de Brézé. It now became the object of
Portuguese policy to obtain the elusive French league, while Richelieu preferred to keep his hands free to make peace with Spain.

Meanwhile on 12 June the mission to Holland had concluded the
ten-year truce, to begin forthwith in Europe and a year later in the
east. The Portuguese would recruit officers and buy munitions in
Holland in return for commercial privileges in Lisbon. These last
included important new concessions: freedom of conscience and
worship in Portugal, which thus limited the jurisdiction of the
Inquisition against protestants, and a monopoly of the right to hire
ships to Portugal, the Portuguese undertaking to use no other foreign
ships to go to Brazil. The Portuguese had asked for the return of the
parts of Brazil and West Africa held by the Dutch, in return for
compensation, either financial or territorial and, if the latter, at the
expense of Spain. The Dutch had pointed out that such a settlement
had no place in a ten-year truce, and the question of Brazil was
therefore omitted from the treaty.

The treaty was much criticized in Lisbon, both because it seemed
to open the legal trade of Brazil to the Dutch and because of the
concession of freedom of worship; but the mood of the Dutch was to
give little and ask much, and John IV had nothing to bargain with.
Meanwhile, the attitude of the States-General had influenced not
only France, but also England. In February 1641 an approach had
been made to Charles I, who received a Portuguese mission on 8
April, despite the objections of the Spanish ambassador. It sought
friendly relations, the restoration of trade, and permission to engage
English troops and to buy arms and ships, no mention being made
of the ancient treaties. In the public audience Charles I expressed
pleasure at the independence of Portugal and urged John IV to
fortify his frontiers. The London merchants were evidently anxious
to resume the Portuguese trade which was to be regarded as 'the very
best branch of all our European commerce'.

The negotiations proceeded smoothly until news was received of the treaty with the Dutch. The English commissioners then demanded most-favoured-nation treatment, particularly in respect of the exercise of their religion in Portugal and the right to supply ships and to trade with Portuguese possessions. The Portuguese gave an assurance that no nation should receive greater privileges than England, a proposition that later led to much scrabbling among documents to find out what precisely could be claimed. The religious issue was referred to the archbishop of Lisbon, and a commission of ecclesiastics ruled that liberty of conscience could not be expressly conceded, but that 'negative action' might be taken, and there could be no objection in principle to granting the English the same treatment as other foreigners. The monopoly of the hire of shipping already granted to the Dutch was obviated by agreement to examine the question in two years: as Luso-Dutch relations deteriorated, the English were able to fill the gap. On 29 January 1642 the treaty was signed, and the ancient Alliance was revived in a new form, though for the moment its effect was limited by the troubles in England between king and Parliament.[1]

The separation of Portugal did not precipitate the collapse of Spain and, as Saint-Pé soon informed Richelieu, John IV was not disposed to rush in to invade the neighbouring country: his Council of War had to start from almost nothing, and his ducal estate of Vila Viçosa was only a few miles from the frontier. Nevertheless, the Treaty of 1 June bound Portugal to conduct active war. The first engagement was a skirmish between the garrisons of Elvas and Badajoz on 9 July, but both sides were most intent on restoring fortifications and accumulating munitions.

Meanwhile, Olivares sought to bring down the Braganças by means of a palace plot, while the Portuguese joined with their allies in an attempt to precipitate the separation of Andalusia. The Hispanophile party in Portugal was small but influential: the duchess of Mantua, held in the convent of Xabregas, remained in touch with her friends. The archbishop of Braga, though he had attended John's

---

[1] A mission to Scandinavia achieved nothing in Denmark, but concluded a treaty of peace, friendship and commerce with Sweden on 29 July 1641, by which Portugal obtained supplies of muskets, pikes, armour and metal, to be paid for in sugar, spices, salt and coin.

coronation, was suspected of siding with her, as were the Inquisitor-General, the marquis of Vila-Real, and others. One small party of Portuguese nobles had gone to Andalusia; others who were in Spain or overseas remained in Philip's service: in this way, Ceuta, the earliest Portuguese possession in Africa, passed under the Spanish flag. The existence of a conspiracy in Lisbon was reported by a treasury-officer who laid information: on 28 July 1641 John summoned the royal council and announced the arrest of the leaders. A month later, four noblemen were beheaded and six commoners hanged: in the case of the young duke of Caminha the only charge was that he had failed to denounce his father. The archbishop died in prison, but the inquisitor was released early in 1643.

During these events preparations were on foot to revolutionize Andalusia in circumstances that remain mysterious. John IV had proposed an attack on Cádiz to the Dutch, and it was for this that de Brézé's fleet arrived in Lisbon on 9 August: it was joined by thirteen Portuguese warships and six caravels. Louis XIII gave his approval to the expedition, but by the time it reached Cádiz the place was garrisoned and guarded. Admiral Gijsels reached the Tagus with a Dutch fleet on 10 September, but by then the attack on Cádiz had failed. Meanwhile, messengers had passed between John and his brother-in-law, the duke of Medina Sidonia. Olivares ordered his arrest, and that of his nephew, the marquis of Ayamonte: the duke declared that he was the victim of the intrigues of a meddling priest and considered John IV a traitor: he was spared, but Ayamonte forfeited his life.

During the excursion against Cádiz a Spanish force of about 8,000 men had attacked Olivença and been repulsed, and in the following year, 1642, the Portuguese under Sancho Manuel, also with some 8,000 men, held the frontier of Beira against the duke of Alba. In April John sent Dom Vasco Luis da Gama (later marquis of Niza) to France to press for the league, pointing out that the failure of de Brézé's expedition had not been the fault of the Portuguese, who had raised 3,000 horse and 20,000 foot in a year and a half with almost nothing to start from. John asked for a guarantee that Portugal would be included in any peace and for a loan of 600,000 cruzados. But Mazarin, like his predecessor, refused the desired alliance.

In September 1642 John again summoned *cortes* and asked them to find 2,400,000 *cruzados*. The three estates met in three separate monasteries and the commoners asked that the subsidy be first apportioned between the three estates, each of which might then consider how to raise its quota. The two privileged classes protested, and although the famous Jesuit, Fr António Vieira, the most vehement orator of the Restoration, recalled the general duty to support the crown from which the nobility derived its titles and the church its monasteries, he pleaded in vain. Finally, the secretary of state undertook to find 900,000 *cruzados* from the royal revenues.

Outside of Spain, the stoutest opposition to Portuguese independence came from Rome, where Spanish influence was strong. John's ambassador, the bishop of Lamego, only reached the Holy See by way of Marseille with a French safe-conduct. Urban VIII refused to see him for seven months, while Olivares demanded the excommunication of John IV, alleging the wrongful imprisonment of the archbishop of Braga and of the inquisitor and the concessions made to foreign protestants. A committee of cardinals rejected the bishop's credentials and his agent's defence of John's claims. On 20 August 1642, when the bishop was with the French ambassador, he was warned that the Spaniards were preparing violent measures, and as he returned to his lodgings accompanied by his friends and servants and some servants of the French embassy, a battle was fought in the streets in which twelve persons were killed. Despite his complaints, the pope would do no more than appoint a guard for his house, still refusing his credentials: he received one audience in his capacity as bishop and left Rome on 18 December, after a year of fruitless applications.

So far the object of Portuguese policy had been not to take the offensive until the league had been achieved. But some were in favour of giving military action priority over diplomacy. Dom João da Costa, later count of Soure, presented a memorandum in which he complained of the want of energy of the four ministers, none of whom had any military experience: the king never attended the Council of War, though he pursued 'occupations less necessary for the defence of the kingdom', and in consequence the council's recommendations were often altered. John accordingly expressed support for the invasion of Spain and promised to join the army in the

Alentejo in the spring, following the example of Philip IV, who now went to the Aragonese front in defiance of the advice of Olivares.

The complaints of the military were chiefly directed against John's secretary of state, Francisco de Lucena, who had worked with the execrated Vasconcelos until shortly before the Restoration. His long experience made him valuable to John, but he had hesitated before accepting office because his son was still in Madrid, and had been arrested. Lucena had treated for his release, with John's consent, but he was nevertheless accused of corresponding with Olivares. John was persuaded to order his arrest, but an investigation revealed nothing. Soon after his release, the commander of a fort at Elvas accused of treating with the enemy implicated Lucena under torture. Although the accuser later retracted, Lucena was again arrested and this time executed (April 1643): his guilt was very doubtful.

In July 1643 John IV went to Évora, near his troops, who were now commanded by the count of Óbidos. Óbidos moved against Badajoz but gave up the attack on the ground that his men were insufficient. He was arrested, and the command passed to Matias de Albuquerque. No major action was fought before the end of the season. However, Philip IV had now at last dismissed Olivares, the author of the fatal policy of centralization by compulsion, and promised to govern, not merely to reign, as hitherto. He still required all his forces to mend the gaps the French had made in the defences of Aragon, but he appointed a new commander to the Portuguese frontier, the marquis of Torrecusa. In May 1644 Albuquerque advanced against the Spanish town of Montijo, and Torrecusa sent 2,500 horse and 8,000 foot to face them. The Spanish attack broke the Portuguese wings, but Albuquerque rallied his men and drove the Spanish troops across the Guadiana with heavy losses. The battle of Montes Claros was the first considerable victory of the war, and caused great rejoicing in Lisbon. In reply Philip IV ordered Torrecusa to take some Portuguese town, and afforded 17,000 men for an attack on Elvas. Albuquerque, now count of Alegrete, foiled a first attempt in November, but as the season closed the danger of a Spanish invasion had not decreased and the strain of continued mobilization was beginning to be felt. Conscription, billeting and requisitioning caused general discontent, and Alegrete was relieved of the command of the Alentejo frontier, which was now given to the count of

Castelo-Melhor, who had won minor successes on the Galician frontier. He hoped to enter Badajoz by surprise, but the Spaniards were forewarned, and nothing came of the intention.

In 1644 general negotiations for peace began at Osnaburgh and Münster. John IV sought representation at both places, though his agent at Osnaburgh soon died and was replaced only just before the conclusion of the Treaty of Westphalia in 1648. His main concern was with the dealings between France and Spain at Münster. Both Spain and Austria refused to recognize the Portuguese delegates, who arrived in the French and Dutch parties. The Spaniards threatened to withdraw rather than discuss the inclusion of Portugal. No progress was made until August 1646, when the French dropped their insistence on the recognition of Portuguese independence. The Portuguese could therefore hope for nothing more than a long truce: in fact, the French conditions on behalf of Portugal were whittled down to the right to assist Portugal in case of attack and the release of John IV's brother.[1] Finally, the negotiations collapsed, and the war between France and Spain was resumed.

John IV again attempted to seek a reconciliation with the pope, sending the prior of Cedofeita to Rome to make representations on behalf of the Portuguese clergy: seventeen sees were now vacant. The prior was attacked in the street in broad daylight, and escaped from his carriage leaving a servant and a horse dead. His mission failed; and by 1649 there was only one bishop left in Portugal, two in Asia, and none in the Islands, Africa or Brazil.

Meanwhile, relations with Holland had deteriorated. Since May 1643 the Portuguese had attempted to get a promise of inclusion in any treaty with Spain, offering to pay up to 200,000 *cruzados* to the *stathouder*: they also sought to convert the truce with Holland into a permanent treaty and to obtain the complete evacuation of Brazil, offering a compensation of up to 2m. *cruzados* to the West India Company. The crucial period for these discussions was from 1644 to 1645, when the contracts of both companies expired. The East India Company was still highly profitable, and there was little chance of

---

[1] John's brother Duarte had entered the service of the Emperor Ferdinand III, following a military career. At the Restoration, the emperor complied with Spanish demands for his arrest. John's attempts to obtain his release failed; and when the present negotiations were broken off, the emperor sold Duarte to Philip IV for 40,000 *cruzados*. Duarte died in prison at Milan in 1649.

success. But the West India Company was in serious difficulties: it could no longer support the expenditures of Johan Maurits, who returned in 1644. There was therefore some hope of recovering Brazil and Angola, though John IV could not afford to redeem the capital of the company. But in May 1645 there came news that the Brazilian Portuguese had revolted against the Dutch. The munificent prince of Nassau had gone, and the Dutch mercenaries, company-directors and usurers inspired little enthusiasm. John was taken by surprise by the outburst of Brazilian patriotism: he evidently did not at first suppose that it would succeed, and feared that it would expose Portuguese shipping and commerce to ruin, as it nearly did. The Dutch demanded that he should punish the leaders of the rising, and he could only persuade them that he was not its author by disowning it and ordering the insurgents to lay down their arms. He also sent Fr Vieira to offer the Dutch 3m. *cruzados* for the abandonment of Brazil: they refused (July 1646).

The Brazilian rising could not be contained. Johan Maurits had succeeded only by lavish expenditure at a time when the West India Company was already deep in debt. The Dutch were soldiers and administrators, not planters: the export of sugar was largely carried on by Jews and its production by Portuguese Brazilians, mulattoes and negroes. These last clearly preferred a society which incorporated them to one which excluded them, and they largely supplied the fighters for 'divine liberty'. But John IV could hardly bear to contemplate the prospect of hostilities with the Dutch by sea simultaneously with the land-war with Spain. In 1646 he made a new attempt to obtain the league with France, this time with a dynastic alliance. It had already been proposed that his heir Teodósio should marry Louis XIII's niece La Grande Demoiselle. John now returned to this scheme, asking no dowry provided that Portugal was included in any peace or truce or assured of military help: Mazarin was offered the bishopric of Évora, worth 7,000 *cruzados* a year. The scheme was rejected; and Vieira was sent to Paris to propose that Teodósio and a French princess should reign in Portugal while John retired to the Azores to reign over Brazil. Vieira had interviews with Mazarin and the French queen-mother, but neither was attracted by this extravagant plan (November 1647).

John's personal inclination to relinquish the crown was perhaps

increased by an attempt on his life. A Portuguese who had fled to
Madrid was bribed to kill him, which he intended to do by taking
lodgings in the middle of Lisbon, boring holes in the walls of the
house, and shooting the king as he passed by in the Corpus Christi
procession. The assassin lost his nerve and was later denounced by
an accomplice and hanged.

Meanwhile the West India Company had resumed its attacks on
Portuguese shipping, causing great havoc to the sugar-fleet: in 1647
and 1648 the number of ships lost was 220. Worse still, the Dutch
made peace with Spain in June 1648, turning from equivocal allies
to undeclared enemies. In order to obtain new help, the queen's
confessor, Fr Daniel O'Daly (or Frei Domingo do Rosário), the
founder of the Dominican house of Corpo Santo in Lisbon, went to
Ireland to raise troops, while an agent recruited Germans at Ham-
burg. Massaniello's rising at Naples suggested the possibility of
stirring up trouble for Spain in Italy, and Vieira departed to offer
the rebels funds for a new attempt. While in Rome he raised with
fellow-Jesuits the possibility of marrying Teodósio to a Spanish
princess, a fantastic scheme which came to nothing.

It had long been clear that the Braganças would only wring
recognition from Spain with the collapse of the latter or after a long
interval, as had occurred with the house of Avis after Aljubarrota.
It was indeed perilous to underestimate the powers of resistance of
Castile; and now the divisions which she had suffered began to appear
in her rival, where the government of Mazarin, weakened by the
defection of the French nobles, seemed for a time liable to emerge
not victorious but vanquished. For the Portuguese the league with
France had long appeared to hold the only clue to success. But now
another possibility emerged. During the last years of the English
monarchy the Alliance had been almost suspended. John not un-
naturally favoured the king, if only because he had risked so much
to become one himself. When therefore, after the execution of Charles
I, Prince Rupert sailed into the Tagus with eleven ships, he was
amiably received (30 November 1649). But Rupert's only source of
income was the seizure of republican ships, and he demanded the
freedom of all Portuguese ports and the right to store or sell his
prizes. To this John replied politely but ambiguously, for the English
merchants in Lisbon included many republicans. Some of these

protested against activities of Rupert, who demanded that they should be arrested. But in January 1650 news was received that the Commonwealth had sent Admiral Blake to Lisbon.

John was unwilling to take sides in the domestic disorders of the English and requested Rupert to depart. He had not done so when Blake appeared in March: he bore instructions to attack Rupert and to make a friendly approach to the Portuguese. His negotiator, Charles Vane, asked the English factory in Lisbon to petition John that both fleets be required to put to sea. But the consul, Chandler, a monarchist, refused to provoke bloodshed; and Vane, having failed to get him removed, had to withdraw. Blake could not face the forts at the mouth of the Tagus, and having molested some French ships, he departed. A few days later Rupert also left and the account was settled elsewhere.

These events obliged John to seek a settlement with the Commonwealth, and he sent an envoy to London. Parliament refused to treat until he accepted six articles indemnifying the English merchants for the losses they had received in Lisbon and paying reparations for the cost of Blake's expedition. John decided that he must accept this imposition, and sent the count of Penaguião to London with instructions to submit and to ask for the renewal of the Treaty of 1642.

The members of the English factory in Lisbon and their principals in London now produced a list of thirty-eight points which they wished included in a treaty. These were reduced to nine additional articles, all of which Penaguião accepted. The English merchants in Portugal were never to pay more than 23 per cent in customs-dues and to be consulted about all increases; they were to be amenable to their own Judge-Conservator for all civil offences, and to have religious liberty and their own burial-ground; merchants of either country were permitted to trade with the colonies of the other, while English warships were permitted to enter Portuguese ports for supplies or repairs (a consequence of Blake's failure).

The Commonwealth Treaty of 1654 determined the 'privileges of an Englishman' in the Portuguese trade for almost two centuries, though it was only after 1700, when the Portuguese acquired sudden and extraordinary wealth, that its advantages became fully apparent. The peculiar feature of the treaty was that a number of concessions, some of them three hundred years old, were raised to treaty rank at a time when they might rather have been expected to disappear. The most important of these was probably that of the Judge-Conservator. In the fourteenth century it had been common practice to grant foreign merchants the right of having their cases settled expeditiously by a certain magistrate, usually the judge of the custom-house, so that their departure might not be delayed by tedious suits. This magistrate became the custodian of the privileges granted to the nation concerned. But now most of the English merchants were resident in Portugal, where they constituted a 'factory': yet they acquired the right not only to have their own judge but to appoint him and pay his salary.

The treaty of 1654 assured Portugal of an ally in case Spain forced France to come to terms. In March 1652 Mazarin, sorely pressed by the rebels of the Fronde, had offered the league for 3m. *cruzados*, but this sum was more than John could pay, and if Mazarin fell or the French were defeated, it would be useless. In 1653 the Spaniards had at last transferred troops from Catalonia to the Portuguese frontier. Their attack was broken in the battle of Arronches, but the threat of invasion forced John to strengthen his defences, and the English treaty came in time to bring men and material. Meanwhile, in Brazil, the Dutch were routed in the two battles of Guararapes, and with the loss of Pernambuco (1654), their occupation was brought to an end.

So in 1655 Mazarin sent the chevalier de Jant to Lisbon to offer hopes of a marriage between Louis XIV and John's daughter, and to ask for money and press the Portuguese to invade Spain, according to the Treaty of 1641. The Portuguese refused, saying that without the league they could not afford to help France, for if the latter made a separate peace, they would need all their resources for their own defence. At last, on 7 September 1655, de Jant signed a treaty by which France would grant the league for 2m. *cruzados*. In doing so, he was influenced by rumours of negotiations between Portugal and Spain: he probably knew that Mazarin would refuse to ratify. By May 1656 Mazarin had returned to his former position: no league unless Portugal invaded and occupied part of Spain.

Having apparently come so near the coveted league, the Portuguese court was not easily put off. Fr O'Daly was sent to France to make soundings and thought that the French might grant the league in return for a marriage with a dowry in money or the cession of Tangier: Mazarin might be bought for 600,000 *cruzados*. John IV was not fully convinced, but allowed O'Daly to pursue the question.

The affair was still pending when John died on 6 November 1656. The first ruler of the house of Bragança was not a brilliant or magnetic character: after Sebastian, this was hardly to be desired. He was cautious and stubborn, and these virtues had their value. However, as he grew older and succumbed to the family affliction of gout, his lack of energy became evident; and the queen and Fr O'Daly took the leading part in the negotiations.

2. AFONSO VI, 1656–68 (D. 1683)

Queen Luisa now became regent: the daughter of the greatest family of Andalusia, she had married the head of the leading house of Portugal without any expectation of becoming a queen. Having by a stroke of fortune attained royal rank, she was determined to secure the future of her children and the continuance of her line. Her eldest son Teodósio had died in 1653 at the age of nineteen: two years earlier he had run away from court to join the army in the Alentejo; he wrote to his father from Elvas urging him to settle the arrears of pay of the troops. John feared some kind of military *pronunciamento*, but at length the prince was induced to return to court, where he was given the title of Captain-General of Arms. When he died of an illness, *cortes* were summoned to confirm the succession of his younger brother Afonso, aged ten. This child had in infancy suffered a disease which left his right arm and leg partly paralysed and affected his understanding. Some hesitated to have him enthroned until his capacities were demonstrated: others held that in such troublous times a king must exist, and nine days after John's death, he was proclaimed.

The old king, bearing in mind the escapade of Teodósio, had not appointed tutors to his younger sons, but kept them by him. Queen Luisa now chose Dom Francisco de Faro, count of Odemira, to govern the king. The result was not very flattering to Odemira, for although Afonso learned to read and write, he spent most of his time in riding, coursing bulls and watching dog- and cock-fights. It seems that Odemira found Afonso ungovernable, and that he was too interested in the intrigues of the palace to discipline the king or to risk offending him. He died in May 1661, when Afonso was seventeen, knew very little, and at once fell into even less recommendable hands.

During her regency, Queen Luisa still pursued the elusive league with France and the dynastic alliance. In December 1656 Mazarin made a treaty with Cromwell, by which England entered the field against Spain. In January 1657 it was rumoured that Philip IV would take advantage of the death of John IV to attack, and Luisa therefore again applied to France for the league and the marriage, offering a dowry of 1m. *cruzados* and either Tangier or Mazagão. There were now reports of a general alliance of England, France and Sweden against Spain, and the Portuguese accordingly applied for admission. But Mazarin realized that such a general alliance would greatly reduce the market value of the league with France: he therefore sent the count of Cominges to Lisbon to offer the league without the dynastic link for 2m. *cruzados* in cash, an annual subsidy of 200,000 for the duration of the war, the cession of Tangier, and the use of six Portuguese warships. Cominges was received 'like one sent from heaven' (18 July 1657), but when his terms were known, the queen was disappointed at the omission of the match and her advisers dismayed by the demands. Cominges himself soon realized that there were limits to what could be expected from 'this kingdom afflicted on all sides'. The state of Portugal was more precarious than he had supposed; elaborate defences were being prepared round Lisbon, but they would take years to complete. The Dutch were cruising off the coast in the hope of capturing ships or demanding money: they had taken Ceylon and were besieging Gôa, and though they had been driven out of Brazil, the States-General would demand a large indemnity as the price of peace.

Queen Luisa's efforts to achieve a dynastic alliance had helped to inflate Mazarin's demands: he now blew cool, and the Portuguese supposed that he might use them as a bargaining counter in peace discussions with the Spaniards. The court was now divided into factions, whose differences were largely responsible for the disadvantageous result of the campaign of 1657. Dom João da Costa was dismissed from the command of the Alentejo front through the efforts of his rivals, and the count of São Lourenço was brought from prison to denounce the now traditional defensive policy and prepare for an invasion of Spain. As he did so, a Spanish force besieged Olivença, bringing up twenty-nine cannon; these sufficed to drive São Lourenço back. He rashly decided to attack Badajoz as a diversion. He did so without effect; meanwhile, Olivença capitulated and was occupied by Spanish forces.

São Lourenço was now dismissed, and the command passed to Joane Mendes de Vasconcelos, who planned to take Badajoz: he was given 17,000 men and twenty pieces of ordnance, but was forced to withdraw by the arrival of Spanish reinforcements. The Spaniards then besieged Elvas in October 1658: they were still there in the new year, when a relief force from Estremós surprised them and forced them to leave. But the war between Spain and France was now in its closing stages. France had succeeded in weakening the Spanish fortresses in Flanders which had long threatened Paris, but in Catalonia the defensive power of Spain had been demonstrated. When Dom João da Costa arrived in France to ask for military aid, he learned that the preliminaries of peace had already been agreed. Louis XIV would marry, not Catharine of Bragança, but a Spanish princess. A secret article in the treaty required France to break off relations with Portugal so that 'the affairs of Portugal shall be placed in the state they were in previous to the revolution'. But all that Dom João was told was that France was compelled by public opinion to make peace. He offered Mazarin 1m. *cruzados* and the bishopric of Évora if Portugal were included. The pass had already been sold. He drew up and had printed a long justification of Portugal's conduct, and he quoted Louis XIII's undertaking 'to establish the king of Portugal in his present state by means of a general peace'. He also followed Mazarin to St Jean de Luz. But on 7 November the Treaty of the Pyrenees was concluded, and France and Spain ceased to be enemies.

All that Costa could obtain from France was permission to raise men in anticipation of a Spanish attack. He engaged as generals an Irishman, Lord Inchiquin, and a German, the count-duke of Schomberg. Inchiquin's ship was captured by Algerine pirates, and Queen Luisa had to ransom him. He proved a difficult fellow and returned to Ireland, disgruntled and unregretted, at the end of 1662. Schomberg accompanied Costa to Portugal with 600 men and set about reforming the Portuguese army. He organized the cavalry in regiments instead of in semi-autonomous companies, and persuaded the infantry to march in columns. The changes were not accomplished without friction, for the experienced Schomberg was *mestre de campo* under the young count of Atouguia: but he built a strong camp at Estremós so that the Spaniards could not advance far without exposing their lines of communication. Thus in May 1662 the Spanish forces, now commanded by Philip IV's son Don Juan José, entered Portugal and occupied the town of Borba; they then took Juromenha to the south and struck north and west to Monforte, Alter and Crato· The heat of the summer and the fevers of the Alentejo forced the Spaniards to withdraw, but in May 1663 Don Juan José returned with 18,500 men, found Évora insufficiently defended and entered it. This was the greatest reverse of the war for the Portuguese: the Spaniards had come a third of the way from Badajoz to Lisbon and occupied much of the eastern Alentejo. There were riots in the capital, and rumours that the enemy was approaching Setúbal. But troops were moved south from Beira, and faced the invaders at Ameixial, near Estremós. Schomberg rapidly raised earthworks, and Don Juan José decided to retire leaving his cavalry to fight a rearguard action. The Portuguese then attacked, won the victory of Ameixial (8 June 1663), and recaptured Évora. The Spanish effort had failed; Don Juan José was dismissed, and three years later, Philip IV having died, his widow at last made peace and recognized the independence of Portugal.

Queen Luisa had attempted to stand aside from the rivalries of her court. The main factions of the nobility were led by the count of Cantanhede, a descendant of the first duke of Bragança, and Odemira, a collateral of a former queen. These two, with three or five other members, formed the council, which took decisions by majority vote. The two Secretaries, of State (Pedro Vieira da Silva), and of the Wardrobe (Gaspar Faria), were not of either faction: the former attended the council and conveyed its recommendations to the queen. But the success of this system was not matched by attempts to educate the king. The governor, Odemira, took care not to cross him. The preceptor, the prior of Cedofeita, could do nothing with him: a polite chronicler could only record that Afonso's 'great memory, though not applied to any lesson, was so prodigious that he had already given admirable proofs of it on certain occasions'. The king took to gazing from the palace window at the children of the lower orders throwing stones in the street, 'favouring one or other partiality of these youthful gladiators'. Presently a youth called Antonio Conti of Ventimiglia, born in Lisbon of Italian parents, a stallholder in the square, took to egging on and leading the band favoured by the king. He was called to the palace and captured Afonso's friendship with gifts of gilt knives and toys. The queen ordered him to be forbidden to enter, but Afonso became so unmanageable that his attendants allowed Conti to return. He soon established himself in a room next to Afonso, invented his own genealogical tree and began to lead the king off on night excursions in which respectable citizens were attacked, and taverns and disorderly houses raided. Odemira made some attempt to interest the king in riding, but with little effect. When Afonso was sixteen, in 1659, Luisa decided to give him a household. Odemira remained governor, but a group of young nobles was appointed, taking turns week by week to attend the king. The duke of Cadaval remonstrated with the king, but only succeeded in setting Afonso against him. When Odemira died in May 1661, Conti assumed all the airs of a royal favourite. Some of Afonso's attendants, not without ambitions of their own, sided with him, and Luisa found the balance of power she had maintained destroyed. She suddenly announced that she wished to give up the regency. It seems improbable that she had any serious intention of doing so: she was anxious to conclude the marriage of her daughter. Her advisers urged her to remain. However she succeeded in separating her youngest son Pedro, and in June 1662 set him up with his own attendants in the neighbouring Corte-Real palace. On the same day, she announced her intention of resigning the regency in two months' time. In response to this ultimatum, Cadaval, who now became the leading supporter of Pedro, offered to undertake the removal of Conti. On 16 June Luisa summoned Afonso, and Cadaval went to Conti's room; the favourite locked himself in, but when Cadaval threatened to break down the door and kill him, he came out, was arrested, and was put on a ship for Brazil.

This done, the nobility, the officials and the representatives of the guilds were summoned before Luisa and Afonso, and the secretary of State read a message in which the queen urged her son to prepare himself to govern, to occupy himself fittingly and to avoid unscrupulous companions. Afonso evinced no sign of interest in this lecture, and according to Ericeira, walked out with a satisfied air, asking if the assembly was the *cortes*. When he realized that his companions had been spirited away, he became very angry and demanded to be told where they were. This was the opportunity for the most ambitious of his attendants, the count of Castelo-Melhor, who suggested that the enemies who had removed Conti might sequester the king himself. Afonso then rode with Castelo-Melhor to Alcântara, where 400 men were gathered for his defence. It only remained for Afonso to summon the nobility and court and announce that he had taken over the reins of government. Most of those summoned appeared to kiss his hand. His mother was then informed that her regency was at an end: only Cadaval, the marquis of Marialva, Soure, Vieira and a few others adhered to her. On 12 July Castelo-Melhor was appointed *escrivão da puridade* or secret secretary: he alone had access to the king and issued orders and decrees in his name. The queen had no choice but to give in. She was required to retire to a convent. On the day of her withdrawal she was to be escorted by her two sons, but care was taken that she should not succeed in speaking to them. When she told her coachman to stop, theirs followed suit; and when she turned about, they galloped off towards Lisbon. Castelo-Melhor purged the court of enemies, and held power for five years.

Before her exclusion, Luisa had completed arrangements for the marriage of her daughter and the renewal of the English Alliance. After the peace between France and Spain, the Portuguese ambassador in England, Francisco de Melo, later marquis of Sande, had been instructed to negotiate a military treaty. This was concluded on 18 April 1660, and Sande obtained permission to recruit men and buy horses. But owing to the English Restoration, this was not ratified. Sande found the new English government willing to send aid, but not to risk war with Spain: he therefore suggested to Monk a league fortified by a royal marriage. England would undertake to defend Portugal against Spain and Holland, and not make a separate peace. Charles would marry Catharine of Bragança and receive a dowry of 2m. *cruzados*, the cession of Tangier and the right to trade with the Portuguese colonies: Bombay was added later. The new treaty was concluded on 23 June 1661, and it confirmed the provisions of the treaties of 1642 and 1654. The English bound themselves to defend Portugal 'as if it were England itself', with no limit of time: the obligation was expressly extended to cover the Portuguese territories overseas.

The 'league' was thus at last attained, though not with France. Charles II was attracted by the munificence of the dowry, from which the Mint coined the first English gold guineas.[1] It sufficed to overcome the opposition of the Spanish ambassador, who proposed alternative matches, bribed the Catholic press to slander Catharine and threatened war. Allegations of rapacity against Charles are not altogether justified, since the terms for a dynastic alliance had been driven steadily upward during the long negotiations with France: Louis XIV later declared that he had urged Charles to accept the match. In Lisbon, Queen Luisa, who had sighed so long for a French marriage, declared that an angel from heaven could not have brought better news. Her counsellors, however, were reluctant to accept the cession of Bombay and Tangier, and when the draft was read to the Council of State, she instructed the secretary not to recite the clause relating to Tangier. The object of the cession was to enable the English to dispatch assistance to Portugal, but it proved costly to maintain, and when the present struggle was over it was futilely abandoned in 1684.[2]

Thus on 25 April 1662 Catharine of Bragança sailed from Lisbon for Falmouth. In return, the English were to contribute two cavalry regiments of 500 men each and two of infantry of 1,000 with arms and supplies, as well as ten warships in case of attack. Most of the land forces had arrived in time to arrest the attack of Don Juan José in the same summer, and more before Ameixial, where a force commanded by Thomas Hood distinguished itself in resisting a charge by the Spanish cavalry.

In the following years Castelo-Melhor pursued the war with

---

[1] The dowry is said to have been almost double what any monarch had received before, Prestage, *Diplomatic Relations*, 140. In its day, the dowry of Isabel when she married the Emperor Charles V was probably a record, 900,000 ducats. Since then more than a century had elapsed in Portugal without any royal marriages.

[2] Pepys' diary contains numerous references to the question of fortifying Tangier: he realized that Gibraltar was much more defensible, and to a degree the episode of Tangier led to the seizure of Gibraltar during the war of the Spanish succession in 1704.

energy. The loss of Évora had produced riots in Lisbon and the agitators were dispersed by a troop of musketeers: its recovery caused general celebrations. By 1664 there were 28,000 men in the field and the frontier fortifications had been improved. The final effort of the Spaniards was in 1665 when Don Juan José's successor, Caracena, with reinforcements from Germany and Italy, left Badajoz to attack the home of the Braganças at Vila Viçosa. Schomberg at Estremós sent his troops forward to divert the advance, and the armies met on the morning of 17 June 1665 at Montes Claros. The Spanish cavalry charged, but was broken by artillery fire. Caracena continued the offensive without shifting the Portuguese positions, and by three in the afternoon his forces were exhausted. A well-judged cavalry attack completed the victory. The Spaniards lost 4,000 dead and 6,000 prisoners; the capture of 3,500 horses crippled their offensive power.

Three months later, in September 1665, Philip IV died, leaving Spain and all its possessions in the feeble hands of his son, the infant Carlos II. Soundings for peace had begun much earlier, and the Spaniards were at least prepared to contemplate a long truce. But Castelo-Melhor would accept nothing less than the recognition of Afonso VI as King of Portugal. He pitched his demands high and stood by them. In fact, peace was not finally concluded until February 1668, when Castelo-Melhor had fallen. The delay was due largely to growing differences between the English and French. The former, having contracted to defend Portugal, were naturally anxious to bring the war to a close as soon as possible. The latter, for whom the Treaty of the Pyrenees was no more than a stage in their long struggle with the Habsburgs, regarded the Portuguese situation as a convenient instrument of diplomacy, worth preserving until they were again at war with Spain. As early as 1662 Turenne had proposed to keep Portugal within the French orbit of policy by marrying Afonso and his brother to French princesses. In 1663 Sande went to France to pursue negotiations, with the consent of Charles II and Catharine. Thus Afonso VI was betrothed to Marie-Françoise-Isabelle of Savoy: Pedro, who had always opposed the influence of Castelo-Melhor, refused the match that was proposed for him and declared that he would not marry. In February 1666 the king's wedding contract was signed in Paris, and in the same month Queen Luisa died, still in retirement: she had summoned Afonso to her side from Salvaterra, where he had been hunting, but he lingered three days on the way and his mother was already dead when he arrived.

His bride reached Lisbon in August. He met her and escorted her to the church, but found the ceremonies boring, and left her to preside over the celebrations while he dined heavily in bed. She could hardly fail to have known his limitations: her object in coming to Portugal was to be a queen and to extend the influence of France. Her confessor, Fr Verjus, a French Jesuit, directed her activities. She demanded and obtained admission to the meetings of the Council of State, while her followers made contact with Schomberg and succeeded in having him appointed commander-in-chief. The marquis of St-Romain, sent by Louis XIV to prevent the conclusion of peace with Spain, was soon able to report that Maria-Francisca had great influence over Afonso and that Castelo-Melhor could do nothing without consulting her. The English ambassador Southwell recorded that she found on her arrival that Afonso was little better than a slave to Castelo-Melhor, and that she was to be excluded from the government. In her efforts to prevent this, she could count on a formidable array of rivals to the minister, including Cadaval and Marialva.

Meanwhile Southwell's predecessor, Sir Richard Fanshawe, remembered as the first English translator of the *Lusiads*, had been moved to Madrid in 1664 with the object of concluding peace with Spain. On the death of Philip IV, he succeeded in concluding a draft agreement, which he brought to Castelo-Melhor, who had affected indignation at the terms and, characteristically, refused to allow Afonso to receive Fanshawe. But Fanshawe and Southwell obtained Castelo-Melhor's counter-proposals, and it was at this stage that Louis XIV sent St-Romain to Lisbon to frustrate the peace by dangling the famous league before the Portuguese. This enabled Castelo-Melhor to use the possibility of an alliance with France to bring the Spaniards to terms. In March 1667 Castelo-Melhor signed a treaty with France by which Louis XIV undertook that if England made peace with Spain, he would declare war within thirty months or alternatively pay Portugal 900,000 *cruzados*: Portugal would then use her energies to fight Spain and receive a subsidy of 600,000 *cruzados* a month until France should be at war. The league would last for ten years, during which neither party would make peace without the other.

This surprising development stimulated England and Spain to new efforts to prevent the resumption of war. Spain, well aware of the object of Louis XIV, came to terms: in August 1667 the regent in Madrid expressed her readiness to make peace and to recognize Afonso VI as king of Portugal. All at last seemed safe. But by using the French league to force his demands on the Spanish court, Castelo-Melhor was himself ensnared: he no longer controlled the sorry king, and before he could accept the olive-branch from Madrid, Afonso summoned him and dismissed him from his service (7 September 1667). The fallen minister fled to Bussaco, seeking shelter in its modest monastery. When a troop of cavalry arrived in pursuit of him, he hid in the forest, which his pursuers would have burned down but for the entreaties of the monks. He later escaped to England, and became confidential adviser to Catharine of Bragança.

Afonso was now in the hands of his queen, his brother and the band of nobles that had formerly favoured his deposition. Pedro again took up residence in the palace, and the municipality of Lisbon petitioned for the summoning of *cortes* with the object of making him regent. Two weeks passed, and no decision was reached. On 11 November the city fathers demanded that *cortes* be summoned in a week, threatening to withhold the war-tax. It was then agreed that *cortes* should meet on 1 January 1668. The Portuguese nobles were by no means unanimously in favour of the French league, and the capital and nation were desperately anxious for peace.

The French party did not give in. It was rumoured first that Maria-Francisca intended to ask for the annulment of her marriage and that she would return to France. On 21 November she and her household left the palace, and she established herself in the Esperança convent. She wrote a letter of farewell to Afonso, expressing regret that she had not been able to play her part to his satisfaction, and asked his permission to return to France, together with the refund of her dowry. When the king heard what had happened, he dashed to the convent and ordered the gates to be opened. The abbess replied that the queen had the keys. Pedro then appeared and proposed that the Provincial of the Franciscans be called. But the gates were still not opened, and Afonso finally returned to the palace: next day Maria-Francisca asked the chapter of Lisbon cathedral to seek the annulment of the marriage.

It remained to persuade Afonso to consent to his own deposition. In a private conversation, the marquis of Cascais explained the need for a successor and urged Afonso to deliver the government to his brother, who would marry and have children. He agreed, and an instrument was drawn up, by which he made over the government to Pedro, reserving for himself the estates of the duchy of Bragança and an annual income. When he had signed this, he became a virtual prisoner. But before the peace could be snatched away, Southwell took steps to make public the Spanish acceptance of the terms demanded by Castelo-Melhor. The judge of the people was apprised of the conditions—recognition, the liberation of prisoners, restitution of property. Pedro, newly established in power, had no desire to incur the displeasure of the people; the bringing of peace would set the seal on his power. In December he gave his approval.

Thus in January 1668 *cortes* assembled in Lisbon to declare Pedro prince and governor and heir to the throne. All the three estates supported the deposition of Afonso and the transference of power to Pedro, but all made different recommendations: the commoners that he should take the throne at once, the clergy that he should be entitled Prince Governor, and the nobles that a committee of theologians and lawyers should decide. Finally, Pedro assumed the title of Prince-Regent.

The *cortes* also asked Pedro not to allow Maria-Francisca to leave Portugal, 'both for the great love these realms bear to her great virtues and for the necessity of succession'. Perhaps the strongest argument was the fact that if she departed, it would be necessary to refund her dowry. The suit of nullity was therefore prepared. Afonso swore that he had done his best to consummate the marriage, and Maria-Francisca took the complementary oath. No oral examination of either spouse was made, as canon law required, but a profusion of indelicate evidence was amassed to illustrate Afonso's incapacity. The day after the royal depositions had been presented, the marriage was pronounced annulled. The industrious Fr Verjus had departed for France to obtain a dispensation from the Cardinal de Vendôme. In view of the lack of contact between Portugal and Rome, this was not unnatural: however, the certificate, which treated the case of nullity as already decided, was issued in Paris nine days before sentence was pronounced in Lisbon. As soon as it arrived, by the safe hand of Fr Verjus, Pedro was married to Maria-Francisca.

3. PEDRO II, PRINCE-REGENT 1668–83, KING 1683–1706

Pedro had been brought to the throne to assure the perpetuation of the monarchy, and Maria-Francisca to secure the continuance of French influence. Their opponents made one or two attempts to restore Afonso, who was at first confined to rooms in the palace at Lisbon. His friends protested to the pope that he had not been allowed to present an advocate in his suit, that the witnesses had been pressed and the judges suborned: since Portugal was still unreconciled with Rome, the appeal must have been facilitated by Spain. It had no effect, but in the following year Afonso expressed the desire to see the open fields of Vila Viçosa, the ancestral home not far from the Spanish border. Instead, he was despatched to the Azores, landing at Angra in June 1669, by night, lest the curiosity of the inhabitants be aroused: he dwelt in three rooms and a gallery in the governor's house, and made the life of his attendants almost as intolerable as his own. Meanwhile in January the succession had been assured by the birth of a daughter to the Prince-Regent and his wife, Isabel-Luisa-Josefa, who was duly recognized as heiress by *cortes* when she reached the age of five.

As the long shadows of the wars of the Restoration diminished, the Portuguese court did its best to remain at peace: it had certainly no desire to be drawn into further quarrels with Spain. But the chief object of French policy was now to dominate the failing Habsburg monarchy, and when Louis XIV claimed the Spanish Netherlands under the trivial pretext of a local law of inheritance and resumed the offensive, England, Holland and Sweden were sufficiently alarmed by his exorbitance to form a Triple Alliance. Thus the two powers on which the Portuguese had relied during the Restoration parted company. The French did their best to carry the Portuguese into their camp by exploiting old grievances against the Dutch: by the Treaty of 1661 Portugal had obtained Dutch recognition of her recovery of Brazil, but had agreed to pay an indemnity now long in arrears. In March 1669 Colbert drew up a scheme by which France offered to help Portugal to recover the trade of the East which had been surrendered to the Dutch. But few Portuguese were prepared to embark on new adventures. When in April 1672 Louis XIV offered troops for the defence of Portugal in the event of her drawing down on herself the hostility of Spain through joining a struggle against the Dutch, the Portuguese government took the attitude that while a war with the Dutch might be a just war, one with Spain would not. A group of Portuguese joined with the Spanish ambassador in Lisbon in a plot to rescue Afonso VI who, it was proposed, would be carried to Spain, where he might marry the Spanish queen-mother. The Portuguese participants were promptly executed, but Pedro thought it prudent to have his brother nearer at hand, and in August 1674 Afonso was brought from Angra to Lisbon, and conveyed to Sintra: here he passed the last nine years of his life, confined in an apartment from which he emerged only to hear mass. One morning in September 1683, he woke up screaming and demanding that mass should be said: he was carried from the chapel to his bed and ended his miserable existence the same day. Thus the Prince-Regent at last became Pedro II: their wife died just over three months later.

Pedro's heiress was now fourteen. Four years earlier, in 1679, Louis XIV had made peace with Spain at Nijmegen and sought to strengthen his influence in the Peninsula by means of new marriages: between Carlos II of Spain and a French princess, and between the Portuguese princess and Victor-Amédée II of Savoy. *Cortes* were summoned in December 1679 to give their consent to the marriage of the heiress.[1] The negotiations were continued until May 1682, when the duke of Cadaval sailed to Villefranche with a fleet of twelve vessels to bring back the bridegroom. The vessels waited for some months for Victor-Amédée, but he finally declared that reasons of state prevented him from leaving his people. The failure of the negotiations in these circumstances gave great offence in Portugal,

[1] Since the Restoration the Portuguese had provided themselves with a written constitution, the better to consolidate the legality of the separation from Spain. This was a compilation of the 'cortes of Lamego' supposed to have been celebrated by Afonso Henriques in 1139, and published under the date 1632. The object of this patriotic deception was to provide proof of the right of John IV, for one of the laws deprived any princess who married a foreigner of all claim to the Portuguese throne. *Cortes* now set aside this supposed law, on the ground that no suitable bridegroom for the princess could be found in Portugal.

and when Pedro II married again in 1687, it was with Maria-Sophia-Elizabeth, a daughter of the Elector-Palatine, Philip-William of Neuberg, outside the French orbit. She gave birth to Pedro's successor, the future John V, in October 1689, and had three more sons and a daughter before she died in 1699.[1]

Since the Restoration, the government had been conducted by the ruler (or, under Afonso VI, in his name) with the aid of the Secretaries and the Councils of State and War. The chief positions were held by noblemen, whose followers came near to forming political parties. However, the jealousies of the leaders, rather than adherence to principles, controlled their activities, so that the factions remained fluid: those suspected of subversion were promptly dealt with by tribunals of *inconfidência*.

One of the effects of the Restoration had been to divide the Portuguese church from Rome. It was only in 1669, after the peace with Spain, that relations were restored, and bishops again appointed. During the breach, freedom of worship was conceded to foreign protestants and the persecution of New Christians by the Inquisition suspended. Similarly, members of the Orders came to discharge functions that had previously been entrusted to bishops: thus Queen Luisa had entrusted her Dominican confessor, Fr O'Daly, and the Jesuit Vieira with all kinds of business of a diplomatic or economic nature. The Jesuits then established themselves as royal confessors, and a contemporary writer notes that in matters which divided the court, the confessor and Vieira would take opposite sides: it was thought deliberately, so that whichever party succeeded a Jesuit would stand well.

Until 1679 *cortes* had continued to meet, the three estates assembling in different monasteries. Their chief function was now to approve and apportion taxation for the war, though they also had the traditional prerogative of recognizing the heir to the throne. But they had never acquired more than advisory functions: the right to convoke or close *cortes* remained with the crown, and the principle that redress should precede supply had never beeen established. Moreover, although the towns were represented, the procurators were appointed by the town councils from among the class of officials, who were at most indirect spokesmen for the populace at large. The

---

[1] Isabel-Josefa, the daughter of Maria-Francisca, died in 1690.

cortes had narrowed in functions and composition, and matters formerly within its province were dealt with either by officials or by the guilds. When the crown wished to obtain the support of the urban masses, it did so through the magistrate (*juiz do povo*) of the guilds of Lisbon, who still had their Casa dos Vinte e Quatro. Between 1679 and 1697 no *cortes* were celebrated, and in 1697 the sole purpose of the assembly was to recognize the heir to the throne. Having done this, *cortes* authorized the crown to make such alterations in the law of succession as might be required in the future without further reference. The crown never summoned *cortes* again: the age of absolutism had begun.

With the Restoration, Portugal had again turned to the great markets of Europe, and sought to restore the position of Lisbon as an emporium. In 1641 John IV had opened the ports to merchants of all countries, who were allowed to enter freely and to take out the profits of their trade. This was attractive to foreign merchants, who brought in arms and supplies, and such staple commodities as dried fish and wheat, taking away sugar, salt and wine. But the monarchy of the Braganças needed capitalists and bankers for the purpose of expanding its overseas trade. The only community which possessed wealth and experience was that of the New Christians: Olivares had already begun negotiations for their possible return to Spain. In 1643 Vieira wrote a memorial for John IV in which he emphasized the folly of persecuting the Jews, but it was not until 1649 that John was able to order the return of the property of New Christians seized by the Inquisition on condition that it was used to provide capital for a new Brazil Company, to be organized according to the Dutch or Spanish models. This company would provide two fleets of eighteen ships each, equipped with twenty or thirty guns apiece, for the defence of Brazil, and would enjoy considerable privileges: its own regime and judge, facilities to obtain ships and supplies in Portugal and the monopoly of dye-wood in Brazil. Some difficulty was found in raising capital, for the New Christian families of Botelho, Carvalho, Serrão and Silveira were less wealthy (or more cautious) than had been imagined, and had to seek additional funds. The Company also concentrated on sugar at a time when the high rate of production was depressing prices, and the English market was reduced by the annexation of Jamaica. In 1658 the company's monopoly was suppressed, and in 1664 it was taken over by the state, which repaid shareholders out of the revenue of the tobacco monopoly.

The Restoration also affected Portugal's internal economy. During the association with Spain she had been able to make good her deficiency in wheat by importing from Andalusia. In the early years of the seventeenth century Entre-Douro-e-Minho had diminished the cultivation of wheat in favour of wine, which was exported to Brazil and elsewhere. But with the Restoration and the conscription of men for military service there was a danger that a serious shortage would develop, particularly in the Alentejo, the region of extensive cultivation, now most exposed to attack and most affected by the decision that each province should organize its own defence. In 1641 *cortes* proposed enforcing the legislation of Dom Dinis by which those who failed to till the land should be dispossessed. During the war, this was not possible, and instead grain was imported duty-free, but after the return of peace demands were heard for the compulsion of labourers in order to remedy the deficiency of wheat.

The task of producing a coherent economic policy fell to Dom Luis de Meneses, count of Ericeira, who in 1675 was appointed Vèdor da Fazenda, and continued to control policy until his death in March 1690. With the end of the war, enforced sobriety was followed by a wave of extravagance, and attempts were made in 1677, 1686 and 1698 to regulate luxury in clothes, jewellery, coaches, lackeys and mourning. At the same time Ericeira attempted to stimulate national production. Silk stockings had become a considerable import: in 1676 he restricted the price of mulberry leaves, and in 1677 ordered the planting of new groves in the district of Lisbon; weavers from Seville were engaged, and Bluteau's work on the rearing of the silk-worm was published in 1679. Two years earlier Ericeira had ordered that only Portuguese hats, ribbons and lace should be worn, and in 1686 the import of woollens of various kinds was prohibited, to be fully enforced within two years. In 1690 a Regulation for the Cloth Industry was published. A little later Dom Luis da Cunha could declare that he had travelled through Europe dressed in Portuguese cloth made at Covilhã and Fundão.

Precautions were also taken to protect existing Portuguese industries. Of these one of the most ancient was the production of salt, long a staple export: the excellence of the salt of Alcácer do Sal is apparently due to a phenomenon of marine biology. The appearance of competition from Galicia in 1695 led to an order forbidding the emigration of salt-workers, followed by another prohibiting the entry of foreigners to learn the secrets of the industry. But within the next decade these measures of careful housekeeping were to be first revised under the pressure of political circumstances and then rendered obsolete by a new and incalculable torrent of opulence.

Although the wealth of Brazil had hitherto derived from sugar, the Portuguese had never ceased to believe that treasures comparable with those of Mexico and Peru must exist somewhere in their vast viceroyalty. Traces of gold had been reported from São Paulo in the sixteenth century, and in 1608 the governor had been made super-intendent of mines, but the revenues were trifling. The first three Braganças had urged prospectors to hasten their work, but it was not until the last years of the century that the first great discoveries were made. The pioneers, known as *bandeirantes*, because they travelled under the banner of their leader, who took with him kinsmen, friends, clients, slaves and friendly Indians, were armed with flintlocks and swords. They wore a padded leather waistcoat capable of keeping off arrows, doublet, cotton hose, a headcloth and a length of baize which served as cloak and blanket. Their travels might last years: in 1674 the *bandeira* of Pais Leme passed through the heart of the future Minas Gerais, the 'General Mines', but found only tourmalines, which they mistook for emeralds. It was only in 1692 that river gold was found in Mato Grosso. Two years later, gold was found in abundance, and in 1697 Leme's son-in-law Borba Gato discovered a site near Sabará from which 900 pounds of gold were extracted. Nearby, the metal was found at Ouro Preto, Black Gold, later known as Vila Rica. The ensuing gold rush drew prospectors from all parts of Brazil, adventurers, nobles, priests, slaves: by 1705 the population of the Mines had risen to 50,000.

At this time Portugal had little to fear from Spain, whose very survival had been called into question by the approaching end of the Habsburg dynasty. Nor was she immediately involved in the passions and ambitions of the other powers. Louis XIV, intent on grasping the Spanish succession, strove to attain his ends by diplomacy and had built up an influential party in Madrid: he hoped also to make his annexation of Spain palatable to the other powers by partitioning some of her possessions. Thus in 1700 he concluded a treaty with Portugal by which the frontiers of northern Brazil and of French Guiana were settled to her advantage, and he offered as part of the general partition, and in satisfaction of the rather tenuous Portuguese claim to the Spanish succession, to give Portugal the towns of Badajoz and Alcântara. In October the last Spanish Habsburg drew up his will in favour of the Bourbon succession, on condition that the crowns of Spain and France should never be united. This encouraged Pedro II to accept the terms of the partition proposed earlier in the year.

On 1 November Carlos II died: Louis XIV's grandson Philip was at once presented to the court of Versailles as king of Spain and within a few weeks the Bourbons were established in Madrid. England recognized Philip V as king of Spain in April 1701. Louis XIV sought to forestall any opposition from Portugal, and when she recognized Philip in June, he also negotiated a treaty which provided for an alliance with France and Spain for twenty years: Portugal would close her ports against enemies of the Bourbon powers, and France promised military and naval support and aid in recovering her former possessions in the east: in July eight French warships reached Lisbon.

But the preponderance of the Bourbons in Spain and Italy and the evasion of the issue of partition now caused England and Holland to form an alliance with the Austrian Habsburgs, the Grand Alliance, concluded in October 1701 for the purpose of driving the French out of Italy and the Spanish Netherlands, and of bringing to the throne of Spain an Austrian Habsburg, the Archduke Charles. Louis XIV retorted by recognizing James III as king of England. This made the Portuguese treaty with the Bourbons incompatible with the existing alliance with England, and Pedro II was obliged to reconsider his policy. His ambassador in London, Dom Luis da Cunha, proposed to ask France for aid on such a scale that she would not comply. But his government was unprepared for war, and in particular for a new war with Spain. It therefore proposed that the English and Dutch should base their declaration of war on some ground that might not involve Spain, such as Louis XIV's recognition of James III. At the same time it raised the question of aid from France. No reply had been received when England, Holland and Austria declared war in

May 1702. Their action was based on the Spanish issue and therefore concerned Portugal.

The English government now sent as envoy to Lisbon John Methuen, who had formerly been minister at Pedro's court, but had been succeeded by his son Paul. He soon found that Pedro was prepared to guarantee the security of the English and Dutch in Portugal, but reluctant to go further without knowing what contribution would be made to the defence of Portugal. In June 1702 he returned to England and hastened the dispatch of a naval division, which was to join the Dutch off Cádiz. When he returned to Lisbon, still no reply had been received to the Portuguese communications with France, and in August Pedro's government denounced the agreements with France and Spain. Negotiations then began for Portugal's adherence to the Grand Alliance. Her situation made it impossible for her to remain neutral. The Bourbon courts could offer to defend her coasts, but they could not protect her shipping or guard her possessions overseas: nor would they guarantee that she should not again be absorbed by Spain. England was already committed to defend her frontiers against Spain and an alliance with both maritime powers assured her commerce of security. Before joining the alliance, Pedro asked for guarantees that no peace would be made until the Bourbons had been driven from Spain and that the Archduke Charles should appear in person to lead his armies. The negotiations continued until April 1703, when Methuen left Portugal. His son concluded them on 16 May. He had no difficulty in completing the defensive alliance, by which the English and Dutch extended guarantees to Portugal. The treaty by which Portugal adhered to the Grand Alliance was more complicated. It provided for the expulsion from Spain of the Bourbons and the imposition of the Austrian Habsburgs. The archduke promised to transfer to Portugal two strips of territory in eastern Spain and Galicia from which the Spaniards had conducted the war of 1640–68, as well as the Sacramento colony on the north bank of the River Plate. The size of the armies to serve in the Peninsula was established at 7,000 horse and 33,000 foot, composed of Portuguese paid by Pedro, Portuguese paid by the allies, and allied troops. The allies would also supply artillery trains and a subsidy of $1\frac{1}{2}$m. *cruzados* for the first year of the war and 1m. thereafter: against this the Portuguese indemnity to the Dutch was scaled down to 850,000. In December 1703 Portugal severed relations with the court of Philip V.

In the following spring the archduke, now known as Charles III, landed in Lisbon and issued a pardon to all Spaniards who joined him within a month. On 30 April Philip V declared war and invaded Portugal. His main army, commanded by the duke of Berwick, moved down the Tagus and entered Castelo Branco on 24 May. The allied forces held Abrantes, and as Berwick crossed the river and occupied Portalegre, the Portuguese commander, the marquis of Minas, sent a force into Spain as a diversion. Berwick then abandoned the places north of the Tagus.

Pedro II and the pretender met at Santarém in May, but it was only in September that they concentrated their armies in Beira and attempted in vain to take Ciudad Rodrigo. The attack failed and Pedro and the pretender returned to Lisbon. In 1705 the allies attacked below the Tagus, taking Alcântara and Albuquerque, but failing to reduce Badajoz. In June the archduke left Portugal for Catalonia: the Catalans, though they had often opposed the Habsburg kings, now set themselves even more bitterly against the centralism of the Bourbons, and the city of Barcelona resisted to the end of the long and arduous war. The campaigns of 1706 and 1707 seemed to bring the allies to the brink of success. In March 1706 Minas advanced from Alcântara and Berwick fell back as he did so. On 6 June he entered Salamanca, and two weeks later Philip V retired from Madrid. The allied cavalry entered the capital on 25 June, and Charles 'III' was acclaimed, though without great enthusiasm. Minas' position in Madrid was spectacular, but unsafe. The archduke was defending Catalonia, and the earl of Peterborough had landed at Valencia, but was not ready to advance. So on 14 August Minas left Madrid to join him, and in October the campaign was suspended for the winter. The Spanish and French troops then returned to Madrid. It was at this moment of apparent success that Pedro II died in December 1706.

VIII

THE AGE OF ABSOLUTISM

I. JOHN V, 1706-50

John V was a youth of seventeen when he succeeded. He had been brought up by his mother almost entirely in feminine society, and had had no opportunity to accustom himself to his duties, but he was the best educated of the Braganças and had the desire to improve himself. He had learnt Spanish, French and Italian, studied mathematics and, like his grandfather, delighted in music. He was not without obstinacy, but he was shy and docile: he chose respectable ministers, but never spurred them to activity. As a result of the alliance with the Habsburgs, he was married to Maria Ana of Austria, the sister of the archduke, in 1708. Three years elapsed before the birth of his first son (who died at the age of two), and John vowed to build a vast and magnificent monastery if heaven should vouchsafe him an heir: the site of Mafra was selected in 1712. His eventual successor was born in June 1714, whereupon John expressed the desire to travel abroad, journeying through Spain, France, Italy, Germany, Holland and England. He planned to travel incognito with a household of 200 persons and body of eighty guards, and supposed that he and his party might achieve their grand tour for the modest sum of 8m. *cruzados*. His ministers had some difficulty in dissuading him, for he insisted that his honour was engaged in not desisting from what he had decided. Finally, the duke of Cadaval reminded him that he could not travel abroad without the consent of *cortes*.[1] The French minister reported that John fell into a profound depression on finding his scheme impracticable, and retired to Vila Viçosa to convalesce in May 1716. In the following year, work was begun at Mafra. Palace, library, basilica and country-seat, this enormous monument sought to rival the Escorial: the basilica was consecrated in 1730, but the whole edifice was terminated only in 1735, having absorbed enormous sums of money.

---

[1] Nor were nobles allowed to travel abroad without first obtaining royal consent, since the defections after the Restoration.

The source of this wealth was the gold of Brazil. The rush of prospectors continued, and in 1708–9 there were violent struggles in Minas between the discoverers and the interlopers (*emboabas*). New towns appeared, and in 1720 Minas Gerais became a separate territory. During this time, the production of gold was probably about 3,200 lb. a year. The crown was entitled to one-fifth of all precious metals mined, though it had difficulty in obtaining it. The royal smelting-house converted gold-dust into bars, retaining the royal fifth, but as the smelting-houses were distant and there was little coin in Brazil, miners and traders used dust instead of coin, reckoning its value at four-fifths. This led to much evasion. Attempts to enforce the payment of the fifth by severe penalties proved useless, and in order not to drive the gold to foreign countries, the crown minted gold coin in Brazil, relaxed the searching of ships for contraband, and authorized the mint in Lisbon to receive gold for coining without inquiry as to its origin. Thus in 1705 a fleet brought to Lisbon about 16,000 lb., of which less than 640 was for the crown. During the period 1700–20, the crown received about 36m. *cruzados*. In 1728 the flow of wealth was increased by the discovery of diamonds in the same area, and in the last twenty-four years of the reign, the crown drew some 71m. *cruzados*. The sum of 107m. *cruzados* spread over forty-four years is not fabulous, but the royal revenues represented only a fifth of what was declared. Evidently the situation of Portugal and Brazil in the first half of the eighteenth century was far removed from the penury of the first Braganças. According to the phrase placed in the mouth of John V: 'My grandfather owed and feared; my father owed; I neither fear nor owe.'

But before the effect of this wealth was felt, there intervened a period of stress as the war against the Bourbons worked itself out. After the death of Pedro II, the struggle in Spain went against the allies. In the spring of 1707 French and Spanish troops advanced to Almansa, where they occupied a strong position and had the advantage of numbers. The Anglo-Portuguese forces in Valencia attacked, but after gaining an initial advantage, they were defeated, and the attempted invasion from Valencia collapsed. It was then planned to advance against Madrid from Beira, but the Bourbon forces occupied Serpa and Moura, the Portuguese territory to the east of the Guadiana. These were recovered, but the prospects of

driving the Bourbons out of Spain were now dim. In 1709 Galway
planned to advance against Badajoz, against the advice and desires
of John V and his ministers: when in April, supported by the marquis
of Fronteira, he began his attack, he was involved in a series of
unsuccessful manœuvres in which he lost his cannon and was in
danger of losing his army. After this no major operations were
attempted from the Portuguese front. Soundings for peace had begun
much earlier, but preliminary discussions at the Hague in May 1709
failed, since the allies still insisted on the expulsion of the Bourbons
from Spain. After Malplaquet in September 1709, negotiations were
resumed, only to fall foul of the same difficulty. In 1710 the pretender,
operating from Catalonia, entered Saragossa and succeeded in taking
Madrid (28 September): he was coldly received, for the Castilians
did not take kindly to the idea of conquest from Catalonia, and reports
of his undertakings to dismember Spain added nothing to his popular-
ity. He was unable to hold the capital, and the Bourbon forces
inflicted two defeats on him. In April 1711 the Emperor died, and he
succeeded to the imperial throne. This changed the whole balance
of forces. At the beginning of the struggle, it had seemed that the
French threatened to dominate Europe; but now the accession of the
Spanish pretender to the Habsburg domains conjured up a vision of
a restored Empire such as had existed in the days of Charles V. In
October 1711 preliminaries of peace were signed in London, and in
January 1712 representatives of the powers concerned met at
Utrecht. The Grand Alliance had failed.

In Portugal it had been necessary in 1709 to sell offices, including
those in the Mint and the Casa da Índia, and by 1711 the pay of
the army was eleven months in arrears. Many of the sources of
revenue were mortgaged, and pensions, annuities and salaries were
paid directly from the custom-houses, tobacco-monopoly and other
royal establishments. The prospects of attaining the advantages
promised by the Grand Alliance were now remote. Just before the
opening of the discussions at Utrecht, Dom Luis da Cunha had asked
the English government for the creation of a frontier province to
serve as a buffer between Spain and Portugal, similar to that by
which Holland proposed to protect herself. But the idea was impracticable, and the Portuguese obtained little satisfaction from the
negotiations. In November 1712 they concluded an armistice, and

in April 1713 a peace-treaty with France. In February 1715 peace was concluded with Spain: the few Spanish frontier fortresses held by the Portuguese were returned, while in America the Sacramento colony was awarded to Portugal, as provided for by the terms of the Grand Alliance.

During the following years the monarchy of John V accumulated wealth and power, advancing towards a form of national absolutism. The model for monarchy was the regime of Louis XIV, his personal power, the ceremonial of his court and the magnificence of Versailles, the patronage of learning and culture by the crown and the centralization of government. In Spain the Bourbons attempted to implant a similar regalism, overriding the regionalism of the ancient domains of Aragon and attempting to mould the existing institutions of Spanish culture or to implant new ones. In Portugal, the problem of regionalism did not exist and the Braganças were not foreigners. John instituted a Royal Academy of History (1720) and endowed the University of Coimbra with an elegant and splendidly decorated library: the library of the palace at Mafra is the most attractive portion of that enormous pile. Under royal patronage there appeared Bluteau's *Vocabulário*, the *Bibliotheca Lusitana*, the *Corpus Poetarum Lusitanorum* and Caetano de Sousa's *História genealógica da Casa Real*. A hundred volumes of documents relating to Portugal were copied in Rome, and the destruction of antiquities was prohibited. The Academy of Portugal was founded for Portuguese artists in Rome. Nor were more practical designs overlooked. The Aqueduct of Free Waters brought to Lisbon the blessing of abundant water, carried a distance of 18½ km. over 109 arches built by Manuel da Maia (1729–44). The handsome street fountains (*chafarizes*) are of this date. So too are the Lisbon arsenal and ordnance factory, the paperfactory of Lousã and the expansion of the woollen industry at Covilhã, originally set up to supply the army with uniforms. New hospitals were raised, and a course in surgery instituted in Lisbon, while Portuguese were sent abroad to study economic practice, mathematics and astronomy.

Much of John's wealth was distributed in gestures of prestige or largesse. When his heir José was married to the Spanish princess Mariana Victoria, and his daughter married the Spanish heir Ferdinand (VI) the extraordinary expenses of the ceremonies were met by a so-called 'voluntary donation' of 7m. *cruzados* from Brazil. Those who came to Portugal or left it in John's service were handsomely rewarded. But he also assisted those in need, whether the queen-mother of Spain, who could not obtain her pension, or a captain who had been victorious against the Turks, or the peasants of the Alentejo, who in 1735 had no seed. His munificence may have been unplanned, but it was not reckless.

John's wealth rendered him independent of the subsidies of *cortes*, which now ceased to be summoned. However, the changing form of society had long since rendered obsolete the ancient institution in which the commoners were represented as an undifferentiated mass. The royal will was made to run in the provinces by the military commands set up during the wars of the Restoration. In the city, the municipality and guilds were the only instruments of representation. Nevertheless, the monarch himself was not a 'sacred catholic majesty': it was impossible to forget that his grandfather had been a mere nobleman and that many of the rest of the class were his kinsmen. He was no less interested than the Bourbons in the dignity of his situation, and not lacking in personal vanity. But unlike the Bourbons, John wished his splendour to be firmly associated with the apostolic tradition. He not only richly endowed the church in Portugal, but expected it and the Holy See to respect his foibles.

Early in his reign, in January 1709, he appointed as his chaplain Nuno da Cunha de Ataide and applied to Rome for dignitaries for the royal chapel. He then sought to raise the chapel to a patriarchate and asked the Holy See first to detach a number of parishes from the see of Lisbon and later to place the whole of the western half of the city under his patriarch, who was soon granted all the honours and prerogatives enjoyed by cardinals, the right to crown kings and finally in 1737 a cardinalate, which was to be conferred on all future patriarchs.

The patriarchate was conferred in 1716 in recognition of John's services against the Muslims. The Turks had seized Morea, and the Emperor Charles VI had declared war on them in May, whereupon the pope appealed to Portugal and Spain to resume their historical crusading mission. Spain, which had still not recognized the emperor, would not actively assist him, but John, as the emperor's brother-in-law, sent six warships, a hospital-ship and other craft. They sailed to Corfu, but the Turks had now retired after the fall of Bucarest and Temešvar, and the Portuguese fleet returned. It had hardly done so when a new appeal was received, and in April 1717 it returned with reinforcements to the Mediterranean, fighting the battle of Matapan in July.

But John's desire to appear beside his brother-in-law as a crusading monarch was compounded with an obstinate zeal to match and eclipse the fervour and piety of the other Catholic courts, not to be baulked even by the pope. The nuncios at Vienna, Madrid and Paris were cardinals. The kings of Poland had attempted to obtain equal consideration, but failed. John now demanded that the nuncio in Lisbon be elected to the Sacred College. He was refused by Clement XI, Innocent XIII and Benedict XIII. Finally in 1725 he obtained a written promise. But the pope refused to promote the nuncio for whom John had demanded the favour, Bichi, and sent in his place one Firrao, whom John refused to receive. There were thus two nuncios in Lisbon, one not recognized by the king and the other not recognized by the pope. When Benedict XIII ordered Bichi to leave Portugal, John ordered him to remain. Two committees of cardinals refused to elevate Bichi, and when he was again passed over, the Portuguese mission in Rome withdrew: in July 1728 relations with Rome were suspended. Finally both Bichi and Firrao left Lisbon, the former with a handsome present. In 1730 Clement XII made Bichi a cardinal: John had already sent him 4,000 *cruzados* for the expenses of his election; he now added 25,000 so that the celebrations might be adequate. A little later John obtained the coveted cardinalate for his patriarch. In effect something akin to a national church had been created under the shadow of the monarchy, in part, at least, the consequence of the persistent snubbing of the Braganças by Rome during the long period of the Restoration.

'Neither owing nor fearing', John V was able to remain unaffected by the shifting combinations of European politics. The attempts of the Spanish minister Fr Alberoni to overthrow the settlement of Utrecht had brought a momentary crisis in 1719, but this was resolved with his fall, and in the following years relations between the two countries improved. In 1728 the Braganças were united to the Spanish Bourbons by a double marriage. However, neither prince enjoyed any influence in affairs until his accession. In Madrid,

Philip V was governed by his second wife, Elizabeth Farnese, who easily excluded her stepson Ferdinand and Barbara of Bragança. In 1735 an incident between the two countries almost led to an open quarrel when Spanish troops in pursuit of a refugee entered the Portuguese embassy in Madrid and seized nineteen servants. John duly sent a company of grenadiers to apprehend nineteen lackeys in the Spanish embassy at Lisbon. There were reports of the movement of troops; and the Portuguese obtained an assurance of assistance from the British ambassador: a British naval division visited the Tagus in June, and the affair was settled early in 1737.

Despite his punctiliousness, John V was not the most active of monarchs, and from 1742 he suffered from what was described as dropsy of the chest: he made frequent visits to take the waters at Caldas, but his energies had been sapped long before he expired in 1750. His abiding fear of death caused him to allow the conduct of affairs to fall increasingly into the hands of churchmen, who were little less lethargic than himself. His reign had seen the rise of the secretaries of state, who were now translated into ministers. The palace had traditionally contained the Councils of State and Overseas Affairs, as well as the treasury, a council consisting of a president and *vèdores*, and the supreme court of appeal. In the days of Afonso VI, who was incapable of governing, his minister Castelo-Melhor had called himself *escrivão da puridade*, an archaic legalism for a private secretary, but implying a vizir or *privado*. Thereafter no minister held absolute power until the time of Pombal; but the secretaries, traditionally not men of the highest nobility, now extended their authority until they were able to eclipse the councils in which the nobles had formerly made their influence felt. The two secretaries became three in 1736, and their business was divided into Home Affairs ('State'), Foreign Affairs and War, and Overseas and Marine (*negócios ultramarinos*). There are few signs of anything resembling a struggle between these departmental heads or ministers and the presidents of the councils: such vain questions as arose from points of precedence could be settled by the munificent monarch.

In John's later years no minister was removed except by death. The office of Minister of State was held by Cardinal da Mota, a personage who was largely responsible for the stagnation and retrogression of those years: he died in 1747, and his office passed to his nephew Pedro da Mota, an invalid. António Pereira, the secretary of naval affairs, died also in 1747, and was followed by Diogo de Mendonça, an agreeable diplomat. The senior minister was Marco António de Azevedo Coutinho who survived until 1749: the control of foreign affairs and war then passed to Fr Gaspar da Encarnação, who in effect held all the reins of government. Behind these, the second Portuguese cardinal, Nuno da Cunha, the Inquisitor-General, exercised an influence only a little less than that of Cardinal Mota. John V's confidential adviser was Padre Carbone, a Neapolitan Jesuit who had come to Portugal on ecclesiastical business and won the monarch's confidence: he died in 1750.

The emergence of this priestly party was largely the consequence of John's illness. Neither the cardinal nor Fr Gaspar were the best candidates available. The royal secretary, Alexandre Gusmão, pointed out the consequences of the inactivity of the government: 'If your Highness were to go about your realms, you will find, not without alarm, many lands usurped, others untilled, and many roads impassable, so that whatever the land produces cannot be used . . . many great places almost deserted, with their manufactures ruined and lost and their trade quite extenuated.' The senior diplomat in the Portuguese service, Dom Luis da Cunha, was well aware of the general state of neglect and of the need for stern measures. In his *Testamento Político* he recommended Sebastião José de Carvalho e Melo 'whose genius, patient, speculative and rather diffuse, though without vice, accords well with that of the nation'. New times were at hand.

2. JOSÉ I, 1750–77

John V died on 31 July 1750 amidst scenes of intense piety and devotion. His widow, the Austrian queen Maria Ana, had assumed the regency during his illness, and it was seen that she would for the moment exert great influence over her son José, who was now thirty-six, but had not been allowed to take any part in public affairs. Nor had he shown much interest in them. His benevolent and rather superficial nature did not admit of intense exertions. His main interests were riding, shooting, cards, the theatre and music: these, with frequent devotions and religious holidays, easily filled an otherwise vacant existence. He had married Mariana Victoria, a daughter of Philip V of Spain and Elizabeth Farnese: she had been betrothed at the age of five to Louis XV, but after two years in France, a quirk of French policy had packed her back to Spain. Her mother had been furious at the slight. She had married José at the age of fourteen, and was more robust and definite than her husband. The royal family consisted of four princesses: the eldest, the future Maria I, was now sixteen.

The Minister of State was still Pedro da Mota, but his health prevented him from doing anything active, and the chief burden of government was borne by Fr Gaspar. Preparations to replace him had already been made, and the most hopeful candidate was Gusmão, whose abilities were certainly above the ordinary. But three days after John's death, his rival Sebastião José de Carvalho e Melo received notice of his appointment as minister, and after a further three days of his assignment to the department of Foreign Affairs and War in the place of Fr Gaspar. Gusmão expressed himself in a fit of prophetic spleen: 'The Pasha has obtained his purpose, such are the ways of the world! The people will suffer for it, and the news will go down to future times, which will admire the effects of his spacious ideas in everything that falls within his own department (if he does not meddle in the others!).'

The Pasha, who in 1759 became count of Oeiras and in 1770 marquis of Pombal, had been born in 1699 of an undistinguished line of rural nobility: his father was a cavalry officer and he was the eldest of three sons and one daughter. Little is known of his early life: he served in the cavalry and as the result of a family quarrel retired to his country home at Soure. He later went to Lisbon to seek official employment with the help of his uncles, one Marco António de Azevedo, the future Secretary of State, and another archpriest in the newly established patriarchate. But Cardinal da Mota would do no more than appoint him to the Academy of History, where he is supposed to have performed researches in the history of the royal family. He then eloped with a niece of the count of Arcos and thus gained reluctant admittance to circles hitherto closed to him. His uncle the archpriest died, leaving him an inheritance, and the cardinal decided to send him to represent Portugal in London, where he was from 1740 to 1744. These were important years in his formation: he decided to investigate 'the causes wherefore His Majesty from the beginning of his reign found the commerce of Portugal in such decay, whereas that of England and of other nations had an excessive expansion'. His more immediate duties were to defend the interests and dignity of Portugal in various naval and commercial incidents. He exercised a forceful and rather overladen style: Benjamin Keene at first thought him 'a little busy pettifogging mind'.[1] When he returned to Lisbon, he endeavoured to persuade his government to float an enterprise on the lines of the East India Company; but those in power, recalling probably the attempts of Vieira, pleaded penury and displayed indifference. In the middle of 1745 Pombal was sent to Vienna to represent John V as mediator between the Empress Maria Teresa and Pope Benedict XIV, a thankless task since both sides suspected him of partiality. He regarded this as evidence of displeasure at his commercial lucubrations. The post was temporary, and he had not relinquished his appointment in London. His first wife died in Lisbon, and he married the daughter of Marshal Daun five months after his arrival in Vienna. She was of ancient lineage but slender resources, and he had to pawn his plate to leave Vienna, arriving back in Lisbon eight months before the death of John V. John was not well-disposed towards him, and he was opposed by Frei Gaspar (who was related to the powerful duke of Aveiro) and by Gusmão. His uncle Marco António died without being able to help him, but he had the support of Dom Luis da Cunha, and his Austrian wife had access to the Austrian queen.

He came to power at the age of fifty-one. The valetudinarian Mota was still Prime Minister, and Pombal had to humour him as well as do his work. His other colleague, Diogo de Mendonça, was a courtier rather than a man of affairs. He was therefore scarcely a rival to Pombal. However, the new minister had to assure himself of the favour of José and to prevent palace intrigues. He was, in fact, to hold power for twenty-seven years, and his rule was coterminous with the reign of the indolent José. He soon took the measure of the king, and José, after at first attending industriously to his new obligations, quickly became content to leave everything to Pombal. Every day, the king and queen rode out to Belém with their company, or played faro, or listened to the opera. They returned to Lisbon at eight or

---

[1] Pombal himself later advised a young diplomat of the importance of dealing with matters according to their moment.

nine in the evening, and in theory José worked with his ministers until midnight: in practice, he rarely appeared before eleven and did little more than sign the papers that were presented to him.

Pombal's power therefore rested on his own resolution and his circumstances rather than on a concern with any institutions, new or old. He did indeed find the machinery of government seized, and determined to make it function differently, but he could not alter things rapidly. On 26 August the French consul noted that the king had set aside three days a week for business, that it was transacted with exemplary speed and that order was beginning to emerge out of chaos. But José quickly lost his enthusiasm, and Pombal found it more advantageous to chat and to explore the king's thoughts than to clear up arrears of business, which were not dealt with until they became pressing, and often not then.

The immediate problems that faced him were negotiations with the Spanish court and the encroachments of the British merchants. In Madrid the accession of Ferdinand VI and his Portuguese queen in 1746 provided a favourable opportunity for the two courts to settle their differences in South America. The Portuguese occupation of the Sacramento colony on the River Plate had led to the growth of an active contraband trade with the Spanish possessions, largely conducted by British ships. It was now proposed that Sacramento should be returned to Spain, which would compensate Portugal by transferring part of Paraguay, now administered by the Jesuits, who had converted the Indians and organized them into thirty missions or 'reductions', and administered the whole territory. The Jesuits, having established a virtual theocracy in the region, were opposed to a bargain which would divide the Indians and expose the missions to raiders from São Paulo. The other objectors were the British, who saw in the treaty a threat to their lucrative trade on the River Plate. The treaty had been negotiated, but not ratified when John V died. Its ratification and the demarcation of frontier led to resistance by the Jesuits and the Indians in a long and obscure campaign in Paraguay and an even more obscure action at the Portuguese court.

As regards the British merchants, Pombal was faced with the fact that much of the gold production of Brazil, which was now showing signs of declining, went to pay for imports from Britain, that the ability of the English to provide goods cheaply stifled Portuguese production, and that the rights of the English to trade were amply protected by a series of ancient privileges expressly revived at the Restoration. He himself was convinced of the importance of trade with Brazil, and while in England had written a paper on the advantages of colonial over foreign trade, but he had thought rather on the lines of the organization of colonial trading-companies. On coming to office, the first task assigned to him was the reformation of the Brazilian gold-trade. John V's ministers had been unable to stop contraband and had reduced the royal fifth to a tenth. As long since as 1734 the mining community had offered to compound for a fixed levy of 100 *arrobas* of gold, but preference had been given to a capitation tax on each miner employed. The effect of this had been to concentrate production at the most prolific points and to discourage prospecting: in 1748 and 1749 over 15,000 negroes had left the mines. Pombal proposed to return to a levy system: he sent his plan to the Overseas Council which expressed opposition (possibly from his rival Gusmão): characteristically, he returned the criticism, informed the council that its functions were purely advisory, and ignored their advice. But although the royal revenues could be improved, it was clear that the production of the mines was no longer soaring.

The export of gold from Portugal had been prohibited in medieval times, but the government of John V had winked at transfers or smuggling, which served to pay for necessary imports. Much earlier, it had been decided not to press too strictly for the royal fifth, for fear of encouraging contraband out of Brazil. However, the smuggling of gold out of Portugal in the later years of John V appears to have been due rather to the general laxity of administration: Gusmão refers to constant smuggling in 1746, and in 1748 there were scandals in the tobacco and pepper trades. Pombal appointed a new head of the custom-house, who in 1752 seized a consignment of bullion belonging to the firm of Burrells, alleging a law of Afonso V by which its export was prohibited. The merchants raised loud protests, as a result of which the British government sent out the former ambassador Lord Tyrawley on a special mission. He soon came to the conclusion that the merchants were making a pother about nothing, and having obtained the return of the bullion to the Burrells, went home. The smuggling was resumed, and in 1755 the tobacco-guards arrested the mate of the Falmouth packet, a Mr Humphrey Bunster, who was found to be carrying four packets of Portuguese coin belonging to Burrells and others. The merchants did their best to have the case brought before the Judge-Conservator, but Pombal insisted that it should go to the usual courts: they decided that the money should be confiscated.

This did not mean that Pombal was opposed to the English: on the contrary, he had seen the effects of capitalism in England, and desired that Portugal should attain a similar prosperity. One of his early measures had been to allow Portuguese merchants to wear swords as the nobility did, thus placing them on a level of social equality with English colleagues and competitors. But a society which consisted of peasants led by a hierarchy of officials and nobles could not overnight be equipped with an active mercantile class. It was clear that the state would have to lead the way, as it had done in the sixteenth century.

When the English merchants had taken advantage of the favourable conditions of the Restoration to re-enter the much-prized 'Portugal trade', they were in the main a crowd of rather young and unruly agents and apprentices who sold dried cod-fish, woollens and hardware and took out wines, almonds and salt. Their affairs were guided by the consul, who governed their association or 'factory', and for two generations they occupied an important, but scarcely a preponderant part in the overseas trade of Portugal. In 1703, Methuen, while concluding the treaties of the Grand Alliance, took the opportunity to negotiate the commercial agreement which bears his name. Its three brief articles gave the English a preferential market for their textiles, and the Portuguese a preferential outlet for their wines. In view of the approaching struggle with France, the opportunity to introduce Portuguese wines into England was evident. The inflow of English woollens adversely affected the Portuguese textile industry, which Ericeira had endeavoured to nurture, and some Portuguese economists believed that their prospects of industrialization had been sacrificed. However, in the conditions of 1703, the market for Portuguese wines in England appeared larger than that for English woollens in Portugal. At that time the flow of gold from Brazil was still only a trickle, and the expansion of Portuguese purchasing-power could scarcely have been foreseen. As the gold flowed into Portugal, the leaders of the British factory acquired considerable fortunes, and families whose forebears had sold dried cod and hardware lived and behaved like merchant-princes. The hey-day of Keene's 'jolly free factory' was in the 1730s.

Their prosperity was not fully reflected in the fortunes of the wine-trade. Port, the fortified wine produced only in the valley of the Douro and long considered a superior product, stimulated a demand for other and cheaper wines, from central Portugal and Lisbon, Dão, Carcavelos, Colares and Bucelas, which came to occupy a progress-ively larger proportion of the trade, while the volume and price of port fell. The pipe of wine worth 60,000 *reis* at the beginning of the century fell to 48,000 in 1731, and to 6,400 after 1750. According to a memorial presented to Pombal, the English merchants had used their monopoly of purchasing and shipping to depress prices, and this had plunged the growers into misery. The causes are probably more complicated than this. The English merchants of Oporto had invested their profits in the purchase of vineyards, and so acquired the profit of the grower; there had also been an undue expansion of the area producing port and a marked tendency to pass over to cheaper wines.

As far as Portugal's trade in colonial commodities was concerned, Pombal found that the system of annual fleets, which had been made compulsory in time of war, now caused the warehouses of Lisbon to be glutted with sugar and tobacco for short periods of the year: prices then dropped, and the goods were withheld until they rose again. It had been proposed to burn the tobacco as a solution—a remedy later adopted in Brazil to maintain coffee-prices, and dignified by the name of valorization. By decrees of January 1751 Pombal offered a reduction of duties for the re-export of tobacco and granted privileges to new sugar-refineries on condition they used the surplus from the Lisbon custom-houses, at the same time simplifying the customs procedure. A similar problem faced the diamond trade. The distribution was controlled by a Jewish monopoly in London and Amsterdam, and by 1734 the market had seemed to be saturated. John V had ordered mining to cease, and then leased the monopoly of trade by contract for periods of four years. In 1749 it was necessary to stipulate that the contractor should not market his stones until the end of the period, so that prices would have time to revive: he permitted extensive contraband, but was none the less bankrupt by the end of his term. Pombal attempted to preserve the monopoly of production, but to force the hand of the Jewish monopoly by setting up a marketing agency in Holland. However, the contractors for 1753 gave up after only two years and their successors after three. In 1771 the trade was taken over by the state.

Pombal's first adventure in state-aided capitalism was the Company for Trade with Asia in 1753, followed by the Grão-Pará Company in 1755. The latter was intended to be the first of three companies which would monopolize the trade of Brazil. Its statutes bore some resemblance to those of Vieira's company of 1648; it was given a Judge-Conservator with priority over the Judge of the English, and its directors were to be all Portuguese. Its monopoly included the export trade, and the wholesale trade. These privileges were obnoxious to the Portuguese merchants already trading to Brazil, as well as to the Jesuits and the British merchants. In Lisbon the Portuguese merchants were loosely organized in an association known as the Mesa do Bem Comum, which now presented a memorandum of protest. It was at once dissolved, and its secretary was banished for thirty years. In 1756 it was replaced by the Junta do Comércio, a body which functioned under the minister, and controlled all matters relating to commerce: it too was given its own court, its judge having priority, and it proceeded to declare a lengthy series of articles to be luxuries, the importation of which was forbidden.

These draconian measures intimidated many. The most active resistance to the minister came from Jesuits, who were on the remotest fringe of the Portuguese world and at its centre. They were still confessors to the royal family, and they still governed the Indians of Paraguay and Pará in virtual independence of the crown. In Paraguay, one of the members of the Luso-Spanish boundary commission had been Pombal's brother, Francisco Xavier de Mendonça. This commission had decided that the Jesuits must move some of their reductions to conform with the new boundaries. Their superiors told them that they must obey, but there had followed a long resistance, after which the Indians were removed by Portuguese and Spanish troops. In Pombal's eyes the Jesuits were responsible for the resistance of the Indians. He now appointed his brother to be governor of Pará and Maranhão in northern Brazil with instructions to enforce the monopoly of the new Grão-Pará Company whatever the objections of the Jesuits, who themselves engaged in trade and maintained that their commercial activities were necessary for the support of their missions.

The first counter-stroke of the Jesuits was a sermon preached in the Patriarcal, with some ironical comments directed at the minister. Pombal pronounced those who criticized royal laws guilty of treason: the preacher was banished and three merchants of the Mesa do Bem Comum were exiled to Africa. There was thereafter little active resistance in Pará: four Jesuits were expelled and arrived in Lisbon in November 1755. The great strength of the Jesuits lay in their intimacy with the crown through the royal confessors, their direct influence over the people, whether through their preaching, their unrivalled collection of relics, or their energy in raising funds. The most remarkable of the Jesuits of Brazil was Gabriel Malagrida, born near Lake Como in 1689: he had gone out as a missionary in 1721 and become famous for his fervent sermons and his strange adventures among the Indians, who, it seemed, had been prevented from eating him only by miracles. His fame as a prophet and saint spread far and wide, and wherever he appeared his ascetic eye, his long white beard and his fiery sermons brought crowds to see him. The faithful gave largely, and he founded convents and rebuilt decaying churches. In 1749 he had returned to Portugal and had been received by John V, who was so impressed that he insisted on dying in his arms. Malagrida had then revisited Brazil (travelling in the same ship as Pombal's brother), but in 1753 he again returned to Portugal and attached himself to the queen-mother, Pombal's former protectress. But his influence now aroused suspicion, and when she fell ill, he was forbidden to enter her apartments. However, in this he was a match for Pombal. He returned to his house at Setúbal, and on 14 August 1754, while preaching a sermon, he broke off to announce the death of the queen-mother: it was, of course, later verified that she had died precisely at that moment. However, it was only a year later that Malagrida was provided with an opportunity to pull out all his stops.

The great Lisbon earthquake occurred at 9.30 a.m. on All Saints' Day, Saturday, 1 November 1755. It was a clear, bright morning, and large numbers of people had crowded to the churches where the altars were ablaze with candles. The city suddenly shook, pitching and rolling like a ship at sea. After a brief pause, there followed a devastating shock lasting two minutes. Churches, palaces and houses came down in a roar of destruction. Then came another shock, and the rising of palls of choking dust. The whole phenomenon lasted about ten minutes. After an interval of perhaps an hour, it was followed by a tidal wave: the waters of the Tagus receded, piled up and then came rolling into the Terreiro do Paço and the shore at Alcântara. There were several aftershocks which brought down shaken buildings. The main shocks were felt throughout the Peninsula and in France, while the tidal wave was felt with force at Cádiz, reached England the same afternoon and the Caribbean in the evening: it was perceived as far afield as Dantzig.

It is impossible to establish accurately the number of those who perished. Many were buried in fallen churches or burnt in the fires that raged. More than 5,000, possibly as many as 15,000, died out of a population of 270,000. The Portuguese nobility lost less than twenty; the English factory lost seventy-seven. The Spanish ambassador was killed as he rushed from his house, and the president of the English Seminary died after being crushed under a bench. The ruins of the great church of the Carmo founded by Nun'Alvares Pereira can still be seen. The palace of the Patriarchate, the Inquisition, the Arsenal, the Casa da Índia all collapsed. The church of São Domingos was the scene of a great fire. The devastation was probably greatest in the centre of the town, and among the palaces and official buildings near the waterfront.

At the time of the catastrophe José was at Belém where the shock was comparatively mild. When he asked what to do, the marquis of Alorna is said to have replied: 'Bury the dead, care for the living and close the ports', and this remark, in the form: 'Bury the dead and feed the living' has since been frequently ascribed to Pombal. Of the other ministers Mota was ill and Mendonça not to be found. Pombal displayed good sense, but he was supported by many others, including José's cousins, the duke of Lafões and the cardinal-patriarch, the marquis of Marialva, Grand-Master of the Horse, the marquis of Alegrete, president of the Lisbon Senate, and the marquis of Abrantes, commander-in-chief, not to mention many officials and parish priests. Added to fears of a recurrence were the dangers of pestilence, starvation and crime. The patriarch consented that the dead should be buried without religious formality, and troops of soldiers recovered bodies from the ruins and sank them in the Tagus. In each of the twelve wards of the city a special magistrate was appointed with full powers. Gallows were erected as a warning to bandits, whose ranks were swollen by the escape of convicts. All food on ships in the Tagus was impounded, and supplies were ordered from the provinces. Prices were fixed and taxes suspended. Emergency canteens and hospitals were opened. A great part of the population took to the fields. It was necessary to stop the flight of skilled craftsmen and to hasten the provision of temporary shelters. José and his family lived in tents at Belém for nine months, at the end of which they moved into a wooden palace. Pombal himself, though his palace was undamaged, lived in huts at Belém. At the end of the month, a survey of the ruins was made, and it was decided to rebuild the centre of the city. The opportunity to execute a bold piece of town-planning was seized, and its results can be seen in the existing Terreiro do Paço and the uniform streets which lead from it to the Rossio.

The neighbouring governments offered assistance in dealing with the crisis. The English parliament voted £100,000 for relief and sent barrels of meat, firkins of butter, rice, flour, footwear and money. The cost of rebuilding the city was provided for by a tax of 4 per cent on all merchandise, to be collected by the Junta do Comércio. Against this the British merchants protested in vain.

The effect of the earthquake on European thought was profound. A host of accounts of the phenomenon appeared in many languages, giving rise to a series of controversies, of which the most far-reaching turned on whether the earthquake was a purely natural phenomenon or a divine visitation. The first published account (Trovão e Sousa, 20 December) contained many exaggerations, which were corrected by the Franciscan António dos Remédios (20 January 1756) and by Bento Morgante (13 February). There followed a commentary composed with great care in Portuguese and Latin by António Pereira de Figueiredo. Other writers emphasized the need for investigation of phenomena and medical and other aspects. But for many the earthquake was a manifestation of divine wrath and afforded an irresistible opportunity to produce thunderous sermons, the purport of which was the special wickedness of the Portuguese and the need for atonement. Exhortations to personal penitence were unexceptionable and salutary: but those who inferred a special collective guilt, if asked why thousands of faithful had perished during mass on All Saints' Day while those in prisons or haunts of vice were spared, could only reply that the designs of Providence were inscrutable. Pombal requested the cardinal-patriarch to restrain the fervour of these priests who sought to represent a national disaster as a pure and deliberate manifestation of divine displeasure.

At the time of the earthquake, Pombal was not yet in name chief minister, though he became so a few months later, when Pedro da Mota died. His elevation brought him supreme power, for the king merely devoted less of his time to hunting and more to religious observances. Pombal filled the vacancy in foreign affairs by calling on Dom Luis da Cunha Manuel, a nephew of the diplomat. The only remaining member of the older dispensation was Diogo de Mendonça, who found himself gradually forced into opposition.

By the spring of 1756 Pombal had consolidated his power: he could now be dislodged only by the king himself, and it seemed unlikely that José would ever oppose the ruthless will of his minister. Aspirants to power had often associated themselves with heirs to the throne. But José's successor was his daughter Maria, princess of Brazil, now aged twenty-two. She would be required to marry in Portugal, and the choice was virtually limited to her uncle Pedro, José's brother, and José's cousin, the duke of Lafões. Those aristocrats who saw in Pombal a threat to their own interests began to frequent the court of Pedro at Queluz: Pedro himself was not in the least ambitious for power; the only danger lay in his manipulation by others. Pombal was suspicious of the circle of Pedro, and particularly of Diogo de Mendonça, the amiable, popular and jealous Minister for Overseas Affairs. The Jesuits who had been deported from Pará had reached Lisbon soon after the earthquake and must have made their complaints to him. José had already requested that the Spanish Jesuit, St Francis Borja, should be appointed patron and protector of Portugal, and Pombal had dispatched the petition to the pope, who readily complied in May 1756: in future, the name of St Francis

Borja was to be invoked in every parish in Portugal on the anniversary of the earthquake.

A month later, in June, Pombal came upon some correspondence which he regarded as compromising, and took the opportunity to arrest Mendonça. He was banished from court and replaced by Pombal's brother, Francisco Xavier de Mendonça, now recalled from Pará. The remaining conspirators included two Italian priests about the palace, a lawyer, Teixeira de Mendonça, who had drawn up a petition of grievances to be presented to the king, and Martinho Velho Oldemburg, of a well-known Luso-Dutch merchant family, who apparently laid the petition before José and urged him to dismiss Pombal, offering suggestions for his replacement. The story thus unfolded was that Oldemburg, in whose houses at Ajuda the king was lodging, approached him under pretext of presenting a scheme for the reconstruction of Lisbon, and cast aspersions on Pombal: he promised to justify these, and produced a memorandum of twenty-eight pages in which many charges were levelled against the minister's family and it was alleged that Pombal himself had wormed his way into the Academy of History to obtain private information with which to undermine eminent houses, and that he had received 50,000 *cruzados* from the gunpowder concession, 600,000 from the diamond contract, and 160,000 in shares of the Grão-Pará Company: the court and kingdom were full of dissatisfaction, and though they had accepted the legislation in the hope that good might ensue, further wrongs were contemplated which would ruin the kingdom by preventing the succession.[1]

José showed the document to one of his two Italian priests, who remarked that if this were true he must be much mistaken in his minister. The king then delivered the report to Pombal, who arrested Oldemburg, the author of the paper, the Italian priests and other suspects. The priests were held at Junqueira and the rest dispatched to Angola. Mendonça was banished from court, then deported and finally imprisoned at Peniche, where he died. Towards the end of 1756, the duke of Lafões was sent to Vienna, where he spent the following twenty years.

[1] 'The legislation' referred to the Junta do Comércio and the trading-companies; 'further wrongs' to Pombal's unwillingness to allow the princess of Brazil to marry her uncle. His wife certainly held shares in the Grão-Pará Company, and he certainly used his power to enrich himself.

Meanwhile, as the anniversary of the earthquake approached, it was suggested that José should make a personal and public manifestation of penitence. During the summer Malagrida composed and published his *Judgement on the True Cause of the Earthquake*, which inveighed against the sins of the people and described as heretics those who professed to believe that the late cataclysm could be 'the pure effect of natural causes and not fulminated specially by God for our sins'. The government pointed out to the nuncio the danger of spreading alarm among the people and obtained the banishment of the prophet to Setúbal.

During this time, Pombal was attempting to establish some large economic interests in Portugal, to balance the interests of the English, Dutch and German merchants. In September 1750 he set up the General Company for Wine-culture in the Upper Douro, with powers to define the port-wine area, to assure the quality of the wine and to prevent the manipulation of prices. It could buy all the wine produced in a given district, and held the monopoly of export to Brazil, and could sell to the merchants and divide its stocks among them. It was thus an instrument of state control, closely linked to the Junta do Comércio, and a trading-company in which anyone might acquire shares. Its directors must be Portuguese, and its judge had precedence over other courts. Neither its moving spirit, Fr João Mansilha, a henchman of Pombal's, nor its operations were above criticism, but the object of 'establishing a powerful company which by the weight and unity of its capital and credit' should counterbalance the foreign merchants, was largely attained: it survived until 1834.

The immediate effect of the launching of the Company was to raise the price of wine in Oporto. The tavern-keepers laid the blame on the government, and on 23 February 1757, Ash Wednesday, a rabble gathered in the streets and marched to the Judge of the People, who appeased them by promising to get the company abolished. The affair of the 'Tipplers' Revolt' was greatly magnified by rumour in Lisbon, and Pombal obtained José's consent to drastic measures. Oporto was surrounded by troops, and a special court investigated the circumstances and tried the leaders: in October thirteen men and four women were hanged, twenty-five were sent to the galleys, eighty-six were banished, and fifty-six imprisoned or fined.

This tigerish persecution was clearly designed to impress Pombal's enemies nearer Lisbon and further afield. He had already scotched the ill-considered Oldemburg plot, split the clique of Queluz and banished Lafões. In May 1757 he ordered the secularization of civil power in Pará, extinguishing the missions and declaring the Indians free. The Jesuits were thus limited to the standing of parish priests: some left their churches and removed the sacred vessels and images, but the state claimed the ownership of these. There were many small incidents between the Jesuits and the functionaries sent to supersede them. The Jesuits were armed with cannon, according to Pombal: according to themselves, they had two small pieces used for saluting distinguished visitors. News of the disorders reached Lisbon in September. When the royal confessor sought the king to express the alarm of the Society, he found access forbidden. At four o'clock next morning the Jesuits of the royal household, including the confessors of José and his brothers, and the tutor of the princess of Brazil, were ejected. They were forbidden to return to court without the monarch's express consent, and their duties were divided among Franciscans, Augustinians and Carmelites. In October, Pombal instructed his cousin, Francisco de Almada e Mendonça, whom he had sent as minister to Rome, to request a secret audience with the pope and press for the reform of the Society on the grounds of its insatiable desire for wealth and of its usurpation of the power of sovereigns. These charges were amplified in February 1758, and developed into a full-scale polemic. Pombal's *Brief Account* represented the Jesuits as militants who had attempted to erect a state of their own and merchants who compelled the Indians to produce tobacco, cotton and sugar for their own benefit. This was translated into French, German, Italian and Latin, and followed by the voluminous *Chronological Deduction* on the same theme. Benedict XIV was slowly dying, and it fell to Pombal's cousin to try to wrest an immediate reform of the Jesuits from him, and at the same time to ingratiate himself with possible successors with gifts. In April, the pope authorized the cardinal-patriarch to reform the Society in Portugal: he died on 9 May. On 15 May the cardinal-patriarch prohibited the Jesuits from engaging in 'illegal commerce', and on 7 June they were forbidden to preach or to hear confessions; in July their superior was banished to sixty leagues from Lisbon. Meanwhile, in Rome, Mendonça bestowed sugar on various cardinals. He could not prevent the new pope Clement XIII from summoning a congregation to consider the appeal of the Jesuits: after much assiduous sweetening, the congregation finally upheld the brief of reform.

There remained still one powerful nucleus of opposition to Pombal, the nobility. The great families had excluded him, refused to acknowledge his capacity, and long resisted his ambitions. His rise had prevented Fr Gaspar da Encarnação from securing for his nephew, the marquis of Gouvêa, the dukedom of Aveiro on the death of the last duke; and in 1752 he had humiliated the marquis of Alorna, who after a victorious career as viceroy of India, was forbidden to appear before the king until his actions had been investigated, and died in disgrace. In 1757 Pombal had struck directly at the prerogatives of the nobility, though in a minor way: various young noblemen had rescued a servant from arrest by royal officials, and when they claimed the immunity of their rank, Pombal upheld the royal magistrates by exiling them from court.

The Portuguese nobility formed a small class, much intermarried, and possibly the most exclusive in Europe. The inheritance of titles was subject to royal confirmation: the dukes all claimed kinship with the king, and there were only nine marquises and thirty-three counts. Most had palaces in Lisbon and possessed estates within reach of the capital: few dwelt in the more distant provinces. They expected to hold offices at court, embassies, governorships or other decorous employment. They were less formidable collectively than they might have been owing to their inveterate jealousies. So far, Pombal had removed the duke of Lafões from Portugal, appointed none of the nobles as ambassadors, and reserved all the plums within his reach to his family and henchmen.

The members of the nobility who were now involved in a mysterious but dreadful collision with the minister were the duke of Aveiro, his son the marquis of Gouvêa, the count of Atouguia, and his wife, and the marquis of Távora and his wife and daughter-in-law, the younger marchioness. Some of these, together with other members of the nobility, had visited Malagrida at Setúbal. And Malagrida had appealed to Clement XIII, writing, as Pombal may have known: 'What a fatal scene! What a grievous spectacle! What a sudden metamorphosis! The heralds of the word of God expelled from the missions, proscribed and condemned to ignominy! . . . And who does this? Not his most Faithful Majesty, son of Dom John V and Dona Mariana of Austria, but the minister Carvalho, whose will is supreme at court. He, yes, he, has been the architect of so many disasters and seeks to darken the splendour of our Society, which dazzles his livid eyes, with a flood of bigoted writings that breathe an immense, virulent, implacable hatred. If he could behead all the Jesuits at one blow, with what pleasure would he not do so!'

The event that was to provide Pombal with the necessary pretext occurred on the night of 3 September 1758, when the king was returning to Belém at about eleven o'clock. His coachman, finding a gate jammed, took a side road. Suddenly three mounted men appeared under the darkness of an arch and fired several shots at the royal carriage. The coachman whipped up his horses; and José, who had been hit in the arm, ordered him to drive straight to the palace surgeon at Junqueira. He thus avoided a second ambush, a group of mounted men, who fired at the back of the carriage.

The king was treated for bullet-wounds at the top of the arm and in the shoulder and chest. Next day, a brief bulletin announced that he had been taken ill, but although rumours circulated that he had been ambushed by the Távoras, nothing more was heard of the affair for over three months. Then, in December, two decrees appeared nominating a special court to investigate the attempted assassination of the king and empowering it to waive all customary forms of legal procedure and to discover and arrest the criminals, pronounce sentence and execute them on the same day. These decrees were accompanied by posters relating the events of 3 September, accusing certain persons of prophesying the death of the king and of conspiring to bring it about, and offering lavish rewards for their arrest. Next day, the House of the Twenty-four expressed the desire of the people for the punishment of the guilty. Troops were sent to apprehend the duke of Aveiro, the marquises of Távora and Alorna, and counts of Atouguia, Alorna and Ribeira Grande: Malagrida and twelve other Jesuits were arrested, and all the Jesuit colleges surrounded with troops. Three days later, the House of the Twenty-four again addressed the king, asking that the trial should take place in secret 'so that the accused might testify without fear', and also that the king should permit the use of torture for the occasion. Pombal and other ministers were present at the interrogations, at which a youth testified to having seen Aveiro bang his pistol on a stone, saying: 'Devil take you, when I have need of you you fail me.' Servants of Aveiro and of the Távoras produced under torture a tissue of evidence which enveloped the whole family: much of this was later retracted. Aveiro confessed under torture and incriminated the Távoras. Távora and his second son withstood the torture and revealed nothing: his elder son and Atouguia confessed and implicated the Távoras, but later retracted.

It appears that the king was in the habit of disappearing on amorous errands attended only by his confidential servant, Teixeira, when the queen and others imagined that he was engaged by affairs of state. One of those who received his attentions was the younger marchioness of Távora, and according to Aveiro's evidence the old marquis had learned of the king's relations with his daughter-in-law on 29 August, and had instigated the attack on the king. The court rejected Aveiro's attempt to implicate the Távoras, because the marquis could not have learned so recently what was common knowledge, and 'the Throne was many spheres above the competency and temerity of vassals': history recorded many similar cases in which the highest families had been involved, and the consequences never were any but silence or dissimulation. These perhaps were the fruits of Pombal's researches in the Academy of History: no further reference was made to José's lapses.

The evidence of the servants sought to establish that Aveiro had borne a grudge against the king for the loss of certain privileges, and had been the chief mover in the supposed plot. He had raised a subscription to pay for the assassins. They had waited for José for ten or twelve nights, but on some occasions the carriage had not appeared and on others it had gone too fast or their courage had failed them. At last Aveiro had gone out himself, placed the men and joined the first group. To cover his retreat an entertainment was held at his house, and he was to appear as soon as the deed was done. According to the evidence, on the day after the crime, he sought an interview with the young marchioness and told her of rumours that her family was implicated: she in return accused Aveiro.

On 16 December the House of the Twenty-four besought José to withdraw his wonted clemency in the case of this crime 'against the anointed of the Lord, and a sovereign of such virtues that he is the

delight of all those who have the good fortune to live under his Most
August Protection'. The wonted clemency was certainly withdrawn:
counsel for the defence was appointed only when the case was complete, and given a day to make out his case, which rested on alibis.
Questions of motive were ruled out and no further witnesses were
called. Sentence was pronounced and executed on 12 January 1759.
On a scaffold raised in the public square in Belém the elder marchioness was beheaded, followed by her two sons, Atouguia and three
servants who were broken on the wheel and strangled. Then amidst
the litter of corpses Aveiro and the old marquis were broken, while
a last asssassin was burnt. The whole scaffold was then set alight and
the ashes scattered in the Tagus.

The special court, with the intervention of the Judge of the People,
had carefully overridden the privileges of the nobility, and the blood
of dukes and servants mingled in the flames. There remained the
ecclesiastical offenders or victims. The verdict asserted that the plot
had been hatched with the collaboration of the Jesuits, and on 19
January all the fathers were confined to their colleges by royal edict:
their possessions were sequestered, and found to be of small value.
Pombal then demanded that the pope should permit the trial of the
Jesuits, and José wrote to Rome to express his intention of expelling
them from Portugal. On 11 April a brief was issued authorizing the
trial of any involved in the affair of 3 September, but rejecting in
principle the trial of priests in secular courts: Clement XIII also
wrote to José praising the Society for its work and urging him not to
condemn the whole for the errors of a few. These messages were sent
to the nuncio, who was to deliver them to José in person and to ask
him to add an ecclesiastic to the tribunal. However, Pombal's cousin
contrived to have them intercepted, and Pombal refused the nuncio's
application for an audience without being informed of their contents.
Thus on 3 September 1759, the anniversary of the royal escape, a
royal edict was published in which the crimes of the Jesuits were
related, and they were outlawed and expelled from Portugal for
ever: it was treason to communicate with them. The Portuguese
fathers were dispatched to Rome, and those from Brazil arrived there
by sea in the following year. Pombal decided to have Malagrida, the
particular object of his hatred, condemned as a heretic by the
Inquisition. The existing Inquisitor-General, a bastard of John V,

would not do for this purpose, and he was retired and sent to Bussaco, his place being taken by Pombal's younger brother, Paulo de Carvalho. Pombal himself drew the indictment in which Malagrida was charged with planning regicide from his house at Setúbal: for good measure, his life of St Ann was declared heretical and a work called a 'Treatise on the Life and Reign of the Anti-Christ' was foisted on him. He was found guilty of treason on 12 January 1761, together with blasphemy, impiety and false prophecy, and was executed publicly on 20 September. The spectacular *auto-da-fé* lasted all day, two hours being given to the reading of Malagrida's sentence. About 124 Jesuits were confined in St Julian's fort near the bar of the Tagus: some died, some probably escaped; forty-five were still there when the death of José set them free in 1777.

Nothing like the Pombaline reign of terror had been experienced in Portugal. For the rest of the reign the minister was the virtual proprietor of the government, sharing his power only with his family and his henchmen. His brother Francisco Xavier was Minister of Overseas and Marine until his death in 1769. His second brother, Paulo, priest of the Patriarchate and sometime Inquisitor-General, was president of the Senate, the corporation of Lisbon, and was succeeded in this office by Pombal's son Henrique. Pombal's sister was abbess of Odivelas. His creatures included the ineffable Fr Mansilha, who presided over the Wine Company and the Junta do Comércio and finally the royal board of censorship, which replaced the ecclesiastical censorship; José Seabra, a brilliant young lawyer from Coimbra, who became at twenty-three judge of appeal at Oporto and so minister, until he quarrelled with Pombal and was banished to Africa; N. Pagliarini, an Italian adventurer who had been burnt in effigy in Rome and was made head of the royal press; and the Abbé Patel, or Parisot, an ex-missionary who was employed to write propaganda. No more persecution was necessary. José devoted himself to his usual pastimes, and everything was left to the minister. There was now no danger from Dom Pedro, and he was married to his niece, the princess of Brazil, on 6 June 1760. The nuncio received no invitation to the celebrations and therefore did not illuminate his house: next day, Pombal declared that he had insulted the royal family and expelled him. The breach with Rome lasted ten years, during which the Inquisition was used as an arm of the civil power, and the crown appointed bishops and supervised the affairs of the church.

The religious question was settled only when the other Catholic courts began to adopt the same posture as Pombal. In November 1764 Louis XV allowed the duc de Choiseul to expel the Jesuits from France, and in 1766 the Spanish minister Aranda made them responsible for the riots against his predecessor, and sent them to Italy. Then Pombal joined with the courts of France and Spain in pressing for the election of a pope who would extinguish the Society. This was Cardinal Ganganelli, who as Clement XIV did his best to avoid the commitment, but in 1769 he complied. Next year a nuncio returned to Lisbon amidst general rejoicings, and Pombal's brother Paulo was made a cardinal. José created his minister marquis of Pombal, and the pope sent him the entire bodies of four saints encased in glass-panelled coffins: they were placed in the chapel of the minister's palace at Oeiras.

But the two decades that had seen such strange and alarming episodes also witnessed another phenomenon, not less fundamental than the Lisbon earthquake. The gold mines of Brazil were slowly withdrawing their support from the regime, and Pombal found himself faced with a growing crisis not of his own choosing. Entries of gold reaching Portugal reached their peak during the years 1736–51, when the average annual royal revenues were 125·4 *arrobas*; from 1752 to 1787 this fell to 86·1; and from 1788 to 1801 to 44·3. The true picture is perhaps less favourable, since inspection was improved after 1750. The effects are to be seen in the decline of the slave-trade after 1771. At the same time, but for other reasons, the sugar-trade dwindled: England, France and Holland were no longer dependent on the sugar of Brazil, but controlled their own supplies. The production of Brazil, which reached £2½m. a year in 1760, fell to £1½m. by 1776. Only tobacco withstood the crisis, as the total exports of Brazil descended from £5m. in 1760 to £3m. by 1770.

In Portugal the contraction of trade was reflected in a decline of the volume of gold currency, apparent after 1769, and in a general stagnation of commerce. Imports had stood at about £1,200,000 a year after 1750, dropped as low as £635,000 and £532,000 in 1771–3. Arrivals of ships fell by about a third. The receipts of the crown were affected as early as 1762, when the *décima* or tithe, which had been reduced to 4½ per cent, was raised to 10 per cent. In 1763 new duties were imposed on sugar, cocoa, pepper and dried cod, and reports began to comment on the paralysis of trade and the spread of misery.

It may be doubted whether at this stage Pombal had considered the economy of Portugal as a whole, or whether he had intended to do more than lay the foundations of a national capitalism, such as he had seen at work in England. It could not be the same, but he expected that large companies created with the support of the state would increase the national share of foreign trade and allow it to be successfully exploited by larger and stronger monopolies. With the fading of these illusions Pombal applied a number of expedients of different kinds. The Junta do Comércio was reformed and extended: by its original statutes it was to supervise trade, issue licences to retailers and recover trade debts, as well as stimulate trade: it was now given charge of the Lisbon silk factory, reformed in 1757, and began to sponsor new ventures. Linen, glass and paper were now manufactured. The Royal Hat Factory was set up at Tomar in 1759, and in 1764 factories were created for cutlery, combs, cardboard boxes, varnish and lacquer: they were followed by ventures in button-moulding, porcelain, tapestry, clock-making and iron-founding. In the fishing industry, a General Company of Fisheries was given exclusive rights to fish off the Algarve for twelve years, and the town of Vila Real de Santo António was laid out at the mouth of the Guadiana to serve as a model fishing village. As the revenues declined, Pombal sought to improve the efficiency of the means of collection, tightening the regulations of the customs-house, pressing for arrears of taxes, and in 1766 creating a central treasury, the Erário Real, to centralize collections and payments. These measures palliated the effects of the crisis, even if they did not abate it. Almost nothing was done to curb the expenses of the court, for José would have noticed any shrinking of his own world of singers and horses. But the army and navy were generally neglected.

When Ferdinand VI and Barbara of Bragança ruled Spain, the peace continued, but in 1759 Ferdinand died and was succeeded by his half-brother Charles III. In May 1760 he proposed that his son Luis should marry the Portuguese heiress, and it was to avoid this that Maria was at last married to her uncle. At this time England and France were engaged in the Seven Years' War, and in 1759

Boscawen had defeated the French fleet off the Portuguese coast. The French commander took refuge in Lagos after losing five of his ships on the coast of the Algarve. The French at once began to demand satisfaction, and Pitt sent Lord Kinnoull on a special mission to Lisbon to offer apologies. He arrived in March 1760, by which time Pombal had received a demand from the French for the return of the prizes. The French pressure continued, and Pombal took the precaution of invoking the English Alliance: he was, of course, assured that it would be honoured in case of hostilities, and advised to attend to the coastal defences. But in August 1761 France drew Spain into the war by renewing the Bourbon Family Pact: under a secret article Charles III would declare war on England by 1 May 1762. At the beginning of the year it was realized that the two countries intended to attack Portugal, and Pombal renewed his appeal to England. The state of his defences gave little cause for optimism. Promotions had been deferred for years, and officers were lacking. But efforts were made to bring the machine into order, and six months' arrears of pay was arranged. In February a French envoy joined the Spanish ambassador in Lisbon and demanded that José close the ports to English ships: an answer was required within four days. The demand was rejected in the name of Portugal's Alliance with England. On 1 April the Bourbon powers presented their ultimatum, alleging the failure of Portugal to obtain restitution of French ships captured by the English in her waters: therefore she must be invaded.

In March, Lord Tyrawley, whose presence had been requested by the Portuguese, arrived in Lisbon, not now as a diplomat, but as commander of an army. He was a rakish old gentleman of seventy, and soon quarrelled with Pombal, alleging that the minister had misrepresented the forces available as 35,000, when there were far less. The Bourbons now announced that they would free Portugal 'from the heavy shackles of Britannic dominion', and José replied that he would defend his country against all invaders. On 30 April Spanish troops entered Trás-os-Montes, and on 18 May José declared war. The Spaniards occupied Bragança and Chaves, but Tyrawley's son O'Hara pushed them back. By now Tyrawley's incapacity for command had been discovered, and Pitt had obtained a vote of £1m. and sent some 8,000 men with arms and supplies to Portugal. They were commanded by Count William of Schaumburg-Lippe, with the earl of Loudoun and General Burgoyne. The Portuguese army had been reinforced, and the allied troops were concentrated in the valley of the Tagus as the Bourbons entered Beira. Although the Spaniards occupied Castelo Branco, Burgoyne seized Valencia de Alcântara and captured the French General Dumberry. In November a truce was declared, and in February 1763 peace was made in Paris. By this settlement Portugal received full restitution, and recovered the Sacramento colony in the River Plate.

After this war, Pombal's regalism found an echo in the Bourbon courts: in 1764 Louis XV was attacked with a penknife by one Damiens, who was put to death with the same brutality as Aveiro and the Távoras: Louis was convinced that the Jesuits were responsible and banished them. Two years later the riots in Madrid were also attributed to the Society, and Pombal proposed that the three courts should together demand its extinction. Whatever their possible errors, the Portuguese Jesuits had exercised control not only of the royal conscience and of the souls of the Brazilian Indians, but also of education. They ruled the academic roost at Coimbra and had their own university at Évora. Their discipline was good, and their curriculum included a sound grounding in Latin, scholastic philosophy, metaphysics and mathematics. The chief inadequacy of their system was its uniformity (which some may consider a merit), and its resistance to innovations (though the Jesuits had once made many themselves). They refused to admit the existence of contemporary thinkers who dealt with philosophy or cosmogony, and even in literature their emphasis on scholastic Latin and preceptive judgements seemed inappropriate in a society that delighted in elegance of vernacular style and nimbleness of wit.

Pombal had not scrupled to close the Jesuit university at Évora in February 1758, and he realized the need to create an instructed middle class. In June 1759 he instituted a free grammar-school in each ward in Lisbon and laid down the programme of instruction: there were to be four schools for Greek and Latin in Lisbon, two in Coimbra, Évora and Oporto, and one in each of the other provincial cities. The best pupils would receive priority in entering the university, and entrance to Coimbra was within eighteen months to be solely by examination. Portuguese grammar was to replace the repetition of Latin verses. A Director-General of Studies was appointed, and some of the classes were started, but it does not appear that an adequate supply of teachers was available, or that the scheme was pressed home, probably for want of money.

In 1761, having destroyed the Jesuits, with whom many of the nobility were educated, Pombal determined to reform the preparation of the aristocracy and founded the College of Nobles, to house a hundred boys from seven to thirteen, and to teach them Latin and Greek, rhetoric, poetry and history, French, Italian and English, arithmetic, geometry, trigonometry, algebra, optics, astronomy, geography, navigation, military and civil architecture, drawing, physics, fencing, riding and dancing. This programme illustrates Pombal's ideas of the accomplishments of a gentleman and by implication his reflections on the shortcomings of the nobility as it existed.

Pombal also arrogated to the state the existing ecclesiastical censorship of books: for this purpose the Royal Board of Censorship was set up in 1768 with exclusive rights to approve all books and periodicals. Three years later this board was granted the direction of all lower education and administered the scheme for state schools: a plan of the masters then available shows 479 teachers of reading and writing, 236 of Latin, 38 of Greek, 49 of rhetoric and 35 of moral and rational philosophy.

In 1772 Pombal launched his most successful educational reform, that of the University of Coimbra: he appointed himself 'lieutenant-general' of the university and spent a month in Coimbra to reorganize its syllabus of studies. To the existing faculties of theology, law and medicine, he added faculties of mathematics and natural sciences, pulling down the old castle to make room for large new buildings on the crest of the hill. He also established laboratories, a natural history museum, a botanic garden and an observatory. Other branches of study which he proposed to advance included the history of law and of the church and biblical exegesis. After his return to Lisbon, he remained in touch with the university and continued to lay down small details of its functioning.

But Pombal was far from being a *philosophe*. He himself had been born as long since as 1699, and there is no indication that he accompanied the evolution of thought in contemporary France. The repression of freemasonry, which had begun after the papal condemnation of 1737, was suspended during the whole of his administration. But his censors continued to proscribe the works of Locke and Hobbes, Spinoza, Voltaire, Rousseau and Diderot. He would have repudiated completely any system which questioned the absolute power of the ruler and his ministers or which advocated any form of equalitarianism. His designs for education imply a social readjustment on an important scale, but he envisaged only the creation of a wealthy mercantile class with behind it the phalanx of officials and clerks necessary to carry on administration and trade. The problem of the elevation of a fundamentally peasant society had to be carried forward to the twentieth century.

He celebrated the apotheosis of his power in June 1775, when the reconstruction of central Lisbon was far enough advanced to embellish the great square of the Terreiro do Paço with the equestrian statue of José I, the first such in Portugal. For the three days of celebrations, the unfinished buildings of the Terreiro were filled in with a front of wood and canvas to give an impression of the final effect. José was able to wonder at his own greatness and glory revealed in the statue of himself proudly mounted on a noble steed with plumes fluttering in the breeze.

On the morning of the inauguration a petard was found under the seat of Pombal's carriage, and the police discovered an infernal machine and false keys to Pombal's stables in the house of Battista Pele, a Genoese. He was executed with the barbarity reserved for regicides, his hands being cut off and his body dragged through the streets by four horses. He gave no clue of his motives. A few days after the festivities of the inauguration José received Pombal's 'Most Secret Observations on the Inauguration of the Equestrian Statue', in which he described the triumphs of the happy monarch and of himself. These were, first, literacy ('before 1750 it was rare to find a person who could write a legible letter, whereas now when a clerk is to be appointed numbers of excellently written letters are received'); secondly, industry (Portugal could now supply herself in textiles, carriages and many articles formerly imported); thirdly, culture (architecture, painting and the other arts flourished, and there was literature in Portuguese, Greek, Latin, Hebrew and Arabic); fourthly, prosperity ('observant foreigners did not fail to remark the millions spent in public and private building after the earthquake.

They saw a most magnificent square surpassing all others in Europe. They saw a costly and unexampled equestrian statue erected in the square. Every foreigner who observed such a reunion of riches could not but be convinced that the capital and kingdom were in the highest state of prosperity and opulence').

This, then, was Pombal's view of his achievements, composed less than two years before his fall. It was not entirely propaganda: much had been done to dismantle the old system of privilege and something to lay the foundations of a new order. Manifestations of culture which in the previous reign had depended on the whims of the court or church were given a more national context, and much was written, composed, painted and built. The 'reunion of riches' was lacking, but the economic crisis was passing, and the modest prosperity of the following reign was perhaps already in view.

Pombal was well aware that his power depended on the peculiar passivity of an idle king, and that it was unlikely to survive the accession of the princess of Brazil and her husband Pedro, in whose circle there were many political enemies. He had attempted to have her son and heir José, born in 1761, educated by persons favourable o his own ideas and seems to have attempted to introduce a salic tuccession so that Maria might be excluded in favour of her son. It is likely that he entrusted the preparation of this delicate case to his protégé Seabra. Maria learned of the plan and pleaded her case with her father. José, as usual, sought the advice of Pombal, who stripped Seabra of his offices and banished him in January 1774: he was later deported to Brazil. It was therefore impossible to proceed with the scheme to exclude Maria. In 1776 José fell ill, and in November Mariana Victoria assumed the regency. The king expressed the wish that his grandson should be married before he died, and the prince was therefore wedded to his aunt Maria Benedicta. On 29 November José lost the power of speech. He died on 24 February 1777: on the following day, when Pombal arrived at the antechamber Cardinal da Cunha met him with the words: 'Your Excellency has no longer anything to do here'.

3. MARIA I, 1777–99 (D. 1816)

On her father's death Maria became the first queen-regnant of Portugal; she had been born in 1734, and married in 1760 to her uncle Pedro (III), then aged forty-three: some years before he had inherited the palace of Queluz, built by a younger son of Pedro II, and this charming seat became the usual residence of the royal family. The new prince of Brazil, José, was born in 1761.

On 5 March Pombal was dismissed from office and went to his palace at Oeiras: he was later banished to the village of Pombal. In his testament, José had bidden his daughter to govern with peace and justice, to pay his debts, to protect his faithful servants and to pardon those guilty of crimes against the state whom she considered worthy of clemency. On the day after José's funeral, the prisons were opened and some 800 victims emerged: the Spanish ambassador was reminded, with palpable exaggeration, of a resurrection of the dead. Aveiro's son, arrested as a boy, emerged a man. The surviving Távoras refused to leave until their innocence was proclaimed. Lisbon eagerly availed itself of the privilege of free gossip: 'at the moment there is no particular news except the continuation of conversations, satires and popular follies against Pombal, reaching such lengths that boys make his effigy and burn it, reading and publishing various sentences, and therewith a thousand fooleries. It is certain that Pombal deserves the general hatred of the public for his cruelty, but the savage persistence of the people is by now reaching a point where that disorder stirred up is out of hand, and may lead to ill consequences', wrote the Spanish ambassador on 8 April.

Maria had appointed as her ministers the marquis of Angeja, an aristocrat of irreproachable character and moderation, who was chief minister until his death in 1788, and the viscount of Vila Nova de Cerveira, whose father had died in prison under Pombal. However, she retained Pombal's Minister of Overseas Affairs, Martinho de Melo e Castro, who had succeeded Pombal's brother in 1772. Her confessor, Fr Inácio de São Caetano, who had had an adventurous career as a soldier and monk, had served under Pombal and sat on his board of censorship: he was a jovial prelate, of whom

William Beckford has left a sympathetic picture. Pombal's Intendant of Police, Inácio Pina Manrique, also remained in office. There was therefore not a complete revulsion against the previous regime. Maria possessed a strong sense of filial respect and hesitated to undo anything her father had done. Those who desired vengeance against Pombal therefore turned to her husband: 'the good Dom P. readily believes everything he is told by the Angejas, Marialvas, Minas, etc., but the Q. is more circumspect in what she says, more prudent, more enlightened in her opinions'. Also the queen-mother was opposed to a reversal of policy: 'Your Excellency is not unaware of the repugnance displayed by the queen-mother in the matter of the release', wrote the Spanish ambassador. But Vila Nova quickly obtained a declaration of his father's innocence and on 17 May Alorna obtained also a promise of restitution. The Távoras followed: the count of São Lourenço demanded the personal visit of the sovereign to release him, failed to obtain it and refused to appear at court. In December the queen-mother returned to Spain and Alorna applied for a revision of the whole of the Távora affair. Maria hesitated, and it was only in August 1780 that she appointed a group of magistrates, who found that the case should be reopened.

The queen's conscience was sorely tried, the prelude to her later madness. 'One morning she awoke very perturbed: she refused to tell her ladies what was troubling her, but when the king her husband came to inquire, she revealed that she was tormented by the delay in reaching the end of the suit and that she had a mind to call at once the judges so that the case might be settled that day'. Dom Pedro pointed out the difficulties, but she insisted, and the judges were gathered and sat all night. They pronounced Aveiro and his servants guilty, and the Távoras, Atouguia and the rest innocent, by a majority of fifteen to three. The assertion of Aveiro's guilt broke down his son's appeal: Maria therefore ordered that he was to be treated as a private person, not as a nobleman, though she gave him a pension. The rehabilitated nobles sought the return of their houses and land. Pombal held Atouguia's estate, and the cardinal, who had been the first bishop to denounce the Jesuits but later abandoned Pombal, had Aveiro's silver. Only when the queen received a new confessor, the bishop of the Algarve, did she sign a decree for the restitution of property to the Atouguias: having done so, she scratched out her signature, 'exclaiming that she was condemned to very Hell': she was carried off to her apartments in delirium.

The final scenes of the drama were played in the small town of Pombal, where the fallen dictator had retired to a long-abandoned mansion. He left his son behind, still president of the Senate of Lisbon, and asked him to discharge a list of debts amounting to forty-five *contos*. Many individuals and bodies began to remember others. But, as Pombal noted in 1778, 'we have a much bigger chest in reserve than I hitherto thought', and Beckford in describing the properties of the second marquis ten years after his father's fall, remarks: 'he possesses one of the largest landed estates in the kingdom—about 120,000 crowns a year'. Despite his eighty years, Pombal took up the cudgels with his old vigour: he was freed from sixteen suits, mostly affecting properties: his *Contradiction* advanced the evidence of popes, emperors, kings and statesmen in defence of his character: he denied that he had received any monies fraudulently and outlined the origins of his fortunes.[1] He asserted that no arrests had been made without the king's signature, and attacked his accusers. His defence caused a general stir, and forced the state to intervene. The court of appeal in the palace held that the defence touched the memory of José and ordered the seizure of all copies of the *Contradiction* and the reduction of the suit in question to its original private nature. In October 1779 two judges arrived in Pombal to interrogate him: they found him bed-ridden, afflicted with sores and diarrhoea, for which his doctor recommended a concoction of seethed viper. But his memory remained as fresh as that of a young man. The first inquiry lasted until 15 January 1780. The Jesuits were then demanding a decision which might affect their appeal for the restoration of their society, and the formal declaration of the innocence of the Távoras revived the issue of Pombal's responsibilities. As the minister's body failed his clear and vigorous mind, the mind of his judge, the poor queen, became more and more unhinged. Eventually, by a decree of 16 August 1781, he was found 'culpable and deserving of exemplary punishment, which however I do not order to be executed in view of his present grave illnesses and

---

[1] By decree of 4 January 1754 (when Pombal was a minister, but not yet supreme), he received 24,000 *cruzados* or 9,600,000 *reis* a year. In April 1754, the salary of secretary of the house of Bragança was set at 360,000 *reis*.

decrepit age . . . and also because the Marquis has begged for pardon and execrated the temerarious excesses he has committed'. He died on 8 May 1782: his family was reproached for the splendour of the funeral.[1]

Nature and the merciful relativity of memory are the great healers, but they do not solve the problems of social organization men set themselves. During Pombal's lifetime, the ideal of royal absolutism was being challenged from another quarter, and seven years after his death the French monarchy slid the whole length of the slippery slope from total power to dissolution. During these years, the Portuguese state rested after its strange experience, and under the mild and benignant rule of the queen, tranquillity was restored and the state recovered its well-being. The Jesuits had applied for restoration in a memorial offered to Dom Pedro. The queen, faithful to her father's memory, refused to admit it, but gave them pensions: they did not recover the favour of Rome until 1814, and were re-admitted to Portugal only in the days of Dom Miguel in 1828. In 1787 the board of censorship passed back to the church, but in 1794, under the influence of the French revolution, its functions were divided into three: the Inquisition dealt with matters affecting the church, and a judge of appeal with political affairs.

The state also abandoned many of Pombal's trading ventures. The Grão-Pará Company paid no dividend after 1766 and was wound up in 1778: that of Pernambuco, considerably in debt, was terminated in 1780; the Port-wine Company lost some of its privileges. In 1777 a board of administration was set up for state undertakings: it reduced the subsidies to the silk industry and handed over the woollen factories of Covilhã and Fundão to private interests.

It had been widely imagined that Pombal had left the exchequer in a highly prosperous condition, and that the state possessed 78m. *cruzados* in reserves. But Pombal estimated the treasury to contain 7m., with 5 or 6m. in rough diamonds: even this included nearly 3m. raised in advance. The confiscated property of the Távoras and the Jesuits had yielded 2½m., but this had long since been spent. Wraxall noted in 1772 that salaries were several years in arrears: the Austrian minister, writing in 1773, wrote that salaries, pensions and

---

[1] Already the third marquis of Pombal had married a daughter of Nuno de Távora, even before the latter's release.

dividends were ten years overdue. Pensions for 1773 were settled in 1786.

The army and navy had also been neglected since 1764. 'No money leaves the treasury for any object, which greatly displeases the people', wrote a Frenchman in May 1777. In the arsenal it was necessary to dismiss 600 out of 3,000 workers, with six months' pay. To reduce expenditure, 2,000 horses and mules, the property of the royal household, were disposed of: royal bull-fights were suppressed and the bulls sold. All public works were suspended. But slowly a recovery followed. With the outbreak of war and interruption of trade between England and France, the market for Portuguese wines improved and the passive balance of trade was rectified.

The king consort, Pedro III, died in 1786: he was 'liberal in his alms, talks much in precepts of goodness and justice, but as he has no knowledge of mankind or business, he is easily governed, right or wrong, by those immediately about him, especially if they belong to the church'. Two years later, in September 1788, the prince of Brazil fell ill of small-pox and died, the queen having refused to have him vaccinated: he was twenty-seven. He had been surrounded by creatures of Pombal, with the result that, although he came to disapprove of the minister, his ideas were thought anti-clerical: Beckford reports a curious encounter with the prince on the hills above Sintra. The same year saw the deaths of Maria's confessor, of her sister, his sister's husband and their child, all of small-pox, and of Angeja and Charles III of Spain.

The office of Prime Minister now passed to José Seabra da Silva (December 1788). The brilliant youth who had been so rapidly promoted by Pombal, only to fall from grace, had been exiled, and on his release in 1776, had cultivated Fr Inácio, the queen's confessor, and accumulated a fortune. Foreign affairs and war were entrusted to Luis Pinto de Sousa Coutinho (later visconde de Balsemão).

In 1789 France, which for a century had been the prototype of centralized government and monarchical absolutism, passed into the financial and moral crisis which was to engender the Revolution. As Louis XVI was stripped of his authority, the Spanish Bourbons attempted by various devices to save him while taking steps to prevent the infiltration of revolutionary propaganda across the Pyrenees. The Braganças, though less intimately concerned with the fate of

Louis XVI, followed events with growing concern. Maria herself became subject to fits of melancholy and nightmares and was possessed by the idea that she was damned: Dr Willis, who had treated the mad George of England, was summoned (having stipulated for a fee of £10,000), but his advice proved unavailing. Maria ceased to govern in 1792, and her second son John, now prince of Brazil, did so in her name, though he assumed the title of Prince-Regent only in 1799.

IX

THE PENINSULAR WAR

1. JOHN, PRINCE-REGENT, 1799–1816

As the troubles in France grew graver, the Portuguese government sought to prevent the spread of revolutionary propaganda and to form an alliance with Spain and Britain against France. The Intendant of Police, the redoubtable Pina Manique, attempted to suppress the circulation of revolutionary papers and books and the revolutionary garb which was fashionable among *afrancesados*: the Spanish government took parallel measures. Early in 1793 the French sent an envoy to try to induce the Portuguese to remain neutral: he was arrested on the frontier and ultimately expelled. By July negotiations with England and Spain were completed, and in September 6,000 Portuguese embarked for the Catalan front, under John Forbes Skellater, a Scotch soldier who had remained in Portugal after the campaign of 1762.

The assault on France brought initial successes, but these were followed by the virtual collapse of the Spanish defences on the Basque frontier. French troops reached the Ebro and threatened Madrid, and in July 1795 the Spaniards made peace at Basle, obtaining mild terms, for the French were determined to use them as an instrument to break the Anglo-Portuguese Alliance and to close the Portuguese ports to English shipping. Godoy, now in control of the destinies of Spain, demanded that Portugal should become the ally of France, and in January 1796 arranged that Charles IV of Spain should meet Prince John on the frontier. The French now demanded commercial rights in Portugal, concessions in Brazil and the payment of an indemnity of 10m. *cruzados*. These terms were refused, but the negotiations continued. In August Spain and France concluded the secret Treaty of San Ildefonso, in virtue of which Spain declared war on England on 8 October. This led to negotiations in Paris for the neutrality of Portugal; but when Jervis, aided by intelligence from a Portuguese frigate, destroyed the Spanish fleet off Cape St Vincent, the French Directory proceeded to expel the Portuguese envoy from France (April), and pressed the Spaniards to invade Portugal.

In March 1797 three regiments of French *émigrés* reached Portugal, and in June 6,000 English troops under Stewart, with Jervis' naval division, arrived in the Tagus. The French now offered Godoy troops for the invasion of Portugal, seeking thus to obtain a foothold in the Peninsula. In August the Directory negotiated with both the English and the Portuguese, hoping to divide them. In Paris, they proposed that Portugal should pay 4m. *cruzados* as an indemnity, and undertake not to aid England, or admit more than six ships of any foreign power at one time in Portuguese ports. This was clearly against the conditions of the Alliance: the negotiations failed, and the Portuguese envoy in Paris was arrested and held until March 1798.

The new Directory of 18 Fructidor increased the pressure on Godoy, but he still hesitated to attack Portugal or Britain, and finally was removed from office in March 1798. The king of Spain attempted to persuade the Portuguese to fall in with the designs of Talleyrand, but in vain. In July 1798 a Portuguese squadron was with Jervis before Alexandria, and Bonaparte declared that 'the Portuguese nation will weep with tears of blood the outrage she has perpetrated against the French republic'. The French defeat in the Battle of the Nile in August took the sting out of these words.

Although the Spanish government obeyed the French in bringing pressure to bear on Portugal, they were deterred from an invasion by considerations of what might happen if revolutionary forces entered Spain. But in 1800, by means of a new Treaty of San Ildefonso, Napoleon again obtained concessions from Madrid and sent his brother Lucien to secure the return of Godoy. He succeeded, and in January 1801 he signed with Godoy a convention by which a joint ultimatum would be delivered to Portugal. She must abandon the Alliance, open her ports to French and Spanish ships and close them to the English, hand over a quarter of her territory as a guarantee for Spanish territories held by England, and pay indemnities. If these terms were rejected, Spain would invade Portugal, and France would contribute at least 15,000 men. In February these terms were delivered to the Prince-Regent, and although a negotiator was sent to Madrid, war was declared.

John had already appealed to England for help, but Hookham

Frere, who arrived in Lisbon as minister in November 1800, could promise no effective aid. The duke of Lafões, head of the army, contracted a Prussian general, von Goltz, but could raise only 2,000 horse and 16,000 foot. There were three English regiments in Lisbon, the French *émigrés* in Trás-os-Montes and Forbes Skellater on the central frontier. Godoy had some 30,000 men, and in April French troops began to enter Spain. On 20 May the Spaniards entered Portugal, and occupied Olivença on the frontier. Godoy, enjoying his first experience of generalship, plucked some oranges near Elvas and sent them to the queen of Spain with the message: 'I lack everything, but with nothing I will go to Lisbon'. The 'War of the Oranges' was quickly ended by negotiations: after this show of force, the Portuguese negotiator at Badajoz agreed in theory to close the ports to English ships, to grant commercial concessions to France and to pay an indemnity of 20m. *livres*, of which only 15m. appeared in the treaty, the rest being divided between Godoy and Lucien Bonaparte.

Napoleon had demanded the partition of Portugal and sent a message to stiffen the negotiators. It arrived on 7 June, the day the terms were agreed: the problem was solved by antedating the treaty. Thus Godoy succeeded in using his 'victory' to bribe Lucien to come to terms, the Portuguese supplying the bribe. Napoleon, furious at the fraud, demanded new negotiations, but finally accepted the situation as he concluded peace with England at Amiens.

Having thus breached the Anglo-Portuguese Alliance, the French set about consolidating their advantage. They sent as ambassador to Lisbon General Lannes, the victor of Montebello, a professional fire-eater, who demanded the dismissal of Pina Manique, the chief obstacle to the entry of revolutionary propaganda. Baulked by the ministers, Lannes demanded direct access to the Prince-Regent. Finally, he sought to gain his ends by leaving Lisbon and refusing to return until the Intendant and Foreign Secretary had been removed. His bluff was called and he at length re-entered Lisbon as the war was resumed.

In June 1803 Portugal declared neutrality with the consent of Great Britain, and instructions were given for British warships to avoid Portuguese ports except in case of necessity. But once French troops had set foot in Spain, Bonaparte had little difficulty in converting the 'indemnities' into a tributary system: in October he forced the Spanish government to pay 6m. *livres* a month for her neutrality and to agree to cooperate in extracting a million a month from Portugal. By dint of threats, Lannes now secured the dismissal of the Foreign Secretary and the Chief of Police, the expulsion of the *émigré* regiments and certain personal privileges. He further demanded a commercial treaty and an 'indemnity', in theory to support the French force at Bayonne which was the direct threat by which the subservience of Spain was assured. The Portuguese government could find no alternative to a policy of appeasement, and in December 1803 agreed to pay 16m. *livres* in sixteen months.

But in 1804 the picture changed. In May Napoleon became emperor, and Godoy too developed modest ambitions to rule, while in England the knowledge that Godoy was subsidizing Napoleon's war-chest caused mounting indignation. In October the British navy seized a Spanish treasure-fleet and brought it in to Plymouth. The French pressed Godoy to declare war, and Godoy sought the promise of a principality in Portugal as the price of his collaboration.

Napoleon now sent General Andoche Junot as his ambassador to Lisbon. Junot saw Godoy in Madrid and urged that the king of Spain should press the Portuguese regent to accept Napoleon's terms. He reached Lisbon in April 1805, bearing a letter in which Bonaparte invited the Prince-Regent to 'bring England to more sane and moderate ideas'. The Portuguese replied by asserting their neutrality, while an English naval force appeared in the Tagus. Napoleon had not expected this resistance, and in October Nelson's destruction of the combined French and Spanish fleets off Trafalgar made the whole Peninsular adventure impracticable for the moment.

The prince-regent of Portugal, torn with doubt between a perilous policy of appeasement to Napoleon and an even more hazardous adherence to the Alliance, seemed for a time liable to be stricken with the melancholia which afflicted his mother. But now it was Godoy rather than Napoleon who was most impatient to intervene, and when Britain made peace with Napoleon in June 1806 she was able to obtain a guarantee of Portugal's independence and integrity. Talleyrand resisted this for some time, on the pretext that France was not at war with Portugal; but the dispatch of an English naval force to the Tagus strengthened the allied bargaining position, and in September 1806 the French accepted. The Portuguese government still hoped to maintain neutrality, and the English fleet accordingly left Lisbon.

These were the months of Napoleon's resounding campaigns in Germany, culminating in the announcement of the continental blockade from Berlin on 21 November. The British counter-blockade of January 1807 made an exception for Portugal in the hope that she would be able to preserve her neutrality. But Napoleon, now dominating the whole continent, could not abide the idea of this Achilles' heel. A Portuguese negotiator sent in March to seek assurances from France could not reach Talleyrand at Warsaw, and on 19 July 1807 the French government formally demanded that the Portuguese ports should be closed to British shipping by 1 September. Junot was placed in command of an army of enforcement at Bayonne, and on 12 August an ultimatum was delivered: 'no people, no government has more reason to complain of England than the people and government of Portugal. The liberties taken by the English government in relation to the commerce and policy of Portugal constitute a veritable outrage against her independence. H.M. the Emperor . . . thinks fit to-day to declare that if Portugal should suffer any longer the oppression of which she is the victim, he would have to consider this as the renunciation of all sovereignty and independence, and both to maintain the dignity of all the continental powers, as well as to satisfy the dearest and most sacred interest of 80m. men, who directly obey his laws and those of his allies, he would be obliged to constrain the government of Portugal to fulfil the duties which his intimate relations with the continental powers impose on him . . .' This masterpiece of cant was accompanied by a Spanish ultimatum. The concrete demands of the continental powers were that Portugal should declare war on England, dismiss the British ambassador, arrest all Englishmen in Portugal, confiscate their wares and close the ports to English shipping.

In Lisbon, the Foreign Secretary, António de Araújo, had notified Lord Strangford of the ultimatum and received a promise that if necessary the Portuguese royal family should be evacuated to Brazil. The Council of State was prepared to close the ports but not to break off relations with the ancient Ally. Thus on 1 October the French and Spanish representatives left Lisbon. On 18 October Junot's troops began to enter Spain, marching through Burgos and Salamanca towards the valley of the Tagus. On 27 October the Treaty of Fontainebleau between Bonaparte and the king of Spain provided for the partition of Portugal into three: France would occupy central Portugal including the vital ports at the mouths of the Tagus and Douro; northern Portugal would form a principality for the displaced king of Etruria, and southern Portugal would be the reward of Godoy.

The vanguard of Junot's army entered Portugal in mid-November. The British government was in no position to defend its ally, and Strangford urged the Portuguese government to depart for Brazil. But such a step could clearly only be taken as a last resort. Araújo still attempted a final negotiation with the French; his envoy found Junot near the river Zêzere, and after a conversation under a tree in pouring rain discovered that there was no prospect of staving off the advance. He returned to Lisbon, accompanied by one Herman, whom Junot entrusted with the task of dissuading the prince-regent from embarking.

Strangford had already gone aboard Sir Sidney Smith's fleet, which appeared in the Tagus on 17 November. The Council of State now decided that the royal family should withdraw to Brazil, and a proclamation was issued to this effect. On the morning of 27 November the Prince-Regent, his family, court, government and retainers went aboard fifteen ships of the Portuguese fleet and various merchantmen. The wharves of Lisbon were crowded with courtiers and functionaries, their families and attendants, and cluttered with their treasure, archives and baggage. Owing to bad weather, it was not possible to cross the bar until two days later, when the fleet departed for Brazil: on the same day posters appeared in Lisbon announcing the arrival of Junot.

He had hastened towards the capital with a small advance guard in the hope of detaining the royal family. Hungry, ill-shod and undisciplined, his men had little of the pomp and arrogance associated with the imperial armies; but by Christmas their numbers had swelled to about 10,000.

Thus began the first of the three French invasions of Portugal. The Portuguese Council of State had designated a council of regency to administer the country during the absence of the royal family, but on 1 February 1808 Junot declared that the house of Bragança had ceased to rule and that the government would pass to Bonaparte, represented by himself. He had composed a boastful account of the wealth and importance of his conquest for the edification of the emperor, who replied warning him to beware of the hostility of the Portuguese and of English landings. The better to forestall a rising, he decided to suppress the national militia and to send a Portuguese expeditionary force to serve in Europe. Symbols of Portuguese sovereignty were removed, and the French flag flew over the castle of St George in Lisbon. Herman was put in charge of the treasury and set to find 100m. francs for the imperial war-chests. In return, Junot's proclamations painted a rosy picture of the benefits to be expected from French domination: 'roads shall be opened, canals shall be dug to facilitate communications and render agriculture and industry flourishing', while the Portuguese army would 'form one single family with the soldiers of Marengo, Austerlitz, Jena, Friedland'. He promised that 'public education would be fostered and diffused so that the provinces of the Algarve and Beira may yet some day come to have each its own Camões'. Junot also embarked on the draft of a constitution which would have asserted the principles of religious tolerance, equality before the law, the separation of powers and the freedom of the person.

2. THE CAMPAIGNS OF INDEPENDENCE

The Portuguese court was to remain in Rio de Janeiro from 1808 until 1821; but only the first four years of this period were occupied by the struggle for freedom. While Portuguese sovereignty in the person of the Braganças was proceeding safely to the New World, the Spanish royal house was faced with the occupation of its northern provinces by French troops and with demands for a new treaty which would render Spain completely subservient to Napoleon. Godoy thought of conveying the court to America; but he was overthrown by a tumult organized by his enemies, and Charles IV was obliged to abdicate in favour of his son. In April Napoleon collected the Spanish Bourbons and Godoy at Bayonne and juggled the crown out of their hands, conferring it on his brother Joseph. But on 2 May 1808, as the last members of the royal family were being conveyed from Madrid for exile in France, the Spanish people rebelled against the invaders and so launched the struggle that was to lead to the liberation of western Europe.

The Portuguese had almost preceded them. When Cotton's squadron blockaded the Tagus, there was a general stir against the invaders. But as the Spaniards rose, Junot was obliged to send troops to assist Murat. On 6 June Oporto arrested its French governor and proclaimed the prince-regent, and there were similar movements in Braga, Bragança, Viana and Guimarãis. In Oporto a provisional junta was set up under the presidency of the bishop, and by the end of June central Portugal had freed itself and the Algarve followed suit: two sailors left in a fragile boat to carry the news to Brazil, where the prince-regent formally declared war on France.

The French now held Lisbon, the fortresses of Peniche and Setúbal to its north and south, the garrison towns of the Tagus valley, Abrantes, Estremós and Elvas, and Almeida further north, maintaining their communications with Spain and France. They had the advantage of organization, for the Portuguese forces had either been sent abroad or dispersed. The junta of Oporto, to which the other local committees finally gave obedience, raised volunteers and recalled the disbanded militia, gathering about 5,000 regulars and 2,000 militia in the city. Both it and the Spanish juntas had appealed to England for active support, and on 1–5 August Sir Arthur Wellesley landed near the mouth of the Mondego, and soon occupied Leiria and Alcobaça. On 16 August he made contact with the French at Roliça on the heights between Caldas and Óbidos, and on the following day forced them back. He then concentrated his force of about 16,700 English and 2,000 Portuguese at Vimeiro, near Lourinhã, while Junot occupied Torres Vedras. When the French attacked Lourinhã on 21 August, they suffered substantial losses, and decided to open negotiations. The agreement concluded and ratified on 30 August, called the Convention of Sintra,[1] provided for the evacuation of Junot's army in British ships. The arrangement by which the French were allowed to escape without capitulating and with their arms and baggage, including much stolen property, was bitterly criticized in Portugal and England, where the poet Wordsworth published his tract on 'the Convention of Cintra'. The Portuguese could only watch with dismay the departure of the

[1] Negotiated in Lisbon.

oppressors and their loot, venting their wrath on the collaborators. An army inquiry in England justified the action of Wellesley's superiors in the light of the general state of hostilities.

Thus in September 1808 the Portuguese flag flew once more over Lisbon. The council of regency instituted in the previous year was restored, but since one of its members was a prisoner in France and two others were dismissed as collaborators, their places were taken by the bishop of Oporto and other representatives of the juntas. Meanwhile in Spain a parallel movement had brought the various committees of independence under a single junta at Aranjuez. The French, suddenly made aware of the reserves of patriotic passion of the Peninsular peoples, perceived that the vague promises of economic benefits with which they had courted the Portuguese were of little avail, and in June 1808 they provided the new king of Spain, Joseph Bonaparte, with not only a crown, but a constitution and *cortes*: in December 1808 Joseph was installed in Madrid while Napoleon himself planned a campaign for the reconquest of Portugal.

The prince-regent now sent messages urging the continuance of the struggle and in January 1809 designated an English officer, William Carr Beresford, to reorganize the Portuguese army, granting him the rank of marshal and commander-in-chief: Beresford trained some 4,500 men in 1809. In Oporto Captain Robert Wilson had already raised the Loyal Lusitanian Legion.

The second French invasion began in 1809 when Soult entered from Galicia, occupied Chaves and moved against Oporto. Although preparations had been made for its defence, his cavalry forced an entry on 29 March: the defenders retired to the south of the Douro by the bridge of boats, which gave way under the press of refugees; hundreds were thrown into the water and many drowned. Portuguese troops under Pinto da Fonseca recovered Chaves, and on 21 April Wellesley again landed in Lisbon. His total forces now numbered 7,000 Portuguese and 17,000 English, and he made his main concentration at Coimbra, planning to send one force northward against Oporto, while another moved to Lamego to cut off the French retreat. When the main allied force reached the Douro, the bridge of boats had been destroyed, but the river was forded and the French garrison evacuated the city and joined Ney in Galicia. As they did so, other French armies crossed Spanish Extremadura, threatening to advance down the valley of the Tagus against Lisbon. Accordingly, the pursuit of Soult was abandoned, and Wellesley moved his headquarters to Abrantes. From this point he marched up the Tagus, entered Spain and in July won the victory of Talavera, after which he was made Duke of Wellington. He could not penetrate further into Spain for want of supplies, and because Soult had now joined Victor to bar the way to Madrid. He therefore returned to Portugal, where he made preparations against a third French onslaught.

He decided to establish a fortified camp in the hilly region round Torres Vedras a little to the north of Lisbon. He must have become familiar with the ground in the autumn of 1808 after the conclusion of the Convention of Sintra. The triple series of fortifications and artillery emplacements made ingenious use of the terrain, and even water-courses were diverted to supplement the natural obstacles. By the spring this improvised fortress was ready to withstand the attacks of the greatest force Napoleon could muster. The supreme command was given to Masséna, whose 'army of Portugal' was divided into three parts under Reynier, Victor and Junot, and comprised some 62,000 men and eighty-four cannon. It left Valladolid in May 1810, reduced Ciudad Rodrigo on 10 July, and entered Portugal in August by the frontier of Beira. The allied forces numbered 52,000, almost equally divided between Portuguese and English. In September Masséna moved from Guarda to Viseu and decided to strike across the hills of Bussaco towards Coimbra, since Wellington's guards held the main road. But Wellington was able to occupy the heights of Bussaco, a position of great natural strength. On 26 September, overruling the majority of his council, Masséna decided to attack. The battle of Bussaco, begun on the misty morning of 27 September, ended in the discomfiture of the French with the loss of some 4,500 men. An obelisk, commanding splendid views over the wooded hills of central Portugal, marks the site of the battle, whose anniversary is fittingly commemorated by the Portuguese army.

Masséna made for the main Oporto–Coimbra road, entered Coimbra and sacked it, leaving a garrison which was driven out by the Portuguese. Wellington continued to withdraw in front of the French until his troops entered the prepared positions at Torres Vedras on 9 October. Despite a first surprise attack, which for a moment endangered the outer fortifications, the French found the positions too strong for assault. They were now far from their sources of supplies and were short of food. Their situation was presently so precarious that Masséna ordered the building of a bridge across the Tagus at Santarém in order to bring supplies from the Alentejo. On 29 October he asked Bonaparte for new instructions, but before these could arrive he had been compelled to withdraw. On the night of 14 November the French troops left Torres Vedras: the next day was foggy, and they had reached Santarém before Wellington was sure that the retreat was not a feint. While Masséna waited at Santarém, Napoleon sent Soult, who had recently occupied Andalusia, to his aid. But Soult lingered on the way to reduce Olivença and Badajoz, and by the end of February Masséna could no longer hold Santarém. On 6 March he moved off towards Coimbra, but avoided the city and marched across Beira to Guarda. Wellington overtook him near Sabugal and delivered a successful general attack on 3 April. Masséna then retreated from Portugal, leaving a garrison in the fortress-town of Almeida: after Wellington had won the battle of Fuentes de Oñoro, this was abandoned early in May 1811 and the French occupation of Portugal thus came to an end. The remaining battles of the Peninsular War were fought in Spain, and in 1813 the struggle was finally carried into France.

In Portugal, the council of regency continued to administer the country, but it was beset by difficulties, especially financial and economic, since the invasions had despoiled the country, while the commerce of Lisbon had been disrupted by the migration of the government to Brazil. These difficulties were enhanced by the existence of a foreigner, Beresford, holding a commission from the crown as head of the army. Much depended therefore on the return of the prince-regent and his government.

But the prince-regent was in no haste to leave Brazil and the American Portuguese were not anxious that he should depart. They had acquired a court and a government, which built palaces and houses and stimulated the economic activity of the country: they had also courts of appeal which avoided the costly and hazardous process of referring cases to Lisbon. The benevolent prince-regent instituted public audiences and complied with the request of a Brazilian that the ports should be thrown open to the trade of all friendly nations.

Junot's occupation of Lisbon made this step inevitable, and the immediate consequence was to stimulate direct trade between Brazil and Great Britain. In April 1808 Canning sent Strangford to Rio de Janeiro with instructions to conclude treaties of alliance and commerce. The first Brazilian journal, Hipólito da Costa's *Correio Braziliense*, began to appear in London in 1808, and the English merchants were no less conscious of their opportunities than the men of the 'Portugal trade' had been in an earlier age. Strangford reached Rio de Janeiro in July 1808 and concluded a treaty in February 1809, though Canning's insistence on several changes delayed the final version until May 1810. It revived all the old treaties, and specifically, the English obtained the right to appoint, subject to royal consent, judges-conservator in Brazil, and the Brazilians received in England (in common with all other foreigners) 'the most strict and scrupulous observance of the laws . . . through the acknowledged equity of British jurisdiction and the singular excellence of the British Constitution'—the phrase 'acknowledged equity' has become a byword in Brazil. Duties on British goods were limited to 15 per cent, though an edict of 1808 had established a general import tariff of 24 per cent for foreigners and 16 per cent for Portuguese (reduced to 15 per cent in 1810). According to the treaty, the special rate was not to be extended to foreigners, while the appropriate regulations by which the duty would be assessed would be drawn up by Portuguese and British in equal numbers. Portuguese goods entering England received most-favoured-nation treatment.[1] There is no doubt that in order to obtain these concessions Strangford harped on the services Great Britain was performing for the Braganças. His government did indeed guarantee their rights in both Portugal and Brazil. At the time of the negotiations the prince-regent's government was composed exclusively of Portuguese, and the treaty was almost entirely the work, on the Portuguese side, of Rodrigo de Sousa Coutinho. It is likely that Strangford did not fully appreciate that he was wresting concessions in Brazil in exchange for

[1] On receiving the treaty, Canning at once noticed that the clause conferring on the citizens of each country the right to acquire land in the other was inadmissible, since under the 'acknowledged equity' of English law only native-born or naturalized Englishmen could hold property and only Protestants could be naturalized. But as Canning pointed out, the question was not of any importance for the Portuguese, whereas it was necessary for English merchants to own estate in Brazil.

advantages in Portugal, a fact which explains the unpopularity of the treaty in Brazil.

Nor can it be said that the peace treaties which followed the war did much to compensate the Portuguese for the ravages their country had received from the French; they were awarded 2m. francs, or under 0·286 per cent of the reparations payable by France. Although the Treaty of Paris of 1814 annulled the Franco-Spanish treaties against Portugal, the Article 105 restored Olivença to Portugal, Spain refused to deliver it, and it remained incorporated in Spanish territory.

X

THE IMPLANTATION OF LIBERALISM

1. JOHN VI, 1816–26

In March 1816 Maria I had died after twenty-four years of insanity and the prince-regent at last became king. He was an amicable, hesitant and rather mistrustful monarch who was anxious to be the father of his people. He had married a sister of Ferdinand VII of Spain, Carlota-Joaquina, a turbulent creature consumed with the desire to rule. They had two sons, Pedro and Miguel, and four daughters, but before departing for Brazil, the queen had shown a disposition to come to power by having her husband declared incapable. They had parted company, and although in Brazil they appeared together on state occasions, John kept his heir Pedro with him, while Carlota-Joaquina lived in a country-house with Miguel. Her ambitions were inflamed by the prospect of having herself declared regent of Spain or of Spanish America during her brother's captivity in France. She was encouraged in these designs by a meddlesome Spanish secretary and by Sir Sidney Smith. Her husband at first hoped that she might depart, leaving him in peace, but he soon became alarmed by her intrigues: she was at least partly disarmed by the removal of her secretary in March 1812.

While her brother Ferdinand remained in comfortable detention at Talleyrand's castle of Valançay, the Spanish council of regency acting in his name had been replaced by a junta, which retreated to Andalusia and summoned *cortes* at Cádiz: this body, acting in the name of Ferdinand, had elaborated the liberal Constitution of Cádiz (or of 1812), in itself a counterblast to the constitution which Napoleon had attempted to foist on Spain. Seeing his Spanish scheme and his own empire on the verge of collapse at the end of 1813, Napoleon offered to release Ferdinand on condition he returned to Spain to prevent the spread of 'anarchism and English influence' by overthrowing the liberal constitution. Ferdinand accepted, and in 1814 entered Madrid, where absolutism was restored and the liberals of Cádiz were dismissed and persecuted.

The division or civil war which Napoleon had hoped to provoke in Spain had no effect on the emperor's own fate, but it effectively prevented Spain from finding a path between Bourbon absolutism and foreign doctrines which, however desirable, had acquired no roots in the country. Ferdinand's natural attachment to Bourbon practices of government was strengthened by the fact that concessions to representative government in Spain seemed likely to stimulate those who were demanding independence in Spanish America, where Buenos Aires and Caracas were in revolt, but the old viceroyalties of Peru and Mexico remained loyal.

The spirit of legitimism was further strengthened by the restoration of the Bourbons in France, where Talleyrand continued to pursue the same object as he had had in releasing Ferdinand VII. Once defeated and purged of the revolutionary contagion, France regained influence at the court of the Braganças. It was possibly with the object of strengthening the forces of legitimacy in South America that Brazil was raised to the rank of a kingdom, and the possessions of the Braganças were described as the 'United Kingdom of Portugal, Brazil and the Algarve'. In 1817 French influence eclipsed English, and all power was exercised by António de Araújo (now count of Barca), who had attempted to appease Napoleon ten years earlier. The bonds between Portugal and the European traditionalists were further tightened by negotiations for the marriage of the heir to an Austrian princess, the Archduchess Leopoldina, who arrived in Rio de Janeiro in November: however, Pedro was a wayward youth and he blossomed forth as the leading liberal in the house of Bragança.

In the Peninsula, the opponents of absolutism were organized in masonic lodges which now began to infiltrate both Portugal and Brazil. In March 1817, a republican movement occurred in Pernambuco: it lasted ten weeks. In May General Gomes Freire, who had commanded the Portuguese army when Junot arrived, had led the Portuguese legion serving under Napoleon, and was now grandmaster of the Portuguese masons, was arrested on a charge of conspiracy and shot. Beresford, still marshal of the Portuguese army, had denounced the conspiracy and was popularly blamed for the severity of the sentences, which aggravated the unrest in Portugal. In June Castlereagh urged that John should return to Portugal or at least send his heir; Canning was sent as special ambassador to receive him, but he waited in vain at Lisbon for the royal return.

The most active centre of Portuguese Jacobinism was now Oporto, where a magistrate, Manuel Fernandes Tomás, founded a lodge named the Sinédrio in January 1818. It soon gathered adherents, but it could not expect to succeed without strong support from the army, which had emerged from the war as the most influential institution in the country. It was, moreover, discontented, for the council of regency was almost insolvent and Beresford was unable to pay his men. In the first days of 1820 a liberal insurrection broke out in Spain, among regiments gathered near Cádiz and awaiting transport for Venezuela: the movement gradually spread until Ferdinand VII was obliged to declare himself in favour of a constitution. Meanwhile, Beresford departed for Rio de Janeiro in the hope of persuading John to return: he warned the king that unless he did so, there was danger of a revolution. But this disagreeable prospect made John, who was aware of the indignities put upon his Spanish brother-in-law, more disinclined than ever to forsake the tranquillity of Rio de Janeiro.

With the departure of Beresford, the influence of the liberals in the army swiftly spread, and by August the conspirators were ready to strike. The council of regency was given misleading reports about the state of opinion among the officers, and on 24 August two colonels read proclamations before their troops drawn up in the Campo de Santo Ovídio in Oporto, a salvo was fired, and the revolution was made. It had resulted from an alliance between a civilian Jacobin club and the higher officers of the Oporto command. The main object of the latter was to remove Beresford and force the Braganças to return. The programme of the revolution was thus limited to the formation of a national junta by the municipal council of Oporto and the dispatch of an appeal to John VI. There was no resistance. The army had given the movement a patriotic, national and conservative cast, considering that even liberal institutions were better than none at all. In Lisbon, the regents condemned the act of rebellion, but accepted the demand for *cortes* and then requested the junta to dissolve, since its object had been achieved. It did not do so, and on 15 September, the anniversary of Junot's departure, Lisbon proclaimed an interim government invoking the name of Gomes

Freire. The regency was thus thrust aside, and on 27 October the juntas of Lisbon and Oporto were substituted by two bodies, one to govern and the other to prepare for the convocation of *cortes*. This arrangement put off difficult decisions.

The revolution had disowned the council of regency because of its incapacity to cope with the financial crisis. Most of the army officers were conservative in outlook and opposed only to Beresford. Others, and particularly the younger officers, were influenced by the example of the revolution in Spain, where the political winds blew ever more extreme. Among the civilians, Fernandes Tomás pinned his faith to the convocation of *cortes*, drawing a rosy picture of a remote past when this institution had 'sustained a perfect equilibrium and concerted harmony between the rights of sovereign and vassals'. Few knew quite when this had been, and none could remember how *cortes* had in fact functioned. What Fernandes Tomás really intended was to take advantage of John's absence to present an accomplished fact, suppressing the absolute powers of the crown and establishing the principle of national sovereignty in their place.

News of the affair reached John VI on 7 October: he was alarmed and asked two ministers and eleven counsellors to give their views in writing. Eight thought that he should send his heir at once to Portugal, but John was not sure where this would lead, and merely sent his royal pardon to the rebels, sanctioned the convocation of *cortes* and promised that he or his son would return at some unspecified date. He had no wish to forsake the hospitable shores of Brazil or to alarm his Brazilian friends: he may have hoped that Beresford, whom he confirmed in his rank, would be capable of bringing the army to reason. But when Beresford arrived in Lisbon in October 1821, he was forbidden to land and had no choice but to continue his voyage to England.

Meanwhile, the junta had taken the bit between its teeth and summoned *cortes*. The Academy of Sciences had enunciated that the *cortes* of three estates were the only body legally capable of altering the system of government, and that while the composition of *cortes* had been fluid, the summons might properly be sent to thirty nobles, twenty-three ecclesiastics and 150 commoners nominated by the municipalities. But Fernandes Tomás and his friends intended to introduce some form of popular suffrage. They proposed that heads of families, traditionally responsible for parochial affairs, should nominate electors in the proportion of one for each 600 hearths. These electors would then choose deputies 'for their scientific knowledge, character, religion, patriotism and honest means of subsistence, being, if possible, natives of the electoral district'. A fortnight before the election of electors, a band of Jacobin soldiers tried to seize power and impose the Spanish Constitution of 1812, but they accepted a revision which reduced the electoral units from 600 to 200 hearths and permitted smaller places to choose *compromissários*, or electors of electors of deputies. It is difficult not to admire such scrupulousness: if the system went astray, this was because the villagers had little interest in, and less control of, national affairs. Those who were interested, political leaders and deputies, resorted to less elaborate methods of reaching power.

The first deputies assembled in Lisbon on 24 January 1821. They were mainly constitutional monarchists of the middle class, with much faith in the efficacy of phraseology. There were no political parties. When they began to elaborate a constitution, there was much to be said on the subject of sovereignty. Article 18 of the draft: 'Sovereignty resides in the Nation', divided the moderates from the radicals. The latter wanted 'in the people': the former wanted to insert 'originally', which was defeated. 'Essentially' was acceptable to both parties, each supposing it supported their concept. It was decided to suppress the vestiges of feudalism, the Inquisition and offices not constitutionally authorized. The church was offended by this; and the Cardinal-Patriarch refused to take the oath. *Cortes* then voted (by 88 votes to 1) to deprive of their citizenship all who refused to swear and (by 84 to 5) to banish all who forfeited their citizenship. On 9 March the nuncio refused to illuminate his palace to celebrate the promulgation of the draft. His windows were broken. The Austrian and Russian ambassadors protested and withdrew. Once the anti-clerical note had been struck, it was amplified, largely through pressure of the masonic political clubs which now proliferated.

John at last decided to return. In December, the count of Palmela, the most experienced of Portuguese diplomats, arrived in Rio de Janeiro, and urged the king to make moderate concessions and send his son to Portugal. On 1 January 1821 a parallel movement broke out in Brazil, and on 26 February a liberal ministry was formed. It was then at last decided that John should go to Portugal, leaving Pedro in Brazil. The news reached Lisbon on 26 March, and he himself arrived early in July. Three days before, the constitutionalists achieved their object of presenting him with a *fait accompli* by publishing a proposed constitution of 217 articles (30 June).

By now the Holy Alliance of Austria, Prussia and Russia had been formed for the purpose of stamping out all traces of liberalism: it had already intervened in Naples and would shortly do so in Spain. Only Great Britain was opposed to this reaction, and she promised to use her influence to prevent interference in Portugal provided that the constitution was a mild one which John VI would have no difficulty in accepting. But in its anxiety to ensure that John should take the oath, the members of the junta subjected him to many annoyances, arbitrarily altering the time of his landing, forbidding Palmela and others to disembark, prohibiting all exclamations except *vivas* for religion, *cortes*, the constitution or the constitutional king: this censorship of jubilation was intended to prevent the cry of: *viva o Rei absoluto!* The population demonstrated great enthusiasm: it cared less whether its rulers were absolute or constitutional than that they were present rather than absent.

The crucial encounter over, it seemed possible that the monarch's moderation might slowly temper the infatuation of the Jacobins. But this was prevented by other circumstances. Although John had left his heir to govern Brazil, it soon became clear that this arrangement would not suffice to regulate relations between the two kingdoms. The Brazilians were apprehensive of any return to a subordinate status, and the sensational bankruptcy of the Bank of Brazil soon after John's departure seemed to lend substance to their fears. Much therefore depended on the reception accorded by *cortes* to the deputies from Brazil. Those of Pernambuco and Rio de Janeiro reached Lisbon in August and September 1821, but the deputies from São Paulo arrived only in February 1822. Their immediate object was to ensure that the courts of appeal and similar institutions remained in Brazil, but their compatriots were already pressing Dom Pedro to grant a constitution and convoke *cortes* in Brazil: on 13 May, amidst the celebrations of his father's birthday, Pedro was awarded the title of 'Perpetual Defender and Protector', thus taking a much magnified view of his functions as regent. A month later, a committee of Brazilian deputies was formed in Lisbon to propose additional articles to the Portuguese Constitution to meet the needs of Brazil: they suggested the creation of three bodies, one for each country and one for both. This project was presented on 15 June, but the Lisbon *cortes* refused even to vote on it.

The Lisbon deputies were indeed too much engrossed with their own sovereign powers to pay much attention to Brazil. When Pedro sent back most of the Portuguese troops in Brazil, they retorted by sending more, which he refused to allow to land. They then affected a rather disingenuous indignation, accusing Dom Pedro of disloyalty to his father and demanding that he should return to Europe to complete his education with a tour of England, France and Spain: Fernandes Tomás asserted that 'we can oblige the first citizen to have the education necessary for the position he is to hold' or dismiss him. The demand reached Dom Pedro by the banks of the Ipiranga in São Paulo on 7 September. His reply was 'independence or death', the 'cry of Ipiranga'. On 12 October he was acclaimed constitutional emperor of Brazil.

The Lisbon government had mistaken the character of the prince and the nature of his problem, but they soon washed their hands of Brazil and resumed the absorbing task of constitution-making. The debates were completed on 23 September, and John VI took the oath. The relationship between power and responsibility had been left unresolved. The 'executive power', the crown and its ministers, had no representation in *cortes* and no power to dissolve it. The 'legislative power'—*cortes*—would now consist of a single chamber, whatever the traditional *cortes* had been. Thus there was no representative of the nobility or clergy in the first *cortes* of the new dispensation (December 1822). The quality of the deputies had declined under pressure of the demagogic clubs; and the appearance of a gutter press, free from censorship, resulted in the election of radicals with loud voices and doubtful principles.

The excesses of the Spanish Jacobins had already provoked the Holy Alliance, and at the Congress of Verona these last had played on the desire of the restored Bourbons of France for prestige and on the vanity of their foreign minister, Chateaubriand, to intervene in Spain: the duke of Angoulême followed by '100,000 Frenchmen calling on the name of St Louis' was deputed to enter Spain and raise Ferdinand VII from his constitutional bed of thorns. During the winter of 1822 a legitimist council of regency was set up on the Franco-Spanish frontier, and bodies of royalist volunteers were organized throughout northern Spain. In Portugal, there were signs of a similar resistance and the count of Amarante, a leading absolutist, set up insurrectionary headquarters at Vila Real in Trás-os-Montes. When the French entered Spain in April 1823 and restored Ferdinand to his natural absolutism (24 May), Amarante sounded the call to arms and there was a military rising at Vila Franca de Xira, a little to the north of Lisbon (27 May). Part of the Lisbon garrison joined the absolutists, and they were soon joined by John's younger son, Miguel.

John's tolerant attitude towards the Jacobins had not been shared by his wife, Carlota-Joaquina, the sister of Ferdinand VII. This determined lady, on returning to Portugal, had refused to join her husband in taking the oath to the constitutional regime and had retired to Queluz. She flatly refused to swear the new constitution in November 1822. The penalty was loss of citizenship and exile, but ten doctors declared her unfit to travel, and she merely removed herself from the rococo charms of Queluz to the palace of Ramalhão on the outskirts of Sintra, a distance of about ten miles. From this convenient place of exile, she carried on a correspondence with her brother in Spain and became the protectress of the counter-revolutionaries.

It is hardly probable that the smouldering Spanish queen would have achieved much had she been alone. But her younger son Miguel was now twenty-one, not very brilliantly educated, but addicted to riding and bull-running, and easily accessible to the younger nobility who saw their prerogatives threatened by the Jacobins. His departure to join the revolt at Vila Franca was the result of a domestic and political intrigue. His father issued a proclamation condemning his action and summoning him to return. He took no notice, and John himself departed for Vila Franca, where he received the submission of the rebels and of Miguel. Having lost control of the royal person, the constitutionalists could only capitulate: only sixty-one intransigents, out of 211 deputies, attended the last session of the radical *cortes*.

The radical regime had removed Beresford and forced the Braganças to return: it had also forced the separation of Brazil, imposed a doctrinaire form of government, humiliated the king, antagonized the nobility, the church and the merchants, and failed to produce any improvement in the economic situation. With its collapse, John appointed moderate ministers such as Palmela, who inclined towards an English aristocratic liberalism, and General Pamplona, now marquis of Subserra, who favoured the Bourbon solution of a 'charter of liberties': he had served with Napoleon in Russia, and had been Minister of War during the Jacobin period, but had quarrelled with these and become adviser to Dom Miguel. A committee was set up in June 1823 to study the future regime, but it was in no haste to reach a decision, and in fact the whole constitutional issue was studiously avoided for the rest of the reign.

In November 1823 there arrived in Lisbon a new Spanish ambassador bearing a note in which the Holy Alliance announced its opposition to any form of constitutional government in Portugal. This view was certainly shared by Carlota-Joaquina, who now drew the absolutist faction round her son. She made another attempt to have her husband declared incapable: it failed, but her faction was strengthened by the fact that Pedro had been declared emperor in Brazil and it seemed likely that Miguel would succeed in Portugal. It was thus clear that if the moderate ministers were to survive they must bring about a reconciliation with Brazil. When Pedro was proclaimed emperor, John had written to him, but without using the title, and the letter was returned unopened. In September 1823 Palmela asked for British mediation, and Canning agreed, but stipulated that no other power should intervene with the exception of Austria. But it was only by the middle of the following year that it became possible to bring representatives of the two countries to meet the British and Austrian mediators in London, and even then progress was painfully slow.

After the Vilafrancada, Miguel had been given the title of *generalissimo*, though his powers were limited and did not go much beyond the gang of bravos who were his familiars. That these were dangerous was revealed in February 1824, when part of the court, including Miguel and his friends, was at Salvaterra, a hunting-box in the Alentejo. There one of John's closest advisers, the marquis of

Loulé, was murdered in circumstances of mystery: an investigation failed to disclose the culprits, but they appear to have been Miguel's cronies. By April the absolutist party was ready to make a bid for power. Part of the Lisbon garrison came out into the Rossio and hailed Miguel as king. The prince then appeared at their head, issued a proclamation alleging the existence of a plot to murder the royal family, and arrested the chief of police and others. Palmela and Subserra were forced to take refuge on ships in the Tagus, and John VI was apparently isolated in the palace of Bemposta. The queen at once descended from Sintra to Ajuda, whence Dom Miguel began to distribute military commands among his supporters.

At this time Marshal Beresford had returned to Lisbon, while France was represented by Hyde de Neuville, a diplomat perfectly devoted to legitimism. He was horrified that his principles should be flouted by the alarming Miguel and rallied the diplomatic body to rescue the king. The gentlemen gallantly penetrated the heavy guard at Bemposta, only to find John VI conversing with Beresford. Finally, the king decided to go aboard a British ship, the *Windsor Castle*, whence he deprived Miguel of his rank and ordered him to present himself without delay. The 'artful and ferocious young man' was arrested and confined in the stern of the ship, while his mother retreated in dudgeon to Sintra.

The crisis, the Abrilada, had lasted five days. John was now persuaded to send Miguel abroad, and the prince departed for Paris, which he later left for Vienna. Even so, the danger of violence was not conjured, and Palmela urged Canning to send troops to Portugal. Canning refused to do more than maintain a squadron of the fleet at Lisbon (though this included 750 marines), making a distinction between the obligation to defend Portugal from external attack and intervention in the domestic affairs of the country. Thus Sir W. A'Court, who arrived as ambassador in September 1824, noted: 'It is not the country that is in danger now, but the government'. The distinction was to prove impossible to maintain.

But the British government was obliged to assume an attitude of detachment in the light of the negotiations between Portugal and Brazil. The discussions in London were suspended in November without result, and Canning decided that nothing would be achieved except by separate negotiations. In March 1825 he sent Sir Charles

Stuart (later Lord Rothesay) to Lisbon and thence to Rio de Janeiro. On 13 May John VI issued a declaration to the effect that 'since the succession to the two crowns, imperial and royal, directly belongs to my above all beloved and esteemed son Pedro', he would concede him the full exercise of sovereignty in Brazil. In June Stuart sailed on to Brazil where he negotiated an agreement by which Brazilian independence was reaffirmed, though the title of emperor was conceded to John during his life-time. Brazil expressed friendship with Portugal and disclaimed any designs on Portuguese Africa. This treaty, dated 29 August 1825, reached Lisbon on 9 November, and a few days later John recognized Brazil as an independent and separate empire, transferring the succession to his son and retaining only the imperial title. Thus at the same time, the separate sovereignty of the two countries was asserted, and the right of the same heir to rule over each.

Given time, this solution might have permitted political passions to subside, and the havoc caused by the Napoleonic upheaval to be repaired. If not a great king, John was a good and loyal man who abhorred violence and desired only the happiness of his people. But he died only four months after the settlement with Brazil, on 10 March 1826.

2. PEDRO IV, 1826–34; MIGUEL, 1828–34; THE WAR OF THE TWO BROTHERS

In the absence of his two sons, John VI appointed a council of regency under the presidency of his second daughter, Maria-Isabel. This body accordingly sent a deputation to Brazil to offer allegiance to Dom Pedro, who was duly recognized by Great Britain, Austria, France and Russia, and by Dom Miguel, still in exile in Vienna. The only dissentients were Ferdinand VII of Spain and his sister Carlota-Joaquina, who did not attend her husband's funeral or participate in the regency.[1]

Pedro did not hesitate to accept his inheritance, and confirmed the regency of his sister, announcing the intention of conferring on

---

[1] The view that Dom Pedro had ceased to be Portuguese on becoming head of an independent state and could not therefore inherit the Portuguese crown, advanced by the absolutists and frequently repeated since, was evidently not considered.

Portugal a constitutional charter of the type prevailing in Brazil and France. This charter, though it precipitated a civil war, nevertheless became the law of the land and lasted with some modifications until the fall of the Portuguese monarchy. It was signed on 29 April, whereupon Dom Pedro announced his intention to abdicate in favour of his infant daughter Maria da Glória, on condition that she were betrothed to his brother Miguel and that Miguel accepted the new constitution. In July 1826 the charter was brought to Lisbon by Stuart, who was later admonished by Canning for exposing himself to accusations of intervening in the internal affairs of Portugal. The charter certainly surprised and alarmed the council of regency, but it was decided to publish the document in the gazette, together with the conditional act of abdication.

Dom Pedro's solution to the problem of the succession was within the traditions of the Peninsula: his grandmother Maria I had married her uncle Pedro III. However, Maria II was only seven and would not come of age for seven years. The charter provided that in the case of a minority the regency should be held by the nearest relative over the age of twenty-five: thus Maria-Isabel would hold power until October 1827, when Miguel would reach the required age and take precedence. This prospect was accepted by Miguel, who disavowed the use of his name by the absolutists, and by the Austrian court, which looked with favour on the succession of a granddaughter of Francis I and her marriage to Miguel, now under the eye of Metternich. The charter itself was the least palatable part of the situation. The young emperor of Brazil had inherited his father's benevolent paternalism, but not his caution. He saw himself as a liberal monarch bestowing vast benefits on his subjects with a stroke of a pen. His impulsive and romantic belief in liberal principles did not in the least prevent him from being a born autocrat. He dashed off his charter and presented it to his Portuguese subjects, whom he had not seen since he was nine, not reckoning with his mother, the absolutist faction, the masses of the population, Spain or the European context.

The decision to accept the charter was due largely to the support of the Minister of War, João Carlos Saldanha, who had served in the Peninsular War and in Brazil, and as a liberal, supposed that the absolutist objections could be easily overruled. But the absolutists, after an attempt at rebellion, crossed the frontier into Spain, where they were sheltered by the Spanish Apostólicos. The Spanish government refused to disarm them, and the Portuguese regency appealed to Great Britain for support. Canning thought that there was danger of Spanish intervention and sent General Clinton to Lisbon with a small force. Absolutist bands which had entered Portugal returned to Spain and were this time disarmed.

Meanwhile, the new form of government was inaugurated in October 1826, when *cortes* assembled. There were now two houses, the upper consisting of 1 duke, 24 marquises, 41 counts, 3 viscounts, 4 archbishops and 11 prelates, and the lower of 111 deputies. This was neither the historical institution of appointed delegates nor the radical unicameral body of 1821. But it was bitterly opposed by the absolutists, who continued to regard Miguel as their leader, despite his oath to accept the charter. In 1827 the tension increased as he approached the age of twenty-five, and advised by Metternich, claimed the regency under the charter. As Miguel's marriage to Maria da Glória could not occur for several years, Metternich sent a mission to Brazil to ask Pedro to appoint Miguel as regent on the ground of his own absence. This suggestion was resented by the ministers of Maria-Isabel, especially by Saldanha, since it was clear that the absolutists would regard Miguel's return as a signal to re-enter the field. Pedro invited Miguel to go to Brazil, and Miguel refused. Canning and Metternich then hoped that Pedro would send Maria da Glória to Portugal, where her presence might unite the moderates. Pedro decided to do this and to appoint his brother his lieutenant in Portugal, asking the king of England and the emperor of Austria to ensure respect for the charter. Thus Miguel left Vienna for Paris and London (carefully avoiding the route through Spain), and so reached Lisbon. He landed on 22 February 1828. Four days later he took the oath to his brother and to the charter and was then installed as lieutenant-general.

Once more Carlota-Joaquina came down from Queluz to Lisbon like the Assyrian cohorts. She had compiled lists of friends and foes and saw that Miguel appointed a ministry of absolutists as soon as he had taken the oath. On 1 March there were serious disturbances. The queen-mother, delighting in her belated access of power, removed the governors of the provinces and the military commanders who were not of her faction. Soon not only radicals but moderates were preparing to flee, and by 12 March English ships in the Tagus were crowded with refugees. *Cortes* had been dissolved, and demonstrations in favour of Pedro or the charter prohibited. Instructions were sent to the municipalities to send petitions for Miguel to assume the crown. In April the ministry convoked the traditional *cortes* of three estates to confirm the legitimacy of Miguel's accession and ordered the towns to send only safe men. The *cortes* met in June and decided that Miguel was the legal heir since the death of his father and that Pedro's charter was therefore invalid: on 11 July Miguel was crowned.

The usurpation did not pass unchallenged. On 7 May the diplomatic body protested against the illegal suppression of the charter and convocation of the 'traditional' *cortes*: the Holy See, Great Britain, Austria, France, Naples, even Spain joined the protest. When Miguel was crowned, all the representatives accredited in Lisbon except those of the United States and Mexico refused to recognize the change and asked for their passports. The moderates who had governed under the regency were already dispersed. Both Palmela, who had believed that Miguel had undergone a change of heart in Vienna, and Saldanha, who had doubted it, had taken refuge in England.

Pedro had now sent Maria da Glória to Portugal, but when her ship reached Gibraltar news was received of the usurpation and she continued to England, where she was received as a queen. On 18 May the garrison of Oporto proclaimed its loyalty to Pedro, Maria da Glória and the charter, and the movement soon spread to Aveiro and other places. When the news reached London, the adventurous Saldanha had the idea of sailing to Oporto. There were funds in London, part of an indemnity paid by Brazil. He chartered a ship, the *Belfast*, and sailed for the Douro, taking with him Palmela, who, though doubtful of success, was made president of the junta in Oporto. Saldanha assumed command of the Chartist army; but it soon became plain that the junta was on the verge of collapse. As the Miguelite forces approached, the junta dissolved, and Saldanha and Palmela retired to the *Belfast*, while Bernardo de Sá (later viscount of Sá da Bandeira) crossed the frontier into Galicia at the head of the remnants of the liberal forces. These were finally shipped to Plymouth, where a warehouse was converted into a refugee camp.

The complexity of Portuguese affairs was matched by the confusion of British policies. Canning had left office in April 1827 and lived only long enough to see the collapse of his policy of non-intervention. On 24 April British troops were recalled from Lisbon in order not to countenance the Miguelite usurpation, but this, combined with the withdrawal of the diplomatic body, simply encouraged the extremists. The long-suppressed fanaticism of Carlota-Joaquina and her adherents made itself felt and the moderate absolutists, led by the duke of Cadaval, were eclipsed. It was soon reported that there had been 115 executions and thousands of arrests and deportations: these accounts lost nothing in the telling by the liberal refugees. The new Tory government was disposed to accept the situation as it was. Wellington, whose ideas of the Peninsula had been formed twenty years earlier, disliked the liberals and thought Pedro a ruffian and his charter odious. The Whigs seized on Miguelism as a stick to beat the government. Their rising spokesman on foreign affairs, Lord Palmerston, in a debate on 1 June 1829, denounced the misdeeds of the Miguelites, laid the blame on the shoulders of the Tories and advocated the Canningite policy of non-intervention: 'that principle is sound: it ought to be sacred'. The sense of this statement may well have mystified his hearers, but the speech was accounted a success: Palmerston became overnight an expert on Portuguese affairs.

A year later the whole complexion of European politics began to alter. In July 1830 the French Bourbons were overthrown, and succeeded by the liberal monarchy of Louis-Philippe. In November Wellington fell because he did not think that the House of Lords needed reform, and his successor, Lord Grey, entrusted Palmerston with the conduct of foreign affairs. At that moment Wellington had been on the point of recognizing Miguel and sending Beresford as ambassador to Portugal. This was stopped, and the policy of non-recognition continued until the following spring. But Dom Miguel was the effective ruler of Portugal, and the Portuguese showed little sign of seeking his removal.

The new French government was anxious to assert its influence in the Peninsula, and began to favour the Spanish liberal exiles. Talleyrand now sounded Palmerston about joint action in Portugal, ostensibly to secure satisfaction for commercial claims. Palmerston had already sent a warship to the Tagus to enforce British claims, and while refusing a joint action, he encouraged the French to follow suit, and refused mediation when Admiral Roussin fired on the batteries at the mouth of the Tagus, anchored off Dom Miguel's palace, and seized two Miguelite warships, a demonstration which naturally strengthened rather than weakened Dom Miguel.

The opportunity to intervene, or to 'non-intervene' (in Palmerston's phraseology) was provided only in April 1831, when Pedro, whose relations with the Brazilian political leaders had become increasingly strained, abdicated the empire in favour of his young son, Pedro II, and took ship for Europe with a view to recovering the throne of Portugal for his daughter. When the Miguelites completed their control of the Portuguese mainland, the little princess had returned to Brazil. The only part of Portuguese territory now faithful to Dom Pedro and the charter was the Azores, and it was from the island of Terceira that Dom Pedro planned to re-enter Portugal, encouraged and aided by Talleyrand. On this occasion William IV refused to receive Maria da Glória as queen, and Wellington and the Tories came out against any interference.

Palmerston had placed himself in an odd position. He continued to proclaim a policy of non-intervention, while in fact conniving at the deposition of Dom Miguel. He refused a Spanish proposal that Dom Miguel should be recognized in return for an amnesty and urged the Spaniards to adopt a policy of non-intervention. He told the Prussians that Great Britain could not acknowledge Miguel or prevent a Pedrite expedition against him. He also encouraged the French to sell the two Portuguese warships they had seized to Pedro, and allowed the Pedrites to acquire ships, volunteers, arms and an English naval commander, Captain Sartorius, despite the protests of Dom Miguel's consul-general in London. In February 1832 the expedition sailed to the Azores.

These preparations perturbed the Spanish government, and when it asked for the withdrawal of British ships from the Tagus, Palmerston pointed to the presence of Spanish troops on the frontier, and the two governments exchanged notes adopting a policy of neutrality so long as neutrality was generally observed. But Palmerston's idea of neutrality was of a piece with his idea of non-intervention. In fact, the removal of Dom Miguel had become a fixed idea with him. He spoke long of fair play: 'we shall expect the play to be really fair'; but repeated that Dom Miguel must go.

There were now three main currents of opinion in Portugal: absolutist, moderate and radical. Each had its constitutional and institutional preferences: the absolutists for no written constitution and the 'traditional' *cortes*, summoned and not elected; the moderates for an *octroyé* charter and parliament of two houses; the radicals for the constitution of 1822 and *cortes* of a single chamber. Because of this conflict about the form of the state, no representative system was possible. Had it been, it is likely that the absolutist view would have commanded an overwhelming majority, since it would have had the support of the country-people, particularly in the north. Both constitutionalist groups derived their support from the towns, the moderates standing in the line of the eighteenth century enlightenment and the radicals being the Jacobins of 1823, now discredited. The moderates who had governed during the last year of John VI had satisfied the less extreme absolutists by leaving the constitutional issue open. But Dom Pedro's charter alienated the absolutists, and enabled the fanatical Carlota-Joaquina and her group to take command: having played her part, the Spanish virago died in 1830. Dom Pedro's charter forced the moderates to align themselves with the conservative constitutionalists of 1820, who had been disillusioned by the ineptitude of the radicals of 1823. The attempted compromise by the elevation of Miguel as lieutenant-general was clearly a mistake. Whether or not he was a reformed character, as some had supposed, the hot-headed prince was easily persuaded of his own legitimacy and made no attempt to resist the plans made for him by his mother and her friends. He had now dismissed large numbers of civil servants and officers who had been associated with either the radical or the moderate regime, and the victims of his purge circulated reports of persecution which they certainly exaggerated.

Thus the moderates and the radicals were thrown together in defence of the Pedrite cause, and when Dom Pedro formed a government at Terceira in March 1832, it included Palmela, as well as Mouzinho da Silveira and Agostinho José Freire: the first of these, by sweeping away customary tributes and dues, hereditary offices, and special courts, changed the spirit of the laws. By the end of June preparations for the invasion of the mainland had been completed, and Dom Pedro left the Azores with 7,500 men, who landed at the mouth of the Mindelo to the north of Oporto. He had little difficulty in entering the city on 9 July, although it had a garrison of 13,000. But there was no general rising in his favour, and little sign of enthusiasm for the liberal cause. Pedro was soon besieged in Oporto, and would have lost it but for the energy of Saldanha. On 29 September the Miguelites attempted to carry the defences by storm, but were driven off. In England both Grey and Wellington thought that Pedro's cause was hopeless. In November there was talk of mediation. Pedro had no money, and Palmela departed for London to offer the island of Madeira as security for a loan. In Lisbon Beresford celebrated Miguel's successes by illuminating his palace, while Palmerston's ambassador, Lord William Russell, became violently but impotently opposed to the government to which he was accredited, By the end of the year Palmerston thought that the only solution was for both brothers to withdraw, leaving the throne to Maria da Glória. with a sufficient amnesty but no constitution.

During these months, it seemed that the solution might lie in Madrid. There Ferdinand VII had by his fourth marriage become the father of a daughter, the future Isabella II. The extreme absolutists, or Apostolicals, had counted on the succession of his brother, Don Carlos, and the liberals therefore necessarily pinned their hopes on the infant princess. In September 1832 Ferdinand fell seriously ill, and his ministers proposed to compromise Isabella's rights by betrothing her to the son of Don Carlos. The king recovered, learned that his daughter had almost been disinherited, changed his ministers and banished his brother, who went to reside in Portugal. Palmerston grasped this opportunity to try to persuade Ferdinand to withdraw his support from Miguel, the host of Don Carlos, and to favour Maria da Glória, whose situation was similar to that of Isabella. But when Stratford Canning arrived in Madrid on a special mission, he found that Ferdinand had no intention of furthering the interests of the Spanish liberals, and when the ambassador tried a direct appeal to the queen, Ferdinand showed his annoyance by removing the more liberal members of his government.

By April 1833 Palmerston was almost ready to accept defeat, and Wellington succeeded in carrying a motion against him. In Lisbon Beresford entertained General Bourmont, now sent by the absolutist powers to assist Miguel, while Lord Russell finally arrived at the conclusion that Pedro was as bad as Miguel, 'governed by a faction of unprincipled democrats who have no more love of liberty and justice than Miguel himself': he noted that there was no great support in Portugal for Maria da Glória. Palmerston suffered from a mysterious illness which might equally have been influenza or a crisis of conscience. But in May 1833 he recovered. The enemy now seemed to be the Holy Alliance, for Metternich had announced that he would recognize Miguel as soon as Oporto fell and sent Bourmont to help to take it, while the presence of Don Carlos in Portugal showed that the issue was not solely a domestic one. By May Palmerston felt that the issue was between constitutionalism and the Holy Alliance: and he recovered his confidence.

In June the deadlock at Oporto was resolved. Bourmont achieved nothing, while Pedro's naval commander, the unenterprising Sartorius, was replaced by one 'Carlo Ponza', otherwise Charles Napier, 'not to be trusted except in the hour of danger, and then he performs prodigies far beyond all calculation'. With the aid of new steamships, he defeated and captured Miguel's fleet off Cape St Vincent, and a liberal army under Terceira landed at Faro in the Algarve. It marched northwards and entered Lisbon on 24 July. Four days later Dom Pedro was in the capital.

Even this success did not end the struggle. The liberals held the two great cities, where alone they commanded a sizeable following. The Miguelites occupied the greater part of the country, and the peasants sent recruits and supplies to Bourmont's armies. The wavering Whig, Lord Russell, could not see that Dom Pedro had the slightest chance of defeating Dom Miguel: far from liberating the country, he had imposed an 'iniquitous despotism', and the Portuguese 'feel that they have exchanged one set of robbers for another ... It is very true that Portugal is suffering severely from this civil war, but I do not know that it is part of the duty of England to rescue all other nations from the consequences of their own folly. We are neither tutors nor the police officers of Europe'.[1]

But far from withdrawing, Palmerston was led by events in Europe to plunge still further into 'non-intervention'. In September 1833

---

[1] Mouzinho da Silveira, who had seized the property of the religious orders, had refused to confiscate the possessions of the absolutists and resigned.

Ferdinand VII died, and his queen assumed the regency for Isabella II, now aged three. Sooner or later, Don Carlos would voice his claim to the throne of Spain, and it seemed necessary to pacify Portugal lest the struggle should spread to Spain. In January 1834 Palmerston proposed to precipitate the defeat of Dom Miguel, which would be followed by an amnesty, the convocation of *cortes*, and the broadening of the government. The question of intervention was put to the British cabinet and provoked a crisis: Grey was with difficulty prevented from resigning. But now a more liberal government had been set up in Madrid, and Spanish troops entered Portugal in an attempt to capture Don Carlos. Intervention had occurred, and the Pedrites urged Palmerston to send troops to suppress the Miguelites and avert a more serious Spanish intrusion. The Spanish ambassador in London was ready to negotiate for the expulsion of Don Carlos, and in April Talleyrand asked to be associated with the conversations. Several months earlier, he had put forward the idea of an alliance between France and Britain, which he intended to be the closing triumph of his career. Palmerston had then refused, but the growing threat of strife in Spain caused him now to change his mind. On 22 April 1834 the constitutional governments of the west were united in a Quadruple Alliance, a deterrent to the Holy Alliance of the east.

Within a month the war in Portugal was brought to an end. Terceira occupied Viseu, Coimbra and Tomar, defeated Miguel at Asseiceira, and forced him to retreat to Santarém, whence he crossed the Tagus and reached Évora. Threatened by Portuguese forces under Terceira and Saldanha and by troops from Spain under Rodil and Serrano, Miguel held a last council on 23 May. He rejected a demand for unconditional surrender, and on 26 May capitulated at Évora-Monte in return for an assurance that his officers should retain their ranks and that there should be a general amnesty for political offences. He himself was to leave the Peninsula within a fortnight, never to return. He embarked at Sines on 1 June on the British frigate *Stag*. On arriving at Genoa, he denounced the agreement as void because signed under compulsion, but he settled in Austria and played no further active part in politics. His uncle Don Carlos embarked for England; but as no one had troubled to invigilate his movements, he at once escaped to Spain to assume the leadership of the absolutists in the Carlist wars.

Meanwhile, Dom Pedro IV had entered Lisbon in July 1833 and restored the charter in the name of his daughter. It was now the turn of the liberals to despoil and dismiss those who had served the previous regime, not only in the civil service and the army, but also in the church. On 31 July an ecclesiastical reform commission was set up, and on 5 August all ecclesiastics who were absent from their benefices or monasteries were declared traitors. On 2 October all clergy appointed by or under Miguel were dismissed. Not a few churchmen were liberals, but Dom Pedro's appointments produced a schism which in some dioceses lasted for years. Many liberals were anti-clerical, and the inescapable fact that the state was bankrupt, combined with the belief (quite unfounded) that the monastic orders possessed enormous wealth, impelled the liberal government to take drastic steps. Immediately after the defeat of Miguel, Pedro and his Minister of Justice, Joaquim António de Aguiar, decreed the extinction of all monasteries and convents, and confiscated their possessions, promising to pay pensions to all the dispossessed until they should be able to maintain themselves.[1] Despite the reluctance of the Council of State, the king and his minister pushed the measure through. It met with little resistance from its victims, partly because the most active ecclesiastics had already been removed as Miguelites and the nuncio had left the country. Far from enriching the state or benefiting the poor, the sequestration served only to modify slightly the disastrous state of the finances during the current year. The properties were occupied by the administration or local government or abandoned, and the land was sold at low prices to those who could afford to buy, thus creating a landed class with an interest in the survival of the liberal system.

The War of the Two Brothers left the state heavily encumbered. The Napoleonic wars had sharply increased its indebtedness: this had happened in other countries, but whereas in England and France the struggle had hastened the process of industrialization, the Peninsula had been a battlefield rather than a factory of munitions. In Portugal, the migration of the royal family and the separation of Brazil

---

[1] The number of religious houses was 402 for men and 175 for women: many of the former were small and in decline. Their total population was 7,000 men and 5,980 women, but these numbers include dependants of various kinds. Cardinal Saraiva put the number of professed of both sexes as low as 3,500 in 1826.

had struck a blow at the commercial economy of Lisbon, on which the prosperity of the state seemed to be founded. Deprived of an important part of its revenues, the state must either reduce its expenditures or disturb the existing distribution of wealth, or both; the creation of new sources of wealth was not immediately practicable. But the civil wars had brought a vast new burden of debt. Pedro's campaign had been financed by the Spanish adventurer Mendizábal, who obtained the aid of Ardouin, and Sanson and Ricardo: the nominal loan was £2m., but the actual rate of interest was 16 per cent. Miguel, having raised a forced loan in Portugal, had recourse to Paris for 40m. francs, of which only 69 per cent was actually paid. By the end of the war, the total indebtedness was £18m.; and in comparison with this, the monastic properties produced only a trifle.

XI

THE CONSTITUTIONAL MONARCHY

1. MARIA II, 1834–53

Dom Pedro survived his victory by less than three months: he died of consumption on 24 September, at the age of thirty-six. He had already summoned *cortes* and arranged that Maria da Glória, who was now fifteen, should be declared of age. Three of the Quadruple Allies were now ruled by young queens: if Maria's task was more complicated than that of Victoria, it was less ungrateful than that of her infant cousin, Isabella II of Spain. She was married to Prince August of Leuchtenberg, the brother of Dom Pedro's second wife: he died soon after reaching Lisbon. In 1836 Maria married a cousin of Prince Albert, Ferdinand of Saxe-Coburg-Gotha, who arrived in Portugal with little experience and a German tutor named Dietz: he presented Maria with eleven children and built her an Arabo-Gothick palace on a pinnacle in the Sintra hills.

Since her infancy Maria had been the symbol of constitutional government. The traditional aristocracy had gone into exile or lived on the margin of political life. The church was divided by a schism, since many ecclesiastics resisted the liberal appointees of Dom Pedro. Rural Portugal, though it had had its fill of civil strife, was none the less Miguelite at heart. The ruling minority of liberal constitutionalists was drawn from the heroes of the civil war, military or civilian, supported by the reformist wing of the aristocracy, the educated middle class of the cities, lawyers, journalists and merchants, and shopkeepers and artisans. The political leaders obtained their backing through the press, most of the newspapers being partisan, and political clubs, largely masonic. In the provinces, political power lay with the governor, the local authorities and the political chiefs. The dominance of the provincial capitals had been secured by a new administrative dispensation, introduced in 1833, by which Portugal was divided into seventeen districts, each named after its chief town.[1] Under the charter, the government consisted of six or seven ministers: presidency, interior (*reino*), foreign affairs, treasury, justice, war, marine. *Cortes* were composed of two houses: a house of peers, comprising those who had 'always remained faithful to their oath' to observe the charter (thus excluding the traditionalist peers, whether extreme Miguelites or not), and a chamber of deputies, chosen by indirect elections, each member representing 25,000 inhabitants.[2] There were at first no formal parties, but the houses were divided between *moderados*, the majority, which supported the principles of the charter, and the radical opposition, which harked back to the brave days of 1823.

Maria's first ministry was headed by Palmela, representing the more conservative moderates, but his fellow-ministers were neither fully agreed together, nor with *cortes*. The financial situation was critical, and in May 1835 the government fell before a budget had been passed. Palmela was succeeded by his rival, the unpredictable Saldanha, who entrusted the finances to José da Silva Carvalho. Silva Carvalho proposed to sell off the rich alluvial lands of the Tagus and Sado valleys, the former estates of the Military Orders, which had been crown property for three centuries. The opposition censured the proposal, and Saldanha's government fell. Its successors were unable to meet the government's liabilities in November, and in May 1836 they fell back on Silva Carvalho's remedy. A loan of £800,000 was raised on the lands, which were finally sold to a limited company of large capitalists. In July, the treasury was (accidentally) destroyed by fire, but this did not prevent the debts from reaching £24m.

Meanwhile, in the elections of July 1836 the radicals, now calling themselves the 'Patriotic Society', had carried Oporto, advocating a return to the first liberal constitution as a remedy for unemployment

[1] These are now 18; the Azores form 3 districts and Madeira 1. The subdivision of the district is the *concelho* or municipality with its *câmara municipal* (council); these now number 272. The *concelho* is further divided into *freguesias* (parishes), of which there are 3,788. The Islands comprise 30 *concelhos* and 178 *freguesias*.

[2] Electors were males of twenty-five, or younger if married, officers, graduates or in Holy Orders. They voted by parishes for Provincial Electors, who were required to have an income of 200,000 *reis*. The Provincial Electors repaired to the provincial capital where they chose the Deputies. There were 16 Deputies for the Minho, 27 for the Douro, 11 for Trás-os-Montes, 14 for Beira-Alta, 14 for Beira-Baixa, 20 for Estremadura, 9 for the Alentejo, 9 for the Algarve, 8 for the Azores, 4 for Madeira.

and financial distress. In August, the Spanish liberals, no less impoverished by the disastrous Carlist War, similarly moved to the left. When the Oporto radical deputies arrived in Lisbon in September, they were greeted by demonstrations in favour of the Constitution of 1822. Part of the National Guard joined the throng, and by next day the ministry had fallen. This was the September Revolution, which led to the formation on 10 September of an anti-chartist ministry led by the count of Lumiares, with Manuel da Silva Passos, the mouthpiece of the Oporto radicals, and Sá da Bandeira.

Passos, an energetic idealist and demagogue, believed, too confidently, that the plight of the country was due solely to the incapacity or egotism of the chartist establishment. He intended to dismiss the placemen who had sought shelter from economic distress under the wings of Chartism, and remarked that his arm was weary with signing notices of dismissal. His remedies, however, were political rather than economic. He intended to restore the constitution of 1822, denounced the charter, and governed semi-constitutionally until March 1838. The agitation for the radical constitution and the disaffection of the troops alarmed the court, which regarded the repudiation of the charter as a threat to the throne. The young consort appealed to the British ambassador, Lord Howard de Walden: Lord Howard, who had been taken by surprise, suspected that the radicals had the backing of the French ambassador and feared 'red republicanism'. On 4 November Maria and her consort left the Necessidades palace for Belém, proposing to go aboard a British warship, as her grandfather had once done. The king of the Belgians even offered to send an expedition to the rescue, the costs being met by the transfer of some of the Portuguese possessions in Africa. The possibility of intervention increased the excitement of the populace and of the troops. The government gave way to a junta, which thrust its authority on Sá da Bandeira. He warned Maria that if she sought foreign aid, she would endanger her throne, and urged her to return to Lisbon. This incident, the Belemzada, left the Septemberists in full possession of the field. The danger to the throne had been much exaggerated: the threat was against the charter. But the Septemberists did not go back to 1822 or restore the hateful doctrine of the 'sovereignty of the people'. Instead, they convoked constituent *cortes* and embarked on a new constitution. They also adopted important reforms, including a penal code, health services and administrative changes.

The Chartists were now aggrieved. That Miguelites should be debarred from the sweets of office was one thing, but that the heroes of the civil war should be deprived was quite another. In July 1837 Saldanha and Terceira took the field in the hope of restoring the charter. The 'Revolt of the Marshals' failed when Sá da Bandeira and Bomfim defeated them at Batalha: Saldanha capitulated in September and agreed to go abroad, his followers being reinstated. Palmerston (who had certainly known of the attempt) granted Saldanha £1,000, since he was supposed to be destitute, and announced: 'We shall not interfere', advising Maria to try to work with the radicals. In fact, she was less disturbed than Ferdinand: as Lord Howard noted, 'She has more bottom, though not so flashy'.

The moderate Septemberists led by Sá da Bandeira were no less responsible than their rivals. The only extremists were a small group centred about the Lisbon Arsenal, who were perhaps less objectionable for their views, than for their inflammatory and defamatory methods. They attempted to gain control of the National Guard, but a minor rising in March 1838 was suppressed without difficulty: its object was to defend the principles of 1822. But the Septemberists did not return to the single chamber: the main innovation of the constitution of 1838 was the replacement of the life-peers (whose political predominance had been assured by the charter) by an elected senate.

But Manuel Passos, the moving spirit of Septemberism, had fallen in June 1837: his enthusiasm and honesty were not equalled by his political talents, and he never held power again. It fell to Sá da Bandeira to dispose of the revolting Marshals and to impose order on the Arsenalists: two officers and a functionary, the directors of this troublesome crew, were persuaded to return to their duties; the fourth, António Bernardo da Costa Cabral, an ambitious young lawyer from Beira, passed quickly to the opposing side. Septemberism was already in decline when Sá da Bandeira's government fell in April 1839. It had retreated from its latent anti-clericalism and had opened negotiations for the restoration of relations with the Holy See, though it was only after four years that the succeeding government would agree to recognize the bishops appointed by Dom Miguel in January 1841, and the closure of the schism was marked by the award of a Golden Rose to Maria II in March 1842.

Not a few former Miguelites were reconciled with constitutionalism as a result of the religious settlement. Most of the liberals of 1820 and 1832 had mellowed. Palmela was already an elder statesman. Almeida Garrett had left behind his youthful and romantic anti-clericalism and was now a viscount and a supporter of the reconciliation with Rome: his energies were largely directed towards the establishment of the National Theatre in 1842. Under the count of Bomfim, who governed from April 1839 to June 1841, radicalism was confined to the clubs; and when Joaquim José de Aguiar, the former *matafrades*, succeeded to power in June 1841 the Septemberist movement was in full decline. The shrewdest conversion was that of Costa Cabral, who now became Minister of Finance: in January 1842 the elections of Oporto showed a markedly conservative turn, and the young opportunist hastened north, placed himself at the head of the movement while still a minister under the constitution of 1838 and forced the resignation of his colleagues: three days later, on 10 February 1842, the charter was restored.

The duke of Terceira now became Prime Minister, while Costa Cabral took over the Interior and made his brother Minister of Justice. Once more the upper chamber was made nominative, and Maria created thirty suitable peers. In August 1842 elections were held for the lower house, and Costa Cabral allowed only six oppositionists to gain seats. Press censorship was restored, the clubs were curbed, and the National Guard was purged of political influences. Costa Cabral, aided by a docile parliament, produced a new administrative code, reformed the municipalities, improved the system of education and established granaries to prevent shortages of food in the towns. His change of front and his rapid rise were not forgotten by his enemies, but it was only when his reforms touched the countryside that the opposition became effective. There had grown up a tacit understanding between the two worlds. In the capital governments rose and fell, parliament debated and divided, administrators regulated and revised, clubs intrigued and vociferated. But the countryside lived its traditional existence little affected by political whims. Some who had once paid rents to the church now paid them to secular landlords or their stewards. But the centralized liberal state had not succeeded in breaking down local independence.

Rural Portugal was deeply attached to its own ways, and it was only the imposition of new administrative methods that stirred it to resist. Costa Cabral hoped to simplify the complex system of taxation to three general impositions, introducing a new method of assessment and placing the cost of building roads on the localities: he followed this with new sanitary regulations which forbade burials in church (18 September 1844). The women of the Minho cherished the idea that their nearest and dearest awaited the final doom in the holy ground of the village church, and began to demonstrate against the authorities. Bands of country-people armed with rural implements marched on the villages and towns, in some places destroying registers and records. The movement of 'Maria da Fonte', a supposed prototype from Fonte Arcada, was supported by the rural nobility and clergy, still Miguelites. The governor of Trás-os-Montes refused to intervene. Costa Cabral sent his brother to Oporto with orders to repress the rebels with all severity, but this was not possible: the movement spread into Beira. The pseudonymous rebellion of Maria da Fonte recalls the long struggle of the Basques in defence of their ancient customs. As it gathered momentum, other enemies of Costa Cabral added their mite. On 20 May 1845, the queen dismissed the minister and entrusted power to Palmela, with Terceira for war and marine and Saldanha for foreign affairs: they were joined later by Sá da Bandeira, Lavradio, and J. A. de Aguiar. The new government rescinded the cemetery regulations, the road tax and the general assessment. Cabral and his brother fled to Spain, and there were extravagant rejoicings in Lisbon.

Although the new government included most of the best-known of the constitutionalist leaders, Palmela had only a small personal following, while Terceira was soon dropped as having been too closely associated with Cabral: Sá da Bandeira, though formerly a radical, had curbed the Septemberists and thereafter lost their full confidence. Meanwhile, the Chartists were divided: some had refused to follow Cabral, and others associated themselves with his regime and were dismissed on his fall. To add to the confusion, Cabral continued to pull strings in Madrid and enjoyed the help of the Spanish ambassador in Lisbon, González Bravo, a man of his own stamp, while the affair of Maria da Fonte had given new hope to the Miguelites: Macdonnel, one of Dom Miguel's old generals, had taken the field in the mountains of the Douro, and his deeds, which did not amount to very much, were greatly enlarged by rumour.

Palmela had called for elections on 11 October. Saldanha, who was now anxious for office, hoped to unite the Chartists with the former supporters of Cabral. But this combination brought the Septemberists out in full cry: on 5 September they produced a manifesto which demanded the sovereignty of the nation, direct representation, the reform of the upper house, the restoration of the National Guard and the abolition of press-censorship. This was too much for Maria II: she summoned Palmela and dismissed him, but prudently kept him on hand in the palace while Saldanha and Terceira went out to obtain the support of the garrison. This done, she asked Saldanha to form a government: the elections were deferred, the National Guard suppressed, and the censorship of the press retained.

The 'ambush of 6 October' infuriated the Septemberists, who saw power snatched from their grasp. They were again particularly strong in Oporto, and when Saldanha sent Terceira there as governor, they arrested him, set up a junta under count das Antas and demanded the dismissal of Saldanha. The queen, who had gambled on the success of her intrigues, was forced to assume full powers, making her consort commander-in-chief of the army. But Saldanha controlled not much more than a third of the regular troops, and his attempts to mobilize all able-bodied men fell flat. Much of the country, with the existing garrisons, adhered to the Septemberist junta of Oporto, the *patuleia*, including Sá da Bandeira and Bomfim. In December 1846 Saldanha forced the surrender of a Septemberist contingent at Torres Vedras, but he could not press home his advantage, and during the rest of the winter the *patuleias* gained ground. In April 1847, boldly following the successful campaign of 1833, they landed in the Algarve and marched north to Setúbal, but they had not the strength to enter Lisbon.

The queen and Saldanha had now contrived by their intrigue to bring the country to the brink of a serious war. Saldanha had appointed Costa Cabral minister in Madrid, and the resourceful politician had encouraged the Spaniards to move troops to the frontier, spreading the rumour that the Septemberists in Oporto were collaborating with the Miguelites, that Dom Miguel was treating with his Spanish counterpart Don Carlos, and insinuating that Saldanha had asked for Spanish intervention. This last prospect alarmed Palmerston, who had been inclined to favour the Septemberists. But Maria and Ferdinand were suspicious of the intentions of the radicals, and their accounts of the situation caused Victoria and Albert to fear for the safety of the Portuguese monarchy. It was decided to send a mediator, Colonel Wylde, who on 28 April obtained Maria's agreement to a complete amnesty and the formation of a transitional government without either Cabralists or Septemberists, preparatory to the holding of free elections. But the junta in Oporto made new demands, and the negotiations failed. The members of the Quadruple Alliance then agreed to intervene on behalf of Maria, and an Anglo-Spanish naval division blockaded Oporto, while Spanish troops crossed the frontier at several places. On 29 June 1847 the junta capitulated by the Convention of Gramido. This done, Saldanha resigned and was replaced by a transitional government composed of his friends, who prepared 'free' elections in order to bring about his return to office.

When in December 1847 Saldanha formed a new ministry, Costa Cabral returned to Portugal and resumed his seat in the house of peers. For a time he collaborated with the erratic marshal, but relations between the two steadily deteriorated, until in June 1849 Saldanha fell, and Costa Cabral returned to power. Soon after this he persuaded Maria to dismiss Saldanha from his post of chamberlain. This was too much. Saldanha now joined the opposition to Cabral's attempts to muzzle the press, and in April 1857 attempted to stage a revolution. His first pronouncement at Sintra fell flat: even the north was hesitant, and he was about to go into exile when the garrison of Oporto gave him its support. Soon after, he was able to enter Lisbon, and Cabral again went into exile. In May 1851 Saldanha returned to power.

Thirty years had passed since the introduction of the first liberal regime, and more than fifteen since the promulgation of the charter. In its broader sense liberalism was suited to the Portuguese temperament, humane, affective and often vague. The parliamentary system was similarly attractive to those who delighted in displays of eloquence. But the working of the constitutional regime was less satisfactory. There were no organized political parties, and the stability of governments depended on the authority or magnetism of a small group of leaders. In place of parties, there existed two distinct concepts of the constitutional system: the Chartist, in which the upper house, nominated for life, and the lower, elected, were only kept in step either by creating batches of peers or by restricting the electorate, and the radical, which postulated direct elections for both houses and the 'freedom' of the clubs and the press, however irresponsible or inept. Neither tendency possessed the key to the essential problems of the country, which were financial and economic, and the difficulty of effecting a compromise was increased by the streak of impenitent anti-clericalism in radical politics and the lack of an independent press. The papers contributed little to the formation of public opinion, and some of them, if uncensored, fell into scurrility. All this might not have mattered if there had existed an agreed means of changing the government. When the crown appointed a minister, he formed an administration from among his friends and proceeded to hold elections to obtain the necessary majority in parliament. When he could no longer command support, it fell to the crown to appoint a successor, who repeated the process. There was much criticism in *cortes*, but it was not directly related to public opinion. Rather frequent changes of government made it impossible for any minister to execute permanent reforms: when Costa Cabral attempted this, it was only by stifling opposition and criticism and virtually halting the constitutional process. The recent crisis had emphasized the perils of civil war: the country had been divided between the central government and the junta of Oporto, each of which had called up men and imposed taxation. Fortunately both sides had avoided bloodshed as far as possible, but the economic dislocation intensified the country's difficulties and added to the burden of the national debt.

It was to Saldanha's credit that in 1851 he recognized the need for a new approach, the 'regeneration'. Modifications were introduced into the charter by the Additional Act of 5 July 1852, and by the application of a new electoral law, which introduced a franchise still limited, but satisfactory to the more reasonable Septemberists. Parties opposed to the dynasty were excluded, and the excesses of the political press and the Arsenalists were checked. Governments became more stable and were accordingly able to devote attention to pressing national problems. The old Chartists were now known as Regenerators, or conservatives, while the liberal and radical opposition continued the traditions of the moderate Septemberists as Progressists or Historicals.

In November 1853 Maria II died in childbed: she was thirty-four, and was survived by her consort King Ferdinand and eight children, five sons and three daughters.

2. PEDRO V, 1853–61

Maria's eldest son Pedro de Alcântara had been born in September 1837 and succeeded at the age of sixteen. He had been carefully educated under the supervision of his parents, and in 1854 travelled through western Europe with his brother Luis. He was imbued with a strong sense of duty and was naturally studious, being resolved never to pass a paper without reading and understanding it. His writings clearly illustrate his solicitude to do well. His father exercised the regency until he was eighteen. In the spring of 1858 he married Stephanie of Hohenzollern-Sigmaringen, who died of diphtheria two months after her arrival in Portugal: Pedro survived her by only three years.

During the regency, Saldanha continued to preside over the government. The queen had created twenty new peers to give him control of the upper house, and the chamber of deputies still contained many soldiers and civil servants. But the mercurial marshal, though capable of lofty ideas, had little understanding of their application: by June 1856 he had lost his majority in the peers and in the country. The young king refused his request for a 'baking' (*fornada*) of new peers, and he resigned. He was sent thereafter to represent Portugal in Rome; in 1865 he attempted to return to political life, but did not succeed, to the relief of his countrymen.

He had placed in charge of the treasury Fontes Pereira de Melo, who later succeeded him as leader of the Regenerators. Fontes consolidated the external debt at 3 per cent, raised a fresh loan and established the new Ministry of Public Works, from which he launched a policy of economic expansion. He undertook the building of roads, completed the first telegraphs and opened the first section of the railway from Lisbon to Oporto in 1856: he also concluded plans for cable services to the Azores and across the Atlantic. In embarking on these schemes, he abandoned the attempts of previous governments to thrust the cost of roads on to local authorities, and deliberately incurred new debts. He also sought to raise new taxes on property and to increase customs duties. The serious outbreak of cholera in 1855, followed by an abnormally wet winter, caused much distress and a general rise of prices. In these circumstances the enthusiasm of the Regenerators flagged, and when Saldanha resigned in June 1856, the young king called on the duke of Loulé, who formed a government of 'Historicals' with Sá da Bandeira.

The only serious incident of the reign was with France. A French slaver, the *Charles et Georges* had obtained 110 workers in East Africa for shipment to Réunion. It was arrested off Moçambique by a Portuguese ship and the appropriate court sentenced the captain to two years' imprisonment. The case was transferred to Lisbon in August 1858, and the captain, though admitting that the first eleven men had gone aboard with their hands tied, still claimed that they had done so willingly. This peculiar version was supported by the French government, which demanded his release and the payment of an indemnity, sending a fleet to the Tagus. The British government, though it had repeatedly blamed the Portuguese for the misdeeds of its subjects, refused its good offices, and Loulé was forced to release the *Charles et Georges* and to submit to Napoleon's pressure, paying a sum of 349,045 francs.

The settlement of this incident was soon followed by the fall of Loulé, and in March 1859 Terceira formed the second administration of the Regenerators. It introduced a new system of individual constituencies and obtained a large majority in the elections of 1860, but the election was followed by the death of Terceira, and differences about the succession to the leadership opened the way for the return of Loulé and the Historicals, who held power until 1865. The disappearance of the heroes of the civil war—Palmela had died in 1850, and Terceira in 1860, and Saldanha was in comfortable banishment, from which he was to make a last spectacular and uninvited intrusion on the political stage in 1869—assisted in the formation of political parties, however amorphous, and professional men and professional politicians began to play a more prominent part in parliament.

Although political passions were now at last canalized, they could still be roused by the ecclesiastical question. The appearance in Lisbon of the French Sisters of Charity led to a press campaign in two papers which was generalized into a debate about monasticism and the national character of the Portuguese church. In September 1858 the government required the Patriarch to separate the Sisters from obedience to their superior in Paris. They refused, and in March 1861 were ordered to comply with Portuguese law, and finally to dissolve.

In October 1861, Pedro V and his two youngest brothers were taken ill with typhoid fever after a hunting trip to Vila Viçosa. Ferdinand and Pedro died in November. The second and third brothers, Luis and John, were recalled from a European tour, and John died at Christmas.

3. LUIS I, 1861–89

The new king succeeded at the age of twenty-three and in the same year married Maria Pia, a daughter of Victor-Emmanuel of Savoy. He played the part of a constitutional monarch, leaving initiatives to the political leaders. The ideal of the autocratic monarchy faded into the past with the death of Dom Miguel in 1866. The fall of Isabella II of Spain in 1868 was followed by the appearance of republican propaganda in Portugal, and by intrigues for an Iberian federation with unexpected overtones. A socialist republican movement made itself felt in 1872, and gained support at the time of the financial crisis of 1876, but thereafter made little progress. Unfortunately for itself, the crown was closely affected by the financial difficulties of the country at large. The constituent *cortes* of 1821 had separated the public finances from the royal treasury and granted the crown an annual 'endowment'. In theory, this was to be revised at the opening of each reign, but in fact no change was made until the fall of the monarchy. When Pedro V acceded, the royal minority seemed to offer the occasion for economies; and when he came of age, it was decided to sell the royal diamonds and invest the proceeds in public debt in order to provide the royal house with an annuity. On the accession of Luis I, the endowment was still not raised, the investments were sold, and the Bragança estates were pledged and two loans raised from bankers.

The public debt, which had been consolidated at £27m. in 1854 after the ravages of the War of the Two Brothers and the *patuleia*, grew rapidly until it reached £47m. in 1869. The movement of the deficits was as follows:

1861–2	— 7,100 *contos*	1864–5	— 3,780
1862–3	— 7,858	1865–6	— 6,120
1863–4	— 5,895	1866–7	— 5,200

The Napoleonic wars, which had stimulated the industrialization of England and France, had devastated the Iberian Peninsula and dislocated its traditional commerce. The civil war had placed the Portuguese treasury at the mercy of foreign bankers. It had brought to power the liberals, who had hoped to induce the economic consequences of the Reformation by despoiling the church. But the effect of their policy had been to create flocks of new landowners, not floods of new capital. The reforms of Mouzinho da Silveira in 1832 had been largely concerned with agriculture: ancient rights and dues had been removed, the final traces of the *forais* abolished, and the practice of entailment attenuated (it was finally extinguished in 1863). These changes, however salutary, facilitated the sale of land; and it had always been the practice of the wealthy to invest their gains in land rather than industry. The reforms of 1832 were followed by the launching of agricultural societies and later by the holding of exhibitions. But the attempt to shift new burdens of taxation on to the countryside had been one of the leading causes of the revolt of the *patuleia*, which had greatly increased the burden of debt. Under the Regeneration, this general policy was changed, and the state, having consolidated its indebtedness, contracted new loans for the purpose of development and undertook to finance necessary works. Governments, faced with massive deficits, spoke in terms of increasing revenues by raising property-contributions, stamp-duties and other taxes. The opposition regularly accused them of maintaining excessive numbers of civil servants and demanded economies, resisting proposals for imposts which might raise prices.

The Historicals, under Loulé, continued in power until 1865, when they foundered on internal differences. Loulé favoured a coalition with the Regenerators, but Sá da Bandeira opposed him, formed a government, was defeated and called elections in June 1865. The result went against him and a 'fusionist' government was formed by António A. de Aguilar for the Regenerators and Loulé for the Historicals. It attempted to introduce a sales-tax in 1867, but the merchants of Oporto refused to present their wares for inspection on 1 January 1868 (the *janeirinha*), and forced the government to resign.

Sá da Bandeira and the bishop of Viseu then formed an administration to pursue a policy of 'reformism', and from July 1868 to August 1869 civil servants were dismissed, the civil list reduced, state institutions suppressed or amalgamated, salaries cut by $2\frac{1}{2}$ to 10 per cent, and subsidies abolished. But the deficit did not diminish, and the government was obliged to borrow 8,000 *contos*. The House of Peers demanded a balanced budget, and the government again fell. In August 1869 Anselmo J. Braamcamp joined the duke of Loulé in a 'fusionist' ministry.

Negotiations for a loan with Fruhling and Goschen had failed, and Stern Brothers would not float a loan unless the issuing-price was reduced to thirty-two. Braamcamp's first task was to reach a temporary accommodation with the money-lenders. His second was to produce a budget. The estimates for 1870–1 were: receipts, 16,636 *contos*; expenditure, 21,931; deficit, 5,295. The main item of expenditure was the service of the public debt, which now amounted to 9,153 *contos*. Without this burden, the budget could be easily balanced, but about 55 per cent of receipts was required to satisfy existing creditors, largely foreign bankers. New indebtedness ran at about 30 per cent of revenues. Portuguese funds were quoted at 36.

Braamcamp hoped to force up the property tax, make heavy increases in direct taxation, and apply an income tax. The government's order for the assessment of all property led to agitation in various parts of the country; and the ministry, being unsure of support, held new elections which produced an amenable majority of Historicals and Regenerators. Neither of the two parties was able to govern alone, and the formation of a coalition placed responsibility in the hands of a group of leaders who were heads of factions. The instability of ministries increased the difficulty of imposing unpopular policies, and this in turn rendered the terms under which loans could be made constantly less favourable.

But if the institutions and the economic consequences of liberalism had failed, the spirit of liberalism had prevailed. On the question of the church, passions were less violent, though convictions were strongly held, as appeared in the controversies about the Sisters of Charity and the introduction of civil marriage. On humane issues, milder and more tolerant ideas, more in keeping with the Portuguese character, expressed themselves in the new civil and penal codes. The death-penalty, which had not been applied since 1846, was now abolished, as was penal labour on public works and solitary life imprisonment. A revival of literature had taken place, and manifested itself in diverse ways: the writers of the romantic movement had suffered exile in the days of Dom Miguel, but had returned with Dona Maria da Glória, and the poet Almeida Garrett had founded the national theatre, while the historian Herculano had defended the liberal point of view in various polemics, brought a new approach to the study of history and given a new dignity to the popular novel. The appearance of illustrated magazines diffused general knowledge, and the classics of Portuguese literature were reprinted. In the field of education, the liberals had proposed to set up grammar-schools (*liceus*) in each provincial capital (1836), with normal schools in Lisbon and Oporto, and an upper primary course which would serve as a link between the general elementary system and the grammar-schools of the towns: this would have brought together, or at least have tempered the separation of the middle class, urban and secondary, and the masses of the population, rural and primary. But in fact, the establishment of the link was long deferred and even the system of *liceus* remained inadequate. In 1859 Fontes set up a General Council of Public Instruction, the forerunner of the ministry of education—overriding the opposition of the University of Coimbra—but this instrument for co-ordinating the educational system was rendered ineffective by constant changes of government and policy and calls for economy. Between 1854 and 1868 the number of public schools for boys rose from 1,146 to 1,965 and for girls from 53 to 348: the total population was about $3\frac{1}{2}$m. In view of the exigencies of the money-lenders, this rate of progress could not be maintained.

While in Portugal the Historical liberals were led by a kinsman of the royal family, the duke of Loulé, and a prelate, the bishop of Viseu. In Spain Isabella II had fallen into the hands of a palace clique and refused to call upon the Spanish Progressists, relying on the personal dictatorship of Narváez: the opposition became revolutionary, and the queen was deposed by the revolution of September 1868. Its leader General Prim began to seek an alternative to the Spanish Bourbons, soliciting the candidature of Ferdinand, the king-consort of Portugal. In January 1869 he sent Fernández de los Ríos to Lisbon to assure Ferdinand of a majority in a Spanish election. It was clear that this invitation would lead to the inheritance of the Spanish throne by Luis I, and Prim declared that 'with this candidate there came a great idea that would undoubtedly satisfy the Spanish *cortes* and the whole nation'. The situation was clarified further in June, when Ferdinand married Elisa Hunsler, later made countess of Edla, there being no question of a Spanish succession through this morganatic connection. In Portuguese eyes, this was sufficient to damn the whole affair; and when Prim proposed a formal approach, Sá da Bandeira refused. Rumours that Fernández de los Ríos was to invite Luis to become king of Spain were denied by Luis, by Fernández and by Prim in September 1869.

But in default of Ferdinand, the strongest claimant was Leopold of Hohenzollern, and the French emperor was prepared to go to all lengths to prevent the installation of a German (other than Ferdinand) in Madrid. In October 1869 the aged Saldanha, hitherto Portuguese ambassador in Paris, suddenly appeared in Lisbon and requested Luis to change his ministers. The government asked him to return to his post, but he disobeyed and began to canvas support for Ferdinand. Early in May 1870 Napoleon III took positive steps in the same sense. Fernández de los Ríos again pressed Ferdinand, and Napoleon wrote to Luis to urge him to support his father's candidature: the letter was carried by a brother of the French minister Ollivier; and as he arrived in Lisbon, the Portuguese opposition left the chamber. Saldanha then rode to the palace at the head of such troops as he could muster, made a *pronunciamento* and declared himself universal minister. Loulé and his colleagues refused to countersign the appointment, but Saldanha contrived to cling to the shadow of power until 29 August, by which time Luis was in a position to dismiss him. Although Luis had replied to Napoleon refusing to put forward his father's candidature, Saldanha urged him to change his mind in order to save the peace of Europe. This appeal was read before the council of the royal family on 9 July, and Ferdinand now gave his conditional consent, asking for a guarantee of the continued separation of Portugal, an assurance of three-quarters of the votes in the Spanish *cortes*, the approval of England and France, and a pension in case he should abdicate. It was clear that Prim would refuse to repudiate the 'great idea' of Iberian unity, and it was in any case too late to save Napoleon's face or even his throne. Napoleon's attempts to force the Prussian court to disown Leopold enabled Bismarck to lure him into a disastrous declaration of war. France was defeated, and the Napoleonic empire passed to Germany. Saldanha was dismissed and sent off to London, to end his days as Portuguese minister there. For Portugal, the danger had not been serious; nevertheless, ideas of Pan-Iberianism, fortified by vague misconceptions drawn from the Italian *resorgimento*, continued to haunt the parties of the Spanish left.

Three years later, the Spanish throne again became vacant after the brief tenancy of Amadeo of Savoy. The Spanish *cortes* could find no other monarch willing to sit on it and declared for a republic. The improvised republicans in Spain adopted the theory of federalism which Pi i Margall had obtained from the last work of Proud'hon. In February 1873 the Spanish minister in London went so far as to assert that there was 'a disposition on the part of the Republican Party in Spain towards a union with Portugal' and that the Spanish government 'might not be able to stop some aggressive movement' (!). Grenville replied that the Spaniards 'could not count on the indifference of England to an external attack on Portugal', and the Spanish minister replied that 'everything depended upon the attitude of England: if England opposed such a plan no attempt would be made: otherwise it was sure to happen'. This cool threat of aggression vanished in the anarchy of the Spanish federal republic. The Spanish army restored order in 1874 and brought back the Bourbons in the person of Isabella's son, the young Alfonso XII.

On the resignation of Saldanha, Sá da Bandeira formed a ministry which received the support of Reformists, Historicals and Regenerators. Elections were held, and the Reformists, now led by the bishop of Viseu, formed an administration, sharing power with the marquis of Ávila, a conservative. This alliance of the two wings added nothing to the stability of ministries. The array of leaders, with their small followings, had made it necessary to govern by coalition, and the uncertainty of political combinations made it difficult to secure any continuity of policy and impossible to apply any rigorous remedy to the country's ills. In May 1871 a group of young writers organized the series of 'Conferências do Casino', lectures on the state of Portuguese society, which, couched in the grandiose and general ideas popular at the time, denounced the errors of the past and present, and defended the future, if only because the lecturers left themselves nothing else to defend. The lectures were suspended by the government in June: the conservatives urged the condemnation of erosive republicanism, while the liberals protested against the suppression of free speech. Ávila resigned, and in September 1871 Fontes formed a government of Regenerators: as he did so, the spokesman of the Historicals urged that the political groups should be resolved into two parties, and this was again attempted.

From 1871 it became the practice for governments to govern as long as they were able, and then to hand over power to their rivals. This system, known as rotativism, survived until the fall of the monarchy. It took note of the fact that it was impossible to govern without a majority in parliament or to maintain a majority while there were small groups and shifting combinations. In the Iberian Peninsula governments made elections, not elections governments. Since fully representative elections were impracticable, the practice was for governments to hold elections for the purpose of obtaining a governing majority, allowing the opposition a minority representation, and to resign when they could no longer govern effectively, whereupon the opposition followed the same procedure. Thus at least the members of each ministry were of the same party and were committed to the same policy, and had a sufficient expectation of life to take responsibilities into their hands. The rotativist method was soon adopted in Spain under the constitutional reform of Cánovas del Castillo (1876).

Fontes held power from 1871 until September 1876. During this period the deficit was reduced by two-fifths, from 4,500 contos in 1870–1 to 2,800 in 1875–6 and Portuguese funds rose from 37 to 52½. The main railway system was completed with the building of the Maria Pia bridge over the Douro at Oporto and the extension of the track to the Minho. There were important improvements in the port of Lisbon, which was linked by steamship services with the Algarve, the Atlantic Islands and Africa: the cable to Brazil was laid. Taxes, stamp-duties and customs-duties were increased, and the floating debt was consolidated. Government receipts rose by about half between 1871 and 1876, and the prosperity of the country was revealed in much new building, in the growth of social activities and in the general air of well-being. There was also a wave of speculation, reflected in the appearance of innumerable banks, particularly in the provincial towns, from 1873 to 1875. This growth was stimulated by the transfer of Brazilian capital to Portugal and by investment in Spanish funds. It was cut short in 1876 when the Spanish interest rate was abruptly reduced. On 18 August many banks suspended payments, and the government was forced to declare a moratorium and contract a new loan: the storm was soon weathered.

In September 1876 the opposition groups, Reformists and Historicals, merged in the 'pact of Granja' to form a single party, the Progressists, led by A. J. Braamcamp and the bishop of Viseu. It took advantage of the somewhat uncondescending attitude of Fontes to advocate the widening of the electorate, decentralization of authority, extension of primary education and reforms of taxation, of the banking laws and of the armed services. This programme was designed to attract popular support; but it lacked cohesion, and on some counts the Progressists had been overbid by the Republicans, who, though disconcerted by the collapse of the Spanish federal republic in 1874, recovered their spirits with the success of the French unitary republic two years later.

Fontes now enjoyed great prestige, and his confidence in the importance of material progress as a necessary pre-requisite to social reform made him a formidable opponent. When in 1877 his administration finally failed, power passed to the conservative marquis of Ávila, who was at first supported by the liberal groups which hoped for a change. But Ávila's personal supporters were few, and he was outvoted at the end of the year, whereupon Fontes again formed a government. He held new elections in 1878, and obtained a majority.

In Oporto a republican was now elected for the first time. When finally in May 1879 Fontes was brought down by a series of attacks on aspects of economic policy, combined with accusations of financial irregularities, Dom Luis at last called on Braamcamp, who formed the first Progressist ministry. After governing for some months in the face of the Regenerator majority, he asked for a dissolution and obtained a parliament consisting of ninety-three supporters to twenty-three oppositionists, including one republican. A batch of twenty-six peers was baked to provide a majority in the upper house. Even so, the Progressist administration failed to hold together, and at the end of 1883 Fontes returned to power, organized a majority and governed until February 1886. The Progressist leader Braamcamp had died three months before, and his successor José Luciano de Castro again held elections to obtain a majority.

In May 1886 the heir to the throne, Carlos, married Amélie, a daughter of the Orleanist pretender, the count of Paris. He succeeded on the death of Luis in October 1889.

4. PORTUGUESE AFRICA

Throughout the eighteenth century Brazil had held pride of place among the Portuguese territories overseas. The possessions in Asia and Oceania—Gôa and its dependencies, Macau and Timor—were, like the still considerable Portuguese-speaking communities in Ceylon and Malaya, evidence of a long tradition of evangelization, settlement and commerce, rather than centres of power or wealth. Between these two zones lay Portuguese Africa, with some of the characteristics of each of the others. In East Africa, the fortress of Moçambique remained the chief settlement and the port of call for ships passing to Asia, but it was inadequately held and possessed little control over the estates of the mainland, where the heirs of the 'donas da Zambésia' were largely of Indian or African stock and ruled their *prazos* as feudal potentates. In West Africa, the most important zone of occupation was Angola, with its two cities, Luanda and Benguela, an agricultural belt and the beginnings of a mining and metallurgical industry established in the time of Pombal by Sousa Coutinho, who had advanced the frontier to Caconda in the Benguela Highlands: his successor had founded the port of Mossâmedes.

The coastal settlements of Angola were linked with Brazil by the traffic in slaves, largely conducted through São Tomé and the Cape Verde Islands. In the old kingdom of Congo there were still missions which maintained the Christian tradition. Further north, the Portuguese possessed only a factory on the Dahomey coast and an establishment in Guinea. Elsewhere the commercial expansion of Holland, France and England had deprived them of their ancient trading-stations, though in places the interlopers dealt with the chiefs of the interior through the medium of detribalized natives who still regarded themselves as Portuguese and preserved their language and religion to a greater or less degree. The diversion of the main stream of Portuguese emigration to Brazil had led to a darkening of the population of the Cape Verde Islands and of São Tomé and Príncipe: the agricultural estates founded in the sixteenth century now passed into the hands of mulatto or black landowners.

When in 1795 the English established themselves at the Cape of Good Hope, and the Dutch settlers began to move their agrarian communities into the interior, some forward-looking Portuguese thought of exploring the territory to the west of Moçambique and setting up trading posts. Dr Francisco de Lacerda set out to explore the way from Moçambique to Angola, only to die at Kazembe's near Lake Mweru in 1798. Four years later, Pedro José Baptista and Amaro José, African Portuguese traders, left Angola, reached the Kazembe, where they were delayed for several years, and finally came out at Moçambique at the end of the decade: they had performed the first recorded crossing of Africa. For two decades, those of the Napoleonic wars and the liberal upheaval, little was achieved, but in 1831 Majors J. Correia Monteiro and A. Pedroso Gamitto visited Kazembe and reported on the possibilities of trade in upper Zambesia. They were not very encouraging, and in these years the invasions of the Zulus and Gazas rendered it impossible to proceed with Lacerda's idea of a chain of posts across the interior.

During the eighteenth century the expansion of the American economies had increased the demand for slaves, both from North America and the Caribbean, which drew chiefly on West Africa north of the equator—a traffic largely controlled from Liverpool and from Brazil, which was supplied chiefly from the Cape Verde Islands, drawing on the Guinea coast, and from Angola. In the settlement of

Utrecht Britain had won the right to supply the Spanish Caribbean with slaves, but a century later, in the peace that followed the Napoleonic wars, she attempted to stamp out the trade by international agreement. The movement against slavery had its roots in sixteenth-century Spain, but it developed in the eighteenth in various European countries, which accepted the idea that no one could be a slave in western Europe. This doctrine was held in England and in Portugal in the days of Pombal. Opposition was then directed against the traffic in slaves and especially against the inhuman conditions under which this was conducted. Thus the traffic was prohibited by Denmark in 1792, made a felony for British subjects in 1811, and condemned by the Congress of Verona in 1814. In the following year an Anglo-Portuguese agreement was concluded by which the traffic was prohibited north of the line, and mixed commissions were set up to judge cases of illegal trafficking: it was also agreed that Portuguese subjects should continue legally to convey slaves from points south of the equator to Brazil 'until the trade shall universally cease'. In 1817 the legitimate trading-area in East Africa was designated as from Cabo Delgado to the bay of Lourenço Marques. Some years later an attempt was made in this area to stimulate new activities to replace the traffic, but owing to financial difficulties the Lourenço Marques Company made little headway.

In 1836 Sá da Bandeira prohibited the slave trade throughout the Portuguese possessions. But in Moçambique the governor suspended the decree on the ground that it was still impracticable. The prohibition of the traffic north of the line and its toleration south of the line had inevitably driven many illicit traders southwards and tempted them to make free use of the Portuguese flag. In 1839 Palmerston authorized British warships to search ships flying Portuguese colours, an interference with Portuguese sovereignty that caused deep resentment. After the Portuguese prohibition (and indeed before it), illicit traders tended to use ports not under European control. The slave-trade was endemic in Africa, and slavery had contributed to support native autonomy, since the chiefs were the main procurers of slaves: the suppression of the traffic naturally hastened the process of European intervention and occupation.

The question of sovereignty in Africa was raised in the first half of the nineteenth century, though it became acute only in the second.

In East Africa, the coastal limits of Moçambique were set in 1817; but no demarcation took place. In 1824 Captain Owen, conducting a hydrographic survey, set up a British flag on the southern part of the bay of Lourenço Marques, and when the Portuguese seized a British trading-ship with an illicit cargo of ivory, forced its release and referred the question to London. But the incident passed, and nothing more was heard of it until 1860. On the west coast, the Portuguese claimed Bolama in Portuguese Guinea, first established in 1607. An English party made an agreement with some natives in 1790, and attempted to found a settlement in 1792, but this failed in the following year. In 1828 the Portuguese made a new agreement with the natives, but their rights were infringed by British ships on several occasions, and the issue was still undecided in 1861, when the Portuguese proposed arbitration and the British refused. Further south, in Angola, Portugal claimed both banks of the Congo and Angola. In the interior she had posts on the Cuanza and in Benguela, whence traders such as Silva Porto went into the unknown territory to the east.

In 1854 Livingstone completed his notable journey from his mission on the northern fringe of the Boer area, to Luanda in Angola. He found at Luanda a city of 12,000, with two cathedrals (one desecrated since the expulsion of the Jesuits and turned into a workshop), many stone houses, a well-managed custom-house, paved streets, plenty of shade from trees planted through the town, and an active fishing-port. He noted that even at Ambaca great numbers could read and write, and even after the missions were depleted or abandoned, the inhabitants still taught one another. Although he carried with him Bowdich's account of the Portuguese discoveries and although he met Silva Porto at Linyati, he remained firmly convinced of his own priority, a belief which was amplified by the rising tide of missionary fervour among his compatriots. He had passed through the most savage regions of the interior of Africa and had been horrified by what he saw. He hoped that some day the light of the gospel would illuminate this barbarism, but he did not hesitate to hold out the hope of wealth to encourage his country-men to intervene. The Portuguese, though they treated Livingstone kindly and admired his achievement, were mystified by his intentions, and even more so by those of the British government. As Livingstone noted, no credit had been given for the stamping out of the slave-trade at Luanda. At Ambriz, which had been occupied by the Portuguese in the eighteenth century and then abandoned, the British government refused to admit Portuguese claims, even though the place was a known centre of American slaving-interests: when a Portuguese expedition occupied it in 1855, the traffic disappeared, but Palmerston instructed the Admiralty to oppose by force any further Portuguese expansion. This attitude was maintained until 1875, the Portuguese being left to guess what it portended: in 1856 Sá da Bandeira noted that the policy of the British seemed to be to establish a sort of protectorate as they had done on the Mina Coast.

In 1860 a British naval force occupied the southern part of the bay of Lourenço Marques, and the Portuguese duly protested. Sá da Bandeira proposed arbitration for both this and the question of Bolama, but this was refused. When at length the British changed their stand and submitted the Bolama dispute to the arbitration of the United States, President Grant delivered a verdict in favour of the Portuguese in April 1870. It was based on prior discovery and acknowledged sovereignty: 'it appearing that the said island of Bolama and the said mainland opposite thereto were discovered by a Portuguese navigator in 1446, that the British title is derived from an illegal cession by native chiefs in 1790 at which time the sovereignty of Portugal had been established over the mainland and over the island of Bolama, that the Portuguese government has not relinquished its claim and now occupies that island with a Portuguese settlement of about 700 persons . . .' When the Portuguese concluded a treaty with the Transvaal Republic, the British government accepted arbitration on the case of Lourenço Marques. This time the British chose President MacMahon of France as arbitrator, and in 1875 he gave his decision in favour of Portugal. Thus in December 1875 Portugal was able to make a new treaty for the building of a railway from Lourenço Marques to Pretoria, and in March 1876 one with the Orange Free State. These acknowledged Lourenço Marques as the natural port for the interior and paved the way for its future prosperity.

The question of rights over the mouth of the Congo had been evaded for thirty years. The king of Belgium had nourished designs on Portuguese Africa even as early as the *patuleia*. His successor

Leopold II held a conference in Brussels in September 1876, at which he launched his 'International African Association' and engaged the traveller Stanley to make agreements in the Congo basin on his behalf. During the same years, the French sent Brazza, an Italian born in Rio de Janeiro, to stake claims on the north bank of the Congo. The effect of these moves was not lost on the Portuguese government. In 1875 Andrade Corvo had raised the question of Cabinda, to the north of the Congo river, and Lord Derby had stated that the Admiralty instructions of 1856 were still in force. Some years were still to pass before the British government changed its attitude. Meanwhile, in 1877 Andrade Corvo sent Capelo, Ivens and Serpa Pinto to Angola, and Serpa Pinto travelled from Bié to the Victoria Falls and so to Pretoria and Durban. These journeys indicated the interest of the Portuguese in the territory between Angola and Moçambique and revived the plans of Lacerda. Meanwhile, in the Congo, Stanley obtained land for Leopold in 1878, and the French founded Brazzaville in 1880.

A new situation was created by the intervention of Germany, which suddenly now became aware of an African destiny. When in 1882 Leopold launched his International Congo Association, the British government agreed, much too late, to open negotiations with Portugal, and while the International Association continued its offensive, Granville concluded the treaty of February 1884 by which Great Britain recognized the Portuguese claim to both banks of the Zaire and Portugal undertook to preserve freedom of navigation and to limit customs-duties: there were at this time forty-nine factories on the Congo, of which twenty-six were Portuguese, twelve Netherlands, seven French and four English.

Leopold at once produced a counter-attack. On 3 April 1884 a German Colonization Association was founded, which at its second meeting decided to oppose the Anglo-Portuguese treaty. Propaganda was quickly spread, and the United States added its opposition. In June the British attempted to compromise by recognizing a German claim to Angra Pequena, and the Kaiser responded by asserting a protectorate over South-West Africa (August 1884). In April the British government still hoped to get the Anglo-Portuguese treaty accepted: by the end of June it was hesitant, and by October it was in retreat. This was largely due to the efforts of Leopold, who had succeeded in ranging the French with the Germans. The latter now seized the initiative. The Portuguese had suggested an international conference in May, but nothing came of it until October, when Bismarck announced a meeting to open in Berlin on 15 November. A week before, Germany recognized the International Association, while France pressed Portugal to accept. Faced with this front, the British government wavered, leaving the Portuguese delegates to resist as best they could: they had finally no alternative but to accept the victory of Leopold. The 'Independent State of the Congo' was created, and the conference closed on 26 February 1885.

In the same month a change of government in Lisbon brought the Progressists to power, with José Luciano de Castro as President of the Council and Henrique de Barros Gomes as Foreign Minister. Indignation at the weakness of the ancient Ally ran high, and Barros Gomes perceived that it would be necessary to secure French and German consent to the remaining Portuguese claims. So in May 1886 he concluded a treaty with France by which the territory of Portuguese Guinea was delimited and France promised her good offices to secure recognition of Portuguese claims to territory between Angola and Moçambique, reserving the rights already acquired by other powers: in December Barros Gomes concluded a treaty with Germany by which the southern frontier of Angola and the northern of German South-West Africa was defined, and the Germans made a similar expression about the territory between Angola and Moçambique, with the same reservation as that expressed in the treaty with France. The 'International Association' had served to win for Leopold and the Kaiser territories over which they had no shadow of historical claim or even the justification of 'effective occupation' laid down by the Conference of Berlin. Their intrusion caused alarm and indignation in Lisbon, but Barros Gomes erred in over-estimating the value of their support, for neither they nor France had any interest in the area he hoped to claim.

The Portuguese now published their pretensions to a coast-to-coast colony, the so-called 'Rose-coloured Map', which united Angola and Moçambique. In England, Lord Salisbury protested against the claim, but was in no hurry to embark on negotiations or to manifest what Britain herself would claim. In June 1887 he stated that his government could not recognize Portuguese sovereignty in territories

305

not occupied with sufficient forces to maintain order. Barros Gomes pointed out that the Congo Free State had had no effective occupation when it had obtained recognition, and that Germany had not occupied South-West Africa when her claims were admitted. He alluded to Portugal's historical claims and the conditional recognition granted by France and Germany. He also construed Salisbury's statement to imply that Britain would negotiate on the basis of an effective occupation, and therefore accelerated this as far as possible. In 1884 Serpa Pinto had travelled from Moçâmedes by the Cunene and Cubango and Barotseland to the Zambezi and Quelimane, which he reached in June 1885, while Dias de Carvalho renewed relations with the Muatianvaa, or king of Lunda, opened by Rodrigues Graça in 1843–7.

5. CARLOS I, 1889–1908

Carlos I succeeded his father in October 1889 and maintained the Progressist ministry of José Luciano de Castro and Barros Gomes. Little had been done to ameliorate Anglo-Portuguese relations since the failure of the treaty of 1884 and the success of Germany at the conference of Berlin. In Portugal the disillusionment of 1885 had been followed by a general assumption that the Rose-coloured Map had been internationally accepted: Lord Salisbury's protest had received little attention, and Barros Gomes remained unshaken in his belief that it was possible to use Germany to win recognition of his claims. This belief was possibly fortified by events in East Africa: in October 1886 the southern limit of the territories of the sultan of Zanzibar was fixed by an Anglo-German agreement without consultation with Portugal and to her detriment, and in 1887 the Portuguese remedied the omission with an ultimatum to the sultan. In England, Salisbury, having negotiated with Germany for spheres of influence in East Africa, turned his attention further south. The danger of a concert between the Boer republics and German South-West Africa had been averted by the occupation of Bechuanaland in 1884; but Salisbury was opposed to the northward expansion of the Boers and rejected the Portuguese claim to Mashonaland and the territories to the north and west of the Zambezi, without putting forward any claim himself or attempting to negotiate. When the Boers were reported to be seeking concessions in Mashonaland, Salisbury concluded a treaty (February 1888) with Lobengula, the chief of the Matabeles, who undertook to grant no concession without reference to the Cape and shortly gave a monopoly of mineral rights to an agent of Rhodes. After this treaty Salisbury began to think of claiming the territory up to and beyond the Central Zambezi as a British sphere of influence. As he did so, the Portuguese government prepared a sizeable expedition to northern Mashonaland, the Shiré and the region of Lake Nyasa. The leaders left Lisbon in July 1888. A month later, the idea of a British-controlled 'Cape to Cairo' route was ventilated by (Sir) Harry Johnston in an unsigned article in *The Times*: this concept, later appropriated by Rhodes, was clearly incompatible with the Rose-coloured Map.

There were at this time two particular points of conflict in British and Portuguese policy. First, Lobengula claimed to be overlord of the Mashonas and Makalolos. His people had moved northward earlier in the century and settled near Bulawayo: they intimidated their northern neighbours, but there were no Matabeles anywhere near Mashonaland, and only one chief appears to have sent gifts to Lobengula. Yet the concession-hunters and subsequently the British government recognized the pretensions of Lobengula. The Portuguese, in addition to their historical claims to the land of the Monomotapa, which Salisbury dismissed as 'archaeological', held that one of their subjects Gungunhana was the effective ruler of the Mashonas, who therefore looked to them for defence. They accordingly protested against the implications of the treaty with Lobengula, and their consul at the Cape published a notice rejecting his pretensions.

Secondly, in the region of Lake Nyasa, there existed two British interests, the Scottish missions at Blantyre and Livingstonia (1875-6) and a small trading concern, the African Lakes Company (1875). The missions were menaced by Arab slave-traders on the Lake, but did not appeal to the Portuguese for help: the Portuguese in return were unwilling to allow the passage of arms up the Zambezi without an acknowledgment of their sovereignty.

In the spring of 1889 Salisbury sent Johnston, who had just been appointed consul in Moçambique, to hold exploratory conversations with Barros Gomes in Lisbon. The Portuguese minister was ready to compromise on the Rose-coloured Map, admitting a British corridor from north to south, and forgoing much of the Mashona territory in return for the Shiré highlands and the southern half of Lake Nyasa. There was no doubt that the Portuguese might reasonably lay claim to a considerable, if ill-defined, area to the north and south of the Zambezi: their *prazos* extended to Tete, and they had reoccupied Zumbo. Johnston's proposal was welcomed by Lister at the Foreign Office, who pointed out that no arbitrator would give Britain so much, but it was rejected by Salisbury because of the political influence exercised by the missions: in Glasgow religion and commerce demanded the take-over of the 'land of Livingstone'.[1]

At this time Salisbury limited himself to warning Barros Gomes that he 'must not go too far', though he did not say how far this was. The Portuguese had now erected Zumbo into the capital of a new district: Paiva de Andrade had traversed Manica and Mashonaland distributing flags, and Victor Cordon had built a stockade at the confluence of the Sanyati and Zambezi. A party under Valadim moving to the east of Lake Nyasa was attacked and murdered by the Yaos. Serpa Pinto's expedition remained in camp near the mouth of the Shiré, where he was met by Johnston in August 1889. In the same month Buchanan, the consul at Blantyre, informed Serpa Pinto that the Makololos were under British protection. Some weeks later he was involved in a skirmish near Ruo. When the news reached London in November, Salisbury sent a note to Lisbon in which he issued a warning. In December Barros Gomes replied that there was no intention to attack the territory of Lobengula, but that he awaited a full account. On 11 January 1890 Salisbury demanded that the Portuguese should withdraw immediately from the territory of the Makololos and Mashonas, under threat of recalling the British minister from Lisbon.

This message—the Ultimatum—caused astonishment and indignation at Lisbon. The Council of State asked for arbitration, which Salisbury refused (28 January): he would accept nothing less than complete withdrawal. The Progressists fell, and the Regenerators came to power and negotiated a treaty, but such was the state of opinion that it was rejected in *cortes*. The general excitement was

---

[1] R. Oliver, *Sir Harry Johnston*, 150 f., shows that Salisbury 'set in motion a deliberately staged demonstration of British [i.e. Scottish] public opinion'.

exploited by the republicans. A non-party government headed by General João Crisóstomo de Abreu e Sousa was formed. In January 1891 it concluded a *modus vivendi* in substitution of the rejected treaty. In the same month a republican revolt in Oporto collapsed after a struggle lasting barely an hour and a half: the small group of soldiers and others who planned to repeat the revolt of 1820 counted on the erosive effect of years of disruptive propaganda and on the recent fall of the Brazilian Braganças. Since the Napoleonic invasion the Anglo-Portuguese Alliance had guaranteed the throne of the Braganças, and Salisbury's ultimatum had struck at the roots of the monarchy. The assumption that the Alliance was a guarantee of security was shaken, and the younger intellectuals sought solace in new theories of society proceeding from France and Germany, in particular positivism, which under the pretence of organizing human destinies had lately disorganized the Brazilian empire. But the small commotion in Oporto was soon forgotten and for a decade the Portuguese Republican Party appeared to achieve little.

The most evident consequence of the crisis of 1890 was the aggravation of the financial situation. The Baring crisis, though born in Argentina, affected both Brazil and Portugal. The Bank of Portugal declared a moratorium, and the government was on the verge of bankruptcy during 1891 and 1892. The public debt had reached 592,000 *contos*, and the trade balance showed a deficit of 23,000. It was possible to raise loans only by pledging particular assets such as the tobacco monopoly. The foreign holders of Portuguese debt formed committees and sought control of the customs: the Germans in particular favoured an international naval demonstration, such as had lately been performed off the shore of Venezuela. Oliveira Martins, the historian, philosopher and socialist, became Minister of Finance in January 1892, but his proposals to reduce the deficit dissolved in a sea of detail and he soon resigned. Early in 1893 measures were produced to raise all kinds of taxes and duties, but the resulting agitation led to the fall of the government. In February 1893 the Regenerators formed a ministry (Hintze Ribeiro, João Franco, Fuschini, Bernardino Machado). It dissolved the commercial and industrial associations which opposed the tax reform When Fuschini and Machado resigned, Hintze Ribeiro and João Franco deferred the elections of 1894 and governed by decree, extending the powers of the Minister of the Interior and preparing a new electoral law by which the system of minorities was terminated. The opposition abstained in protest from the elections of November 1895, but Hintze could not control the upper house and fell when the king refused to 'bake' peers for him. The Progressists then came to power, and held office until 1900.

During this period Dom Carlos visited England, France and Germany with a view to improving relations and lessening pressures against Portugal. The financial situation remained precarious, and it was expected that the decision of an arbitration committee at Berne might precipitate a crisis.[1] In May 1897 Chamberlain offered to guarantee the Portuguese possessions and to extend a loan to meet the anticipated Berne award in return for virtual control of Lourenço Marques (and thus of access to the Boer republic). This proposal was rejected, and some time later the governor-general of Moçambique, Mouzinho de Albuquerque, visited London, Paris and Berlin to discuss the raising of funds. He recommended an approach to the British government, but no sooner had the latter begun to consider the question of a loan with a view to controlling the external communications of the Boers than the Germans demanded to be associated in a parallel loan to Portugal to be secured on customs revenue, 'it being understood that in selecting places where these revenues were collected, we should be establishing a footing which, in case of certain eventualities, would decide the destiny of the territories in question': the so-called 'inchoate rights' would 'only come to maturity in case Portugal fell to pieces'. The Germans offered southern Moçambique to Britain on condition that the region to the north of the Zambezi fell to Germany: 'he would also ask on the western side of Africa for the colony of Angola'. When Salisbury remarked that these demands were very large, the German replied that 'I must not tell him later on that we had rejected this proposal on account of the extravagance of his demands, because if we objected to them he was quite ready to consider our objections'. For good measure, the German added that the Republic of Liberia was

---

[1] As a result of Salisbury's ultimatum, the Portuguese terminated the MacMurdo concession for a railway from Lourenço Marques to the Transvaal: the shareholders claimed large damages. Finally, however, the Berne court fixed the compensation at less than £1m. in 1900.

in financial straits and that German subjects were injured by its insolvency.[1]

At the end of June 1898 it was clear that the Portuguese government would need £6m. to meet its debts and £2m. for Moçambique, which might be secured on the customs, valued at £300,000 a year. Salisbury, while clearly aware that Germany intended to encourage 'bad administration and sedition' with the object of gaining control of the Portuguese colonies, nevertheless thought it necessary for political reasons to admit the German demands, and embarked on a series of discussions on the hypothesis of 'a change of territorial ownership . . . wholly contingent on their abandonment by Portugal, a contingency which we most earnestly deprecated'. On 8 August Salisbury had an interview with the German ambassador of which no record exists: he then went abroad leaving the Foreign Office to Balfour, who on 30 August signed a convention with Germany governing the conditions of loans to Portugal and providing for the eventual consignment of custom-houses to the two signatories. Balfour had noted that it was almost impossible to enter into an agreement of this kind without suggesting that the parties desired the dismemberment of Portugal's colonies, which, so far as his government was concerned, was the opposite of the truth: it was 'their earnest wish to maintain the integrity of Portugal, and it was only in the event of our king being unable to attain this result that ulterior eventualities had to be provided for. The German ambassador, Hatzfeldt, assured me that his government were not less anxious than our own to maintain the status quo'. However, the Kaiser was declaring that 'colonial expansion had become a necessity for Germany. He would infinitely prefer to obtain what he wanted by a friendly arrangement with England, but if this were not possible, he would have to . . . place himself under obligation to other Powers'. The emperor, whining and bullying, left no doubt that he regarded the ulterior 'eventualities' as entirely desirable. The main object of Salisbury and his nephew was to remove German influence from the

---

[1] 'His Excellency claimed from England a benevolent examination of the propositions he was making on the ground that in past negotiations Germany had been of great service to this country. When I [Salisbury] pressed him to specify these incidents which my memory did not enable me to recall, he said that Russia and France were very much disposed to attack us on the subject of the Suez Canal, and had only been prevented by the disapproval of Germany.'

approaches to the Transvaal. The method of achieving this object was lacking in dignity, even though the Portuguese minister in London knew all about the secret agreement and Salisbury knew that he knew. The Portuguese government in fact desisted from raising a loan, and the convention remained inoperative.

It was in fact negotiating with French financiers, but their demands were excessive, and in the spring of 1899 Salisbury found it necessary to 'rescue Portugal from the clutches of France and those numerous political and financial sharks which at present hover round it'. A small loan raised privately in London met immediate needs. But in August 1899 the German minister in Lisbon pressed the Portuguese government to borrow, confiding in his British colleague that he 'understood his instructions to convey that one of the objects of the Anglo-Portuguese agreement was to induce the Portuguese government to contract a loan in order that, when its proceeds had been extravagantly wasted, we should remain with a claim on the control of the Portuguese colonial customs'.

Relations between Britain and the Boers steadily deteriorated during the summer of 1899, and Salisbury now took up the question of preventing supplies from reaching the Transvaal. In reply to this, the Portuguese minister Soveral drafted a note in which allusion was made to mutual obligations under the ancient treaties. But this did not satisfy Salisbury, who pointed out that the mutual defence of possessions did not cover the case of the Transvaal, over which Great Britain neither claimed sovereignty nor sought to establish it. He therefore demanded that Portugal should declare war on the Boers, thereby cancelling the Portuguese-Transvaal Treaty of 1875: the alternative, Salisbury added, would be a British blockade of Lourenço Marques. It was therefore at the behest of the British that the Alliance was restored in the words of the treaties of 1642 and 1661—'each of them to favour the other and to use one another with friendly offices and true affection, and that neither of the said most renowned kings, their heirs and successors, by himself or by any other, shall do or attempt anything against each other or their kingdoms, by land or by sea, nor shall consent nor adhere unto any war, counsel or treaty in prejudice of the other', and on the part of the British crown 'to defend and protect all conquests or colonies belonging to the Crown of Portugal against all his enemies as well future as present'. A secret declaration to this effect was signed on 14 October 1899; the Boer war had begun three days earlier.

The discovery by the Germans and French that arms could not be shipped to the Transvaal through Lourenço Marques precipitated a wave of agitation in the Portuguese press, which was inclined to see in the British campaign in South Africa a repetition of the imperialism which the Portuguese had suffered ten years before. The German government threatened that any violation of Portuguese neutrality would lead to the cessation of German neutrality, but without effect. In December 1900 the British Channel Fleet visited Lisbon, and the Alliance was publicly reaffirmed. This caused the Germans to inquire whether the secret Anglo-German agreement was still in force: they were told that the reaffirmation of the old Alliance ('of which everyone was aware') left the secret agreement exactly where it was.

The new century saw the return to power of the Regenerators and the collapse of the rotativist system. Hintze Ribeiro had quarrelled with João Franco, who in 1901 left the Regenerators with twenty-five followers and two years later founded the Centro Regenerador Liberal. In 1899 Oporto had elected three Republicans: when the election was annulled, they were again returned with an increased majority. But Hintze Ribeiro was less concerned with this challenge than with the secession of Franco. It became almost an obsession with him to crush his rival, and having dissolved parliament, he redistributed the constituencies in thirty-three circles in order to dilute the urban vote: by this manoeuvre he eliminated the Republicans and all but one of the followers of Franco. In 1902 Edward VII visited Lisbon and reaffirmed the Alliance, and an agreement was finally reached with the foreign bondholders, who accepted the conversion of all debt into a single issue at 3 per cent drawn from the customs revenues.

But Hintze Ribeiro had no policy of reform, and in 1903 Franco's faction denounced the rotativist system and adopted a programme of financial restrictions, decentralized administration and popular education. Although Franco held meetings up and down the country, his programme was more effective in splitting the Regenerator party than in attracting support from the Republicans, who offered more sweeping changes. When Hintze fell in 1904, the Progressists returned to office, but José Luciano de Castro was now ill and unable to provide effective leadership: an internal quarrel led to the fall of the Progressists in February 1906. Hintze Ribeiro held elections in April, but could not face parliament, and when he resigned Dom Carlos offered power to Franco. The leaders of the two main parties themselves were discredited, and the king thought that rotativism had outlived its usefulness and that a new leader, 'a man of character', would conquer opinion with reforms.

Franco now sought the aid of the Progressists in forming a 'liberal concentration', and agreed with José Luciano on reforms of the electoral system, of the public accounts and of the law of ministerial responsibility. But he also denounced the old party system and at the same time proclaimed free elections. In consequence, the Regenerators struggled against him for their very existence, while the Republicans adopted and amplified his accusations. In June 1906 they elected four deputies in Lisbon and proceeded to create tumultuous scenes in parliament. Their chief onslaught was directed against the crown, which they accused of receiving illegal advances from the treasury: it was indeed stated in the upper house that sums totalling 131 *contos* had been advanced since 1902. The vociferous demands of the Republicans for an inquiry led to their expulsion from the chamber, and in 1907 the failing of a doctoral candidate at Coimbra was converted into a political issue and followed by a strike and the closure of the university. In April Franco prepared a new press law to harness the Republican newspapers, and having closed the parliamentary session, proceeded to govern by decree. In protest the Progressists ceased to support Franco and went into opposition with the old Regenerators. José Luciano asked for a meeting of the Council of State, but Dom Carlos was only willing to receive each counsellor separately: there followed a series of protests from politicians and municipalities, and the Republicans redoubled their propaganda. In August Hintze Ribeiro died, and Júlio de Vilhena was elected leader of the Regenerators.

On 8 September 1907 each of the main parties delivered condemnations of Franco's dictatorship. A week later, Dom Carlos identified himself with Franco in an interview for *Le Temps*. A little before, the minister had decided to settle the question of advances to the civil list and to transfer the royal yacht, the royal Coach Museum and other properties to the state. This decision, taken against Carlos's better judgement, increased the pother of the Republicans. In December Franco announced elections for April of the following year, but the Republicans made an attempt at revolution on 28 January. It was unsuccessful, but the Minister of Justice obtained powers to exile those accused of various political offences. On 1 February, as the royal family crossed the Terreiro do Paço in Lisbon in an open landau, it was attacked by a group of assassins. A young man shot the king in the head. The queen rose to her feet with a bunch of flowers in her hand, and the coach started, but at the corner of the square a bearded man raised a carbine and shot the heir to the throne, Prince Luis Filipe. His younger brother, Dom Manuel, was wounded in the arm. It was the first regicide in Portuguese history.

The assassins were members of a political secret society, and it was claimed that they had decided to murder the king on hearing of the decree of exile for political crimes. Two years earlier a group of anarchists had attempted to murder the young king of Spain on the day of his wedding: the method of political assassination, if devised by Russian revolutionaries, had been advocated by the French anarchist Sorel. Although there was no question of the involvement of the Republican leaders, they were at little pains to dissociate themselves from the spirit that had produced the murder, and subscriptions were promptly opened for the families of the regicides.

6. MANUEL II, 1908–10

The sudden disappearance of Dom Carlos and his heir brought to the throne a prince who had not been expected or trained to rule, and who was much shaken by his horrifying experience. The Council of State was summoned, and Franco resigned and went into exile: he was replaced by Admiral Ferreira do Amaral who formed a cabinet which included both Regenerators and Progressists and promised to institute an 'English' monarchy. But he and his friends were too old to start a new style, and after the elections in April the parties began to intrigue in their usual manner: Vilhena, the new leader of the Regenerators, was eager for power and inclined to undermine the coalition. As a result, when Ferreira do Amaral resigned in November, the new king passed over Vilhena and asked Campos Henriques to form a government of Regenerators with Progressists. This ministry fell in February 1909 on the financial issue, and Sebastião Teles formed a ministry of Progressists with dissident Regenerators: it lasted less than a month. By March both parties were again split into two factions, and in January 1910 Teixeira de Sousa emerged as chief of the Regenerators, while Campos Henriques headed a conservative faction and Vilhena remained excluded. Among the Progressists the main body led by Venceslau de Lima faced a group of dissident followers of João de Alpoim. The only group to benefit by these quarrels was the Republican party, which had now recruited several prominent monarchists. One of these, A. J. da Cunha, confessed to having been the first to make unauthorized advances to the crown, thus reviving a favourite Republican theme. In April 1908 Lisbon had elected four Republican deputies, Setúbal two and Beja one, and in November the Lisbon Municipal Council passed under Republican control: the mob in the capital had now been won over, but Oporto and Coimbra remained monarchist. Until the end of 1908 the directorate of the Republican Party was in the hands of moderates, led by Dr Bernardino Machado, a former Regenerator minister; but they were now outvoted and replaced by a group of activists. These were in close touch with the secret masonic societies, the most virulent of which, the Carbonária, established cells in the armed services, particularly the navy, and among students, sergeants and journalists. Attempts by Teles to suppress secret societies had little effect.[1]

The workings of the secret masonry were as usual attended by an anti-clerical campaign, directed chiefly against the Society of Jesus. As this propaganda increased, the government tried to meet it by adopting an anti-clerical attitude: an order for the suppression of Jesuit houses was signed by Dom Manuel on 3 October, the day before the revolution.

But the monarchist parties had demoralized themselves. The Republicans won only fourteen seats in the elections of August 1910, and of these eleven were for Lisbon. Outside the capital, they had little

---

[1] The link between the Republican party and the Carbonária was Dr A. J. de Almeida. The Carbonária was governed by a supreme lodge, the 'Alta Venda', which included Machado Santos and António Maria da Silva.

support except through the ramifications of the Carbonária: their only perilous success was in the navy. Machado Santos, a second-lieutenant (paymaster) in the navy, but prime mover of the Carbonária, was reported to have desired a revolution for 14 July 1910, but the government was forewarned and sent several of the ships to sea: the same manoeuvre was repeated a month later before elections were held on 28 August: these gave the Regenerators a small majority. There was little sign that the Republicans were more than a noisy minority which had contrived to seduce the mob in the capital: the governor of Lisbon complacently believed in the absolute fidelity of his garrison.

On 1 October the appearance of the president of the Brazilian Republic, Marshal Hermes da Fonseca, who arrived in the cruiser *São Paulo* after a visit to Germany, provided the pretext for elaborate Republican demonstrations. These were part of a plan concluded on 25 September. The Republicans now had on their side an admiral, Cândido dos Reis. The presence of the Brazilian warship made it improbable that the government would send to sea the naval units which had been implicated. It was proposed to use these ships to bombard the Palace of the Necessidades. On the night appointed for the *coup* Admiral Reis was to go to the docks and await a launch to convey him to the rebellious ships. But one of the ships failed to rebel, the launch did not appear, and Reis, convinced that the revolution had collapsed, committed suicide. However, Machado Santos had taken an infantry barracks and occupied the Rotunda (the present Praça do Marquês de Pombal). On hearing of the death of Admiral Reis most of the officers desisted, but Machado Santos remained at the head of his men.

When at 11 a.m. on 4 October the two rebellious warships began to bombard the palace, Manuel asked for cannon to fire back, but the few officers at the palace advised him to retire. At 1 p.m. the loyal warship *Dom Carlos* was taken, and at 2 p.m. Dom Manuel left by car for Benfica and Mafra. Troops in the Rossio remained loyal to him, and another force marched from Benfica on the Rotunda. This attack, pursued with little energy, failed. On 5 October revolutionary sailors were reported to be landing at the Terreiro do Paço, and at 7 a.m. the German chargé d'affaires requested an armistice so that German subjects might retreat. The German went with a white flag to the Rotunda, and under cover of this the revolutionary troops advanced down the Avenida da Liberdade. The monarchist commander complained of this, and Machado Santos replied that the armistice (for an hour) was due to begin at 8.45: it was still only 8.44. This peculiar intervention assured the success of the Republican cause.

Dom Manuel, assured that there was nothing further to be done, was joined by his mother and grandmother at Mafra, and went to the neighbouring fishing-village of Ericeira, where he took ship in the yacht *Dona Amélia* for Gibraltar and England. He settled at Twickenham and he devoted himself to his splendid library: he died in 1932.

XII

THE REPUBLIC

I. PROVISIONAL, 1910; CONSTITUENT, 1911; CONSTITU-
TIONAL, 1912–15; AND 'DEMOCRATIC', 1915–17

The provisional government formed on 5 October 1910 had as its president, Dr Teófilo Braga, the archdruid of positivism and prolix historian of Portuguese literature. His Minister of the Interior, António José de Almeida, had embraced Republicanism at the time of the Ultimatum, then pursued his medical career in Africa for a dozen years, and having returned to political activity in 1904, played a leading part in organizing the republican revival. Bernardino Machado was entrusted with Foreign Affairs: he had been professor of philosophy at Coimbra and a minister under Hintze Ribeiro, but had gone over to Republicanism and had been elected president of the party in 1902. His standing, wealth and ineffable courtesy gave the movement respectability. Its vehemence and ruthlessness came from Afonso Costa, lawyer, demagogue and fanatical anti-clerical, who became Minister of Justice.

Dominated by the dogma of positivism, the fathers of the republic regarded the throne, church and nobility as a complex of irrational and indefensible institutions and were resolved to replace the ancient system of loyalties by the rule of law, formulated in a written constitution and administered by an aristocracy of ability and intellect, themselves. They abolished titles of nobility and all decorations except the Torre e Espada, and opened careers to the talented by erecting new universities at Lisbon and Oporto, for which fees were nominal or nil. But their jacobinism fell far short of social revolution. They were content to denounce the indebtedness, extravagance and corruption of the old regime and to demolish the apparent barriers of unmerited privilege. They sanctioned the right to strike and modified the tenancy laws. But their ideas contained much of superficial optimism, grandiloquently clad.

They were also more or less hostile to the church and to religion. Disestablishment was a principle of Republican policy, and it fell to

319

Afonso Costa to apply it. He believed that religion was destined to disappear and set out to justify this theory. He divested the state of every manifestation of faith: religious oaths ceased to have legal force, religious instruction in schools and the teaching of theology in the universities were abolished. The army was forbidden to participate in religious observances and saints' days were no longer to be kept as holidays. Costa restored the legislation of Pombal against the Jesuits and of J. A. de Aguiar against the Orders. In order to achieve this it was necessary to dismiss the rector of Coimbra University, whose place was taken by Dr Manuel de Arriaga. When the prelates protested in a pastoral, Costa ordered its suspension: the bishop of Oporto instructed his clergy to ignore the order and was therefore deposed. In April 1911 a Law of Separation (i.e. disestablishment) vested the administration of churches in lay committees (*associações cultuais*) and restricted their revenues to the offerings of the faithful, less one-third to be deducted for lay charities, a triple tithe in reverse. Bequests to the church were prohibited, but in theory the state provided pensions for priests and their dependants who might lose their livelihood.

On 28 May 1911 the provisional government held elections for a Constituent Assembly of 210 deputies. There was still only one Republican party, and local committees drew up lists of candidates, about half of whom were unopposed. Machado Santos demanded that there should be a contest in Lisbon, and one was held: the Republican vote was 18,853; socialists, 407; radicals, 577; independents 100 (population 350,000). The voters were mainly party members, officials, and aspirants to office. Opponents of the revolution abstained, and the monarchists abandoned political life as the Miguelites had done eighty years before. There was thus no opposition when in June the Assembly met, banished the Braganças, and replaced their blue and white flag with the red and green that had flown over the Rotunda, now embellished with the addition of the armillary sphere in gold. It decided to separate the functions of president of the republic from those of the prime minister (or president of the council) and to have the former chosen by parliament, not elected by the people. He would hold office for four years, but would not have the right to dissolve parliament (a right discredited by the constant dissolutions of the previous regime). On

24 August the benign and elderly Dr Arriaga was appointed first president of the republic. The Assembly further decided in favour of a bicameral legislature, the lower house being elected by direct suffrage. But the Constituent Assembly resolved itself into the first Republican parliament, electing a third of its members as senators: the remaining two-thirds automatically composed the lower house.

Many moderates had been antagonized by Dr Costa and his spate of controversial and oppressive decrees, and Dr Arriaga included no members of the provisional government in the first constitutional cabinet. He offered the premiership to Sr João Pinheiro Chagas, a pamphleteer, journalist and Republican of long standing. Although there was still only one Republican party and machine, three groups had already formed, round Brito Camacho, editor of *A Luta*, A. J. de Almeida, whose views were publicized in *A República*, and Afonso Costa, whose followers were called 'democráticos' and whose organ was *O Mundo*. The first two groups had elected Dr Arriaga by 121 votes to 86 for Bernardino Machado, and Chagas' cabinet was drawn from them, including two soldiers: General Pimenta de Castro, War, and Sidónio Pais, Development. In September and October there were monarchist stirrings in the north; and when congress decided to try those responsible, Pimenta de Castro left the government. The monarchists were now regarded as outside the law. Moreover, the caucus of the Republican party elected a new directorate of radicals, and Chagas resigned. The unity of the Republicans was thus lost, and the party machine fell into the hands of Costa and his supporters. Dr Augusto de Vasconcelos formed the new government, a 'ministry of concentration' including three Democrats. The new Minister of Justice resumed the anti-clerical policy of the Law of Separation. The patriarch and prelates were exiled. Meanwhile, Almeida's followers, the Evolutionists, appeared as the more conservative party, and Camacho and the Unionists held a middle position. Machado Santos, the hero of the Rotunda and head of the Carbonária, emerged as an independent whose individualistic views were expressed in the *Intransigente*.

 Meanwhile, the monarchists, Manuelites and Miguelites, were reconciled by the Pact of Dover of February 1912, by which Manuel's claim was to pass to a descendant of Dom Miguel. A monarchist attempt at a counter-revolution, led by Captain Paiva Couceiro, consisted of an unsuccessful incursion innto northern Portugal, followed by many arrests. The government then brought in a law for the defence of the republic, limiting freedom of speech and of the press (10 July), restrictions they had loudly denounced under the monarchy.

The Republicans had legalized the right to strike, and early in 1912 the workers of Lisbon began to avail themselves of the weapon. There were also disturbances at Évora, where the governor used troops to occupy the premises of the labour organizations. The next government, formed by Professor Duarte Leite in June 1912, consisted of two Evolutionists, two Unionists and three Democrats, and vainly strove to hold a balance. The Democrats pressed for the release of the arrested labour leaders, while the others urged the need for reconciliation and an understanding with the church. The prisons were now crowded, and relatives of political prisoners began agitating for their release by writing to friends abroad and making all kinds of allegations about the treatment of the arrested monarchists. A British duchess held a protest meeting in London, but when Sir A. Hardinge went to investigate, he arrived at the conclusion that the charges were exaggerated. In December 1912 Dr Arriaga asked Professor Leite to release the prisoners, but the latter, under pressure from the left-wing extremists, replied that the moment was not opportune and presently resigned (January 1913).

It was now clear that the more moderate Republicans, themselves divided, could not withstand the aggressive demagogy of the Democrats. These last depended on the lower middle classes and the artisans and labourers of Lisbon and Oporto. They were supported by secret societies such as the Carbonária, clubs, meetings and mobs. The professional men who had made the republic, now outnumbered and outmanœuvred by the demagogues, had failed to foresee how precarious their authority would be. Meanwhile, the monarchists, filled with belated piety, found themselves without support either from the church or the countryside, both traditionally conservative. Eighty years before, both church and countryside had been deeply attached to Dom Miguel, but they could not feel the same affection for the liberal monarchy. The countryside had made its last protest in the days of Maria da Fonte, and it had been ignored. Nor could the traditional institutions find common ground in opposing the republic: the church, though persecuted by the Democrats, was more

likely to be defended by conservative Republicans than by monarchists who had failed their own cause so miserably. The nobility, first
divided by the schism of the two brothers, had then been so diluted
by life-peerages of a purely political nature that it had lost its
institutional value.

The doctrines of the Portuguese Republicans were drawn from
France and Brazil. Many Republicans had vehemently denounced
the Alliance with England in 1890. Yet Britain had recognized the
republic very quickly, and it had soon been decided that the ancient
Alliance was between peoples rather than between crowned heads.
The monarchists were disappointed by the readiness of the British
government to deal with their enemies; but they overlooked the fact
that any hesitation on Britain's part would have intensified German
ambitions. The Germans, despite their perhaps decisive part in the
events of the Rotunda, now professed to disapprove of the excesses
of the Portuguese Republic and revived their propaganda in Africa.
The German campaign of vilification was begun early in 1911,
according to General Norton de Matos, who went as governor of
Angola in the following year.[1]

In July 1911 the Germans had attempted to force a way into
Morocco with the Agadir incident, but in the face of British opposition, they recognized the French protectorate in that area, receiving
a 'compensation' in the Cameroons. Both Belgium and Portugal
feared new demands in Central Africa. The British government then
sent Lord Haldane to Berlin to make soundings about 'the possibil-
ties of a rearrangement of interests in Africa'. Haldane's conversations were purely exploratory and came to nothing, though von
Tirpitz represented that 'Haldane began to hold out hopes of a great
colonial empire in Africa for us . . . exaggerated offers of colonial
possessions which did not belong to England and which they had
no right to dispose of'. The next German ambassador to London,
Lichnowski, opened negotiations for a new convention about Africa,
and reached the point of signing in May 1913. But at this stage Grey
refused to conclude unless the previous secret agreement of 1898-9
were published. The Germans were unwilling to accept this, and
when they at last agreed, the Serbian crisis occurred and Europe
was plunged into war.

[1] *Memórias e trabalhos da minha vida*, I, 3rd ed., 1944, 137.

Given these antecedents, the Portuguese, who had good reason to fear a policy of appeasement, had no hesitation in siding with the allies. Spain had already declared neutrality, and there was no danger of direct military involvement in Europe. The ancient Alliance was not invoked, and when Lisbon consulted London, Grey asked only that there should be no declaration of neutrality. On 7 August 1914 the Portuguese parliament granted the government powers to act as the interests of the nation required. Both Angola and Moçambique bordered on German colonies, and steps were taken to reinforce them, the first expeditionary forces leaving Lisbon in September. In southern Angola there were small brushes on the frontier, and on 23 November the government was granted authority to enter the war if necessary. But the frontier incidents did not spread, and a year passed before Portugal was directly involved.

During this time the political and social tensions within the country remained unresolved. Costa's Democratic dictatorship was now exercised to the exclusion of other policies. The president was increasingly troubled by it, and the only solution seemed to lie with the army. When a military rising was stifled and the government proposed to disband the regiments involved, these appealed to General Pimenta de Castro, and Dr Arriaga took the opportunity to dismiss the Democrats and asked Pimenta to form a ministry. This was supported by the Evolutionists and by Machado Santos, and it included officers and non-party civilians. Since parliament was not in session, the Democrats protested, expecting to bring the government down as soon as the session began. But on 4 March 1915 the government shut the parliament buildings, and the deputies replied by meeting elsewhere and declaring themselves a legally constituted assembly. Pimenta held power for four months, during which the persecution of the church was ended and the monarchists were amnestied and permitted to form an association. The Democrats held anti-clerical protest-meetings, and the Unionist party, which had at first supported the dictatorship, disowned Pimenta for his tolerant attitude towards the monarchists, and accused Almeida and Machado Santos of betraying the revolution. On 15 May 1915 there occurred another overturn. The Democrats now seized power with the aid of the bravoes of the Arsenal, the Republican Guard and the navy. Pimenta and Machado Santos were sent to the Azores, and on

17 May a new ministry was formed by Chagas, now reconciled with the Democrats. Dr Arriaga, having supported the overthrown regime, announced that he would resign the presidency, and on 26 May he was replaced *ad interim* by Dr Braga. Parliamentary elections were held, and as the defeated parties abstained, the Democrats occupied the vacant field. Political tension remained high: Chagas was shot at by a political opponent and lost the sight of an eye, while Costa, travelling in a tram, took the jolting for an infernal machine, jumped through the window and fractured his skull. It mended, and on 29 November he was prime minister.

The return of the Democrats brought the reinforcement of the anti-clerical measures and the revival of the lay committees. The impassioned tone of Republican politics may be ascribed to the fact that religion had now become a fundamental issue—not religious tolerance, but anti-religious persecution.

It was at this time that Portugal entered the war. Her services to the allies during the period of non-belligerency had caused much tension with Germany. She possessed valuable equipment, but was not prepared for war in Europe, and her economy, being dependent on overseas trade, was vulnerable. She had no hope or expectation of territorial or economic advantage from participation in the struggle. Therefore, unless the Alliance were invoked, her only clear ground for becoming belligerent was the defence of her African territories. The Unionists considered that this limitation should be accepted. But the Democrats now favoured intervention on a broader footing, Costa perhaps for political reasons, Chagas from attachment to France, and Norton de Matos in consideration of longer-term African interests. They sounded the British government about collaboration, and received undertakings for defence on condition that the German shipping then standing in Portuguese ports was requisitioned. On 24 February 1916 the government took over thirty-six German ships, and on 9 March Germany declared war.

On entering the war, the Democrats attempted to form a 'sacred union'. Almeida, the Evolutionist leader, formed a cabinet consisting mainly of Democrats, with Costa as Minister of Finance, Norton de Matos for War, Azevedo Coutinho for Marine and António Maria da Silva for Labour. The Unionists stood aside, adhering to their former position. It fell to Costa to negotiate the conditions of participation, and an Expeditionary Corps for service in Flanders was soon under training at Tancos. It sailed for France in January 1917 under General Tamagnini de Abreu e Silva. The force of 25,000, later raised to 40,000, was organized as a corps of two divisions. It occupied the sectors of Ferme du Bois, Neuve Chapelle and Fauquissart.

The 'sacred Union' dissolved in April 1917 with the resignation of Almeida. Costa again became Prime Minister and formed a government of Democrats, refusing invitations to set up a national government. The consequences of the call-up, the requirements of the allies, the disruption of trade and shortages of commodities now began to make themselves felt. When the unions struck for higher pay, the government replied by mobilizing various services. In April there was a lack of food, accompanied by strikes and protests. By the autumn the situation was more serious. The Democrats were now intensely unpopular. The opposition formed a committee which was presided over by Major Sidónio Pais, who had been professor of mathematics at Coimbra, had held office under Pimenta de Castro and had been minister in Berlin until Portugal entered the war. He was supported by the Unionists, by Machado Santos, by part of the armed forces and by the many enemies of Costa. On 5 December 1917 he made a revolution in Lisbon, and overturned the Democratic faction.

2. THE NEW REPUBLIC, 1917–18; THE RETURN OF THE DEMOCRATS, 1918–26

Sidónio Pais seemed to many what Manuel II might have been but was not. He had gravitated into the abandoned position of leader of the opposition. He had the necessary experience, academic, military, administrative and republican. He first formed a triumvirate of officers with Machado Santos and Feliciano da Costa, joined by three Unionists and three independents. He and his friends dismissed and exiled President Machado and General Norton de Matos and arrested Costa. They abolished the lay committees and annulled the order of banishment of the cardinal-patriarch and the bishop of Oporto. Sidónio Pais toured northern Portugal, the Alentejo and Algarve, where he received as enthusiastic welcome, reaching the hearts of many who had renounced all hope of the 'old' republic. He could count on the support of new political thinkers who had reacted against the vaporing positivism of 1910, but he could not hold together the politicians who had joined him or win over those who were opposed. The Unionists remained anxious to limit the war commitment, and their enthusiasm diminished when they found that Sidónio Pais was less concerned about this than to reform the political morass: they finally broke with him in March 1918 and refused to present candidates for his parliament.

The most evident weakness in the Republican system was its lack of cohesion and authority. The president had either to wrestle with the Democrats, as Dr Arriaga had done, and been thrown, or to be ruled by them like Dr Bernardino Machado. Sidónio Pais' solution was a 'presidentialist' system like that of Brazil and the United States. He thus became president and Prime Minister. His 'new republicans' held the majority in both chambers, and as the old republicans abstained, the minority went to the young monarchists. But fortune was against him. On 9 April 1918 in Flanders the German Sixth Army Corps launched one of the heaviest attacks of the Ludendorff offensive against the Portuguese Second Division, holding a front of some eight miles, and the neighbouring British 40th and 55th Divisions. The front line troops suffered heavy losses in the battle of the Lys, but the situation was slowly stabilized.

At home, economic difficulties mounted. The *escudo*, with a par value of 4s. 5½d. had remained at 4s. in 1917, but fell to 2s. 10d. in 1918. This was only a foretaste of what was to come. Sidónio dismissed his Finance Minister and was compelled in October to remodel his cabinet. There followed an attempt at revolution, and the prisons which had lately been filled with monarchists were now occupied by Democrats. On 5 December there was an unsuccessful attempt on the life of the president, who decided to institute military committees in northern Portugal as rallying-points. But as he entered the main station in Lisbon, he was shot and fatally wounded by a fanatic (14 December). He had won wide support outside the ranks of professional politicians, but no one was now able to take his place, either to carry forward the New Republic, or to revise it. Rear-Admiral Canto e Castro, formerly Minister of Marine, was elected president of the Republic, and he appointed General Tamagnini

Barbosa as Prime Minister. This was the end of the innovation, and was in effect a transition to the old system. On 30 March 1919 the Democrats regained power, and the republic entered upon a period of extreme instability.

The post-war chaos lasted seven years. The forces of revolution were now felt in many countries. The communist upheaval launched by the Germans in Russia brought in its train alarming disturbances in Germany and other defeated powers. Even in Spain, which had remained neutral, a violent labour crisis centred chiefly in Barcelona, lasted from 1919 to 1923. In Portugal the *escudo* continued to depreciate, and as prices rose there were repeated strikes. In 1919 the railwaymen were on strike for two months and metal-workers and municipal employees for shorter periods. In 1920 civil servants, tramwaymen, seamen, printers, electrical workers and others came out, and the office of the General Confederation of Workers was closed. Governments had no solution to offer, and did not last long enough to follow any consecutive policy. There were four reshuffles in 1919; seven in 1920, and five in 1921. There were signs too that the Democratic leaders were losing control over their adherents in favour of secret societies and gangsters. On 19 October 1921 a band of a dozen men in sailor's uniform abducted and assassinated the Prime Minister, Dr A. Granjó, Machado Santos, Carlos de Maia, a minister under Sidónio Pais, and others. The first murderer, a leading-seaman with a prominent gold tooth, was arrested and sentenced to imprisonment: he claimed the sole responsibility for the crime.

There followed a quieter period. António Maria da Silva, a leader of the Carbonária, formed a government on 5 February 1922 and remained in power until November 1923 with only two reshuffles. Dr Almeida now became the first of Portugal's six presidents to complete a term of office, and Teixeira Gomes, lately minister in London, was elected to succeed him. At this time the *escudo* had fallen to 2½d., or less than a twentieth of its par value, and the foreign debt had been swollen by war charges. The cost of Portuguese operations in Africa had been paid by recourse to the printing-press, but the Expeditionary Force in Flanders had been supplied by Britain and Costa had arranged that its expenses should be charged to a sterling account in London. They now amounted to £80m. Under Costa's agreement of 1916 this was less than 400,000 *contos*: it was now 8m. *contos*, or three years' revenue. In 1923 a loan was obtained, the terms being such that the effective rate of interest was 13 per cent. The total deficits between 1919 and 1926 reached 1,548,760 *contos*, and were met by borrowing from the Bank of Portugal and the national savings and pensions fund. The fiduciary circulation mounted from 87,767 *contos* to 791,024. By 1920 the price level of 1910 had been multiplied by 12, the index of wages by less than 4½. These problems extended to Angola. General Norton de Matos had been sent as High Commissioner with a considerable degree of autonomy in order to accelerate development, but too much was spent on too many schemes which could not be brought to fruition: the indebtedness of the colonial government increased tenfold.

In 1925 there was a renewal of instability, with five Democratic governments in the course of the year. At the end of it Teixeira Gomes, who had been unable to curb the quarrels and jealousies of the politicians, resigned the presidency, and his place was taken by Bernardino Machado.

At this time a lurid light was thrown on the prevailing system by the affair of the Banco de Angola e Metrópole, known in England as the 'Portuguese Bank-note Case'. A group of tricksters, using notepaper obtained from the Bank of Portugal, instructed the London firm of Waterlow to print 580,000 500-*escudo* notes. The conspirators obtained delivery of the notes and passed them into Portugal through the Venezuelan diplomatic bag. They then floated a bank to unload the proceeds. Suspicion was aroused by the boldness of its policy, and confirmed by the appearance of notes with duplicate numbers. The Bank of Portugal called in both series. The Banco de Angola e Metrópole was liquidated, and the Bank of Portugal sued Messrs Waterlow for the sum still outstanding. Counsel for Waterlow's sought to argue that damages should be limited to the actual costs involved, but the House of Lords rejected this, and Waterlow's were required to find £610,932. Although this scandal did not directly involve responsible politicians, it could scarcely have been perpetrated unless in a period of inflation and administrative confusion.

The only institution capable of ending this sorry state of affairs was the army. A first attempt at a military rising on 5 March 1925 was stifled with the arrest of the ringleaders. On 18 April a second attempt also failed, and on 19 July a third, led by Captain Mendes Cabeçadas, likewise. Special courts were set up to try those concerned, and when General Sinel de Cordes and his colleagues defended their action with a bitter attack on the politicians, they were acquitted. By the beginning of 1926 the Democratic regime was failing, and on 28 May it was finally overthrown by General Gomes da Costa, Portugal's best-known general of the Great War. From Braga he addressed an appeal to all citizens of dignity and honour, and a committee was quickly formed in Lisbon. The only resistance was at Santarém and Caldas da Rainha: it amounted to little, and President Machado resigned on 30 May.

General Gomes da Costa entered Lisbon in triumph on 3 June 1926. He formed a triumvirate with General Gama Ochoa and Captain Mendes Cabeçadas. Another general, António Oscar de Fragoso Carmona, was entrusted with Foreign Affairs. But Mendes Cabeçadas was not prepared for a break with the old political parties, and Gomes da Costa was soon deposed, sent to the Azores for a year and later promoted marshal, as befitted a popular but not particularly perspicacious war hero. From July 1926 the head of the government was General Carmona, who in November became acting president of the republic. He was elected in March 1928 and re-elected in 1935, 1942 and 1949, dying in office in 1951.

3. THE NEW STATE

Many of the leaders of the republic were men of ability and even rectitude, but the regime itself was ineffective and corrupt. Politicians must live under the heaven of political theory and on the earth of administration: it is easy for them to lose sight of the limitations of their calling, and these limitations are best set by institutions which represent permanent factors in the life of the nation. In Portugal, the institutions of the monarchy had been demolished. Those of the republic were merely ideas, some sound, some impracticable, some false. The republican parliament achieved agreement about abstractions, but not about actions. The deliberations of parliament were heated and often disorderly, and the power of decision was exercised if at all by the Carbonária and other gangs of agitators. One institution had survived from the monarchy, the burden of debt, now intolerable. The republican budgets had often been cooked, and Commander Filomeno da Câmara, who first took over the Ministry of Finance, discovered that the deficit for 1925–6, budgeted as 63,565 *contos*, was in fact 330,000. On 9 July General Sinel de Cordes became minister and began negotiations for a revision of the war debt in London. On 31 December (Sir) Winston Churchill signed an agreement by which the sum owed was scaled down to £23m. Even this sum could not be paid, and General Cordes made soundings about pledging the tobacco-monopoly for a loan. He was recommended to apply to the Finance Committee of the League of Nations, which had granted loans to the defeated countries. Portugal was the first of the allies to apply, and she asked for £12m. The defeated powers had been required to submit to certain measures of control, and it was surprising and shocking to the Portuguese military government to find themselves treated no better than the defeated enemy. The League proposed a commission to supervise the collection of customs-dues in Portugal. The displaced politicians did all in their power to prevent a loan from being concluded, but the new government decided not to sell its honour and attempted a new solution.

The portfolio of Finance had been briefly offered to Dr António de Oliveira Salazar, then professor of economics at Coimbra, in June 1926, but there had been a reshuffle before he could take office and he had returned to his university. In April 1928, when General Carmona was already president and General J. V. de Freitas Prime Minister, he was asked to assume responsibility for finance. The cabinet was now partly military and partly civilian, and Sr Duarte Pacheco, a close friend of Dr Salazar, was Minister of Education. Dr Salazar himself was unknown outside the circle of the university. He had been born at Santa Comba, a small town in the valley of the Dão, between Coimbra and Viseu. He went to Coimbra in 1908 and after graduating began to lecture on political economy: his early associations were with the Academic Centre of Christian Democracy, a group of Catholic students influenced by the *Rerum novarum*. He had been elected a deputy in 1921, but returned to Coimbra after one session. His works included a thesis on the gold *agio* and papers on the wheat problem and the control of public expenditure. In 1928 he was able to obtain the terms he needed for his work: full control of revenue and expenditure, and a prohibition that any other minister should incur expenditure without first consulting him. His first object was to secure a unified system of accountancy and a balanced budget. By pruning expenditure and applying new taxes, he achieved a budgetary surplus in his first year and repeated it annually thereafter. The deficits of 1917–28 had totalled 2,574,000 *contos*; the surpluses of 1928–39 reached 1,963,000. The resources thus gained were devoted to public works, social assistance and rearmament, and to long-range economic plans for communications, the development of ports, irrigation, hydro-electric development and education. The public debt, 692,000 *contos* in 1910, had reached 7,449,000 in 1927, of which a third was floating. This last was extinguished, and the total debt reduced, by conversions, by over 1m. *contos*. Interest rates paid by the state fell from $6\frac{3}{4}$ per cent to $3\frac{1}{2}$.

At the same time Dr Salazar set out to remedy Portugal's deficit of external payments. The shortage of wheat, of ancient origin, had lately involved a drain of as much as 200,000 *contos* a year: as a result of the wheat campaigns begun in 1929, a large surplus was achieved in favourable years. Boards and regulating commissions were set up to meet the problems of export industries, such as fruit, for which there were no established standards, and sardines, affected by irregular cycles of production and excessive competition; rice, formerly little grown, was now extensively cultivated throughout southern and central Portugal.

These measures brought Portugal through the general economic crisis of 1929–31, if not unscathed, at least in better shape than other countries. They would not have been possible without a stable administration, pursuing a consciously realized goal. In Dr Salazar's analysis the key to Portugal's troubles lay in the solution of ancient economic problems. This was an essential preliminary to a greater social stability, which in turn would allow a more responsible political process. He himself had been brought to office because of his technical preparation, and he had little sympathy for those who had made a profession out of politics.

In November 1932 Dr Salazar became Prime Minister (President of the Council), and by the following year the groundwork of his reforms was sufficiently advanced for him to produce a new constitution, together with a statute of labour and a Colonial Act. The constitution provided for a unitary republic of which the overseas provinces formed an integral part. The president would be elected for seven years by popular suffrage (in 1961 it was decided to return to the former system of election by parliament). The president of the republic appointed the President of the Council, and other ministers on his recommendation, and approved legislation and convoked parliament. The Council of Ministers or cabinet consisted of ministers for the Interior, Justice, Finance, War, Marine, Foreign Affairs, Public Works, and Communications, Overseas, Education and Economy, this last including commerce, industry and agriculture: variations on this pattern have taken place from time to time. The National Assembly, first constituted with ninety members, was increased to 120 in 1945 and later to 130. Deputies are elected by block-list by direct suffrage and sit for four years. The Assembly holds sessions from November with recess at Christmas, and may pass or amend legislation and amend the constitution: it deliberates in detail on the budget, but may not normally initiate money-bills. In addition, the upper house or senate is replaced by the Corporative Chamber, a consultative body in which the main aspects of the nation's life are to be represented, economic, professional and intellectual. The Chamber is ultimately to comprise representatives of twenty-four corporations or groups of activities.

The experience of the unicameral parliament of the first republican constitution pointed the need for an upper house. The old peerage had been destroyed, and there seemed little justification for a territorial basis, so that representation was now to be linked to economic and professional responsibilities. But the corporations were to be formed only gradually, since the bodies which would give them substance would depend on voluntary association. Employers' interests would be drawn together in Federations and employees' in Unions, the professions being constituted in Orders. The federation consists of local Guilds of employers, and the union of Syndicates of employees. These bodies come into existence when half those engaged in a particular activity in a particular region are agreed. When this occurs, they negotiate about wages and conditions and arrive at collective contracts, which require the consent of a member of the government responsible to the Prime Minister. Although membership

333

is not compulsory, contracts are binding on members and non-members alike. Strikes and lock-outs are forbidden, and employers and employees are required to collaborate in the study of problems of the improvement of conditions, unemployment and professional training. Special provision is made for fishermen and labourers, in the *casas do povo* and *casas dos pescadores*, which serve as community and welfare centres.

Dr Salazar's reforms required, as has been seen, a long period of internal peace. After the events of the first republic, this was not difficult to establish. However, the international scene was increasingly disturbed. In Spain, the economic crisis led to the fall of General Primo de Rivera in 1930 and of the monarchy itself in the following year. The Spanish republic collapsed in the midst of civil war after only five years, and the struggle in Spain was followed after an interval of months by the second Great War. In Portugal the inception of the Spanish republic encouraged the Democrats to attempt a revolution in the Azores and Madeira. A group of politicians and professional revolutionaries who had been deported to the Azores launched an oratorical outburst in the grand manner and on its collapse sailed to Madeira; the 'Atlantis republic' lasted only a few weeks.[1] The more disquieting aspect of Spanish affairs was the resurgence of Pan-Iberianism in the parties of the Spanish left. The notion of Pan-Iberian federalism still lingered in Catalonia, where it was fancied that the association of Portugal in an Iberian federation would assure Catalan autonomy by offsetting the centralizing influence of Castile: this theory had, of course, no attraction for Portugal, which could only lose by it. But when a leading Portuguese publicist interviewed prominent Spaniards, he heard categorical professions of Pan-Iberianism in Catalonia and few express repudiations of it in Castile. During the conservative period of the Spanish republic (1934–5), Portugal had no cause for alarm, but in February 1936, the Spanish Popular Front, formed in imitation of that of France, which was communist-inspired, came to power. The Spanish communist party, hitherto insignificant, suddenly became active and infiltrated the powerful socialist movement. Between February and

[1] It is described by Ferro Alves in *A mornaça*, Lisbon, 1935. The author was a professional revolutionary and his account throws an amusing light on the outlook of himself and his companions.

July public order in Spain disappeared in a wave of 'general strikes' and church-burnings. In July the murder of Sr Calvo Sotelo was followed by a military insurrection. The domestic affairs of Spain became international property as one side obtained support from Italy and Germany and the other from the international Marxist organizations and adherents of the Popular Front policy. France and Britain attempted to limit the conflict through a policy of non-intervention. This was accepted by the Portuguese government, which had no wish to see the expansion of German or Italian interference but believed, as did Mr Churchill, that the Spanish nationalists would avoid falling under the heel of Hitler or Mussolini: whether the republicans would be able to curb Russian influence was more problematic. Portugal therefore regarded a victory of the Spanish Popular Front as a matter of grave disquiet, and suspended relations with Madrid in October 1936. She then became the target for Russian accusations. In general her policy was aligned to that of Great Britain, and in March 1937 she admitted a party of British observers to invigilate her frontier with Spain: when Britain appointed an agent to the Burgos government, Portugal extended recognition.

As the Spanish war drew to an end, Dr Salazar took the opportunity to conclude a treaty of friendship with the new Spanish regime, by which both parties agreed to respect one another's independence and territory, to assist one another in case of attack by a third party, and to enter into no alliance or treaty directed against the other (17 March 1939). This treaty was to be one of the chief safeguards for Spanish neutrality in the coming struggle. The pact between Hitler and Stalin for the partition of Poland plunged Europe into the second Great War. Hitler's aggression against a Catholic nation, in alliance with Russia, did much to weaken his influence in Spain. The sympathies of the Portuguese were clearly on the side of the allies, and Portugal adopted an attitude of 'juridical' neutrality as in 1914. In October 1939 negotiations took place with a view to accommodating Anglo-Portuguese trade to British plans for economic war. But Hitler's conquest of France in June 1940 brought his troops to the Pyrenees and enabled him to exert unanticipated pressure in Spain. It fell to Dr Salazar to undertake 'the difficult and delicate task of securing from Spain certain political assurances regarding her intention and ability to remain neutral.'[1] General Franco had declared himself 'non-belligerent' on 12 June, but he met Dr Salazar and on 29 July signed a protocol providing for consultations as a means of safeguarding the independence of the two countries and reaffirming existing treaties. The foundations of Spanish neutrality were laid, but Hitler continued to press Spain, and in September General Franco's Axophile brother-in-law Serrano Súñer told Hitler that Spain would join him if her supplies could be guaranteed: as her industry was paralysed and her bread-ration reduced by a disastrous harvest, the condition could not be fulfilled. In December 1940 Hitler suddenly informed the Spanish government that he wished to send German troops into Spain in January, but a few days later he changed his plan and the crisis passed.

In June 1941 the situation again became dangerous as Hitler ordered the invasion of Russia. He hoped now to gain support in the anti-communist Peninsula, and Admiral Raeder recorded on 25 July that he would enter Spain and Portugal if the United States occupied the Spanish or Portuguese islands. The first signs of pressure on Portugal came in October when the Germans, having cut off their supplies of oriental wolfram by attacking Russia, began a desperate campaign to extract it from Portugal. Their agents forced up the price from £2,500 a ton to £6,000 in a month, hoping that country-people would prospect everywhere and sell their finds to German agents. Dr Salazar, well aware of the disruptive effects of this on the Portuguese economy, tried to limit production by fiscal and other means. But the Germans were prepared to go to all lengths to obtain wolfram, and on 12 October they openly sank a Portuguese merchant-man eighty miles off the coast, the first neutral ship to be sunk on the trans-Atlantic run. In December they torpedoed a second ship. The German threat against the Portuguese merchant navy made it impossible to resist, and in January 1942 Dr Salazar signed an agreement to sell wolfram to Germany, having indicated that he could not hold out against threats to the merchant marine.

The Japanese had now entered the fray with their assault on Pearl Harbour. They had previously shown some interest in the Portuguese part of the island of Timor, and in order to forestall a Japanese descent, Australian and Dutch troops occupied Portuguese Timor

[1] Medlicott, *Economic Blockade*, I, 513.

on 17 December. Dr Salazar was not notified until the plan had been executed and was much annoyed lest the Peninsular policy be jeopardized. The Japanese occupied Timor in February 1942.

Hitler was now losing his grip on Russia and beginning to concentrate on the so-called 'fortress of Europe'. When the question of an allied campaign in the Mediterranean area arose, it became necessary for the allies to consider the use of the Atlantic Islands. Admiral Raeder records that in June 1942 Hitler planned to meet an American landing with the use of submarines. Although he no longer appeared capable of overrunning the Peninsula, he was still in a position to attack merchantmen and to disrupt supplies. The question of the renewal of wolfram purchases led to prolonged negotiations, but in the spring of 1943 supplies were renewed. In June the British government invoked the ancient Alliance, requesting the use of the Azores by British forces. Dr Salazar complied at once, and details of the facilities to be provided were negotiated, the British government promising to give all possible aid in the event of an attack on continental Portugal. In October British troops landed. The German ambassador in Lisbon was informed immediately before the publication of the Azores agreement, but although he protested sharply, it became clear that the Germans would not retaliate. In consequence of the Azores agreement Portugal received guarantees of the integrity of her possessions from the United Kingdom, the Dominions and the United States.

When finally in the spring of 1944 the allies pressed Dr Salazar to suspend all deliveries of wolfram to Germany, the Germans reminded him that their threats of violence to Portuguese shipping were still valid by stopping a cargo-liner in mid-Atlantic and forcing passengers and crew to abandon ship. But a few days later the Portuguese government declared a total embargo on wolfram exports and shortly closed all mines. When the war ended, Dr Salazar had succeeded in upholding the policy of 'juridical neutrality' in Europe and in reconciling it with the requirements of the ancient Alliance; the single exception was in Timor, which was presently liberated from the Japanese. In Portugal itself there had been severe shortages, but inflation had been checked and the prices of essentials fixed. Transport and communications had been particularly affected by the lack of fuel, vehicles and supplies.

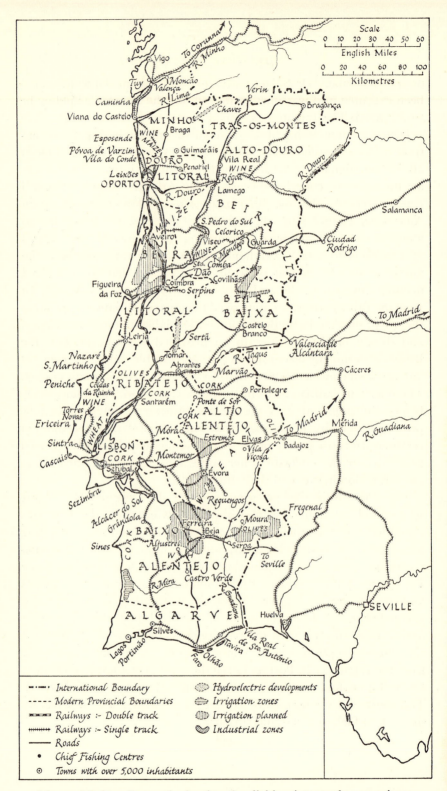

Map 7. Modern Portugal, showing the division into modern provinces, communications, and hydro-electric and irrigation works.

Dr Salazar's government pursued his policy of reform and development, though for ten years the abnormal conditions of war in Spain and Europe kept him occupied with questions of foreign policy. The return of peace enabled him to embark on development programmes long held in view. During the war he had extended unlimited credit to Britain, and the sum now owed by Britain to Portugal was about £76m. The war had shown the inadequacy of the Portuguese merchant-fleet, and it was now proposed to build or buy half a million tons of shipping: by 1953 fifty-one new ships were in service and the tonnage had been increased by about 70 per cent for an investment of £40m. New roads and bridges were built, including the great span across the Tagus at Vila Franca. The lack of fuel was remedied by a large programme of electrification: in particular the damming of the Zêzere at Castelo de Bode and of the Cávado in the extreme north brought power to all parts of the country and quickened the pace of industrialization. The control of water led to irrigation schemes of particular benefit in the arid region of the Alentejo. The proportion of cultivable land was also increased by afforestation schemes, which have made timber and wood products a valuable export and the basis of new industries producing pulp, paper and plastics. The electrification schemes were crowned with the building of three dams on the international stretch of the Douro, supplying power to eastern Portugal and to Leon and Castile. A new stage of industrialization was reached in 1961 with the opening of a steelworks and a factory for motor-vehicles.

INDICATIONS OF ECONOMIC GROWTH, 1940–60

	1940	1950	1960
Population (millions)	7.7	8.4	9.1
General index of industrial production (1953 = 100)	60	92	157[1]
Electrification (million kWh)	386	780	2,694
Cement (1,000 tons)	270	573	1,202
Fertilizers (1,000 tons)	192	324	662
Paper pulp (1,000 tons)	7	6	84
Value of imports (1,000 contos)	2,583	7,879	15,695
Value of exports (1,000 contos)	1,683	5,334	9,408

[1] 1959.

These changes have been accompanied by a steady growth of the towns. Although the proportion of those engaged in rural activities remains high, the building of rural schools and the extension of literacy have greatly bettered the prospects of the country-people. The two great cities have expanded rapidly, and the outskirts of Lisbon have been covered with new housing while the building of a bridge across the Tagus, the longest in Europe, assures the future expansion of the industrial suburbs on the south bank and the area between it and Setúbal.

Overseas this expansion extended to the Portuguese possessions in Africa and the east. Angola, brought to the verge of bankruptcy under the regime of autonomy, had received a loan from the home government and its exchange operations were subordinated to a control commission. During the war its economy developed rapidly, and in the succeeding period there was a notable growth of colonization. The capital Luanda became an important city, while the advances in tropical medicine made it possible to settle areas hitherto considered unhealthy. Thus the Benguela highlands, formerly regarded as the most suitable part of Angola for white settlement, were eclipsed by the region to the north and north-east of Luanda. Even so the average density of population remains less than ten to the square mile. The possibilities of Angola were greatly enhanced by the substitution of poor crops such as maize by cotton and coffee.

Dr Salazar continued to regard the political *détente* as essential to social and economic advance, and was strongly opposed to a return to the old party system. The adherents of the government were grouped in a National Union which was intended to be a loose movement rather than a political party. Ministries were composed of men who had shown ability as administrators or technicians rather than of prominent party men. The National Assembly criticized government policy rather than the government. Although opposition lists of candidates could be submitted for government approval and could campaign if they were found to be free of Marxist infiltration, those who proposed to run usually withdrew. The resulting plebiscites showed general support for the existing regime. In the presidential elections various opposition candidates were put forward: in 1949 General Norton de Matos, the octogenarian colonialist and administrator, decided to oppose General Carmona, but at the last moment

340

changed his mind. His supporters included a Marxist element which unsuccessfully attempted to perpetuate a political organization after the campaign.

The most active opposition to the Portuguese government now came from the Indian Union, which demanded the cession of the Portuguese territories of Gôa, Damão and Diu. The inhabitants of Gôa itself showed no sign of desiring to be annexed, but there were of course many persons of Goan descent long settled in the Indian Union: some of these and some political expatriates sided with the Indian government. Left-wing elements in the Indian Union now organized bands of agitators who entered Goan territory. Although these propaganda invasions were halted, the Indians overran two small enclaves, Dadrá and Nagar Aveli. Although Mr Nehru refrained from placing himself in a position to take responsibility for the invasions, he made his views on self-determination quite clear: 'we will not tolerate the Portuguese, even if the Goans want to keep them' (September 1954). The opportunity was not lost on the Soviet Union, whose leaders, Bulganin and Khrushchev, visited India in November and made inflammatory statements in favour of Indian demands. Mr Foster Dulles replied with an unequivocal assurance that 'all the world regards it [Gôa] as a Portuguese province' (December). The Indian attacks abruptly ceased, and nothing more was heard of them for four years. In 1955 Portugal brought a case before the International Court of Justice at the Hague, seeking access to the occupied enclaves.

The association of the Marxists with the neutrals in a policy of militant 'anti-colonialism' took shape at the Bandung conference in 1955. Until this time orthodox Marxism had hammered vainly at the more advanced countries, and communist parties for colonial territories had been usually dependent on the metropolitan communist parties. The aggressive policy of China, which succeeded in bringing about the partition of Indo-China, led the orthodox Marxists to reconsider. They now proceeded to proclaim 'anti-colonialism' everywhere, except in the Russian empire, and to alter the constitution of the United Nations in order to make colonies 'illegal'. The ability of the Marxists to make propaganda was greatly extended by the confusion of the West which followed the Egyptian seizure of the Suez canal and its consequences. A sizeable flock of Afro-Asian territories had been given the status of nations and admitted to the United Nations, and the Marxist delegates clamoured and harried to good effect.

Meanwhile, in Portugal General Francisco Craveiro Lopes had been elected president for the period 1951–8: of the two opposition candidates, one, Admiral Meireles, a former supporter of the regime, withdrew, and the other was disqualified as a tool of the illegal communist party. General Craveiro Lopes was thus returned unopposed with a vote of about 78 per cent. During these years a proposal for the reform of the constitution was discussed, whereby the president would be elected by the Assembly and Corporate Chamber according to the Italian (and former Portuguese) system. The office of Minister of the Presidency, evidently intended as a deputy to the Prime Minister, was created in 1950, but filled only in 1955. The first six of the long-awaited corporations were brought into being in 1956.

One of the less fortunate effects of the long identification of national unity with the National Union had been to lump disgruntled opponents of the government with dangerous revolutionaries. In the post-war presidential campaigns communists or fellow-travellers supported the opposition candidates and attempted to circumvent the restraint on political organization by prolonging the temporary associations formed for electoral purposes: thus the Movement for Democratic Union (MUD) and its successors were dissolved on grounds of infiltration. This was not to say that all opponents of the regime or even all members of these bodies were communists or fellow-travellers. The regular infiltration of opposition groups had led to some feeling in favour of the founding of a Christian Democratic party, but this was disallowed, since it could only have served to divide the existing National Union and to afford a precedent for less desirable groups. At the presidential election of 1958 Admiral A. R. Tomás, the government candidate, had at first two opponents. Eventually, the communist-supported one withdrew in favour of Brigadier H. Delgado, and Admiral Tomás was elected with $77\frac{1}{2}$ per cent of the votes cast to $22\frac{1}{2}$ per cent for Sr Delgado. The latter had declared his opposition to the existing regime and constitution, and later departed for Brazil. Admiral Tomás duly confirmed Dr Salazar as Prime Minister.

At this time, the Marxist block had turned its propaganda to the African scene, hoping to take advantage of opportunities provided by the Afro-Asian group. Attempts to form a communist party for Angola go back to about 1954, but did not get beyond Paris. At about the same time anti-Portuguese propaganda began to be launched in various places in Europe and America, not to mention the usual source in the Indian Union. The general Marxist penetration of Africa was intensified after the Anglo-French withdrawal from Suez in 1956: the Chinese in particular quickly established relations with Egypt and the neighbouring states and began to outpace the Russians. When in 1958 the French granted political independence to their African territories, the Marxists attempted to force the creation of large and weak states or federations in which they would be able to function freely and if possible launch civil war. As this possibility faded, they supported international conferences and labour organizations, the latter often being thinly disguised political parties. One territory, French Guinea, dominated by the Marxist Sékou Touré, seceded from the French community and constituted a point of Marxist infiltration, the communist group for Angola being reconstituted there in 1959.

Meanwhile, Mr K. Nkrumah came to power in Ghana and aspired to spread his wings over his neighbours. In April 1958 he held a conference at Accra which was attended by P. Lumumba from the Belgian Congo and H. Roberto, born in the Portuguese Congo (the northern edge of Angola) but domiciled since childhood in Belgian territory where he was educated and employed as a clerk. Lumumba, formerly of moderate views, was impregnated with Marxist 'activism', and on his return to Belgian territory provoked riots at Leopoldville. In consequence of his activities, plans for the independence of the Belgian Congo were brought forward to June 1960. Scarcely had Belgian rule ended when the country fell into anarchy, and in the face of tribal fighting and massacre and of possible Marxist intervention, the United Nations was obliged to send a force to impose order.

Early in 1960 an attempt was made in New York under the patronage of the American Committee on Africa (not officially classified as a communist-front organization) to assert the existence of disturbances in Angola, but as the territory was demonstrably quiet, this

343

fell flat. However, in the following months the Afro-Asian and Marxist designs were gradually coordinated. In April the International Court at the Hague delivered its verdict on the Portuguese claim to have access to the occupied enclaves of Nagar Aveli and Dadrá. Although the court granted the Portuguese peaceable access, the Indian Union refused to comply.

In October Mr Khrushchev appeared in New York to proclaim *urbi et orbi* his support for 'anti-colonialism'. A month later the American presidential elections gave the Democratic candidate a narrow victory: it was already clear that Mr Kennedy's government would be, at least at first, more uncritical about Afro-Asian demands than its predecessor. Members of the Afro-Asian block prepared to declare the situation in Angola a 'threat to peace'. Elsewhere, attempts were made to organize the evidence. A Captain Galvão, a former supporter of Dr Salazar who had fallen from grace, had organized opposition propaganda and had been sentenced to prison for attempted revolt, had gone to Venezuela, where he formed a band of adventurers, chiefly Spaniards and South Americans, and seized the Portuguese liner *Santa Maria*, shooting the officer of the watch in cold blood. His object was to broadcast attacks on the Portuguese government and to announce troubles in Angola. An attempt to start a riot in Luanda to synchronize with this *coup* was suppressed without difficulty. The motion to declare Angola a 'threat to peace' was suddenly presented to the Security Council of the United Nations by the Liberian delegate: it failed to secure the necessary majority despite the fact that the American delegate took the unprecedented step of voting with the Russians. On the same day, bands of armed men invaded Angola from camps in the neighbouring (Belgian) Congo, and several hundreds of Angolans, black and white, were massacred. A massive press campaign was mounted to represent the invasion as a rising in Angola. In fact, there was no doubt that the invaders crossed the frontier after having received some training in Congolese territory: many doubtless were, like Roberto, born in Angola, but had lived most of their lives in or near Leopoldville. There were several thousand of these expatriates, many of them unemployed since the troubles in the (Belgian) Congo, and therefore easily recruited.

For a brief period part of northern Angola (the Portuguese district of Congo) was overrun, but the Portuguese, both black and white, were able to regain control during the succeeding months. Roberto's movement had little influence outside BaCongo territory and had no claim to be considered national. The Marxist MPLA, which had now moved its headquarters from Conakry to Leopoldville, did its best to take over control and the two groups soon came to blows.

By the summer the effects of the intensive propaganda campaign were wearing off, and left-wing elements in the Indian Union pressed for action against Gôa before the west recovered its conscience. The Marxist anti-Portuguese propaganda was repeated, and used by the government of Ghana to bring charges against Portugal before the International Labour Office: these were investigated and effectively disposed of in a report which finally appeared in April 1962. Meanwhile in the summer of 1961 the Indian government sponsored a 'seminar' in New Delhi for the disposal of the Portuguese possessions. Mr Nehru found himself pressed off the high moral ground on which he had long posed, largely through the efforts of Mr Krishna Menon. Indian troops were concentrated at the beginning of December and in spite of attempts to impose restraint and Portuguese demands for the dispatch of observers, the invasion and occupation of Portuguese India was executed. The Russian president arrived in New Delhi at the moment of the attack; and when the Portuguese brought this flagrant act of aggression and conquest before the Security Council in New York, the Russian delegate interposed his veto and so prevented further discussion and condemnation of the aggressor. The invasion of Gôa caused much distress in Portugal, both because of its flagrant injustice and of the flouting of international order and of the inconstancy, weakness and lack of principle of the western powers. The Americans had abruptly reversed a declared policy, while the inhabitants of the United Kingdom seemed unconscious of the fact that the Commonwealth had been augmented by force at the expense of the ancient Ally.

345

BIBLIOGRAPHICAL NOTE

This refers more particularly to works that have appeared since the publication of my earlier *History of Portugal.*

No convenient bibliography of Portuguese history exists, though the Portuguese Academy of History has issued the first part of a *Guia de bibliografia histórica portuguesa* (1959). For current books, there is the *Boletim Internacional de Bibliografia Luso-Brasileira* (1 = 1960). In English, the late W. B. GREENLEE's article 'A descriptive bibliography . . .' appeared in the *Hispanic-American Historical Review*, XX, 1940: it should be supplemented by DORIS V. WELSH's *Catalog of the William B. Greenlee Collection,* listing the books in the splendid collection of the Newberry Library, Chicago.

The standard histories remain FORTUNATO DE ALMEIDA, *História de Portugal* (6 vols, Coimbra, 1922–9), with booklists for each chapter, and the *História monumental de Portugal,* edited by DAMIÃO PERES and ELEUTÉRIO CERDEIRA (8 vols, Barcelos, 1928 etc.), In English, recent works include CHARLES NOWELL, *A History of Portugal* (New York, 1952), and J. B. TREND, *Portugal* (London, 1956). Essays on various aspects of the Luso-Brazilian world are contained in *Portugal and Brazil: an Introduction,* dedicated to EDGAR PRESTAGE and A. F. G. BELL and edited by the late W. J. ENTWISTLE and myself (Oxford, 1953).

Among recent reference works mention should be made of the completion of the *Grande Enciclopédia Luso-Brasileira* and of the launching of an *Enciclopédia Luso-Brasileira da Cultura* (1 = 1963). The articles of the *Dicionário da História de Portugal* (1 = 1961), edited by J. SERRÃO, are by many hands.

The Academia Portuguesa da História has since 1937 published a *Boletim,* two sets of *Anais,* several volumes of *Subsídios,* and commemorative and miscellaneous volumes. The Centro de Estudos Históricos Ultramarinos in Lisbon has published *Studia* since 1958, and at Coimbra the Instituto Dr António de Vasconcellos publishes the *Revista Portuguesa de História* (1 = 1941). Other relevant publications include those of the University of Lisbon, the *Revista* of the Faculty of Letters; the *Revista de História* of the University of São Paulo; and the *Bulletin des Études Portugaises* of the French Institute in Portugal (1 = 1930).

PREHISTORY AND ANTIQUITY

There is no very satisfactory general conspectus of Portuguese archaeology. The older works of LEITE DE VASCONCELOS and A. A. MENDES

CORREA can be supplemented from results of investigations in the *Revista de Guimarães, Arqueólogo português* (new series, 1 = 1951), *Conimbriga,* etc. Important contributions include: ABBÉ J. ROCHE, *Le gîsement mésolithique de Moita do Sebastião* (Lisbon, 1950); G. and V. LEISNER, *Antas do concelho de Reguengos de Monsaraz* (Lisbon, 1951); and the articles by AFONSO DO PAÇO and E. JALHAY in *Anais* of the Academy. D. FERNANDO DE ALMEIDA has a good monograph on *Egitânia* (Lisbon, 1956).

S. LAMBRINO illustrates the Celtic origins of the Lusitanians in 'Les Lusitaniens', *Euphrosyne,* I, 1957, and T. DE SOUSA SOARES has marshalled the arguments for a distinct Lusitania in pre-Roman times in *Reflexões sobre a origem e fundação de Portugal,* I (Coimbra, 1962). The late FR PIERRE DAVID's important studies include especially *Études historiques sur la Galice et le Portugal* (Coimbra, 1947). F. J. VELLOZO discusses Swabian Portugal in 'A Lusitânia Suévico-Bizantina', *Bracara Augusta,* II, 1950, IV, 1952. The late PAULO MERÊA's *Estudos de direito visigótico* (1948) was followed by two volumes of *Estudos de direito hispânico medieval* (Coimbra, 1952–3).

In addition to the Portuguese periodicals, relevant material appears in: *Zephyrus* (Salamanca) and *Cuadernos de Estudios Gallegos* (Santiago de Compostela).

MEDIEVAL PORTUGAL

FR L. GONZAGA DE AZEVEDO's revision of Herculano's classic history was completed by D. M. GOMES DOS SANTOS: *História de Portugal* (6 vols, Lisbon, 1940–4: to 1250). TORQUATO DE SOUSA SOARES has revised and expanded H. DA GAMA BARROS's *História da administração pública em Portugal* (12th–15th centuries), the original four volumes having been extended to eleven (Lisbon, 1945–54).

RUY PINTO DE AZEVEDO has published important collections of documents, royal and private, *Documentos...* (I, 1958; II, 1952; III, 1947). The publication of the *Crónica de cinco reis* by the late A. MAGALHÃIS BASTO (Oporto, 1945) and of the *Crónica dos sete primeiros reis de Portugal* by C. SILVA TAROUCA (3 vols, Lisbon, 1952–3), has led to discussion about their relationship to the lost works of FERNÃO LOPES, for which see MAGALHÃIS BASTO's *Fernão Lopes e a crónica de 1419* (Coimbra, 1960) and articles by A. BRÁZIO in *Anais.* L. F. LINDLEY CINTRA has edited and studied the *Crónica geral da Espanha de 1344,* with an important introduction (3 vols, Lisbon, 1951–61). SILVA TAROUCA has also published the *Crónica de D. Denis* (Coimbra, 1947).

The period of the national crisis of the second half of the fourteenth century has been studied very fully by P. E. RUSSELL, *English Intervention in Spain and Portugal in the time of Edward III and Richard II* (Oxford, 1955).

SALVADOR DIAS ARNAUT has contributed *A batalha de Trancoso* (1947) and *A crise nacional, I: A sucessão de D. Fernando* (Coimbra, 1960).

BIBLIOGRAPHY

VIRGÍNIA RAU, whose *Subsídios para o estudo das feiras medievais* appeared in 1943, studied the *Sesmarias medievais portuguesas* (1947) and *A exploração do comércio do sal de Setúbal*, I (1951). Her *Casa dos Contos* (Coimbra, 1951) is an important contribution to administrative history. MARCELO CAETANO has made two valuable contributions with *A administração municipal de Lisboa durante a 1ª dinastia, 1179–1383* (Lisbon, 1951) and *Subsídios para a história das cortes medievais* (Lisbon, 1963).

THE FIFTEENTH CENTURY AND THE DISCOVERIES

Numerous publications have been inspired by the quincentenary of Prince Henry the Navigator in 1960. Pride of place must be given to the splendid *Portugaliae monumenta cartographica* of ARMANDO CORTESÃO and AVELINO TEIXEIRA DA MOTA (5 vols, 1960–3). There are four volumes of *Comemorações* (Lisbon, 1961–3). *Monumenta henricina* (5 vols, Coimbra, I = 1960) prints documentary and other sources relating to the Prince and his household, adhering rather to the protagonist than to the topic of discovery, for which see JOÃO MARTINS DA SILVA MARQUES' *Descobrimentos portugueses* (I and Suplementos, 1944; this was followed by II, *O Algarve e os descobrimentos* by ALBERTO IRIA, 1956). A. J. DIAS DINIS, who edited AZURARA's *Crónica dos feitos de Guiné* (2 vols, Lisbon, 1949) has produced two volumes of *Estudos henriquinos* (Coimbra, 1960). A selection of documents on the discoveries is V. MAGALHÃIS GODINHO's *Documentos sobre a expansão portuguesa* (3 vols, 1943, 1945, 1956): the same author has written an *Economia dos descobrimentos henriquinos* (1962).

The most notable general account of the discoveries has been JAIME CORTESÃO, *Descobrimentos portugueses* (2 vols, Lisbon, s.d.). DAMIÃO PERES, whose *História dos descobrimentos portugueses* appeared in 1943, has edited the *Viagens de Cadamosto e de Pero de Sintra*, and DUARTE PACHECO PEREIRA's *Esmeraldo de Situ Orbis* (1954). He has also printed the *Regimento das cazas das Indias e Mina* (Coimbra, 1947), comprising the original regulations of 1509 and additions to 1697.

FRANCIS ROGERS has studied the career of Prince Henry's elder brother in *Infante Dom Pedro* (Harvard, 1961). LUIS SUÁREZ FERNÁNDEZ studies the relations of Portugal with her neighbour in *Relaciones entre Portugal y Castilla en la época del Infante D. Enrique, 1393–1460* (Madrid, 1960), and, with A. DE LA TORRE, *Documentos referentes a Portugal durante el reinado de los Reyes Católicos* (1958 etc.).

SIXTEENTH AND SEVENTEENTH CENTURIES

Recent works on the Portuguese renaissance include: JOAQUIM DE CARVALHO, *Estudos sobre a cultura portuguesa do século XVI* (2 vols, Coimbra, 1947–8); CARDINAL CEREJEIRA's *O renascimento em Portugal* (Coimbra,

348

1949); MARCEL BATAILLON, *Études sur le Portugal au temps de l'humanisme* (Coimbra, 1952); and L. DE MATOS, *Les portugais en France au XVIe s.* (Coimbra, 1952).

The late J. M. QUEIRÓS VELLOSO's *D. Sebastião* (3rd ed., 1943) was followed by his *Reinado de D. Henrique* (1946); *Estudos históricos do século XVI* (1950) and *Interregno dos governadores* (1953). M. A. NUNES DA COSTA has edited PEDRO DE FRIAS' *Crónica d'el-rey D. António* (Coimbra, 1955). In Spain A. DÁNVILA has dealt with Philip II's relations with Sebastian; *Felipe II y el Rey D. Sebastián* (Madrid, 1954) and *Felipe II y la sucesión de Portugal* (1956). E. W. BOVILL describes *The Battle of Alcazar* (London, 1952).

The centenary of the Restoration was celebrated by the publication of many works and documents, particularly by the Academy of History. HIPÓLITO RAPOSO published his biography of *Luisa de Gusmão; duquesa e rainha* in 1947. VIRGÍNIA RAU, whose *D. Catalina de Bragança* came out in 1941, published letters from Catherine in 1962. C. R. BOXER has dealt with *The Dutch in Brazil, 1624–54* (Oxford, 1957) and with *Salvador de Sá and the Struggle for Angola and Brazil* (London, 1952).

On the economic aspects of the period, see: DAMIÃO PERES, *História monetária de D. João III* (Lisbon, 1957); F. MAURO, *Le Portugal et l'Atlantique au XVIIe siècle, 1570–1670* (Paris, 1960); J. GENTIL DA SILVA, *Stratégie des affaires à Lisbonne entre 1595 et 1607* (Paris, 1956); and M. LOPES DE ALMEIDA, *Memorial de Pero Roiz Soares* (Coimbra, 1953).

EIGHTEENTH CENTURY

For the reign of John V, EDUARDO BRAZÃO has published *D. João V: subsídios para a história do seu reinado* (1946) and the VISCONDE DE CARNAXIDE, *D. João V e o Brasil* (Lisbon, 1952). C. R. BOXER has studied *The Golden Age of Brazil, 1695–1750* (California, 1962), and JAIME CORTESÃO has made a definitive study of *Alexandre de Gusmão e o Tratado de Madrid* (8 vols, Rio de Janeiro, 1950–9).

SIR T. D. KENDRICK discusses the moral consequences of *The Lisbon Earthquake* (London, 1956) and S. CHANTAL describes *La vie quotidienne au Portugal après le tremblement de terre de Lisbonne de 1755* (Paris, 1960).

JORGE DE MACEDO discusses the economy of eighteenth-century Portugal in *Problemas de história da indústria portuguesa no século XVIII* (Lisbon, 1963) and *A situação económica no tempo de Pombal* (1951).

NINETEENTH CENTURY

The late SIR MARCUS CHEKE followed his biography of Pombal with a racy account of *Carlota Joaquina, Queen of Portugal* (London, 1947). A study of Portugal during the Peninsular War (as distinct from the events of the

War itself) is still wanting, but JORGE DE MACEDO has studied *O Bloqueio continental: economia e guerra peninsular* (Lisbon, 1962).

SIR CHARLES WEBSTER's *Foreign Policy of Palmerston* (2 vols, London, 1951) throws a somewhat one-sided light on Portuguese affairs: it has drawn comments from F. P. Langhans. The close correspondence between Maria II and her husband and Victoria and Albert has been edited by R. ANDRESEN LEITÃO, *Documentos do Arquivo de Windsor* (Lisbon, 1949), and *Mais documentos . . .* and *Cartas de D. Pedro V ao Principe Alberto* (1954).

Little has been published about the later years of the monarchy. ALVARO RIBEIRO's *Os positivistas* (Lisbon, 1951) is a useful introduction to the ideas of the period.

For the negotiations relating to the partition of Africa, MARCELO CAETANO's *Portugal e a internacionalisão dos problemas africanos* (Lisbon, 1963) supplies the deficiencies of some of the standard works with regard to Portuguese problems. R. OLIVER's *Sir Harry Johnston* (London, 1959) throws some light on the antecedents of the Anglo-Portuguese crisis of 1890, and the settlement of the following year is fully examined in JOSÉ DE ALMADA's *Tratado de 1891* (Lisbon, 1947). The events of the following decade are studied by P. B. WARHIRST, *Anglo-Portuguese Relations in South-Central Africa, 1890–1900* (London, 1962).

THE REPUBLIC

The fullest account is J. PABÓN, *La república portuguesa*, I from D. Carlos to Sidónio Pais; II from Sidónio Pais to Dr Salazar (Madrid, 1941–5). To the publications of the republican leaders should be added GENERAL NORTON DE MATTOS', *Memórias e trabalhos da minha vida* (4 vols, Lisbon, 1944–5).

The earlier works on Dr Salazar's regime by FREPPEL COTTA, MICHAEL DERRICK and F. C. C. EGERTON, the last dating from 1943, have not been followed by corresponding accounts of the subsequent twenty years. L. STOTT HOWARTH's *A Aliança luso-britânica* (Lisbon, 1956), deals with the wartime period in outline, and some wartime problems are touched on in W. N. MEDLICOTT's *Economic Blockade* (London, 1952–9). The British and American guarantees to Portugal were printed as state papers.

A recent outline of Portuguese economic problems is A. PASQUIER's *L'Économie du Portugal* (Paris, 1961).

R. VON GERSDORFF, *Portugals Finanzen* (Bielefeld, 1961) is an account of Dr Salazar's reforms, with a short bibliography. Dr Salazar's speeches are available in five volumes (Coimbra, I = 1937).

Much of what has been written in English recently on Portuguese Africa is so tendentious as to be worthless. F. C. C. EGERTON's account of *Angola in Perspective* (London, 1957) is perhaps the most reliable book on that country. The most credible account of the troubles in 1961 is HÉLIO FELGAS, *Guerra em Angola* (Lisbon, 1961). A recent account of Moçambique is C. SPENCE, *The Portuguese Colony of Mozambique* (Cape Town–Amsterdam, 1951).

Portuguese experiences of the United Nations are briefly and ably laid forth by DR FRANCO NOGUEIRA, *Portugal and the United Nations* (London, 1964): see also ADRIANO MOREIRA, *Portugal's Stand in Africa* (New York, 1962).

(a)

(b)

(c)

I (a) and (b) Roman thoroughbreds: Roman mosaics from Torre de Palma;
(c) medieval vinegrowing and winemaking, from the *Apocalipse* of Lorvão

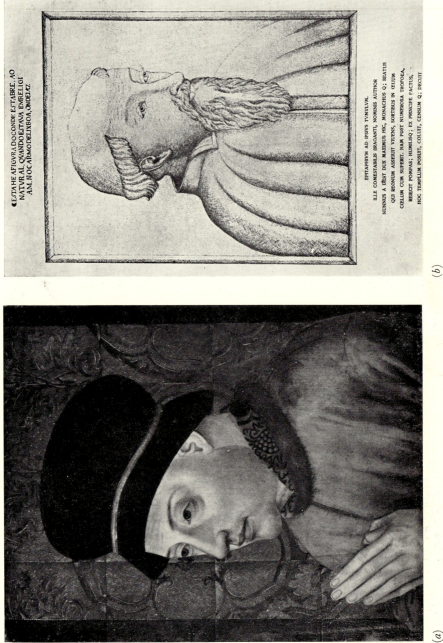

ESTA HE A FIGVRA DO CONDE ESTABRE. AO NATVRAL. QVANDO ESTAVA EM RELIGI AM. NO CAR MO DE LIXBOA. ON DE I EZ.

EPITAPHIVM AD IPSIVS TVMVLVM.

ILLE COMESTABILIS BRAGANTI, NOMINIS AUTHOR

NUNNUS A B ̄EST DUX MAXIMUS HIC, MONACHUS Q; BEATUS

QUI REGNUM ASSERUIT VIUENS, SORTIBUS IN OEIUM

COELUM CUM SUPERIT. NAM POST NUMEROSA TROFOEA,

REIECIT POMPAS; HUMILISQ; EX PRINCIPE FACTUS,

HOC TEMPLUM POSUIT, COLUIT, CENSUM Q; DECUIT

(b)

II (a) John I; (b) Nun' Álvares Pereira, the Holy Constable

(a)

III   John I entertains John of Gaunt

IV   The Monastery of Batalha

V   Triptych of St Vincent, attributed to Nuno Gonçalves: painel do Arcebispo

VI   Torre de Belém, Lisbon

VII   Tomar: the Great Cloister

VIII   Coimbra: the University Library

(a)

(b)

IX (a) John V; (b) John VI

X   The Peninsular War: the Anglo-Portuguese victory at Bussaco

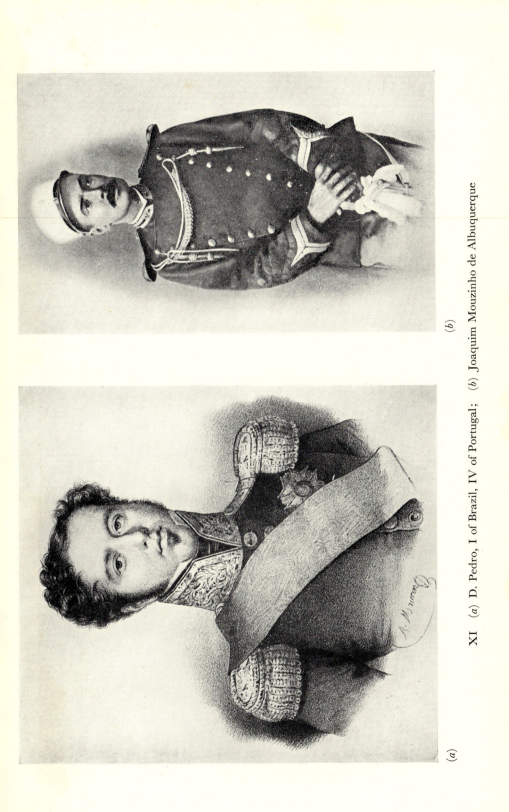

(a)   (b)

XI (a) D. Pedro, I of Brazil, IV of Portugal; (b) Joaquim Mouzinho de Albuquerque

XII   Dr António de Oliveira Salazar

INDEX

Abarbanel, Isaac, 125, 166
'Abbāsids, 35
Abbeville, Jean d', Cardinal, 75
'Abdu'l Mu'min, 52, 56
'Abdu'r-Raḥman I, 35
'Abdu'r-Raḥman III, 37
Abelhart (Valarte), 119
Abrantes, 254
Abrilada, 267
Abu Ya'qub, 64
Abu Zakariya, 52
A'Court, Sir William, 267
Aden, 129, 142
Aeminium (Coimbra), *see* Eminio
Afonso I (Henriques), 9, 10, 46, 48, 49, 50, 51, 52, 53, 54, 55–63, 64, 65, 66, 86
Afonso II, 71, 72, 73, 74, 84
Afonso III, 75, 78, 79, 80–4, 87
Afonso IV, 88, 89, 92, 93, 100
Afonso V, 113, 115, 119, 120, 121, 122, 123, 128
Afonso VI, 173, 185–96, 197
Afonso, Count of Ourém, 115
Afonso, son of Afonso III, 88
Afonso, son of John I, *see* Bragança, Afonso, 1st Duke of
Afonso Sanches, son of Dinis, 88, 89
Agadir, 135, 323
Aguiar, Joaquim António de, 278, 284, 285, 293, 320
Ajax, Bishop, 25
Alans, 22, 23
Alarcos, battle of, 71
Alba, 3rd Duke of, 161, 162
Alba, 6th Duke of, 177
Alberoni, Julio, 210
Albert, Cardinal Archduke, 164, 165
Alberto, Mestre, 67
Albuquerque, Afonso de, 141, 142
Albuquerque, Matias, de, 179
Alcácer do Sal, 20, 55, 62, 65, 70, 75, 200
Alcácer-Quivir (al-Qaṣr al-kabir), 135, 157, 158, 163
Alcácer-Seguir (al-Qaṣr as-saghir), 120, 135, 149
Alcáçova Carneiro, Pedro de, 151, 153, 159, 164
Alcáçovas, Treaty of, 122

Alcañices, Treaty of, 88
Alcântara, battle of, 162
Alcobaça, 62, 69, 90, 127, 153
Alcoutim, Peace of (1371), 95, 96
Aldana, Francisco de, 157, 158
Aledo, 43
Alegrete, Count of, *see* Albuquerque, Matias de
Alenquer, 101
Alentejo, 2, 4, 5, 7, 20, 69, 188, 200
Alexander III, Pope, 65
Alexander VI, Pope, 131
Alfarrobeira, battle of, 116
Alfonso I, of Aragon, 46, 47, 50, 52
Alfonso I, of Leon, 34
Alfonso II, of Leon, 35, 36
Alfonso V, of Leon, 37, 38
Alfonso VI, of Leon, 40, 41, 42, 43, 44, 45, 52
Alfonso VII (Raimúndez), 45, 46, 47, 48, 50, 51, 52, 61, 63
Alfonso VIII, of Castile, 63
Alfonso IX, of Leon, 71
Alfonso X, *el Sabio*, of Leon and Castile, 79, 80, 81, 84, 85, 86, 88, 92, 132
Alfonso XI, of Castile, 89, 90, 93
Alfonso, son of Juan II of Castile, 120, 121
Algarve, 2, 4, 7, 8, 9, 20, 33, 54, 56, 65, 70, 80, 136, 252
Algarve, Bp of, *see* Melo, José Maria de
Aliseda (Cáceres), 13
Aljubarrota, 62; battle of, 103, 105
Allard, 61
Almada, 70
Almansa, 206
Almansur (al-Manṣūr), 37, 39
Almeida, António José de, 319, 321, 325, 326, 328
Almeida, Francisco de, 131, 139, 140, 141, 154
Almeida Garrett, 284, 294
Almeirim, 146
Almería, 12
Almohads, 51, 52, 56, 57, 62, 63, 64, 65, 66, 70, 71, 75
Almoravids, 9, 42, 43, 45, 47, 51, 52, 55, 56, 57, 62
Almourol, 62

Herculano, Alexandre, 10, 44, 294
Herman, François-Antoine, 250, 251
Hermenegild, 28
Hermenegildo Gonçalves, 36
Hermeric, 23, 24
Herminian Mountains (Serra da Estrêla), 15, 17
Hervey de Glanvill, 57, 60
Heytesbury, 1st Baron, *see* A'Court, Sir William
Hintze Ribeiro, Ernesto Rodolfo, 309, 310, 313
Hispania Citerior, 17
Hispania Ulterior, 14, 16, 17
Historicals, 289, 290, 292, 293, 296
Hither Spain, *see* Hispania Citerior
Hohenzollern-Sigmaringen, Leopold, of *see* Leopold of Hohenzollern-Sigmaringen
Hohenzollern-Sigmaringen, Stéphanie of, *see* Stéphanie of Hohenzollern-Sigmaringen
Honorius, Emperor, 22, 23, 24
Hospitallers, 85
House of Twenty-Four, *see* Casa dos Vinte e Quatro
Hugo, Bp of Oporto, 48
Hydatius, Bp of Chaves, 24, 25, 26, 31

Ibn Qasi, 56, 62
Idanha, 27
Idrisì, 54, 55, 65
Iliberri, Council of, 21
Imino, *see* Eminio
Inchiquin, Earl of, 187
Inês de Castro, 90, 91, 98, 100, 101, 102, 105
infanções, 38, 67, 68, 80
Innocent III, Pope, 73
Innocent IV, Pope, 78, 80, 102
Innocent XIII, Pope, 210
inquirições (of Afonso II), 74; (of Afonso III) 84: (of Dinis), 84
Inquisition, 126, 134, 147, 149, 165, 175
Isabel (St), of Aragon (m. Denis), 84, 88, 89
Isabel, Duchess of Burgundy (dau. of John I), 107
Isabel Luisa Josefa (dau. of Pedro II), 196
Isabella, of Portugal (m. Afonso V), 115, 119
Isabella, of Portugal (m. Charles V, Emperor), 145

Isabella I, of Spain, 121, 122, 131, 134, *see also* Ferdinand and Isabella
Isabella II. o Spain, 275, 277, 291, 295
Isidore (St), of Seville, 29, 32
Ivens, Roberto, 304

Jaffuda Cresques (Jaime de Mayorca), *see* Cresquer, Jaffuda
Jant, Chavalier de, 184
Jervis, John, *see* St Vincent, Earl of
Jesuits, 137, 148, 149, 150, 198, 215, 219, 220, 223, 226–7, 228, 230, 235, 242, 316, 320
Jews, 125, 126, 127, 133, 134, 136, 147, *see also* New Christians
Joana, of Portugal (m. Henry IV of Castile), 119, 120; Joana, her dau., 120, 121, 122
João das Regras, 102, 106
John I (Master of Avis), 91, 100, 101, 102, 103, 104, 105, 106
John II, 119, 122–31
John III, 135, 145–51, 156
John IV, 171, 173–85
John V, 198, 205–12
John VI, 245–68
John, son of Inês de Castro, 101, 102, 105
John, son of John I, 107, 115
John, son of John III, 151
John, of Austria (son of Charles V, Emperor), 153
John, of Austria (son of Philip IV, of Spain), Juan José, 188, 192
John, of Gaunt, 96, 98, 104
John XXI, Pope, 83, 105
John XXII, Pope, 86
Johnston, Sir H., 307
Jorge, son of John II, 132
José I, 208, 212–38
José, son of Pedro III, 239, 243
Jourdan, 61
Juan I, of Castile, 97, 98, 99, 100, 101, 103, 104
Juan II, of Castile, 106, 110, 111, 114, 115
Juan Manuel of Castile, 89
Juana, 'la Beltraneja', *see* Joana
Julian, of Ceuta, 32
Julião, Mestre, 67
Julius Caesar, 17
juniores, 68
Junius Brutus Callaicus, Decius, 16
Junot, Andoche, Duke of Abrantes, 248, 249, 250, 251, 252, 254

Seabra da Silva, José de, 231, 238, 243
Sebastian, 151–62
Sebastianism, 165–7
Seia, 39
Sena, 155
Senegal, River, 112, 156
Septemberism, 282, 283, 284, 286, 287
Sequeira Diogo Lopes de, 142
Sequeira, João Lopes de, 135
Serpa, 63, 65
Serpa Pinto, Alexandre, Viscount of, 304, 306, 308
Sertorius, Q., 16, 17
Servilius Caepio, Q., 15
Setúbal, 2, 7, 173
Seville, 27, 34, 36, 55, 126, 151
Silingians, 23
Silva, António Maria da, 328
Silva Porto, António Francisco Ferreira da, 302
Silveira, Francisco da, see Amarante, Francisco da Silveira, 1st Count of
Silves, 55, 56, 63, 70, 81
Simon, of Dover, 57
Sinédrio, 260
Sinel de Cordes, General, 330, 331
Sintra, 43, 55, 61, 132, 252, 265
Sintra, Pedro de, 119
Sisebut, 29
Sisnand, Count of Coimbra, 39, 41, 43
Skellater, John Forbes, 245, 247
Smith, Sir Sidney, 250, 258
Socotra, Island, 141
Sofala, 129, 139, 154, 155
Soult, Nicholas, Marshal, 253, 254, 255
Soure, 47, 51, 54, 56, 62, 85
Soure, João da Costa, Count of, see Costa, João da
Sousa, Coutinho, Rodrigo de, 256
Sousa, Martim Afonso de, 146
Sousa, Tomé de, 149
Southwell, Sir Robert, 193
Soveral, Marquis of, 312
Stanley, Sir Henry Norton, 304
Stéphanie, of Hohenzollern-Sigmaringen (m. Pedro V), 289
Strangford, 6th Viscount, 249, 250, 256
Strozzi, Philippe, 164
Stuart of Rothesay, Sir Charles, Baron, 268, 269
Stukeley, Sir Thomas, 157, 158
Suevi, see Swabians
Sulpicius Galba, S., 15

Swabians, 22, 23, 24, 25, 26, 27, 28, 29, 36, 40
Swintila, 29, 30

Tagus, 1, 2, 6, 7, 10, 11, 12, 14, 16, 20, 21
Talleyrand-Périgord, C. M. de, 246, 249, 258, 259, 272, 273, 277
Tamagnini de Abreu e Silva, General, 326, 327
Tâmega, 5
Tancos, 326
Tangier, 32, 112, 113, 120, 135, 149, 154, 158, 186, 190, 191, 197
Tarasia, see Teresa
Tarouca, 38
Tarraco (Tarragona), 19
Tarraconensis, 17, 18
Tartessos, 13
Távora, family, 227, 228, 229, 230, 239, 240
Teixeira de Sousa, António, 316
Teixeira Gomes, Manuel, 328, 329
Teles, Leonor, see Lenor Teles
Telo, Count João Afonso, see Barcelos, João Afonso Telo, Count of
Templars, 51, 56, 62, 70, 80, 85
Teodósio, son of John IV, 181, 185
Terceira, see Azores
Terceira, Duke of, 276, 277, 285, 286, 290
Teresa, Countess of Portugal, 44, 47, 48, 49, 52
Teresa, dau. of Afonso I, 62, 66
Theodemir, King, 27, 28
Theodoric I, 24
Theodoric II, 25, 26
Thierry, of Alsace, 62
Timor, 299, 336, 337
Toledo, 26, 30, 33, 34, 35, 42, 44
Toledo, Councils of, 29, 30, 31
Tomar, 62, 70, 85, 233
Tomar, Count of, see Costa Cabral, Antonio Bernardo da
Tomás, Adm. Américo, 342
Tordesillas, Treaty of, 139, 145
Toro, 40, 121, 122
Torrecusa, Marquis of, 179
Tôrres Vedras, 252, 254, 255
Toulouse, 23, 25, 26
Trancoso, 79, 102, 104
Trás-os-Montes, 4, 5, 45, 68
Trastemires, Gonçalo, 38
Tristão, Nuno, 116, 117
Tucci (Martos), 16